Command Language Cookbook for Mainframes, Minicomputers and PC's:
DOS/OS/2 Batch Language, CLIST, DCL, Perl, and REXX

Hallett German

VNR VAN NOSTRAND REINHOLD
New York

Copyright © 1992 by Van Nostrand Reinhold

Library of Congress Catalog Card Number 92-1388
ISBN 0-442-00801-5

Printed in the United States of America.

Van Nostrand Reinhold
115 Fifth Avenue
New York, New York 10003

Chapman and Hall
2-6 Boundary Row
London, SE1 8HN, England

Thomas Nelson Australia
102 Dodds Street
South Melbourne 3205
Victoria, Australia

Nelson Canada
1120 Birchmount Road
Scarborough, Ontario MIK 5G4, Canada

16 15 14 13 12 11 10 9 8 7 6 5 4 3 2 1

Library of Congress Cataloging-in-Publication Data
German, Hallett.
   Command language cookbook for mainframes, minicomputers, and PC's:
DOS/OS/2 batch language, Clist, DCL, Perl, and REXX / Hallett German.
      p. cm.
   Includes index.
   ISBN 0-442-00801-5
   1. Programming languages (Electronic computers)   I. Title.
QA76.7.G45   1992
005.13—dc20   92-1388
                                                          CIP

To:
Sweet Baby Chelsea Olivia German,
who wasn't around the first time:
"Whatever living being there may be . . .
born or coming to earth—may all beings have happy minds."

Contents

7. Command Language Advisor—Perl   247

8. Command Language Cookbook—the Grand Tour of the Major Command Languages

Preface

After completing *TSO/E CLISTs: Basics, Applications, and Advanced Techniques,* I took a year off and worked on various projects. One was to prepare a presentation on command languages for the third annual Northeast SAS® Users' Group Conference. (A group I founded in more energetic days.) I became aware that there is a real need for a book on the major command languages; the approach should emphasize that the application being developed determines the command language components to use; and using such an approach would result in 30 to 40 percent of the application's development being completed before a single line of code is written, thus helping you avoid common bottlenecks. I hope that this book proves useful to you.

There are many people along the way who helped this book come to light. I greatly appreciate all their efforts. Many topics were enlarged or clarified because of reviewer comments. The wonderful reviewers who took time out of their busy lives include Dave Carter of GTE Laboratories Inc., Lowell ("Jim") Mercier of Private Health Care, and Mason Kelsey of Bank of America. Gerry Pauline of Pace University, a reviewer who went far beyond the confines of the REXX chapter, gave many useful insights.

The vendor support for this project was outstanding. This includes Ed Gaudet and his staff at Boston Business Computing, Ed Spire of the Workstation Group, Bill Hawes of Wishful Thinking Development Corporation, and Robert Jones (creator of pCLIST). Cathie Dager of Stanford Linear Accelerator Center introduced me to many good sources on REXX. Steve Belczyk of GTE Laboratories patiently answered my Amiga questions. Tom Button of Microsoft Corporation, Chuck Hoffman of GTE Laboratories, and Larry Wall of NetLab Inc. provided good ideas.

I would like to thank the following people for giving me permission to use original material: Jwahar Bammi (Atari St Perl notes) David Grubbs (Amiga Perl notes), Tom Haapanen (MS Windows Frequently Asked Questions), Robert Jones (pCLIST User's Guide), Mason Kelsey (REXX Symposium 1990 paper), Len Reed (MS-DOS Perl notes), and Kai Rommel (OS/2 Perl notes).

Cicely, Stanley, and Robbyn German cheered on this project the entire way. Vovo Olivia and Mamae Miranda sent their prayers and support from afar. The teachings and life of Sakyamuni Buddha inspires me to help others through this and other efforts. Dianne Littwin at Van Nostrand Reinhold was a helpful editor. The anonymous reviewers gave good ideas on the book. The production staff excelled at converting my manuscript into a book.

Alessandra Rose German and her newborn sister Chelsea Olivia German got me to laugh and slip into their world, and they gave me a chance to practice my reading stories voice. Most of all, I thank Raquel Miranda German my wife for her support, love, and help throughout this effort; this is as much her work as it is mine.

Command Language Cookbook for Mainframes, Minicomputers and PC's:
DOS/OS/2 Batch Language, CLIST, DCL, Perl, and REXX

1

A Road Map

WHAT ARE THE GOALS OF THIS BOOK?

One trend in data processing is the dramatic rise in distributed computing. Sites that were once mainframe strongholds are replacing or supplementing them with minicomputers/workstations and personal computers. The result is that users, MIS staff, and system integrators increasingly have to deal with getting two or more operating systems to "talk with each other" or some form of interoperability. Part of this "dialog" usually involves **command languages**, or **CLs**. These command languages, which use English-like commands, offer the user a relatively easy means to ask the operating system to perform one or more tasks. Thus, the questions that usually arise in developing a command language application are: When I have a choice between two command languages, which one do I choose?, how do I convert my **command language programs** (or **CLPs**) to another command language?, is there a better approach that I can use to develop my command language application?, and how do I port my command language program to another platform? Unfortunately, few sources help answer these questions. This book tries to alleviate this by meeting the following goals:

- To offer a one-stop guide to the major command languages. Plenty of books summarize the major programming languages, but none do the same for command languages. This is not a tutorial nor a reference on command language syntax. Many good tutorials already cover each of the command languages. (The references at the end of Chapters 3 through 7 have further information.) *It is a "how-to" reference and tutorial once you have selected your command language and type of application.* Basic knowledge of and some experience with the command language is assumed.
- To provide, for the first time, a reference that objectively compares the strengths and weaknesses of the major command languages. One complaint is that many reviews of a particular command language tend to be overly enthu-

siastic and rarely critical. Balanced reviews of most command languages are rare, which is not the case for programming languages. This book attempts to remedy this. Equivalence command tables are also provided. This will help in converting existing applications to another command language.

- To provide an approach for developing command language applications that can be used with any command language, an approach that also follows the structure of the book.

The approach consists of four basic tasks:

1. Each command language application is one of three types. The first step is determining which type your application belongs to.
2. Knowing the command language type and other information (such as preferred operating system and data formats to be used by the application) determines the command language to be used.
3. Knowing the application type determines the command language components to be used by a proposed application.
4. Knowing the command language components determines which commands for a particular command language will be used to build an application. You can then read up on these particular commands once they are chosen.

- Once you have selected a command language and the type of application that you want to develop, this book provides "real world," ready-to-run examples using handy sequences needed to do the job.

This is true whether having different command languages on two or more operating systems or two or more command languages on the same operating system. Moving a command language program to a different operating system will also be discussed.

WHO SHOULD READ THIS BOOK?

This book is targeted for:

System integrators. They need to get various operating systems talking to each other. A good part of this effort includes converting programs between command languages and porting the same command language program to a different operating system.

End-users. They are familiar with a command language but need to know how to code a particular sequence for an application. They are also concerned with converting programs between command languages and porting the same command language program to a different operating system.

A special group of end-users. They have more than one command language available to them. For example, DOS has versions of UNIX shell languages, CLIST, Perl, and DCL. Also, UNIX supports various shell languages, Perl, DCL, and REXX.

One trend is that more and more you no longer have to migrate to a different operating system just to use a command language. These users need to know "which command language should I use?" The answer is, in part, "what type of application are you trying to build?"

HOW SHOULD I READ THIS BOOK?

Here is a suggested reading order depending on which of the groups you fall into:

Audience	Suggested Order of Chapters
System integrators and special group of end-users	8,1,2, and chapter on the appropriate command languages.
End-users familiar with the language and command language application developers	1,2 and chapter on the appropriate command languages.

THE APPROACH USED IN THIS BOOK

This section presents the general framework of the book and includes a diagram showing the process of designing an application and the corresponding chapters on each step.

Chapter 2 gives an overview of command languages. A typology of popular command language applications and an approach in developing applications are proposed.

Chapters 3 through 7 show real-world, ready-to-run sequences you can use in developing your applications. Part of the chapter discusses when it is appropriate to use each language and how to extend each language. Porting to another command language or other operating systems is also discussed.

Chapter 8 compares and contrasts the various command languages discussed in Chapters 3 through 7. Some flow diagrams on choosing a command language and command equivalence charts are also included.

Appendix 1 helps in finding commercial software for the command language that you have chosen.

If you are developing an application, you may want to consider the following process outlined in Figure 1-1 and look at the corresponding chapters:

Note the sequence:

1. Determine the type of application and appropriate command language.
2. Review the components generally used with the application type.

Step	Related Chapters	Related Sections
What type of application do I have?	2	Components of command languages Types of command language applications
⇓		
Which CL should I use?	8	A comparison of command languages Choosing a command language
Review flow diagram on selecting CLs.	8	A comparison of command languages Choosing a command language
⇓		
Review when to use each CL.	3–8	When to use the CLIST language When to use the REXX language When to use the Digital command language When to use the DOS or OS/2 batch language When to use Perl Choosing a command language A comparison of command languages
⇓		
Which CL components will I need?	2,8	Components of command languages Types of command language applications Comparing commands across command languages
⇓		
Which CL commands match these components?	2	Which commands are right for my application?
⇓		
Where can I learn more about these commands?	2–7	Which commands are right for my application? When to use the CLIST language through Other CLIST program concerns When to use the REXX language through Other REXX exec applications When to use the Digital command language through Other DCL command procedure concerns When to use the DOS or OS/2 batch language through Other DOS or OS/2 batch language concerns When to use Perl through Other Perl concerns

Figure 1-1. A general method for developing command language (CL) applications

3. Examine the commands in the selected command language that correspond to the particular command language component.
4. Learn more about the command. (And then create your program.)

All this is completed before a single line in the program is created. The result is that you are more than one-third done with your application, having avoided common dead-ends and traps. Using this approach, you'll never have to say "I don't know how to start my application."

Note that because this book is comprehensive, a topic such as built-in functions may span several non-contiguous sections. A detailed index and listing of related sections throughout the book help reduce the time to look for this information.

COMMAND LANGUAGE VERSIONS USED IN THIS BOOK

All efforts were made to keep this book as current as possible. These were the versions numbers at the time of publication:

Command Language	Version
CLIST	TSO/E Version 2 Release 3
DCL	VMS 5.4
DOS batch language	DOS 5.0
OS/2 batch language	OS/2 1.3
Perl	Version 4.0 patch 19
REXX	Version 4.00

2

Command Languages and Applications—an Introduction

Before developing a command language application or reading further on a particular command language, you'll find it helpful to have a good understanding of command languages. To do this, let's first define the term command language, then describe its characteristics. Next, we'll examine the components of a command language and types of command language applications. The chapter concludes by providing the crucial links in the proposed command language application development cycle—showing the relationship between the command language application type and command language components—and more important, showing the commands corresponding to each component.

WHAT IS A COMMAND LANGUAGE?

The term **command language**, or **CL**, was first used in the late 1960's or early 1970's. A common definition is *a series of commands that were entered at the keyboard and executed immediately on some type of time sharing operating system.* For examples of this definition see Dolotta 1983, p. 236; Moran 1981, p. 5. Other terms that have been used for command languages are interactive command languages, operating system control languages, response languages, and control languages.

A time sharing operating system means that multiple users can run interactive sessions simultaneously. However for each user, only one interactive program such as executing a **command language program** or **CLP** can be running at a time. However, you could have multiple jobs running in background or batch mode at the same time.

Moran (1981) points out the main problem in defining a command language—differentiating it from a job control language or a programming language. This is getting harder to do because command languages tend to contain more and more elements of the other two common types of languages. However, learning more about the other types of languages will be useful in attempting to define what a command language has evolved into today.

The common definition of **job control language**, also called **JCL** or batch command language, is *a set of commands used to "ask" the operating system—sometimes called command system—to perform a series of tasks in a batch (background) mode.* Part of this "asking" includes providing user-supplied primary and secondary values such as file names. See Jardine (1975) for a good overview of job control languages. This frees users to submit another job control language program, prepare or run an interactive command language program, or do something else on their terminal.

In comparison, *a programming language is a high-level, English-like series of commands usually compiled with the entire program processed as one unit rather than one at a time.* Beech (1980) observes that the major difference between programming and command languages is that the latter emphasizes interacting with the operating system and the former does not. Programming languages were mentioned by Gram and Hertweck (1975) and others as having the following strengths over command languages:

- More data types including strings, pointers, integers, and imaginary numbers.
- More data formats for values such as hexadecimal, octal, scientific format, exponents, and decimals.
- Better numerical precision partly due to more data types.
- Faster speed because of compiled programs.
- Easier to learn because of more consistent syntax.
- Easier and better to use for database applications, complex file manipulations, customized reports, and multi-dimensional array manipulation.
- More flow control structures such as C's SELECT-CASE and FOR, FORTRAN's conditional GO TO and arithmetic IF, and PASCAL's CASE.
- More built-in functions including identical functions for each data type.
- More powerful subprocedure and function structures, which gives programming languages greater extensiveness than command languages. This includes the ability to pass back more than return codes to the main program—such as arrays, pointers, and character strings.

With the arrival of recent command languages (such as Perl and REXX), many of these criticisms are less true today and the differences between command and programming languages becomes increasingly less apparent. In fact, a study by Hauptman and Green (1983) surprisingly showed that there are no significant differences between command languages, natural languages, and menus in the amount of time and number of errors in doing a task. Command languages are no longer second-rate—they are starting to come into their own. Recent trends include:

1. *Availability of the same command language on an increasing number of operating systems.* This allows for the possibility of cross-platform command language development. Examples include all the command languages examined in this book plus others such as Icon and Python. This number has a healthy rate of growth each year.

2. *Attempts to create compilers for the more popular command languages,* in spite of their lack of conventional flow control structures and data types.

3. *Existing command languages are purposely kept small and generally only incremental changes are added.* This is the explicit philosophy for Perl and REXX—despite that some users insist features be added to their favorite command language that would substantially change its nature.

4. *More sophisticated command languages* including graphics and object-oriented programming while supporting graphical user interfaces (GUI) as well as operating systems. Examples include a MS-Windows interface for MS-DOS REXX interpreters, X Windows/Curses interfaces to Perl, and Frontier on the Macintosh.

5. *Existing command languages have or will soon have interfaces to other areas* such as databases, for example Oracle interfaces exist for both Perl and REXX and communications (a TCP/IP library for REXX (MVS) and the socket (Interprocess Communication or IPC) built-in functions of Perl.

6. *Command languages standards are starting to appear such as UNIX shells (POSIX 1003.2) and REXX (ANSI X3J18).* Others will follow in time.

Today each major operating system has or soon will have a command language that serves as a liaison between the user and the operating system.

One of the last holdouts, the Macintosh, is about to have several command languages available. Each of these will support the same underlying structure—the Open Scripting Architecture. This architecture is a set of evolving guidelines on using AppleEvents, a collection of built-in system calls to perform various operations on the Macintosh. The command ("scripting") languages that have been announced are Apple's AppleScript (no announced availability date), Userland's Frontier, Simple Software's Control Tower, and CE Software CE/IAC.

To some less sophisticated users, the command language *is* the operating system. A working definition consistent with recent trends in command languages is:

A programming language consisting of a series of high-level, English-like commands entered interactively—for example, a keyboard, mouse, or other input device—or noninteractively—that is, created with an editor, saved to a file, and executed in foreground or background. An interpreter or compiler for the command language then determines which of the user-defined operating system tasks to perform and processes them using corresponding task values.

There is a valid opposing viewpoint about defining command languages. In his excellent book on defining command languages, Beech (1980) reviews the argument that command languages should not be viewed as a language in their own right but as the means to interface to various other languages, editors, and environments. As you will see in a later section, components of a command language, the interfacing to external environments is a very important part of what a command language does. But in my opinion that does not in itself deny that command languages are languages in their own right.

CHARACTERISTICS OF COMMAND LANGUAGES

It is far easier to describe the characteristics of a command language than to define the language as a whole. The following is a list of characteristics common to the command languages described in this book.

- *Command languages are usually interpreted languages.* This means the interpreter or **command language interpreter** (CLI) scans the syntax of each command, performs the necessary symbolic substitution, and executes the command language program *every time it is invoked.* The result is that command languages are ideal for quick and dirty prototyping because you can create a fairly sophisticated example of an application fast. They are also ideal for new users because these users can immediately verify if a command language program worked and add incremental changes if necessary.

  Only a few command languages have any sort of compiler (REXX and Icon). Prachl (1990) and others outline reasons why there are so few:

  Most command languages have GOTO statements that can enter or exit inner/outer loops, functions, and subprocedures. It is hard to write a compiler to correctly handle such behavior.

  Some command languages (like REXX and PERL) do not have variable declarations or limited data types. If a compiler was built to handle the lack of such features, it would generally be large and slow to run.

  Thus, the command language's greatest strength of non-procedural, open-ended programming would be its greatest liability in creating a compiler. Even if a compiler was created, it would probably offer only marginal speed improvements over a comparable interpreter, such as Perl under MS-DOS.
- *Command languages are usually executed in foreground mode.* Command language programs are usually stored in a file or dataset and the interpreter processes the program one line a time. Sometimes, commands are entered at the terminal, one command at a time. In either case, you are usually unable to perform anything else in foreground mode while the command language program is being processed. (However, one or more programs can be running in background mode.) This may reduce your overall session productivity.
- *Command language commands are composed of English-like verbs describing the task to be performed, such as WRITE or READ.* They usually have accom-

panying parameters, modifiers, and submodifiers that supply values and further define the task to be performed. That is to say, command language commands usually have a hierarchical format. This structure generally makes command languages easy to learn and speeds up the time in looking up the appropriate command to perform a task. (Studies on command language grammars include Gram and Hertweck 1975, Moran 1981, Hauptmann and Green 1983, and Payne and Green 1989.) The following example may clarify this. Listed is the DCL (or Digital command language) command to display a file. DCL is currently available for VMS. However, DCL emulators exist for MS-DOS, MVS, and UNIX.

TYPE A.TEXT /PAGE

KEY: 1 = Verb (*TYPE*)—describes the task to be performed (i.e., display the file).

2 = Parameter (*A.TEXT*)—a positional value that describes which file to perform the task on.

3 = Modifier Delimiter (*/*)—signals that a modifier immediately follows.

4 = Modifier (*PAGE*)—Also called keyword operand. Usually a type of noun or adjective that further defines a task by enabling or disabling some attribute of the system task, in this case, display the file a screen at a time.

- *Command languages programs either directly include operating system commands such as DOS/OS/2 batch, CLIST, and DCL or indirectly include them through a particular CL command such as Perl's exec or system functions and REXX's ADDRESS instruction.* This reduces the need for operator intervention or knowing operating system internals just to perform a task. Command languages such as Perl and some implementations of REXX include built-in functions that simulate system commands such as CHDIR to change the current directory.
- *Command languages usually provide the capability for users to extend the language through subprocedures, functions, and interfaces to external environments, such as editors, session managers, and compiled programs.* No command language can satisfy all your needs. But the ability to customize a command language to do exactly what you want increases its usefulness and power.

COMPONENTS OF COMMAND LANGUAGES

This section builds on what has been discussed so far in the chapter by reviewing the components found in most command languages. The functions and subfunctions of these components are also mentioned. Knowing about these components is a cru-

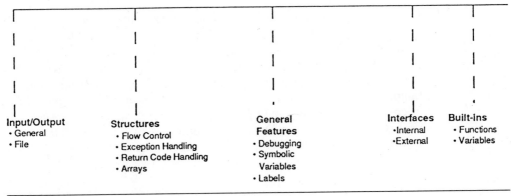

Input/Output	Structures	General Features	Interfaces	Built-Ins
• General	• Flow Control	• Debugging	•Internal	• Functions
• File	• Exception Handling	• Symbolic	•External	• Variables
	• Return Code Handling	Variables		
	• Arrays	• Labels		

Figure 2-1. Diagram of Command Language Components

cial part of the approach proposed in this book for application development as shown in the sections that follow. Figure 2-1 shows how the components of command languages can be grouped into five distinct areas.

Table 2-1 further details the major components of command languages (under the five areas) and their functions.

TYPES OF COMMAND LANGUAGE APPLICATIONS

Most applications for command languages can be placed into one of three types. Knowing the application type will determine the command language components (and corresponding commands for the selected command language). After reading this and the following section, you will be ready to read the appropriate chapters (3 through 7) and sections detailing the task that you wish a command language application to perform.

WHICH COMMANDS ARE RIGHT FOR MY APPLICATION?

This section tries to synthesize the discussion on command languages so far. This will be done in two steps: First, showing which command language components are appropriate for each type of application. Second, listing the commands that correspond to each of these components. Having this knowledge, you are more than one-third done in developing your command language application—*all before having written a single line of code!* You can then read the appropriate command language chapters (3 through 7) for further information. (It may help also to review Figure 1-1 to see where we are in the application development cycle. Also look at Chapter 8, especially the section comparing commands across command languages for further information of commands by function.)

Table 2-1. Major Components of Command Languages and Their Functions

Component	Function
	Input/Output
General Input & Output	Output to screen (messages, menus, & input prompts). Output to a printer (files and reports). Output to a file. Input from the keyboard or other device. Input from the command line.
File Input/Output	Opening and closing a file. Sorting a file. Reading, writing, updating and deleting records in a file.
	Structures
Flow Control Structures	Unconditional flow control (i.e. GOTO). Conditional flow control (e.g. IF-THEN). Multi-conditional flow control (e.g. SELECT-CASE, multiple IF-THENs) Loop testing (e.g. DO-WHILE, iterative DO, compound DO, FOR, WHILE)
Exception & Exit/Return Code Handling	Sequences for various types of errors. Sequences on pressing Escape, Attention, or other keys. Sequences for capturing exit/return codes from command language statements and operating system commands. Sequences for passing and receiving exit codes from another command language program, function, or subprocedure.
Array Operations	Add, update, delete, or retrieve values from an array.
	General Features
Trace/debugging facility	Assists in debugging a command language program by doing the following: • Traces to the screen which commands are being executed including the results of symbolic substitution and return codes from commands. • Sets up breakpoints to see how a particular sequence performs and to display values of variables at the breakpoint. • Traces to the screen which labels are being processed.
Macros or symbolic variables	Performs substitution of symbols with user-defined values.
Labels	Identifies the start of a command sequence. This is useful for exception handling, flow control, and debugging.

Table 2-1. *(continued)*

Component	Function
	Interfaces
Internal interfaces	Functions or subprocedures written in the same command language.
External interfaces	Interface to operating system commands. Providing input/output to a load module or executable written in a programming language.
	Built-Ins
Built-in functions	Functions when supplied with the correct arguments perform the following tasks:
	• string manipulation
	• session information
	• date/time information
	• operating system information
	• external environment information
	• file information
	• network information
	• data type conversion
	• mathematical operations
	Return codes are usually given by functions to indicate success or failure.
System variables	Variables that keep information about the session, system, and command language program location. Some of these may only be set by the system. These also may be called global variables or environment variables.

The following lists the command language components that are characteristic of each application type:

- Front-end
    - Operating system commands
    - Environment Interfaces (invoking executables)
    - General Input/Output (input/output to/from an executable or operating system command)
- System and utilities
    - System variables (system information, session information, dataset information)
    - String operations (parsing a dataset name)
    - Clear a screen

Table 2-2. Types of Command Language Applications

Type	Function
Front-end	Provide input to or receive output from other applications and programs.
	May also perform the necessary housekeeping tasks for an application such as allocations and deletions.
	Startup/login programs also fall into this category.
System and utility	Similar to front-end applications but emphasis is on performing system and utility operations.
	Performs system operations tasks such as archiving or recovering files.
	Also include general-purpose utilities that can be used as a function or subprocedure in the "main" command language program, such as a function that returns the modification date of a file.
Self-contained	Such as creating a customized extract or a travel expense report.

  Batch operations
  Dataset/file operations (plus those components found in front-end applications)
 • Self-contained
  Capture command line values
  Exception handling
  Data validation (flow control & string operations)
  User input and validation
  Text case operations
  Date/time operations
  String operations
  Functions/subprocedures (Plus those components found in front-end and system/utilities applications)

  Table 2-1 shows further information on which command language components are appropriate for each application type. Note that command language components may be used by more than one type of application. The type of command language components may vary depending on the command language selected, familiarity with the command language, and other factors.

Table 2-3. Command Language Applications and Components

Front-end	System & utility	Self-contained applications
Operating system	Operating system	
External interfaces: Sending input/Receiving output from an executable	External interfaces: Sending input/Receiving output from an executable	External interfaces: Call external executable functions
Utility functions	Utility functions	General subprocedures/functions
Input/output: File operations	Input/output: File operations	Input/output: Record operations
	Printer operations	
Command line input	Command line input	Keyboard/input
Exception & return code: handling: emphasis on return codes and command errors	Exception & return code handling: emphasis on return codes and command errors	Exception & return code handling: emphasis on user input errors
Built-in functions: system & session	Built-in functions: system & session	Built-in functions: string & data
		System variables
Conditional flow control statements	Loop testing and conditional flow control statements	Multi-conditional flow control statements and loop testing.
	Arrays	Arrays

Table 2-4 lists the appropriate command for each command language component. Further information on each command is given in chapters 3 through 7 and sections in the selected chapter.

Table 2-4. Appropriate Command for Each Command Language Component

Command Language Component	CLIST	REXX	DCL	DOS/Batch	Perl
Input/Output					
• *General Input/Output:*					
> Keyboard Input	Read	Pull (Really Parse Pull)	Inquire or Read	None: but there are many shareware programs that do this.	Getc, <STDIN>
> *Command Line Input* (parsing command line input)	Proc	Parse Arg	Placed in symbols P1–P8. Use lexical functions if further parsing is needed.	Placed in variables %0–%9.	Placed in $Argv[0]– $Argv[$#Argv].
Output to the Screen	Write	Say	Write or Type	Echo	Print, Printf, Sprintf
• *File/Input/Output*					
> Open a file/directory	Openfile	Execio, Linein, Charin	Open	N/A	Open, Dbmopen, Opendir
> Close a file/directory	Closfile	Execio, Finis, Lineout, Charout	Close	N/A	Close, Dbmclose, Closedir
> Sort a file/directory	TSO Sort command	Use operating system command.	Sort	DOS Sort command	Sort
> Read a record from a file. Read a directory	Getfile	Execio, Diskr, Linein, Charin	Read	Find "*string*" *file*	Readdir, Read, Sysread
> Write a new record to a file Write a directory	Putfile	Execio, Diskw, Lineout, Charout	Write	Echo and I/O redirection	Write, Syswrite

Table 2-4. *(continued)*

Command Language Component	CLIST	REXX	DCL	DOS/Batch	Perl
> Updating an existing record in a file	Putfile	Execio Diskru/ Diskw, Lineout, Charrout	Write/Update	Echo and I/O redirection and Find.	Print, Printf, Sprintf
> Deleting a record from a file.	Putfile	Execio Diskru/ Diskw	Read/Delete	N/A	Delete
Deleting a directory				rmdir	Rmdir
> I Prove if file exists	&Sysdsn	Stream(), Lines(), Sysdsn()	F$Search()	If Exist/If Not Exist	if (-e $file), open
Structures					
* Exception & Return Code Handling:					
> Sequence on Pressing Escape, Attention, or Other Keys	Attn	Signal on Halt	On Control_Y	Break On, then DOS takes over.	$SIG('ABRT') $SIG('QUIT') $SIG('INT')
> Sequences for various types of errors	Error	Signal on Error, Signal on Novalue, Signal on Syntax, Call on Error, Call on Halt, Call on Failure, Call on Notready	On Warning On Error, On Severe_Error	If Errorlevel	Warn Die
> Sequences for capturing return codes	Exit, Return and &Lastoc	Exit, Return and Rc for external commands	Exit and $Status	If Errorlevel	Die, Exit, $? for backtick and system $! /$@ error number or string.

Table 2-4. *(continued)*

Command Language Component	CLIST	REXX	DCL	DOS/Batch	Perl
• *Array Operations*	Double amper-sand symbolic variables. No real array operators or functions.	Compound variables. Can set value of entire array.	Use symbols with letter and number. No real array functions or operators.	% parameters. Use Shift and For commands to manipulate.	Two types of arrays: indexed (LIST) and associative. Multi-dimensional arrays indirectly possible. System array variables and array/list functions are available.
* *Flow Control Statements*					
> Unconditional Flow Control	Goto	None	Goto	Goto	Goto
> Conditional Flow Control	If-Then	If-Then	If-Then-Endif	If (no Then)	If
> Multi-conditional flow control	If-Then-Else-Select-When-Otherwise-End	If-Then-Else-Select-When-Otherwise-End	If-Then-Else-EndIf OR F$Locate and Goto	Multiple Ifs	If-Elsif-Else
> Loop testing	Do-to-While, Do-to-Until, Do While, Do Until, Do Number, Do Forever	Do-to-While, Do-to-Until, Do While, Do Until, Iterative Do, Iterate	While counter is less then last value, increment counter: Uses: —label —counter —If-then	For-In-Do	Do-*Block*-While/Until/ Unless *Expression*, While Do *Block*, Do *Expression*, For, Foreach (arrays)

Table 2-4. (continued)

Command Language Component	CLIST	REXX	DCL	DOS/Batch	Perl
		Interfaces			
• *Internal Interfaces* > Functions	Can nest many clists. Just enter clist name. Can also call REXX execs.	Can have internal or external functions. Can also call Clists. Function is name followed by parentheses and arguments.	Internal functions in same command procedure, invoked by Call.	Name of next batch file does not return to main batch file. Command/c or Call to return to main batch file (Don't use with environment variables.)	Use Sub command with a Return in it. Invoked by Do or *&function*
> Subprocedures	Subprocedures in the same clist and identified by label. Can return a value or result (SYSREF)	Can be internal or external. Invoked by Call or Call On condition. Result in system variable Result.	GoSub to invoke subprocedure. Nest up to 16 levels. Identified by level.	Can simulate it with environment variables and Goto.	Use Sub command with no return in it. Invoked by door *& function*. Can have external subroutine library. (Do and subroutine name in single quotes.)
• *External Interfaces* > Interface to Operating System	Just place the TSO, Session Manager, ISPF command in the clist.	Address access, operating system and other environment such as ISPF, XEDIT.	Place command in command procedure.	Put commands in batch file	Exec and System functions.

Table 2-4. *(continued)*

Command Language Component	CLIST	REXX	DCL	DOS/Batch	Perl
> Provide input to executables	TSO Call command with parameters as symbolic	Address command. TSO Call command.	Define SYS$INPUT as your terminal. /OUTPUT qualifier to send to a file.	Invoke executable with parameter.	Use exec and system functions
> Provide output to executables	Invoke CLIST with parameter as CLIST operand (Proc.)	Invoke exec with parameters. (Parse Arg)		Use Errorlevel or environment variables to pass to batch file.	Use environment variables, exit codes.
Built-Ins					
* *Built-in Functions*	15 functions: string, double-byte characters, utility	60+ functions: String, bit, date/time, utility	35 functions: String, session, system, utility	0 Functions, available as shareware	90+ functions: String, array, system, networks
• *System variables*	36 variables: system, session, clist processing	3 Special variables: RC, Result, Sigl	4 common file logicals SYS$Command, Sys$Error, Sys$Input, Sys$Output. Many others (local and DEC-supplied) are available,	3 environment variables: %Comspec%, %Path%, %Prompt%. 2 more in DOS 5.0: %Temp%, %Dircmd%	31 special variables such as $_ (All are two characters and start with a $.) 5 Special arrays: @ARGV, @INC, %ENV, %INC, %SIG
			3 Symbols: $Status $Severity $Restart		

Table 2-4. *(continued)*

Command Language Component	CLIST	REXX	DCL	DOS/Batch	Perl
General Features					
* *Macros/Symbolic Variables*	Variables start with one or more ampersands. Default value is Null. 99 levels of substitution.	Symbols may start with most characters. Default value is symbol name in upper case. Interpret performs 1 level of substitution.	Symbols may start with A–Z. Default value is blanks. Use single quotes or ampersands to perform 1 level of substitution.	Parameters are %0–%9. Environment variables start and end with a %. Both have a default value of blank. and perform 1 level of substitution.	Scalar variables start with a $ followed by the variable name. Default value is Null. Double quoted and backtick strings indicate 1 level of symbolic substitution.
• *Labels*	Up to 31 character label name (TSO/E) with a colon immediately after the name.	No limit label name with a colon immediately following after the name.	Up to 255 character label name with a colon immediately after the name.	Up to 8 character label names and starts with colon.	No limit on label name with a colon after the name.
• *Trace/Debugging Facility*	Conlist, Msg, Symlist, List Write *value*	Trace Say *value*	Set Verify Write or Type *value*	Echo On Echo *value*	perl -d, Print, Printf, or Sprintf *value*

Commands may not be available for all operating systems, such as REXX's LINEIN function.

SUGGESTED READINGS

Barron, D.W., and I.R. Jackson, 1972. The Evolution of Job Control Languages. *Software Practice and Experience.* 2(2), pp. 143–164.

Beech, David, 1980. What is a Command Language? *Command Language Directions: Proceedings of the IFIP TC 2.7 Working Conference on Command Languages.* David Beech (ed). New York: North-Holland Publishing Co. pp. 7–31.

Cohen, Raines, 1991. "Apple and Userland Set Open Scripting Plan," *MacWeek,* June 4, p. 4.

Dolotta, T.A., 1983. Command and Job Control Languages, *Encyclopedia of Computer Science and Engineering.* 2d ed, Anthony Ralston and Edwin D. Reilly Jr. (eds). New York: Van Nostrand Reinhold, pp. 232–240.

Gram, Chr. and F.R. Hertweck, 1975. Command Languages: Design Considerations and Basic Concepts, *Command Languages.* C. Unger (ed). New York, N.Y.: North Holland Publishing Co., pp. 43–70.

Hauptmann, Alexander G., and Bert F. Green, 1983. A Comparison of Command, Menu-Selection, and Natural-Language Computer Programs. *Behaviour and Information Technology.* (Great Britain), 2(2), pp. 163–178.

Jardine, D.A., 1975. The Structure of Operating System Control Languages, *Command Languages.* C. Unger (ed). New York, N.Y.: North Holland Publishing Co., pp. 27–42.

Moran, Thomas P., 1981. The Command Language Grammar: A Representation for the User Interface of Interactive Computer Systems, *International Journal of Man-Machine Studies,* 15, pp. 3–50.

Payne, Stephen J., and T.R.G. Green, 1989. The Structure of Command Languages: An Experiment on Task-Action Grammar, *International Journal of Man-Machine Studies,* 30, pp. 213–234.

Prachl, Walter, 1990. CMS REXX: Compiler & Library, *Proceedings of the REXX Symposium for Developers and Users.* Stanford Linear Accelerator Center Report 368, pp. 33–58.

3

Command Language Advisor—CLIST

The CLIST language, available since the early 1970s, was one of the earliest command languages in popular use. **CLIST** (pronounced "*see-list*") is short for command lists—that is, a series of TSO and other commands that "ask" the operating system to perform one or more tasks. CLIST programs are stored in sequential or partitioned datasets (or PDSs). As a historical note, until the early 1980s CLIST programs were called command procedures, which now refers to compiled load modules. A CLIST program is also called a CLIST, which makes it hard to distinguish language and program. Consequently the terms CLIST language and CLIST program will be used through this book.

An MS-DOS version of the CLIST language interpreter called pCLIST has been available since August 1988. Current release 1.08c has most of the features of the TSO/E Version 1 Release 4 CLIST interpreter. Most CLIST programs not relying on TSO features can be easily converted to work with pCLIST. Examples of CLIST programs that work with pCLIST are presented throughout this chapter. Information on obtaining pCLIST can be found in Appendix 1.

WHEN TO USE THE CLIST LANGUAGE

Consider writing your application using the CLIST language under these conditions:

When your in-house expertise is mainly in the CLIST language and you need a program relatively fast.
When an application is expected to be used only in the short term. Long-term TSO applications should be converted to REXX.

25

When you are using TSO commands with subcommands such as EDIT.

When portability is not a major concern, unless it is portability to MS-DOS.

When at least two levels of symbolic substitution are needed.

When the data is either character, numeric, or double-byte characters and not decimals or exponents.

When string parsing sequences do not need to be sophisticated and parsing emphasizes substrings rather than words.

When a more powerful alternative to the MS-DOS/OS/2 batch language is needed.

HOW TO INVOKE CLIST PROGRAMS

A CLIST program may be invoked in either foreground (i.e. interactive) or background (i.e. batch). Here is how to do either method:

Invoking a CLIST Program in Foreground

You may invoke a CLIST in foreground either implicitly or explicitly. The explicit method uses the EXEC command, while the implicit method does not. Either way can be used at TSO's *READY* prompt or the *COMMAND* ===> field in an ISPF or PDF panel.

Implicitly Invoking a CLIST Program (TSO)

If the CLIST program is in a sequential or partitioned dataset allocated to SYSPROC concatenation, then the EXEC command is not needed. Here are two different formats you can use:

1. Member name *without* percent sign prefix:
   ```
   removel data.data
   ```
2. Member name *with* percent sign prefix:
   ```
   %removel data.data
   ```

   Tips and Traps:
   1. Data.data, an operand value, is not in single quotes.
   2. The *percent sign* (%) tells TSO to search only the SYSPROC concatenation (resulting in less system overhead). Without the percent sign, all the system libraries and program areas are searched *before* the SYSPROC concatenation.
   3. After the CLIST executes, the READY or COMMAND ===> (from ISPF and PDF) prompt reappears.

Explicitly Invoking a CLIST Program (TSO and MS-DOS)

The following are ways using either the EXEC or EX command (TSO and TSO/E) and the pCLIST command (MS-DOS) to explicitly invoke a CLIST program.

TSO

1. Fully-qualified sequential dataset name with no operands:
   ```
   exec 'hhg1.runprog'
   ```
2. Partitioned dataset with member and two operands:
   ```
   ex utils(cleanup) '25 nocopy'
   ```
3. Sequential dataset with a quoted operand value:
   ```
   ex runit'''yes'''
   ```
4. Partitioned dataset member:
   ```
   ex (regress)
   ```

MS-DOS

1. From DOS prompt:
   ```
   pclist strings 23
   ```
2. Using command mode:
   ```
   pclist (from the DOS prompt)
   ==> strings 23
   ```

Tips and Traps:
1. After the CLIST executes, the READY (TSO), COMMAND ===> (from ISPF and PDF), or C:\ (MS-DOS) prompt reappears.
2. In examples 2–4, the first (usually *userid*) and last qualifier (dataset type of *CLIST*) are implied. Listed below are the fully qualified dataset names:
   Example 2 `'userid.utils(cleanup).CLIST'`
   Example 3 `'userid.runit.CLIST'`
   Example 4 `'userid.CLIST(regress)'`
3. In example 1, the dataset is not part of the SYSPROC concatenation and needs to be fully qualified (i.e. the complete dataset name).
4. In example 3, the operand value '*YES*' is contained in double quotes. To produce double quotes, use three quotes to produce one, six quotes to produce two, etc. Note in example 2 that multiple operand values are separated by blanks.
5. In the MS-DOS examples a file extension of *.CLT* is implied (so the CLIST program is in *strings.clt*). The complete file specification such as *c:\CLIST\ strings.clt*) is needed only if the CLIST program is a directory or subdirectory that is not part of the current path, which is assigned by the DOS PATH command.

6. In TSO/E Version 2 Release 1 and later, you may also specify a *CLIST* keyword operand with the EXEC command. If you do not do this, it takes TSO/E longer to determine if your program is a REXX exec or CLIST program. The following is how example 2 would be invoked with this format:

```
ex utils(cleanup) '25 nocopy' CLIST
```

Invoking a CLIST Program (TSO) in Background

Consider running a TSO or TSO/E CLIST program in background when any of these conditions are present (note that pCLIST does not have a background capability):

1. Your CLIST program is in a stable state and will be changing little in the future.
2. You wish to have a CLIST program processed but without dedicating a foreground session.
3. When you can predetermine what the values to all prompts will be. For example, if your CLIST program archives designated datasets, then it would be a good candidate for background processing if you know in advance the datasets to be archived. Then you can "hard code" them into the batch program.

The following is the "skeleton" of the JCL—job control language program needed to run a CLIST program in background:

```
1. //jobcard
2. //STEP1       EXEC PGM=IKJEFT01,DYNAMBR=30
3A. //SYSTSPRT    DD SYSOUT=A
        Or
3B. //SYSTSPRT    DD DSN=dataset,DISP=OLD
4A. CLIST invocation or
TSO command.
        Or
4B. //SYSTSIN     DD DSN=dataset,DISP=SHR
5. //SYSUDUMP     DD SYSOUT=A
```

Statement by statement explanation:

1. The *job card* includes all the necessary processing information to run the job. Visit your computer center for this information—don't just blindly copy your neighbor's.
2. The *IKJEFT01* program needs to be invoked to process TSO commands or CLIST programs in background. (If you wish to end an IKJEFT01 program before going to the next step, IJKEFT1A is also invoked.) DYNAMBR is the maximum number of dynamic dataset allocations allowed for the job step. Values can be between 1 and 1635.

3. *SYSTSPRT* sends the job's output (which includes the processing of the TSO command or CLIST program) to a printer (3A) or a new/existing dataset (3B).
4. Place *EXEC* or other *TSO commands* here (4A) or in a single dataset (4B). Note that there are various TSO commands and CLIST statements that are not allowed or behave differently during background processing. These include: - READ, READVAL, TERMIN, &SYSDLM, &SYSDVAL, &SYSUID, &SYSPREF, &SYSLTERM, and &SYSWTERM.
5. A useful tool in debugging is having a dump of the user areas. The *SYSUDUMP* statement (5) generates a dump if an error occurs.

Tips and Traps:
These CLIST statements are useful for CLIST programs running in background:

&NRSTR, &STR   To create the JCL program
DATA PROMPT-ENDDATA   For providing values to TSO command prompts
&SYSENV   Returns a value of BATCH, and can be used to conditionally process a sequence only if a CLIST program is executing in background.
&LASTCC   Captures the return code of the last TSO command or CLIST statement processed, good for exception handling
&SYSOUTTRAP and &SYSOUTLINE   Captures TSO command line output

THE FUTURE OF THE CLIST LANGUAGE

In 1987, IBM announced that all its current and future computers (from mainframes to microcomputers) would adhere to a set of emerging procedures and standards called **SAA**, or **System Application Architecture**. An important part of SAA was selecting REXX (or REstructured eXtended eXecutor) as the command language for all IBM computers. This is also called SAA programming language or SAA/PL. In theory, one could run the same program with little modification across all IBM machines. This means that the CLIST language will receive few if any future enhancements and will be not supported in any future TSO/E release. In reality, because there is no conversion software from CLIST programs to REXX execs, the migration process has been slow and painful for many sites. Yet the arrival of pCLIST and four recent books on the CLIST language should renew some interest. So, the CLIST language should continue for some time. However, any new long-term projects should be created with the REXX language.

DEVELOPING CLIST APPLICATIONS

Chapter 2 discussed three different types of common command language applications. The next sections of this chapter provide basic and advanced CLIST sequences to perform the various tasks that an application requires. These sequences are listed under the type of application where it is most commonly used. However, there is no reason why a particular CLIST sequence could not be used by any type of application. The last section in this chapter discusses some major concerns when developing an application. It also looks at porting CLIST applications between MS-DOS and TSO/E and to other command languages.

FRONT-END CLIST APPLICATIONS

Two popular uses of the CLIST language are "housekeeping" for load modules and other applications (such as freeing and deleting files) and startup tasks when logging into a TSO session. This section reviews the sequences necessary to perform both.

How To Access TSO/MS-DOS Commands In a CLIST Program

To access a TSO command, simply place it in a CLIST program. The following sequence prompts the user for a dataset name to delete. The dataset name is placed directly in the TSO command (DELETE) and the dataset is deleted.

TSO

```
WRITE Which dataset do you want to DELETE? (Full name NO quotes)
READ DSET /*Ampersand is not needed for &DSET*/
SET &DSET = &STR('&DSET') /* Quotes are added to &DSET*/
DELETE &DSET /*TSO command with symbolic substitution*/
```

To access a MS-DOS command, simply place it in the pCLIST program. pCLIST also has a *DOS* statement which creates a second COMMAND.COM process. (However, it does not recognize existing settings for environment variables such as PATH and PROMPT.) Here is the MS-DOS version of the sequence:

MS-DOS

```
WRITE Which dataset do you want to DELETE? (Full name NO quotes)
READ DSET /*Ampersand is not needed for &DSET. Quotes not needed.*/
DEL &DSET /*DOS command with symbolic substitution*/
```

How To Get a Return Code From TSO/MS-DOS Commands Or CLIST Statements in a CLIST Program

The result of each TSO command or CLIST statement is placed in a control (system) variable called &LASTCC. Since the value of &LASTCC changes every time a TSO command or CLIST statement is processed, it is recommended to save the desired value of &LASTCC to another symbolic variable to "freeze" the value. Common names for this other symbolic variable are &LCC, &LCD, &RC, &RCD, &CD, and &CODE. Here is how you can do this:

```
                                TSO
ALLOCATE F(OLDDS) DA(OLD.DATA) SHR
  SET &RCD = &LASTCC /*Freezes ALLOCATE &LASTCC */
  SELECT /*Previous &LASTCC Changed*/
    WHEN (&RCD = 0) THEN WRITE ALLOCATE WORKED
    WHEN (&RCD = 12) THEN WRITE ALLOCATE FAILED
    OTHERWISE WRITE SYSTEM OR USER CODE &RCD
  END
```

Notes:

1. Use multiple IFs instead of SELECT if you have TSO/E Version 1 Release 3 and earlier.

2. For pCLIST users, only a small number of DOS commands have return codes (or **ERRORLEVELS**). Under DOS 5.0, these include BACKUP, DISKCOMP, DISKCOPY, DOSVER, FORMAT, GRAFTABL, KEYB, REPLACE, RESTORE, and XCOPY. If an errorlevel is returned from a MS-DOS command, it will be stored in &LASTCC. Note secondary processes cannot return ERRORLEVELS so the value will always be 0.

3. The above example would not work for pCLIST because: a) pCLIST uses the ALLOC command, b) pCLIST currently does not support SELECT, and c) ALLOC returns the message "ALLOC: Dataset does not exist" and does not give a return code unless you have an ERROR statement (e.g., *error set rc=&lastcc*) preceding the ALLOC. Under release 1.09, you will be able to capture the return code directly after an ALLOC or FREE statement.

4. For both TSO and MS-DOS: You can also use the control variable &MAXCC to determine the highest return code found in the CLIST program so far:

```
                                TSO
ALLOCATE F(OLDDS) DA(OLD.DATA) SHR
SET &RCD = &LASTCC      /*Freezes ALLOCATE &LASTCC*/
```

```
IF &RCD<&MAXCC OR &RCD = &MAXCC THEN WRITE HIGHEST RETURN CODE IS -
&MAXCC
    ELSE IF &RCD>&MAXCC THEN WRITE HIGHEST RETURN CODE IS &RCD
```

How To Capture Output From a TSO or MS-DOS Command in a CLIST Program

Of the two different ways to do this, the first is that if Session Manager is installed at your site, you may use the TSO **SMCOPY** command to put *all or part of your interactive session* to a dataset for later manipulation. Here is a typical way to do this:

```
SMFIND 'ALLOC' STREAM(TSOOUT)  /*Finds where the first ALLOCATE was -
used */
SET &LOCATE = &LASTCC  /* Store the ALLOCATE line in &LOCATE */
      /* Copies from the ALLOCATE until line 999 and stores it in
userid.SESSION.DATA */
SMCOPY FROMSTREAM(TSOOUT) TODATASET(SESSION.DATA) LINE(&LOCATE:999)
```

Tips and Traps:
1. Your entire TSO session is stored in a data "stream" named TSOOUT. By manipulating that stream, you can decide how much of your session to save.
2. If you are not going to copy the entire session, then using SMFIND to find the starting and ending lines to save is invaluable. Also consider using the various SMFIND operands such as ALL (All instances of a string. The default is FIRST.), ASIS (case-sensitive search), and FORWARD/BACKWARD. (Direction of search in STREAM. The default is backward.)

The second approach is that if you do not have session manager installed at your site, then use the control variables **&SYSOUTLINE** and **&SYSOUTTRAP** to *capture output from a TSO command*. Note that this is identical to the OUTTRAP built-in function in TSO/E REXX. You must have TSO/E Version 1 Release 3 and later to use these control variables. &SYSOUTTRAP is the maximum number of lines to save from the command output. Note that this has *no effect* on the actual number of lines saved. &SYSOUTLINE, where the command output is stored, is also the number of lines saved. This sequence stores the values from the TSO LIST-CAT command:

```
SET &SYSOUTTRAP = 10000 /*Maximum number of command output lines to -
store*/
SET &OUTP = &STR(&&OUTP)      /* To reduce the number of double amper-
sands used */
```

```
/* The TSO command listed below displays all cataloged datasets that -
have GR00 as their first qualifier */
/*and TEXT as their third qualifier */
LISTC LVL('GR00.*.TEXT')
SET &NUMLINE = &SYSOUTLINE      /* Number of lines of command output */
DO &CNT = 1 TO &NUMLINE  /* Use DO-WHILE for TSO/E Version 1 Release 3 -
and earlier*/
  SET &OUTP&CNT = &&SYSOUTLINE&CNT /*Transfer command output to &OUTP1 -
onward*/
END
```

Tips and Traps:

1. Neither approach will work with the pCLIST. Instead, use the redirection operator (>) after the DOS command. If you want to append to an existing file, use (>>).

   ```
   dir c:\>dirlist.txt /*Redirects a listing of the root directory of -
   the C drive to a file named dirlist.txt.*/
   ```

2. Use the second approach if you are executing a CLIST program in batch (background). Note that approach uses the array symbolic variable &SYSOUTLINE 1 to &SYSOUTLINE*n* with *n* as the value of &SYSOUTLINE (the total number of command output lines). The preceding example takes these values and stores them in the array &OUTP1..&OUTP*n*. Doing this "freezes" the current values of the &SYSOUTLINE array but still allows use of &SYSOUTLINE.

3. A DO loop may not be needed if the &SYSOUTLINE array is small. Just use WRITE statements to display the captured command output lines such as those listed below.

   ```
   WRITE LINE #1 IS... &SYSOUTLINE1
   ```

4. Be careful when using &SYSOUTLINE while the trace facility is enabled (such as CONTROL LIST CONLIST LIST MSG). Because this results in more command output lines being produced, &SYSOUTTRAP may have to be increased to capture all the command line output.

What To Include In a Startup CLIST

A special type of front-end CLIST program is the **startup**, or **logon**, CLIST program (the name is site-dependent). This gets processed before you see the READY prompt or the Session Manager screen. These types of CLIST programs can be as creative as you want them to be. The following types of operations are usually found in startup CLIST programs:

1. *Housekeeping commands:* These are usually allocations of datasets used by CLIST and ISPF programs. Here is an example of some typical TSO and ISPF library allocations:

```
FREE F(SYSPROC ISPPLIB ISPMLIB ISPSLIB ISPTLIB ISPPROF ISPSFILE +
ISPLLIB)
FREE F(SYSEXEC)
ALLOC F(SYSPROC) DA('SAY2.APP.CLIST' -        /*personal CLIST dataset*/
                    'SYS1.SYSTEM.CLIST') SHR REUSE /*system CLIST -
dataset */
ALLOC F(SYSEXEC) DA('SYS1.SYSTEM.EXEC')/*system REXX execs*/
ALLOC F(ISPPLIB) DA('PROD1.APP.ISPPLIB') SHR REUSE /*ISPF panel -
library*/
ALLOC F(ISPMLIB) DA('PROD1.APP.ISPMLIB') SHR REUSE /*ISPF message -
library*/
ALLOC F(ISPSLIB) DA('PROD1.APP.ISPSLIB') SHR REUSE /*ISPF skeleton -
input library*/
ALLOC F(ISPTLIB) DA('PROD1.APP.ISPTLIB') SHR REUSE /*ISPF table input -
library*/
ALLOC F(ISPPROF) DA('PROD1.APP.PROFILE') SHR REUSE /*ISPF panel -
library*/
ALLOC F(ISPLLIB) DA('PROD1.APP.ISPLLIB') SHR REUSE /*ISPF load -
library*/
```

Other examples of housekeeping programs are commands that set up a Session Manager environment and an EXEC that invokes the initial CLIST program or ISPF application (usually for specialized applications or less sophisticated users).

2. *Welcome commands.* These commands humanize a TSO session. For example:

```
SET &HOUR = &SUBSTR(1:2,&SYSTIME) /*Get current hour*/
IF &HOUR GE 12 AND &HOUR LE 24 THEN DO
    SET &TIMEOD = P.M.
       SET &HOUR = &HOUR - 1 /*Set to 12 hour format*/
END
ELSE SET &TIMEOD= A.M.
WRITE HELLO HAL, IT IS &HOUR &TIMEOD /* Example: Hello Hal It Is 2 +
P.M.*/
WRITE TODAY IS &SYSDATE /*Example Today is 12/01/90*/
WRITE NOW GET BACK TO WORK!!!!
```

Tips and Traps:

1. If the housekeeping part of the startup CLIST fails it is usually because: (1) the continuation character (dash) is omitted, or (2) a dataset name is misspelled or missing quotes. If this part fails, it may mean you are unable to access some system/local TSO or ISPF commands (because they cannot be found if the dataset they are in is not allocated). To resolve this problem, you may have to log on to another account. Once logged on, you can change your start-up CLIST.

2. Placing *EXECUTIL SEARCHDD(NO)* in the startup CLIST program searches only SYSPROC datasets instead of SYSEXEC datasets before SYSPROC.

3. pCLIST (DOS) cannot replace AUTOEXEC.BAT but can be called from an AUTOEXEC.BAT so it is the next command processed. Before Version 1.09, character forms of operators (e.g. GE, AND) could not be used—only the symbolic equivalent (e.g. >= and &&).

Invoking a Load Module

To invoke a load module, use the CALL command followed by the dataset name and up to 100 comma-delimited parameters in any case with TSO/E Version 1 Release 2 and later. Here are some examples of invoking load modules:

```
                              TSO
/* Invokes userid.DEMO.LOAD(UTIL1) along with parameters placed in a -
symbolic variable.*/
1. CALL DEMO(UTIL1) '&UPARMS'

/*Fully-qualified load module must be in single quotes. Three comma-
delimited parameters are also passed*/
2. CALL 'SYS1.SYSTEM.LOADMOD(MOD1)' '23,HAL,555-1222'

                              DOS
/* Invoking a DOS executable named RUNIT in pCLIST */
1. RUNIT HAL.TXT
```

Tips and Traps:

1. Use the IKJEFT01 program when invoking CALL in batch. It uses the following skeleton:
```
//STEP1 EXEC PGM=IJKEFT01,DYNAMBR=30
//SYSTSPRT DD SYSOUT=H —put in hold queue
//SYSTSIN DD *
allocate f(sysin) da(test.data) old — (data used by the load module)
call (num 1) —call userid.load(num 1)
/*
```

Getting the Return Code From a Load Module

To obtain a load module's return code, use the WHEN SYSRC command:

```
CALL TEST(RUN1) '88'
WHEN SYSRC(EQ 0) CALL TEST(RUN2) '89' /*Invoke next load module*/
```

```
WHEN SYSRC(= 12) EXEC ERRLIST /*Execute error routine*/
WHEN SYSRC(> 12) SEND 'UNKNOWN ERROR' U(HHG1) /*Send a message*/
```

Tips and Traps:
1. The operator can be symbolic (=) or word (*EQ*). The value it compares to must always be a whole number (EQ 4). No "then" condition is necessary since the default is to end the CLIST (so *WHEN SYSRC(=0)* is valid). If such a condition is included, it is always a TSO command. In any case, a WHEN SYSRC always ends CLIST processing.
2. To include a WHEN SYSRC in a SELECT structure, enclose it in a WHEN-DO-END statement.
```
SELECT (&OPTS)
WHEN (5) DO
  call demo(mod1)
        WHEN SYSRC(GT 0) EXEC ERRLIST
END
END
```

Although not heavily used, some DOS commands such as BACKUP, REPLACE, RESTORE, and XCOPY in DOS 5.0 and executables pass back a return code (or ERRORLEVEL) with a value between 0 and 255. If there is such a return code, pCLIST will have placed its value in the &LASTCC unless the DOS command was included in a DOS statement, which starts up a second COMMAND.COM process. Note that secondary processes cannot return ERRORLEVELS, so the value will always be 0.

SYSTEM/UTILITY CLIST APPLICATIONS

System & Utility CLIST applications are similar to front-end applications but have a different emphasis. These CLIST programs instead perform various system and general utility operations. The sequences that follow are mostly concerned with getting information about one or more datasets.

How Can I Determine If a Dataset Exists?

Before performing various operations on a dataset and producing unwanted errors, it is necessary to determine if the dataset exists. Here are some ways to do this:

```
/* #1 For TSOE Version 1 Release 2 and later*/
1. IF &SYSDSN('HHG1.TEST.DATA') = OK THEN DELETE 'HHG1.TEST.DATA'

/* #2 FOR TSO/E Version 1 Release 3 and later.*/
2. LISTDSI 'HHG1.TEST.DATA'
```

```
IF &LASTCC GT 4 OR &SYSREASON = 24 THEN WRITE DATASET DOES NOT EXIST.
/* #3 Using &SYSOUTLINE*/
3. LISTDS 'HHG1.TEST.DATA'
SET &CNT = &SYSOUTLINE
 IF &CNT <= 1 THEN WRITE 'HHG1.TEST.DATA DOES NOT EXIST'

/* #4 For any version of TSO or TSO/E or pCLIST*/
4. ERROR DO
      SET &RC = &LASTCC
        IF &RC = 400 THEN WRITE DATASET DOES NOT EXIST
      CLOSFILE FILE1
      FREE F(FILE1)  /*pCLIST version: free file1*/
 END
ALLOC F(FILE1) DA('HHG1.TEST.DATA') SHR /*pCLIST version: alloc file1 -
hhg1.dat*/
 OPENFILE FILE1 INPUT
 GETFILE FILE1
 CLOSFILE FILE1
 FREE F(FILE1)     /*pCLIST version: free file1*/

/*#5 pCLIST (MS-DOS)*/
5. IF &SYSDSN(TEST.DAT) = OK THEN WRITE DATASET EXISTS
```

Tips and Traps:

1. These are placed in descending order of reliability. Nos. 1 and 5 are the most direct ways. Also note symbolic variables could be used in any of the above examples and a THEN condition besides a WRITE could be used. This is closer to a "real-world" example:

   ```
   WRITE Enter the name of the dataset to delete:
   READ DSET
   IF &SYSDSN('&DSET') = OK THEN DELETE &DSET
   ```

2. In No. 2, a return code (&LASTCC) for LISTDSI greater or equal to 4, means that LISTDSI had problems processing the dataset, highly likely because it does not exist. A reason code of 24 also means that the dataset does not exist.

3. In No. 3, LISTDS produces four or more lines if a dataset exists. Using &SYSOUTLINE, you can determine how many output lines were produced. (You can enhance this process by comparing &SYSOUTLINE1 or &SYSOUTLINE2 to a predesignated string.)

4. In No. 4, an ERROR routine is needed to capture &LASTCC on an OPEN-FILE if an error occurs—an *IF &LASTCC > 0* statement will not be processed.

5. The examples for pCLIST (MS-DOS) in 4 and 5 are nearly identical to the TSO version (except for the file name and the lack of FILE and DA operands for ALLOC and FREE commands).

File Operations

Both the TSO and MS-DOS CLIST interpreters support dataset operations in either interactive or batch TSO. These operations are performed using the queued sequential access method (or QSAM). Throughout the chapter, you will see the term "CLIST QSAM facility" referring to how the CLIST interpreter performs dataset operations. Datasets are either sequential datasets or members of partitioned datasets. These datasets are usually no larger than 50,000 records. Each record in the dataset is a collection of related values that has no index (or key). Here are skeletons for the basic dataset operations:

READ FROM A DATASET

```
/* Place an error routine here*/
FREE F(DATA1) /*pCLIST free data1*/
ALLOC F(DATA1) DA(DATA.DATA) SHR /* pCLIST alloc data1 data.dat shr*/
OPENFILE DATA1 INPUT
SET &CNT = 1
SET &CL = &STR(&&CL)
DO WHILE &CNT <= 10 /*Read first ten records*/
    GETFILE DATA1/*Get record. Assign to symbolic variable below*/
    SET &CL&CNT=&STR(&DATA1) /*Set &D1..&D5 =record*/
    SET &CNT = &CNT + 1 /*Bump counter. Could also have DO = 1 TO 10*/
END
CLOSFILE DATA1 /*Close the file*/
FREE F(DATA1) /*pCLIST free data1*/
```

WRITE TO A DATASET

```
/* Place an error routine here*/
FREE F(DATA1)/*pCLIST free data1*/
ALLOC F(DATA1) DA(DATA.DATA) MOD /* pCLIST alloc data1 data.dat mod*/
/*Use SHR to overwrite existing records*/
OPENFILE DATA1 OUTPUT
SET &CNT = 1
SET &CL = &STR(&&CL)
SET &CL1 = &STR(Record1)
SET &CL2=&STR(Record2)
SET &CL3=&STR(Record3)
DO WHILE &CNT <= 3 /*Append three new records*/
    SET &DATA1 = &STR(&CL&CNT) /*Set &D1..&D5 =record*/
    PUTFILE DATA1 /*Write record. Capture from symbolic variable -
above*/
    SET &CNT = &CNT + 1 /*Bump counter. Could also have DO = 1 TO 10*/
END
CLOSFILE DATA1 /*Close the file*/
FREE F(DATA1) /*pCLIST free data1*/
```

Here are tips and guidelines when performing dataset operations using the CLIST QSAM facility:

1. For both PUTFILE and GETFILE, use the built-in functions of &STR, &NRSTR, and &SYSNSUB to read special characters and JCL statements.
2. GETFILE and PUTFILE *always* convert text to uppercase regardless of whether you are using CONTROL ASIS or CAPS. This is not documented in many versions of the CLIST user's guides.
3. Use OPENFILE UPDATE to update an existing record and OPENFILE OUTPUT to add or append a new record.
4. Include error routines to handle unexpected end-of-file and other error conditions. (See the section, Exception Handling, in CLIST Programs for further information).

How Can I Obtain DCB Information About a Dataset?

Available since TSO/E Version 1 Release 3, the LISTDSI command stores data control block (DCB) information about a dataset in 25 symbolic variables (also called LISTDSI control variables). You can then copy the information in these symbolic variables to your own symbolic variables. The examples that follow show how you can use this to your advantage.

```
/* #1 Take information from one dataset to allocate another*/

1. LISTDSI TEST.DATA
      SET &RCD = &LASTCC
   ALLOC F(NEWDATA) DA(TEST2.DATA) DSORG(&SYSDSORG) +
      DIR(10) LRECL(&SYSLRECL) BLKSIZE(&SYSBLKSIZE) NEW +
      SPACE(&SYSPRIMARY,&SYSSECONDS) &SYSUNITS RECFM(V B)

/* #2"Dataset at a glance. Only most common symbolic variables are
shown.*/

2. LISTDSI TEST.DATA
      IF &LASTCC = 0 THEN DO
            WRITE ****************Dataset at a glance******
            WRITE *** Dataset Name - - &SYSDSNAME

            WRITE *** Accessed on &SYSREFDATE
            WRITE *** Device is &SYSUNIT and Volume is &SYSVOLUME
            WRITE *** DSORG - - &SYSDSORG and RECFM - - &SYSRECFM
            WRITE *** LRECL - - &SYSLRECl and BLKSIZE - - &SYSBLKSIZE
            WRITE *** Allocated - - &SYSALLOC vs Used - - &SYSUSED in +
            &SYSUNITS units.
      END
/*#3 - The pCLIST version of 2. Only the symbolic variables listed -
below are available.*/
3 LISTDSI TEST.DAT
      IF &LASTCC = 0 THEN DO
            WRITE ****************Dataset at a glance******
```

```
WRITE *** Dataset Name - - &SYSDSNAME with these attributes: -
&SYSATTR
WRITE *** Updated on &SYSREFDATE at &SYSREFTIME
WRITE *** Bytes Allocated - - &SYSALLOC vs Used - - &SYSUSED
```

Tips and Traps:

1. Using LISTDSI, you can expand number 2 to a space utilization report on designated datasets.
2. The TSO ALLOCATE command with the LIKE or USING operands or the ATTRIB command performs a similar function of allocating a dataset with predefined values as number 1.
3. Look at the LISTSP.CLT and the LISTS.CLT included with pCLIST as additional examples on how to use LISTDSI.
4. The following is sample output from 2 and 3.

EXAMPLE 2 (TSO)

```
*******************Dataset at a glance******
*** Dataset Name - - HHG1.TEXT.DATA
*** Accessed on 1990/288 (Note:julian date)
*** Device is 3380 and Volume is VOL12
*** DSORG - - PO and RECFM - - FBA
*** LRECL - - 80 and BLKSIZE - - 6160
*** Allocated - - 21 vs Used - - 21 in TRACK units.
```

EXAMPLE 3 (pCLIST)

```
*******************Dataset at a glance******
(note that the full path is not shown such as C:\HHG1.DATA)
*** Dataset Name - - HHG1.DATA with these attributes:..A.. (Note:
Archive dataset)
*** Updated on 10/14/1990 at 15:22:30
*** Bytes Allocated - - 100 vs Used - - 100
```

5. Note you cannot directly use &SYSRECFM in an ALLOCATE since ALLOCATE expects spaces between the letters (example LISTDSI returns FBA but ALLOCATE expects F B A).
6. &SYSATTR was added to pCLIST in Version 1.08c. It is a six-character string that has a value of either period (.) or the file attribute (such as R [read-only], H [hidden], S [system], A [archive], D [directory], and L [label].

How Can I Parse a Dataset Name?

The following is a general-purpose subroutine for parsing a dataset name. The subroutine could be converted to a subprocedure or stand-alone CLIST program. It checks if quotes are used or not and can be used only with TSO/E Version 1 Release 3 and later.

TSO

```
PROC 1 DSET
SET &DSLEN = &LENGTH(&STR(&DSET))
/***STRIP_Q- - removes quotes from a dataset name if they are present*/
STRIP_Q:-
   IF &SYSINDEX(&STR('),&DSET) = 0 THEN SET &DSET2 = &STR(&DSET) /*if no -
   quotes*/
      ELSE DO /*If Quotes Found....*/
      SET &Q_LOC = &SYSINDEX(&STR('),&DSET,2) /*Set &Q_LOC to second quote -
      location*/
      /*Reset &DSET without quotes*/
      IF &Q_LOC > 0 THEN SET &DSET2 = SUBSTR(2:&Q_LOC-1,&DSET)
   END
/*Dataset without quotes*/
      SET &DSLENN = &LENGTH(&DSET2)/* Capture new length of &DSET2*/
/****MEM_PAR- -parses member name*/
MEM_PAR:-
  SET &RIGHTP = &STR()) /*Set &RIGHTP to)*/
  SET &LEFTP = &STR (( /*SET &LEFTP to (. Right parenthesis is not needed*/
  IF &SYSINDEX(&STR(&RIGHTP),&DSET2) > 0 THEN DO /* If member found...*/
      SET &LPAREN = &SYSINDEX(&STR(&LEFTP),&DSET2) /*Find left parenthesis*/
      IF &LPAREN > 0 THEN DO /*parse to get member name*/
          SET &MEM = &SUBSTR(&LPAREN+1:&DSLENN-1,&DSET2)
          SET &DSET2 = &SUBSTR(1:&LPAREN-1,&DSET2) /*Dataset name without member*/
          SET &DSLENN = &LENGTH(&DSET2) /*Length of remaining dataset name*/
      END
      ELSE DO
          WRITE MISSING LEFT PARENTHESIS ON MEMBER NAME
          EXIT
      END
  END
  ELSE SET &MEM = /*Set &MEM to blank if no member*/
D_PARSE:
  SET &P = &SYSINDEX(&STR(.),&DSET2) /* Find first period in dataset name*/
  SET &P2 = &SYSINDEX(&STR(.),&DSET2,&P+1) /*Find second period in dataset name*/
  SET &FIRST = &SUBSTR(1:&P-1,&DSET2) /*Dataset name up to first period (first -
  qualifier)*/
/*Dataset name second qualifier (if second period is present)*/
  IF &P2 > 0 THEN DO
          SET &SECOND = &SUBSTR(&P+1:&P2-1,&DSET2)
          SET &THIRD = &SUBSTR(&P2+1:&DSLENN,&DSET2)/*Dataset name - - dataset -
          type */
  END
  ELSE THIRD = &SUBSTR(&P+1:&DSLENN,&DSET2)/* If no second qualifier*/
/* If the dataset name was 'HHG1.TEST.DATA(MEM1)' then FIRST=HHG1, SECOND = -
TEST*/
/* THIRD= DATA and MEM=MEM1*/
```

Here is the version for DOS files:

MS-DOS

```
PROC 1 DSET
SET &DSLEN = &LENGTH(&STR(&DSET))
STRIP_Q:-
IF &SYSINDEX(&STR('),&DSET) = 0 THEN SET &DSET2 = &STR(&DSET)   /*If no -
Quotes.*/
ELSE DO
    SET &Q_LOC = &SYSINDEX(&STR('),&DSET,2) /* Set &Q_LOC to second quote loca-
    tion*/
     IF &Q_LOC > 0 THEN SET &DSET2 = &SUBSTR(2:&Q_LOC-1,&DSET)
END
SET &DSLENN = &LENGTH(&DSET2)
SET &P = &SYSINDEX(&STR(.),&DSET2) /*Find first period in dataset name*/
SET &FIRST = &SUBSTR(1:&P-1,&DSET2)/*Dataset name up to first period (first -
qualifier)*
SET &SECOND = &SUBSTR(&P+1:&DSLENN,&DSET2) /* second qualifier*/
/* If file name is AUTOEXEC.BAT then &FIRST = AUTOEXEC and SECOND = BAT.*/
```

Tips and Traps:
1. These sequences are still rather simple. They could include validations for the second parentheses or quotes.
2. The idea of parsing is rather simple. Find some unique character (such as a period or parenthesis) and use that character to break up the string into recognizable components. Let us take a statement from the preceding example:
```
SET &SECOND = &SUBSTR(P+1:P2-1,&DSET2)
```

If written as a sentence, it would read "Assign &SECOND the substring in &DSET2 starting one character past the first period and ending one character before the second period." So if &DSET is HHG1.TEST.DATA, &SECOND has a value of TEST. In addition, it may help to look at Tables 3-1 and 3-2 in creating your parse routines.

How Can I Decide What Is a Dataset's First Qualifier (TSO)?

Your system's security software (i.e. RACF, ACF2, TOP SECRET) decides the default prefix (or first qualifier) that is used when a dataset is not fully qualified (that is, the dataset name is not in quotes). This prefix is stored in the CLIST control variable &SYSPREF. Userid, a common value for the first qualifier, is stored in the control variable &SYSUSID. The following prefix will use &SYSPREF only if it is not blank or equals &SYSUID.

```
IF &STR(&SYSPREF) ¬= OR &STR(&SYSPREF) = &STR(&SYSUSID) THEN DO
    SET &DSET1 = '&SYSPREF..TEST.DATA' /*Remember it takes 2 periods -
    to produce 1*/
END
allocate f(DSET1) da(&DSET1) shr
```

How Can I Find Out Information About My System?

If you are new to a site, using a CLIST sequence similar to the following can be helpful to tell you what is available:

```
PROC 0
WRITE TSO/E Level               &SYSTSOE /*TSOE Version 1 Release 3 -
                                and later*/
WRITE Is RACF on this system?   &SYSRACF /*TSOE Version 1 Release 2 -
                                and later*/
WRITE RACF Level                &SYSLRACF /*TSOE Version 1 Release 3 -
                                and later*/
WRITE Is HSM on this system?    &SYSHSM /*TSOE Version 1 Release 3 -
                                and later*/
WRITE Default dataset prefix.   &SYSPREF /*TSOE and TSO*/
WRITE Userid                    &SYSUID /*TSO and TSOE*/
WRITE Logon Procedure           &SYSPROC /*TSO and TSOE*/
```

Table 3-1. Parsing a String into Two Variables

Variable	Start	End
1	Position 1	Up to the first delimiter (e.g. &DLM1 −1)
2	1 past the first delimiter (e.g. &DLM1 +1)	End of string (e.g. &LENGTH(&STR(&TEXT))

Table 3-2. Parsing a String into Three Variables

Variable	Start	End
1	Position 1	Up to the first delimiter (e.g. &DLM1 −1)
2	1 past the first delimiter (e.g. &DLM1 + 1)	Up to the second delimiter (e.g. &DLM2−1)
3	1 past the second delimiter (e.g. &DLM2 + 1)	End of string (e.g. &LENGTH(&STR(&TEXT))

The following is typical output from such a CLIST program:

```
TSO/E Level                    2030 (Note: Version 2 Release 3.0)
Is RACF on this system?        AVAILABLE
RACF Level                     1040 (Note: Version 1 Release 4.0)
Is HSM on this system?         HSM
Default dataset prefix         HHG1
Userid                         HHG1
Logon Procedure                LOGONA
```

How Can I Find Out Information About My Session?

Use a CLIST program sequence similar to the following to gather information about your current session:

```
PROC 0
WRITE ISPF is                           &SYSISPF /*TSOE Version 1 -
                                        Release 2 and later*/

WRITE CLIST mode is                     &SYSENV /*TSO and TSOE*/
WRITE CLIST is nested                   &SYSNEST /*TSO and TSOE*/
WRITE CLIST name (IMPLICIT only)        &SYSICMD /*TSO and TSOE*/
WRITE Last TSO command executed         &SYSPCMD /*TSO and TSOE*/
WRITE Last TSO subcommand executed      &SYSSCMD /*TSO and TSOE*/
WRITE Highest return code in CLIST      &MAXCC /*TSO and TSOE*/
WRITE Terminal length                   &SYSLTERM
                                        /*TSOE Version 1 Release 2 and -
                                        later*/

WRITE Terminal width                    &SYSWTERM
                                        /*TSOE Version 1 Release 2 and -
                                        later*/


ISPF is                                 NOT ACTIVE
CLIST mode is                           FORE
CLIST is nested                         YES
CLIST name (IMPLICIT only)              (Note: Null because explicitly
                                        invoked.)
Last TSO command executed               EX (NOTE: EXEC last TSO command
                                        executed.)
Last TSO subcommand executed            (Note: Null because EXEC has no
                                        subcommands.)
Highest return code in CLIST            0
Terminal length                         24
Terminal width                          80
```

If you are using pCLIST (MS-DOS), then you can modify the preceding CLIST program. However, of the program's control variables, only &SYSNEST and &MAXCC are available.

What Version of TSO/E Do I Have?

Knowing your TSO version is important in learning about what enhancements are available, knowing if you need to update your documentation, and determining any known bugs and fixes through IBM's IBMLINK (USA) or Dial IBM (available elsewhere) database and other sources.

Here is an easy way to do this:

```
WRITE MY TSO/E VERSION IS &SYSTSOE
Displayed:
MY TSO/E VERSION IS (NOTE: Null or error message is TSO or TSO/E Ver-
                           sion 1 Release 1 or 2)
MY TSO/E VERSION IS 1030 (NOTE: Version 1 Release 3)
MY TSO/E VERSION IS 1040 (NOTE: Version 1 Release 4)
MY TSO/E VERSION IS 2010 (NOTE: Version 2 Release 1)
MY TSO/E VERSION IS 2020 (NOTE: Version 2 Release 2)
MY TSO/E VERSION IS 2030 (NOTE: Version 2 Release 3)
```

The current version of pCLIST (MS-DOS), 1.08c, cannot be captured from a control variable. This will probably be added in a future release.

How Do I Clear a Screen?

You may need to clear a screen while running an application. If your site does not have a command to do this, use either of these:

1. If Session Manager is installed at your site, issue a DELETE WINDOW or CHANGE.STREAM CLEAR to erase or remove the current screen.
2. Compile an assembly language program with a STLINE0 LINE=1 macro.

For 3270-type terminals, this erases the screen and starts the next display on line 1. There is an example on how to do this in IBM's guide *TSO/E Programming Services* (SC28-1875).

For pCLIST (MS-DOS) users, place the MS-DOS command CLS right in your CLIST program.

SELF-CONTAINED CLIST APPLICATIONS

Self-contained CLIST applications are one or more CLIST programs oriented to end-users instead of computer center staff. Sequences presented in this section are concerned with capturing and validating user input; passing and receiving values and return codes from subprocedures and nested CLISTs, and miscellaneous operations such as date and time operations and case operations.

Capturing User Command Line Values

The following shows some of the options in parsing the values supplied when a CLIST program is invoked.

```
    From READY:
EX CRUN HHG1.DATA PDS OPERAND3(15) OPERAND4(10) BATCH
    In CLIST:
PROC 2 OPERAND1 OPERAND2 OPERAND3( ) OPERAND4(20) BATCH LIST
IF &OPERAND4 = 20 AND &BATCH = BATCH THEN WRITE EXEC WORKED!
```

Tips and Traps:

1. The CLIST program expects two **positional** operands (OPERAND1 and OPERAND2). Note that positional operands can be up to 252 characters, have no default values, are entered in order, and are prompted if a value is not supplied. After the PROC statement is processed, 'HHG1.DATA' is assigned to &OPERAND1 and PDS is assigned to &OPERAND2. The IF statement shows to process either a positional or keyword operand symbolic variable—just like any other symbolic variable.

2. In the preceding example, up to four **keyword** operands may be specified. Keyword operands may be up to 31 characters, are optional (not prompted if not supplied), may have default values, and can be entered in any order. In the example, &OPERAND3 had no associated default value and is assigned a value of 15. A value would be prompted for if one is not supplied. Also &OPERAND4 has the default associated value of 20 overridden with a value of 10. &BATCH is an example of the other type of keyword operand without a default value and is assigned a value of BATCH. Although &LIST is specified on the PROC line, it is not used and is assigned a value of null.

3. If a CLIST is explicitly invoked, all operands must be enclosed in single quotes. Operands are delimited by blanks. Note that you will have to use two single quotes to produce one in the explicit form. Associated keyword operand values can be placed in single quotes (such as dataset names).

4. For pCLIST (MS-DOS) users, keywords operands can be entered in either upper or lower case. (For TSO users, it is upper case only.)

How To Create Menus, User Prompts, and Confirmation Messages

WRITE and WRITENR—short for WRITE NO RETURN—play an important role in self-contained applications. Note that the two statements are nearly identical but WRITENR keeps the input cursor *on the same line* while WRITE puts it on the *next line.* The following approach can be used in either TSO or MS-DOS CLIST programs and shows three common uses of WRITE and WRITENR statements:

WRITE FOR PROMPTING INPUT:

```
1. WRITENR What is Your State of Residence?
   displayed:
   What is Your State of Residence? WASHINGTON
```

WRITE FOR MENUS

```
2. WRITE *********************************************
   WRITE * Please select ONE of the Following:    *
   WRITE * T - Travel Expense Report               *
   WRITE * W - Word Processing                      *
   WRITE * P - Programming                          *
   WRITE *********************************************
   WRITENR Enter Your Choice (P,W,T):
   displayed:
   *********************************************
   * Please select ONE of the Following:    *
   * T - Travel Expense Report               *
   * W - Word Processing                      *
   * P - Programming                          *
   *********************************************
   Enter Your Choice (P,W,T): P
```

WRITE FOR CONFIRMATION MESSAGES

```
3. WRITENR The report from &DSET1 is queued to print on
   WRITE printer &PRT1 displayed:
   The report from 'GROO.DATA(MAY88)' is queued to print on printer PRINTER1
```

Tips and Traps:

1. Note that WRITENR is ineffective under Session Manager because: (1) the input will always be placed on the line following the WRITENR, and (2) to process a null value, a user has to go through the process of pressing the Erase to End of Field (or EOF) key and then the Return Key.

2. As a general guideline, use WRITENR for (a) displaying text that goes on multiple lines, (b) prompting for user input and (c) prompting for a menu selection. Use WRITE for everything else.

3. Add several WRITEs if you need to guarantee that some text will fill up the screen.

How to Capture and Parse User Input

Often accompanying WRITE and WRITENR statements, READ and READ-DVAL can be used to capture user input and pass it to one or more symbolic variables. The following are some examples on using these statements (these can be used for either TSO or MS-DOS CLIST programs):

ONE VALUE

```
CLIST:
WRITE PLEASE ENTER YOUR AGE
READ AGE
WRITE YOUR CLAIMED AGE IS .... &AGE
WRITE THE VALUE OF SYSDVAL IS.... &SYSDVAL
Displayed:
PLEASE ENTER YOUR AGE
22
YOUR CLAIMED AGE IS .... 22
THE VALUE OF SYSDVAL IS.... (Note: Null because READ has a symbolic
                                   variable.)
                           Long value with blanks
CLIST:
WRITE ENTER A LONG MESSAGE WITH BLANKS
READ
WRITE SYSDVAL IS ...&SYSDVAL

Displayed:
ENTER A LONG MESSAGE WITH BLANKS
A LONG MESSAGE WITH BLANKS
SYSDVAL IS ...A LONG MESSAGE WITH BLANKS (Note: Entire line is
                                           retained)
```

MULTIPLE MULTIWORD VALUES

```
CLIST:
WRITE PLEASE ENTER YOUR FIVE ALL-TIME FAVORITE TELEVISION SHOWS.
WRITE USE WRITE UNDERSCORES (_) BETWEEN WORDS, COMMAS BETWEEN SHOWS:
READ
READDVAL SHOW1 SHOW2 SHOW3 SHOW4 SHOW5 (Note: Parses &SYSDVAL)
WRITE SHOW #1 is......&SHOW1
WRITE SHOW #2 is......&SHOW2
WRITE SHOW #3 is......&SHOW3
```

```
WRITE SHOW #4 is......&SHOW4
WRITE SHOW #5 is......&SHOW5
WRITE SYSDVAL IS...
```

Displayed:
```
PLEASE ENTER YOUR FIVE ALL-TIME FAVORITE TELEVISION SHOWS.
USE WRITE UNDERSCORES (_) BETWEEN WORDS, COMMAS BETWEEN SHOWS:
M*A*S*H, OTHERWORLD, QUANTUM_LEAP, STAR_TREK, NOVA
WRITE SHOW #1 is......M*A*S*H
WRITE SHOW #2 is......OTHERWORLD
WRITE SHOW #3 is......QUANTUM_LEAP
WRITE SHOW #4 is......STAR_TREK
WRITE SHOW #5 is......NOVA
SYSDVAL IS...M*A*S*H, OTHERWORLD, QUANTUM_LEAP, STAR_TREK, NOVA
```

Tips and Traps:

1. Use two commas or single quotes to assign a null value in a READ statement:
   ```
   READ VAR1, VAR2, VAR3
   ```
   Entered by User:
   ```
   3,,2 (Note: &VAR1 = 3, &VAR2 =, &VAR3=2)
   '3' " '2' (Same result as above)
   '3' " '2' (Note: Results in 3 " 2)
   ```

2. A symbolic variable is set to null if a user does not specify a value in a READ or READDVAL statement. If there are more values than symbolic variables, then the extra values are ignored.

3. The user must enter a space, or comma to delimit between multiple values.

4. The preceding example should drive home the difference between READ and READDVAL. READ can directly take user input either storing it in user-defined symbolic variables or &SYSDVAL. Once it is in &SYSDVAL, READDVAL can be used to parse the input. (For example, everything from the first character up to the first blank is placed in the first READDVAL symbolic variable and so forth.)

5. Use an underscore or some other non-blank character to read multiple words as one value. Otherwise, READ will assign the value after the first blank to the next symbolic variable (if there is one) or discard the rest.
   ```
   READ VAL1
   User Enters:
   Really One Long Value (Note VAL1 is assigned a value of REALLY. The
   rest is dropped.)
   ```

How To Validate User Input

Once the CLIST has captured and parsed user input using one of the approaches discussed in the previous section, then the next step is to validate the input. Validation usually consists of one of the four types (These can be used for either TSO or MS-DOS CLIST programs):

1. *Checking the data type*
```
ST_VAL: WRITE: Enter your STATE OF RESIDENCE:
READ &ST
IF &DATATYPE(&ST) NE CHAR THEN GOTO ST_VAL
AGE_VAL:WRITE: Enter your AGE:
READ &AGE
IF &DATATYPE(&AGE) NE NUM THEN GOTO AGE_VAL
```

Tips and Traps:

1. pCLIST uses ^= for "not equals." Release 1.09 supports character formats of operators (such as GE).
2. Decimals (such as 1.1) are seen as CHAR not NUM.

2. *Checking for specific values:*
```
MENU1:
(Menu not shown)
WRITENR Enter your selection (A, B, C)
READ SEL
IF &SEL ¬= A AND &SEL ¬= B AND &SEL ¬= C THEN DO
 WRITE INVALID CHOICE PLEASE REENTER
  GOTO MENU1
END
```

Tips and Traps:

1. pCLIST uses ^= for "not equals." Release 1.09 supports character formats of operators (such as AND).
2. For TSO/E Version 1 Release 4 and later, you can also use a SELECT:
```
SELECT (&SEL)
WHEN (A|B|C) /*Go to END*/
OTHERWISE WRITE Invalid Selection. Must be A-C
END
```

3. *Checking for a number range*
```
MENU1:
(Menu not shown)
WRITENR Enter your selection (1-5)
READ SEL
IF &SEL LT 1 OR &SEL GT 5 THEN DO
 WRITE INVALID CHOICE PLEASE REENTER
  GOTO MENU1
END
```

Tips and Traps:

1. For TSO/E Version 1 Release 4 and later, you can also use a SELECT:
```
SELECT (&SEL)
WHEN (1:5) /*If in the range, go to END*/
OTHERWISE WRITE Invalid Selection. Must be 1-5
END
```

4. *Checking for blank/nonblank:*
```
IF &SEL = /*Checking for blank input*/
IF &SEL NE /* Checking for non-blank input - - TSO*/
IF &SEL ^= /* Checking for non-blank input - - pCLIST*/
```

How To Obtain the Current Date And Time

The following CLIST sequence shows you how to access the current date and time using control variables:

```
WRITE MMDDYY Format             &SYSDATE Note: (Sample: 12/01/90)
WRITE YYMMDD Format             &SYSSDATE Note: (Sample: 90/12/01)
WRITE YYDDD Format (Julian)     &SYSJDATE Note: (Sample: 90:335)
WRITE HHMMSS Format             &SYSTIME Note: (Sample: 15:10:21)
WRITE HHMM Format               &SYSSTIME Note: (Sample: 15:10)
```

Tips and Traps:

1. &SYSJDATE, &SYSSDATE, and &SYSSTIME are available for sites running TSO/E Version 1 Release 2 and later.

2. pCLIST supports all of the above.

3. Use &SUBSTR to extract the desired date or time substring.

4. Except for the WRITE statement, &STR or &SUBSTR you must enclose date and time values within a built-in function because they contain the special characters of colons and slashes.

5. Limitations:
   a. No easy way to change the date or time to a different format (you have to parse the string and then reconcatenate it).
   b. No mmddyy or yymmdd function without slashes. This would be useful for date calculations.
   c. No control variable that returns AM or PM although you can easily create your own.
   d. No control variable for each component of day and time such as just current hour. Again, you can easily do this on your own.
   ```
   SET &HOUR = &SUBSTR(1:2,&SYSTIME)
   ```

How Do I Change Text To Upper/Lower/Mixed Case?

For sites using TSO/E Version 1 Release 2 and later, CLIST programs can specify the case of a string. Here are some guidelines to produce the desired results:

1. To produce text in all caps (uppercase).
   a. Use CONTROL CAPS or include a SET &SYSASIS=OFF (TSO/E Version 1 Release 4 and later) statement.

   b. After doing a, just enter text in either upper- or lowercase. All text will be converted to uppercase.

2. To produce text with some lowercase characters:

   a. Use a CONTROL NOCAPS, CONTROL ASIS, or SET &SYSASIS=ON statement.

   b. After doing a, lowercase characters are not converted. Use &SYSCAPS to reset specified characters to uppercase. Here is an example of capitalizing a first name:

```
CONTROL ASIS
SET &FNAME = &SYSCAPS(&SUBSTR(1,&FNAME))+
             &SYSLC(&SUBSTR(2:&LENGTH(&FNAME),&FNAME))
```

3. Additional tips and traps:

   a. Neither &SYSCAPS or &SYSLC converts special characters (hexadecimal codes 00-FF), numbers, national characters (#,@,$), and double-byte characters (but is supported in TSO/E Version 1 Releases 2 and 3).

   b. GETFILE and PUTFILE are always converted to uppercase regardless of the CONTROL CAPS setting. This is not documented in some CLIST user guides.

   c. If working with input or data of unknown case, convert everything to uppercase using the preceding methods.

```
CONTROL CAPS
WRITE WHAT IS YOUR SEX?
READ SEX
IF &SEX = FEMALE THEN DO /*won't fail if &SEX = female*/
```

   d. Use a CONTROL statement to temporarily change an existing setting.

   e. When using &SYSLC or &SYSCAPS with another built-in function, always have either one enclose that function.

   f. pCLIST can do all of the preceding but has no CONTROL NOCAPS. Use CONTROL ASIS instead. This also can be set with a *set pCLIST=a* statement executed from a batch file or entered at the DOS command prompt.

How Do I Add Trailing Blanks to a String?

Use the following approach if you wish to add trailing blanks to a string. This is useful if you wish to keep all the values of a symbolic variable the same length.

```
/* Makes sure that &CITY always has a length of 20 */
SET &BLANK="                    "/*20 blanks*/
SET &CITY = ATLANTA
SET &CITY = &STR(&CITY&SUBSTR(2:21-&LENGTH(&CITY),&BLANK))

   Or
SET &CITY = ATLANTA
```

```
SET &LEN=&LENGTH(&STR(&CITY))-1
SET &CITY=&STR(&CITY&SUBSTR(2:20-&LEN,"        "))
```

How Do I Pass Information Between CLIST Programs?

A good CLIST programmer will use **modular programming** for all types of applications. The idea is to create easily identifiable modules that perform one or two related functions. These modules can be identified by a CLIST label in a CLIST program or reside as an external (or multiple or nested) CLIST program called by the main CLIST program.

Note that both nested CLIST programs and subprocedures are limited because (1) they do not support concurrent (or synchronous processing) where the main and nested CLIST programs execute in parallel, (2) unlike FORTRAN, there is no means to specify which statement in the nested CLIST program or subprocedure to execute. This is also true for statements in the main CLIST program after the nested procedure or nested CLIST program ends processing.

The following are the three ways that a nested and main CLIST program can pass information to each other, (the CLIST program that the nested CLIST program was invoked from can be used by TSO and MS-DOS CLIST programs)

1. Passing positional and keyword operands when *invoking a nested CLIST program.*
   ```
   %NEST2 12 AGE(15) NOMAYO
   ```
2. *Using EXIT* passes a return code to the main CLIST program:
   ```
   Main CLIST program:
   %NEST2    /*pCLIST version: pCLIST nest2*/
     SET &RCD = &LASTCC
     IF &RCD = 0 THEN WRITE Nested CLIST program WORKED!
       ELSE WRITE Nested CLIST program FAILED - - LASTCC is &RCD

   NEST 2 CLIST:
   (CLIST statements)
   EXIT CODE(&MAXCC)
   ```
3. Using global variables.

Global variables provide a way for all accessed CLIST programs to pass values to each other. Keep these rules in mind when dealing with global variables:

1. It is the *number of global variables in the first CLIST program* ("main") that determines the number of available global variables. So if the first CLIST has a *GLOBAL A B C D* statement, the nested CLIST cannot have more than four global variables. (You also get the message IKJ56535I NESTED CLIST GLOBAL PARMS SPECIFIED EXCEED THE MAX DEFINED BY THE FIRST-LEVEL CLIST.) Therefore, always have some surplus global variables in your main CLIST program, but usually no more than five.

2. *It is the position not the name* of the global variable that decides its value. So, you could have a main CLIST program with a *GLOBAL A B* statement and a nested CLIST program with a GLOBAL B A statement. Thus, &B in the nested CLIST program receives the value of &A from the main CLIST program. I strongly recommend a global variable "scorecard" placed in each CLIST program header:

```
/* GLOBALS:           */
/*
/* CLIST    Pos1    Pos2 */
/* MAIN1    A       B    */
/* NEST2    B       A    */
```

3. Global variables are *cumulative*. So there are *seven* global variables available for your use if the main CLIST program has a GLOBAL A B C D E statement and the nested CLIST program has a GLOBAL F G statement.

Tips and Traps:
1. Use the control variable &SYSNEST to detect if you are in a nested CLIST program.

```
IF &SYSNEST EQ YES THEN EXIT(&MAXCC) /*If nested logic*/
   ELSE EXIT
```

2. Standardize on global variables as much as you can at your site.
3. CONTROL MAIN or CONTROL NOFLUSH preserves the input stack if an ATTN or ERROR routine is invoked.
4. Place the heaviest used global variables first to reduce the number of global variables you have to define in a nested CLIST program.
5. When to use a nested CLIST program as opposed to a subprocedure: (1) when multiple CLIST programs access the same sequence, and; (2) when efficiency is less of a concern.

How Do I Pass Information Between a CLIST Program And a Subprocedure?

While nested CLIST programs are in a different dataset or member than the main CLIST program, a **subprocedure** is a sequence that is part of the main CLIST program, identified by a CLIST label and available for all sites running TSO/E Version 1 Release 4 and later and pCLIST users. The following are ways to pass values between a main program and a subprocedure:

1. Using the *SYSCALL and PROC* statements:
   SYSCALL is placed in the main CLIST program and the PROC statement is placed in the subprocedure. The following statement would invoke a subprocedure called SUB1 with three symbolic variables:

```
SET &Q=1
SYSCALL SUB1 SAD Q &Y
```

```
/*Q is the variable NAME not &Q. &Y is the VALUE of &Y */
SUB1: PROC 3 VALUE1 VALUE2 VALUE3 /*Required to parse the SYSCALL*/
    SYSREF VALUE2 /*Says Q is a variable NAME not value*/
    RETURN CODE(&MAXCC)
    END /*Required*/
```

2. Using the *RETURN* statement to pass a return code to the main CLIST such as *RETURN CODE(&MAXCC)*.

3. Using the *NGLOBAL* statement in the main CLIST program. It does not have some of the limitations of GLOBAL. Namely, the subprocedure does not require an NGLOBAL statement and NGLOBAL variables are determined by variable name and not by position. Here is a simple example of an NGLOBAL statement:

```
CONTROL MAIN   /*This example works under pCLIST */
NGLOBAL Q
SET &Q = 1
SYSCALL SUB1
SUB1: PROC 0   /*Proc statement is required*/
    WRITE &EVAL(&Q+1) /*2*/
    RETURN /* return to the main CLIST*/
END
```

4. *Using the SYSREF statement and value* changes a value in the main CLIST program. Beware! Here is an example of this:

```
CONTROL MAIN MSG CAPS
MAIN101: -
SET &STATE = &STR(NEW JERSEY)
SYSCALL SUB1 ST1 OTH2
  IF &LASTCC NE 0 THEN WRITE THE SUBPROCEDURE FAILED.
WRITE &ST1 /* New York! */
SUB1: PROC2 VALUE1 VALUE2
    SYSREF &VALUE1 /* So you can modify &ST1 */
    SET &VALUE1 = &STR(NEW YORK)
    RETURN CODE 0
END
```

Tips and Traps:

1. END is required to terminate the subprocedure and return to the main CLIST program. Otherwise the following message is displayed: END OF FILE ON CLIST INPUT OCCURRED BEFORE ALL PROC STATEMENTS WERE CLOSED.

2. After a subprocedure is completed, the main CLIST program continues with the next statement after the one that invoked the subprocedure.

3. Use subprocedures over nested CLIST programs when (1) efficiency is a concern or (2) only one program heavily uses a subprocedure.

4. pCLIST currently does not support the SYSREF statement. It is intended to be added in a future release, possibly 1.09.

How Do I Create Reports Using CLIST Programs?

Although the CLIST language is not a report-generation language, it could be used to create some types of reports. These include reports about their current session; a report on the MVS system at the current site; and reports from flat dataset databases (generated by the CLIST QSAM facility). The code to produce an error log dataset is shown in the section Exception Handling in CLIST Programs. For reports about datasets, see the section How Can I Parse a Dataset Name for More Information.

These techniques could be used by the CLIST programs that generate reports:

CLIST QSAM facility to obtain the correct records on perform database transactions (such as adding or modifying a record). This can also be used to generate a customized report by using arrays.

Various *string operations* such as parsing, concatenating, and building arrays

Control variables and *built-in functions*

Symbolic substitution to generate customized reports

OTHER CLIST PROGRAM CONCERNS

This section deals with topics that are appropriate for all types of CLIST applications. This includes porting TSO CLISTs to be used by the pCLIST program (MS-DOS).

How Do I Debug a CLIST Program?

The following is a general approach when debugging a CLIST program:

What happened?
  Describe action—what happened, what was supposed to happen?
  Record all error messages.

Gather more information about the problem:
  Where exactly is the error happening—on invocation, at a certain label, when invoking a subprocedure or multiple CLIST program?
  Getting the problem to occur in a consistent fashion makes it easier to resolve.

Make an educated guess about what caused the problem and a way to test it.

Perform the test. If it works, there is no need to go further. Otherwise return to the step to gather more information.

Using the preceding approach, here are some techniques you can use in debugging a CLIST program:

1. Liberal use of WRITE statements—check the value of a symbolic variable before an operation. Check flow control (WRITE GOT PAST LABEL101).

2. Examine &LASTCC—did an operation give a zero return code?

3. Check your TSO Version (WRITE &SYSTSOE). This may be useful in knowing if there are problems that may take place for your release.

4. The CLIST trace facility
   a. Invoked by CONTROL statement that includes one or more of the following keywords: **CONLIST**—CLIST statement after symbolic substitution; **SYMLIST**—CLIST statement before symbolic substitution; **LIST**—TSO statement after symbolic substitution; **MSG**—error and informational messages. Putting NO in front of any of the above keywords disables that trace feature.
   b. Can also be invoked by assigning any of the following control variables a value of ON (TSO/E Version 1 Release 4 and later) &SYSCONLIST, &SYSLIST, &SYSMSG, and &SYSSYMLIST. In addition, pCLIST (PC DOS) users can enter the following from the DOS command prompt or execute from a batch file: *set pclist=c* (CONLIST on), *set pclist=l* (LIST on), and *set pclist=s* (SYMLIST on).

Elements of CLIST Program Style

After writing CLIST programs for a while, you begin to develop your own "fingerprint" or style. This section discusses some of the elements of a good style. Read the Kernighan and Plauger (1978) or the Dilorio (1989) references for further information. The following are general rules that apply to all types of CLIST applications (use them based on your personal and site preferences):

1. *Make your CLIST programs readable:*
   a. *Break your CLIST sequences into modules* that perform only one or two functions. Use label names that describe these functions. These modules can be placed in nested CLIST programs or subprocedures.
   b. *Indent* two or three spaces for (1) code under a label, (2) a IF &LASTCC under TSO command or CLIST statement, (3) READ after a WRITE, and (4) the CLIST statements contained within flow-control structures such as DO-WHILE-END and IF-THEN-ELSE-END.
   c. *Line up* all DOs and ENDs, IFs and ENDs, SELECTs and ENDs, along with Subprocedure Labels and ENDs.
   d. Use *blank space* to separate modules (label and a sequence of code until the next label) and flow control structures.
   f. Some *commenting* to self-document the CLIST program is necessary. Comments have no effect on the speed of CLIST program processing. Make sure they always match the current CLIST program's features. There are various styles of commenting:
      1. Comment only complex sequences.

2. Create a header that lists the program name, what the CLIST statements for each label does, any nested CLIST programs used, any GLOBAL variables used, and CLIST program history.
3. Comment next to each appropriate CLIST statement.
4. One or more comments before each CLIST label statement.
5. My own preference is the "jump start" axiom—*write as much documentation to allow you (after some time) or another person to understand quickly how the CLIST program works.*

g. *Use mixed and lowercase as much as possible.* Possible locations include TSO commands and WRITE text except for emphasis. Try to do this consistently throughout the application so as not to confuse the user.
h. Use *meaningful* names for CLIST programs, labels, symbolic datasets, and so on.

2. *Make your program as effective as possible:*
a. *Leave the environment the way you found it.* Delete temporary datasets. Free appropriate datasets. Close opened files, etc.
b. *Redo a flow control structure if it is not easy to understand.*
c. *Avoid unconditional GOTOs* (GOTO not preceded by an IF-THEN). Ask yourself if GOTO is really needed. Generally avoid GOTOs as a way to get out of or jump into a flow-control structure.
d. *Add parentheses for mathematical operations* if you want an operation to be processed a certain way.
e. *Always check user input* for blanks, valid values, valid range, and valid data type.
f. Have one common exit point that takes errors away from the main part of the program.

How Can I Extend the CLIST Language?

IBM's (SC28-1872) *TSOE Customization Guide* contains a section on how to create your own built-in functions and statements for the CLIST language. Local built-in functions start with &SYSX followed by up to 248 other characters. Local CLIST statements have no such prefix. You have some degree of flexibility in creating error messages (return codes are predefined). The Carstairs (1990) article has a documented example of creating a built-in function.

If you create your own TSO command—many are already in the public domain—you may want to consider accessing CLIST or REXX variables (Version 2 Release 1 and later) from a program. You can access the CLIST Variable Access Module or IKJCT441 to (1) create a CLIST/REXX variable (if not existing), (2) assign a value to a CLIST/REXX variable, (3) return the value of a CLIST/REXX variable. Here are some tips on using IKJCT441:

a. You must reset &SYSOUTLINE to 0 after each TSO command is processed.

b. Have your command, not the CLIST program or REXX exec, perform complex numerical processing. Sections on invoking a load module and getting the return code from a load module show one way that command processors and CLIST programs can pass values and return codes to each other.

c. Return codes from a command can range between 0 and 76.

d. IKJCT441 starting in TSO/E Version 2 Release 1 must be used in the TSO/E area of MVS only.

How Can I Learn More About the CLIST Language?

Here are some suggestions to learn more about the CLIST language. One is the semi-annual proceedings of IBM user groups SHARE, GUIDE, and SEAS (Share Europe):

COMMON, 111 E. Wacker Drive, Chicago, IL 60601; (312)644-6610.
SHARE, 111 East Wacker Drive, Chicago, IL 60601; (312)822-0932. Especially of interest is the MVS group of the operating systems support division.
GUIDE, 111 East Wacker Drive, Chicago, IL 60601; (312)644-6610.
For Europe, Middle East, and Africa: Share Europe Association (**SEAS**) 17 rue Pierres Dulviton, 1207 Geneva, Switzerland; (41) 22-35-40-66.
For Australia and Asia: **Austrlasian SHARE/GUIDE** Ltd. P.O. 62, Turramurra, New South Wales 2074, Australia; (61) 2-449-6848.

The annual proceeding of the SAS User's Group International (SUGI) and the Northeast SAS Users Group have good examples of CLIST programs:

SUGI, c/o Publications Department, SAS Institute, SAS Campus Drive, Cary, NC 27513; (919) 677-8000.
NESUG, c/o Marge Scerbo, University of Maryland at Baltimore, 610 West Lombard Street, Baltimore, MD, 21201; (301)328-8424. Note only a limited number of proceedings are available to non-attendees.

The monthly *Enterprise Systems Journal* (formerly *Mainframe Journal*) is free to qualified readers and has good articles on CLIST, REXX, ISPF, and much more.

Enterprise Systems Journal, Thomas Publications, 10935 Estate Lane, Suite 375, Dallas, TX 75238; (214)343-3717.

TSO Times is published periodically by Chicago-Soft Ltd. with a mix of articles on CLIST and REXX. It is free.

TSO Times, Chicago-Soft Ltd., 738 North LaSalle Street, Suite 2, Chicago, IL 60610; (312)525-6400.

Exception Handling in CLIST Programs

The following are some tips and tricks when writing ERROR and ATTN routines:

1. Place the ATTN or ERROR routine before the CLIST statement it is associated with, usually near the start of the CLIST program. ATTN routines are invoked when the ATTENTION (PA1 or ATTN key) is pressed.
2. Avoid GOTOs in an ATTN sequence. Instead call the same CLIST program as follows:
```
ATTN DO
      %SAMECLIST
END
```
3. When working with nested CLIST programs, use unique return codes to identify if ERROR and ATTENTION routines were invoked.
4. Use CONTROL MAIN or NOFLUSH otherwise many statements will not work (such as RETURN) or will be ignored (such as ATTN after a READ).
5. Some statements (like DOs) ignore ATTN routines regardless what CONTROL is set to.
6. An error routine is invoked when an ERROR, ERROR ON, or ERROR DO is active and a non-zero return code occurs for the associated TSO command or CLIST statement.
7. If possible, give the user another chance to reprocess the offending statement by prompting them for the missing or invalid information. Here is an example:
```
ERROR DO
  SET &RCD = &LASTCC
   SELECT (&RCD)
      WHEN (400) THEN DO
        WRITE DATASET DOES NOT EXIST
        WRITE DO YOU WANT TO TRY AGAIN? (Y/N)
         READ CHOICE
           IF &CHOICE = Y THEN RETURN ELSE EXIT
      END
       OTHERWISE EXIT
  END
END
```
8. Let the user know that an error has occurred. Use WRITE statements to do this.
9. Consider logging errors to a dataset. Here is one way to do this:
```
ERROR DO
   SET &RCD = &LASTCC
   ALLOC F(LOG1) DA(TSO.LOG.DATA) MOD /*Append to existing file*/
```

```
   OPENFILE LOG1 OUTPUT
   SET &LOG1 = &STR(&RCD &SYSUID &SYSTIME &SYSDATE)
   PUTFILE LOG1
   CLOSEFILE LOG1
   FREE F(LOG1)
END
```

10. To avoid problems: (1) generally avoid including a CLOSFILE in an ATTN or ERROR routine because you may close a file that was not open, (2) include error routines for subprocedures and nested CLIST programs.

The following is reprinted with Robert Jones's permission from Summary of TSO CLIST/pCLIST Differences, which accompanies the pCLIST documentation (it is in a file named TSODIFF.DOC). CLIST below refers to CLIST programs.

A difference exists between TSO CLIST and pCLIST in how variables are accessed in ERROR routines. In TSO, an ERROR routine in the main CLIST which is invoked by a nested CLIST or subroutine has access only to the main CLIST variables. In pCLIST, the ERROR routine has access to the variables in the routine where the error occurred. It is intended that pCLIST be compatible with TSO. This will require a major design change and will be implemented in a future release. To be compatible with future releases, ERROR routines that are intended to be used in this manner should only reference GLOBAL or NGLOBAL defined variables. Also, each subroutine or nested CLIST should have its own ERROR routine.

THE ATTN statement for intercepting user attention interrupts is not fully functional at this time. It is recognized, and will not be correctly interpreted. However, it cannot be activated as no hot key assignment has been assigned. A future release will provide hot key activation of the ATTN routine.

Note ERRORLEVELs for .COM and .EXE will be assigned to &LASTCC.

Portability of CLIST Programs

The following are tips and traps when converting TSO/E CLIST programs to MS-DOS or the reverse:

1. Right-from-the start differences:

Different file names. TSO CLIST dataset names can be up to 44 characters (not including member name) and have a file type of CLIST. MS-DOS CLIST file names are 11 characters long with a default file type of .CLT.
    TSO CLIST datasets are EBCDIC characters and have line numbers. MS-DOS CLIST files are ASCII characters and have no line numbers.

2. Non-portable features:

The following TSO CLIST statements, control variables, and built-in functions are not available in the MS-DOS CLIST language:

- Most TSO statements except ALLOC and FREE (needed only for OPEN-FILE/CLOSFILE statements).
- JCL statements.
- ATTN, DATA-ENDDATA, DATA PROMPT-ENDDATA, SYSREF, and SELECT.
- For pCLIST users before 1.09, use of character operators (GT instead of >)
- ¬= for not equals.
- Double-byte characters and their built-in functions: &SYSONEBYTE, &SYSTWOBYTE, &SYSCLENGTH, &SYSSUBSTR.
- &SYSNSUB.
- Some control variables: &SYSLTERM, &SYSWTERM, &SYSUID, &SYSPREF, &SYSPROC, &SYSCPU, &SYSHSM, &SYSSRV, &SYSISPF, &SYSRACF, &SYSLRACF, &SYSTSOE, &SYSCAN, &SYSENV, &SYSICMD, &SYSPCMD, and &SYSDLM.

The following pCLIST features are not supported under TSO/E CLISTs:
- pCLIST environment variable
- The DOS statement
- DOS commands

These statements behave slightly differently between the two operating systems:

- ERROR.
- Keywords (i.e. OPENFILE) in CLIST statements can be in any case in pCLIST but must be in uppercase for TSO.
- TSO commands and CLIST statements can be up to 32,756 characters; pCLIST has a 250-character limit.
- Labels can be up to 8 (TSO and TSO/E Version 1 Releases 1–3) or 31 characters (TSO/E Version 1 Release 4 and later). pCLIST has a 70-character limit (same for variable names).
- pCLIST has limited ALLOC, FREE, and LISTDSI commands, which do not have DA or F keyword operands.
- pCLIST has no CONTROL NOCAPS (use CONTROL ASIS instead).
- pCLIST's &DATATYPE does not return MIXED or DBCS.

Porting CLIST Programs to Other Command Languages

Both TSO and MS-DOS support some of the other command languages in this book (TSO supports versions of REXX and MS-DOS supports versions of REXX, DCL, DOS batch language, Perl, and UNIX shells such as the C shell and the Bourne shell). However, the bad news is there are currently no converters between the CLIST language and any of the command languages mentioned. This section will deal with these questions: When should I consider converting my CLIST programs? Which command language should I convert to? What should my conversion strategy be?

When Should I Consider Converting My CLIST Programs?

When any of the following becomes a need: When values include decimals, scientific format, and hexadecimal characters; When complex string operations are required (such as operations on words).

As mentioned earlier, IBM has stated that future development will be on REXX, not the CLIST language. So, the idea of converting CLIST programs is inevitable.

What command language should I convert to?

The obvious answer is REXX, but let us look at the other possibilities.

1. *A compiled language program* is a strong possibility for subprocedures and nested CLIST programs. When it is combined with the IREXCOM, IRX-EXEC, IRXIC, and IRXJCL modules, you could use both REXX execs and command procedures (this is for TSO/E only).
2. *The DOS batch language* is available only for MS-DOS and would result in a loss rather than gain of features.
3. *DCL (Digital command language)* would be a possibility if you are migrating to VMS and want to recycle some existing CLIST programs. With Boston Business Computing providing a DCL product (named VCL) for MS-DOS, and UNIX, portability of programs is possible. However, a look at Figure 2-2 in Chapter 2 shows the CLIST language is as strong as DCL. So, unless portability or migrating to VMS is a concern, there would be at best minor improvements in converting to DCL such as improved string handling and decimals.
4. *Perl* is a good possibility for MS-DOS—and OS/2—but currently is unavailable for TSO. (With the source available, it may be possible to convert.) Once available for TSO, Perl would offer strong advantages and could be considered an alternative to REXX.
5. For reasons stated earlier, *REXX* would be the most common choice for migration. REXX offers major improvements over CLIST especially in the areas of data types, string manipulation, and portability.

What Should My Conversion Strategy Be?

Based on the preceding information, a compiled language, DCL, Perl, and REXX are the only choices that would offer improvement over the CLIST language and be available for both TSO/E and MS-DOS. The rest of this chapter will discuss the major issues in converting from the CLIST language to DCL, Perl, and REXX.

CLIST language to DCL (Digital command language)

Look at Figure 2-2 in Chapter 2 and Chapter 8's section on comparing commands across command languages for equivalent commands in DCL.

• The following are tips and traps in converting from CLIST programs to DCL command procedures:

1. The following CLIST statements have no equivalent in DCL and probably should not be converted:
   a. DATA-ENDDATA and DATA-PROMPT-ENDDATA
   b. LISTDSI
   c. NGLOBAL, SYSREF
   d. &NRSTR, &SYSNSUB, &SYSONENBYTE, &SYSTWOBYTE, &SYSCLENGTH, &SYSCSUBSTR
   e. All the control variables not listed below

2. Here are recommendations on CLIST components that can be easily converted to DCL equivalents:
   a. PROC positional operands to P1–P8
   b. WRITE and READ to INQUIRE or READ/PROMPT
   c. &SYSINDEX TO F$LOCATE
   d. &LENGTH to F$LENGTH
   e. &SUBSTR to F$EXTRACT or F$ELEMENT or F$EDIT
   f. &DATATYPE to F$TYPE
   g. &EVAL to F$INTEGER and &STR to F$STRING
   h. &SYSSTIME and &SYSDATE to F$TIME or F$CVTIME
   i. Subprocedures (invoked by SYSCALL) to subroutines (invoked by CALL or in simple cases GOSUB)
   j. &LASTCC to $STATUS
   k. Statements that have the same names and perform similar functions, but not necessarily the same syntax: EXIT, GOTO, Labels, IF-THEN-ELSE, READ, RETURN, and WRITE.
   l. CTRL Y is the VMS version of the attention (ATTN) key. You can use *ON CONTROL*_Y to handle when it is pressed.
   m. VMS error messages are divided into three types: warning, error, and severe error. You can use the_ON WARNING, ERROR, and *SEVERE* ERROR command for exception handling.
   n. CONTROL to F$ENVIRONMENT
   o. CONTROL CONLIST etc to SET VERIFY. &SYSCONLIST etc. to F$VERIFY
   p. OPENFILE to OPEN and CLOSFILE to CLOSE
   q. Harder but not impossible to convert: SELECT to multiple IFs, DO statements to a loop sequence
   r. &SYSDSN to F$SEARCH and F$GETDVI(EXISTS)
   s. &SYSCAPS and &SYSLC to F$TRNLNM and SET TERMINAL /UPPERCASE or /NOUPPERCASE

t. SET to Assignment statement

u. &SYSWTERM to F$GETDVI("TT","DEVBUFSIZ")

3. These useful DCL concepts and commands have no equivalent in the CLIST language:

a. Learn to use **logicals,** an alias for a file, tape, or disk device, or another logical. It may help you to substitute the word location when thinking about logicals and symbols, alias for a command, character string, another symbol, or lexical function. It may help you to substitute the word "action" when thinking about symbols. For TSO/E, a logical is similar to the FILE() operand of TSO commands such as ALLOCATE and FREE—an alias for one or more files. (But the life of the logical can be for the whole session while the life of the FILE() operand is just while the command is being processed.) For MS-DOS users, it is similar to using environment variables or the SUBST command, where you can assign an alias to be a directory or file name. Symbols are similar to the idea of regular and global CLIST symbolic variables.

b. These lexical functions: F$CONTEXT, F$CVSI, F$CVUI, F$DIREC-TORY, FFAO, FFILE_ATTRIBUTES, F$GETQUI, F$GETDVI, F$GETSYI, F$LOGICAL, F$MESSAGE, F$PARSE, FPID, FPRIVI-LEGE, F$SETPRV, F$TRNLNM (some), and F$TYPE

c. Global symbols: $SEVERITY and $RESTART

d. STOP

CLIST to Perl

Look at Figure 2-2 in Chapter 2 and Chapter 8's section on comparing commands across command languages for "equivalent" commands in Perl.

The following are tips and traps in converting from Perl scripts to CLIST programs:

1. The following CLIST statements have no equivalent in Perl and will have to be added after the CLIST is converted:

a. DATA-ENDDATA and DATA-PROMPT-ENDDATA (the file handle DATA and the system variable _END_ are somewhat equivalent)

b. LISTDSI

c. NGLOBAL, SYSREF

d. All functions and control variables not listed below

e. Double ampersand symbolic variables

2. The following CLIST commands/functions can be easily converted to Perl equivalents:

a. PROC positional operands to @ARGV for main scripts and @_ for subroutines

b. Local/global symbolic variables to environment variables

    c. SELECT to multiple IFs

    d. DO-WHILE, DO UNTIL or Iterative DO to do *block* while and do *block* until

    e. DOS or TSO commands to exec/sys and the command

    g. EXEC CLIST, or *CLIST*_name. to Perl *script*_name

    h. A subprocedure (SYSCALL) to a subroutine or function (sub)

    j. &LASTCC to $?

    k. WRITE to print

    l. PROC to if $ARGV[..]

    m. &SYSDATE to gmtime/localtime

    n. &SYSTIME to gmtime/localtime

    o. Statements that have the same names and perform similar functions (but not necessarily the same syntax): GOTO, Labels, IF, DO

    p. The signal sequences as indicated by the $SIG array are the equivalent of the attention (ATTN) key being pressed. These include ABRT (abnormal script terminal), ILL (illegal command), INT (equivalent to CTRL/C and CTRL Break), QUIT (quit script), and TERM (termination request)

    q. CONTROL CONLIST etc. to Perl -d

    r. &SYSDSN to -e

    s. &SYSTSOE to Perl -v

    t. &SYSCAPS to tr/a-z/A-Z/ and &SYSLC to tr/A-Z/a-z/

3. These useful Perl concepts and commands have no direct equivalent in the CLIST language:

    a. Environment variables. These are similar to global symbolic variables. Environment variables can/are used by pCLIST (MS-DOS) but not by TSO/E.

    b. Converting DOS commands to TSO

    c. Math functions

    d. Networking functions

    e. Awk to Perl, C header files to Perl, and sed to Perl converters

    f. Setuid and setgid scripts

    g. Associative arrays

    h. Report variables

    i. Binary file mode

CLIST language to REXX (Restructured Extended Executor)

Again, look at Figure 2-2 and Chapter 8's section on comparing commands across command languages for equivalent CLIST statements in REXX.

The following are tips and traps in converting CLIST programs to TSO/E REXX execs. (The emphasis is on TSO/E CLISTs.) Note some of the REXX instructions for TSO/E are not portable to other operating systems. These are discussed in Chapter 4. Some of the information below is printed from a letter of Mason Kelsey with his permission. (Another good reference on this topic is Hoernes (1992).)

1. These REXX concepts and commands (also called instructions) have no equivalent in the CLIST language:
   a. Error handling and flow control: DROP, ITERATE, LEAVE, SIGNAL. These are cleaner to use than CLIST ERROR or ATTN routines.
   b. EXECIO, NOP, OPTIONS
   c. Queue operations and statements, DROPBUF, MAKEBUF, PUSH, PULL, QUEUE, QUEUED built-in function
   d. Numeric Precision: NUMERIC, built-in function: DIGITS, FORM, FUZZ, and SIGN (only SIGN is supported in TSO/E)
   e. Environments and packages: ADDRESS and SUBCOM. For CLIST programs, you don't need ADDRESS because most commands from other environments can be placed in the CLIST "as is."
   f. Keywords can be in any case (also true for pCLIST, not TSO/E users)
   g. All REXX symbols (i.e. names of symbolic variables) are initialized to the symbol name in uppercase. The initial value of CLIST symbolic variables is null.
   h. Most REXX built-in functions: ABBREV, ABS, ARG, B2X, BITAND, BITOR, BITXOR, CENTRE, COMPARE, CONDITION, COPIES, C2D, C2X, DELSTR, DELWORD, D2C, D2X, ERRORTEXT, FORMAT, INSERT, LASTPOS, LEFT, MAX, MIN, OVERLAY, RANDOM, REVERSE, RIGHT, SOURCELINE, SPACE, SUBWORD, SYMBOL, TRANSLATE, TRUNC, WORD, WORDINDEX, WORDLENGTH, WORDS, XRANGE, X2B, X2C, X2D. Note that CLIST string operations are character-oriented rather than word-oriented (like REXX).

   Note Some of these functions can be done in CLIST programs, but it would take from several lines of code to a subprocedure. An example may clarify this point. Here are the equivalent CLIST statements to do the DELSTR function:

```
/* User enters similar to the following: DELS 1 2. Note that posi-
tional parameters are required, so */
/* non-blank values are not possible. */
PROC 2 STARTPOS ENDPOS /*Different than REXX - - ENDPOS required */
WRITE Enter string
  READ
SET &DELS= &STR(&SYSDVAL)
SET &LEN = &LENGTH(&STR(&DELS))
IF &STARTPOS < 0 OR &STARTPOS > &LEN OR &ENDPOS >= &LEN THEN EXIT
   IF &STARTPOS > 1 THEN SET &DELSTR = -
    &SUBSTR(1:&STARTPOS-1,&DELS)&SUBSTR(&ENDPOS+1:&LEN,&DELS)
ELSE IF &STARTPOS = 1 THEN SET &DELSTR = -
    &SUBSTR(&ENDPOS+1:&LEN,&DELS)
```

    i. Many REXX operators such as string concatenation (blank, $||$), Boolean (&, $|$, &&, Prefix), and character relational (==, ¬=).

    j. Immediate commands to override processing. This is available in TSO/E and CMS REXX only.

2. These are CLIST statements and components that can be easily converted to REXX equivalents:

    a. All TSO, ISPF, PDF commands to ADDRESS

    b. PROC to ARG. You will have to create a sequence to deal with keyword operands (see Chapter 4 for such a sequence).

    c. SYSCALL to CALL, nested CLIST programs and subprocedures to internal/external functions and subprograms

    d. CONTROL CONLIST etc. to TRACE

    e. These statements have the same names and perform similar functions (but may have a different syntax):
- Flow Control statements: all DOs, SELECT (slightly different syntax), all IF-THENs
- EXIT and RETURN

    f. WRITE to SAY, READ to PULL

    g. ERROR and ATTN routines to SIGNAL

    h. CLIST statements, TSO/E commands control variables and built-in functions:
- &SYSDATE, &SYSSDATE, &SYSJDATE to DATE
- &SUBSTR to SUBSTR
- &LENGTH to LENGTH
- &SYSTIME, &SYSSTIME to TIME
- CONTROL MSG, &SYSMSG to MSG (TSO/E REXX only)
- LISTDSI TSO/E command to LISTDSI (TSO/E REXX only)
- &SYSINDEX to POS and LASTPOS
- CONTROL PROMPT, &SYSPROMPT to PROMPT (TSO/E REXX only)
- &SYSDSN to SYDSN (TSO/E REXX only)
- CLIST control variables to &SYSVAR (TSO/E REXX only). The 17 (out of 37) CLIST control variables supported are &SYSCPU, &SYSENV, &SYSHSM, &SYSICMD, &SYSISPF, &SYSLRACF, &SYSLTERM, &SYSNEST, &SYSPCMD, &SYSPREF, &SYSPROC, &SYSRACF, &SYSSCMD, &SYSSRV, &SYSTSOE, &SYSUID, and &SYSWTERM.
- WRITE &A to VALUE
- &SYSLIST, &SYSCONLIST, &SYSSYMLIST etc. to TRACE
- &SYSCAPS, &SYSLC to TRANSLATE

    i. OPENFILE, CLOSFILE,GETFILE, PUTFILE to EXECIO (TSO/E and CMS REXX) or CHARIN / LINEIN (DOS, OS/2, UNIX REXX, and a future release of both MVS and CMS)

3. The following CLIST statements have no equivalent in REXX and probably should not be converted:
    a. DATA-ENDDATA and DATA-PROMPT-ENDDATA
    b. NGLOBAL, SYSREF
    c. &NRSTR, &SYSNSUB, &SYSONENBYTE, &SYSTWOBYTE, &SYSCLENGTH, &SYSCSUBSTR
    d. All the control variables/built-in functions not listed above

SUGGESTED READINGS

Carstairs, Frank, 1990. Use control variable to extend CLIST language. *TSO Times,* 2(1), pp. 1–2.

Cowlishaw, Michael F, 1990. *The REXX Language: A Practical Approach to Programming,* 2d ed. Englewood Cliffs, N.J.: Prentice-Hall.

Digital Equipment Corporation, 1988. *VMS DCL Dictionary.* Maynard, Mass. AA-LA12A-TE.

Digital Equipment Corporation, 1988. *Guide to Using VMS Command Procedures.* Maynard, Mass. AA-LA11A-TE.

Dilorio, Frank, 1989. Good Code, Bad Code: Strategies for Program Design, *NESUG '89: Conference Proceedings,* pp. 260–266.

Elston, Jay, 1982. CLIST Esoterica—Advanced Examples, *Share 59 Proceedings,* pp. 1857–1865.

German, Hallett, 1990. The Grand Alliance: Using TSO/E CLIST and REXX Command Languages in the SAS® Program Development Cycle. *NESUG '90: Conference Proceedings,* pp. 216–210.

German, Hallett, 1990. *TSO/E CLISTs: Basics, Applications, and Advanced Techniques.* New York: Van Nostrand Reinhold.

Hoernes, Gerhard E., 1992, REXX for CLIST Programmers In The REXX handbook. Gabriel Goldberg and Philip H. Smith III (eds), New York; McGraw-Hill pp. 557–596.

IBM Corporation, 1990. *TSO Extensions Customization.* SC28-1872.

IBM Corporation, 1990. *TSO Extensions CLISTs.* SC28-1876.

IBM Corporation, 1990. *TSO Extensions Programming Services.* SC28-1875.

IBM Corporation, 1990. *TSO/E Programming Guide.* SC28-1874.

IBM Corporation, 1990. *TSO/E Extensions Version 2 REXX Reference.* SC28-1883.

IBM Corporation, 1988. *TSO Extensions Version 2 REXX User's Guide.* SC28-1882.

Jones, Robert, 1990. *Letter to Hallett German,* December 8.

Jones, Robert, 1991. *Letter to Hallett German,* January 31.

Jones, Robert, 1990. *pCLIST User's Guide.*

Jones, Robert, 1990. *Summary of TSO CLIST/pCLIST Differences.*

Kelsey, Mason, 1990. *Letter to Hallett German,* November 29.

Kerninghan, Brian W., and P.J. Plauger, 1978. *The Elements of Programming Style,* 2d ed., New York: McGraw-Hill.

Kusnierz, Thomas E., 1986. CLIST Tips and Techniques. *SHARE 67 Proceedings,* pp. 1–19. (Handout).

Kusnierz, Thomas E., 1989. REXX in MVS. *SEAS 89 Proceedings,* pp. 1–23. (Handout).

4

Command Language Advisor—
REXX

REXX, which stands for REstructed eXtended eXecutor, is one of the most popular command languages today as well as one of the most portable. It was created in 1979 by Mike Cowlishaw in his spare time at IBM Laboratories near Hursley, England as a simplified version of PL/I. He then placed a note in the tools section (which deals with tools development for VM) of IBM's internal network—called VNET—asking for reactions on what was then called REX. Many replies came back and at least 30 versions were developed and rigorously tested between 1979 and 1982—REXX 2.00 in 1980; 2.50 in 1981; and 3.00 in 1982. This makes it one of the few languages developed by electronic committees! REXX is now the most popular *programming language* (not just command language) used internally at IBM with more than 3 million lines of code. See Cowlishaw (1985, pp. 12–14; 1990a, pp. 15–16; and 1990b, pp. 1–2, 8–11) for more on the history of REXX.

The first public version (REXX 3.20) was included as part of VM/SP (virtual machine/system product) for CMS (conversational monitor system) in 1983. It soon replaced EXEC as the preferred command language. Then 1985 brought the first PC-DOS version by Mansfield Software and the publication of Cowlishaw's (1985) and O'Hara's and Gomberg's (1985) books on REXX (version 3.50).

In 1987, IBM announced a set of evolving procedures and standards called Systems Application Architecture. In theory, compliance with SAA meant a similar "look and feel" across IBM's product line of mainframes, minicomputers, and personal computers. Part of SAA was selecting REXX as the SAA Procedure Language (or SAA/PL) that would be available on all SAA computers. By 1990, REXX could be found in AmigaDOS, part of Version 2.0 and later, as a separate product called ARexx; MVS (TSO/E); OS/2, part of Standard Edition 1.3 and later and Extended Edition 1.2 and later, OS/400; Tandem (called TREXX); UNIX; VM (CMS); and VMS (limited release).

Other developments include:

- The first REXX compiler (for VM) from IBM.
- Two more REXX interpreters for MS-DOS by Kilowatt Software and Tritus Inc. The Tritus interpreter had preliminary documentation at the time of publication, so only Kilowatt and Quercus REXX interpreters are documented in this book.
- Another edition of the Cowlishaw (1990) and the O'Hara and Gomberg (1990) books for REXX 4.00.
- The first annual REXX Symposium discussing REXX issues across platforms (1990).
- The formation of an ANSI technical committee (X3J18) to develop a REXX standard.
- The elevation of REXX to a project at SHARE.
- Quercus Systems taking over the development and support of Personal REXX from Mansfield Software in 1991.
- A second VM REXX compiler by Systems Center called ProREXX.
- The first comprehensive book on REXX issues in 1992, The REXX Handbook by Gabriel Goldberg & Philip H. Smith III.
- Support by Quercus and Kilowatt DOS REXX interpreters for developing MS-Windows applications. These products should appear in late 1992.

Throughout the chapter I will refer to REXX 3.50 and REXX 4.00 (called 3.5 and 4.0 for short). Most interpreters and compilers run REXX 3.5. As of publication date, only the following partly or fully support REXX 4.0 features: CMS compiler 3.46, Personal REXX (Quercus) 3.0, ProREXX, Portable REXX (Kilowatt), OS/2 1.2 Extended Edition and later, OS/2 1.3 Standard Edition and later, OS/400 REXX Interpreter, Tritus REXX, TSO/E REXX with an APAR, and SAA REXX.

Unless otherwise stated, all examples can be used by nearly all REXX interpreters. Information about operations on specific platforms will be highlighted by a change bar.

WHEN TO USE THE REXX LANGUAGE

REXX, a good general-purpose programming language, can be used in most situations including as a first language. (Yes, it is a floor wax AND a dessert topping!) Here are situations where a REXX exec can be especially useful, in no particular order:

- When the data manipulation is word- or substring-oriented and sophisticated string parsing capabilities are needed.
- When portability across platforms is a concern, especially when working with SAA-compliant computers.

- When you need to quickly create a prototype for an application. This prototype can later be converted to a compiled language or be further streamlined.
- When you need to do date and time operations.
- When you need a preprocessor for a compiler. REXX is perfect for this but few compilers take advantage of it.
- When you need to learn a programming language that combines ease of use with strong capabilities. REXX is an ideal first language because: (1) It is English-like and free-form; (2) Most limits are imposed by your REXX interpreter, not by the REXX language; (3) You don't have to worry about "the little things" like declaring variables, opening files, and much more—REXX does it for you; (4) REXX has strong natural datatyping so SAY 2+2 (all numerics) or SAY '2' + 2 yields the same result: 4! This makes string and numeric comparisons more trouble-free.
- When you need to build your own XEDIT subcommands or ISPF/PDF EDIT macros. REXX combined with these macro languages gives the capability of creating powerful commands from rather small REXX execs.
- When an alternative to the DOS batch language is needed.
- When you need to build your own system/utility commands.

HOW TO INVOKE REXX EXECS

REXX execs are usually invoked in foreground but on some operating systems may be invoked in background (batch) as well.

Invoking a Foreground REXX Exec

Invoking a REXX exec in foreground is done differently across operating systems. Listed below are some of the different formats used:

AMIGA (AREXX)

```
rx prog1.rexx [See notes below.]
```

CMS (COMPILER)

```
rexxc prog1 or rexxd prog1 [Please see the notes below on using the
compiler.]
```

CMS (INTERPRETER)

```
prog1 (EXEC handler sees type of EXEC and invokes interpreter. The
EXEC command is optional.)
```

OS/2 (IBM)

cmd prog1.cmd (First line in EXEC *must* be */*REXX*/*, else it is executed as an OS/2 batch file.)
pmrexx prog1.cmd [Or drag the .CMD file to PMREXX.EXE under the Desktop Manager]

MS-DOS (KILOWATT SOFTWARE'S PORTABLE REXX)

ex c:rexx\prog1.rex (Non-resident version only. Processes PROG1.REX)

MS-DOS (QUERCUS SYSTEMS'S PERSONAL REXX)

rexx prog1 (Non-resident version Processes PROG1.REX)
rx prog1 (Resident version. Processes PROG1.REX. Must first enter *REXX/R*)

TSO/E

exec prog1.exec (Invokes *userid*.PROG1.EXEC)

UNIX (WORKSTATIONS GROUP'S UNI-REXX)

rxx prog1.rex (Note: Explicit form for both interpreted and compiled execs.)
rxc prog1.rex (Compiles exec. Used mainly to hide code rather than for speed.)
PROG1 (Implicit form for most UNIX flavors. EXEC must have the following first line: *#!/USR/LOCAL/BIN/RXX* [or the appropriate location] and be marked as executable. Exec may be either interpreted or compiled.)

VMS (LIMITED DISTRIBUTION FROM MANSFIELD SOFTWARE)

$ exec prog1.rex

Tips and Traps:
1. Any of these REXX interpreters may include operating system commands in the exec. Also, parameters may be supplied when the exec is invoked.
2. Most of these interpreters expect the exec's file name to have a default file type. However, in some cases, any name can be used if it is fully specified.

Operating System/ Environment	Default File type	Can other name be used?
AmigaDos	REXX	Yes, recommended to use same extension as application it supports.
CMS	EXEC	No, and also must include a /*REXX*/ statement in the first line. However, REXX compiler programs can be stored in a module that requires a file type of TEXT.
OS/2	.CMD	No, /*REXX statement*/ must start in column 1, line 1.
MS-DOS (Kilowatt)	.REX	No
MS-DOS (Quercus)	.REX	Yes, if fully specified
TSO	EXEC	Yes, if fully specified in quotes.
UNIX	.REX	Yes
VMS	.REX	No

3. Many operating systems allow you to invoke REXX from a C, Pascal, or another compiled language. See the section on subcoms, packages, and REXX for further information.

Amiga (ARexx)

1. Before invoking ARexx, run REXXMAST to make it resident. This can be placed in the startup-sequence file, so it is automatically invoked on booting your Amiga. Note that RXC makes ARexx no longer resident.
2. The default search path for an REXX program is the current directory and the :REXX directory if it exists.

CMS (Compiler)

1. A REXX compiler also exists. The IBM C/370 Library and certain versions of the VM/SP or VM/XA operating systems are prerequisites for the compiler. The compiler can be invoked as a full-screen dialog or from the command line.
2. To invoke the compiler from the command line, you usually enter *rexxc filename*. (*Filename* is the REXX exec to be compiled) The following are some common options when invoking the compiler:

CEXEC	Results in compiled file with the file indentifier that you specify
COMPILE	Enables/disables generating compiled code
DUMP	Diagnostics (dump) produced
FLAG	Sets severity level of errors. Default is that all messages are displayed.

LINECOUNT	Sets number of lines in each page of the compile listing. The default is 55 lines per page.
OBJECT	Produces a TEXT file
PRINT	Enables/disables compile listing and if it goes to a file or a printer
TERMINAL	Enables/disables messages to the screen as well as the listing
XREF	Enables/disables a variable cross listing

3. You can also invoke the REXX compiler as a full-screen dialog. You usually enter *rexxd filename* (*filename* is the name of the REXX exec to be compiled). This allows you to use all the options that you can specify from the command line using REXXC.

REXX (Interpreter)

1. The EXEC interpreter looks at the first line of a program to see if it is a REXX exec, EXEC program, or EXEC2 program. A comment in the first line (/* *comment* */) will identify a program as a REXX exec.

OS/2

1. You must have OS/2 Standard Edition 1.3 (or later) or Extended Edition 1.2 (or later) to use REXX.
2. PMREXX offers the advantage of running REXX programs as a full screen application which offers these advantages:
   - Input and output in their own windows. You can also select the font and size of the output.
   - Cut and pasting between the REXX output in the clipboard and an application
   - A full-screen debugging (trace facility) (/T)
3. Both CTC and Mansfield had their own OS/2 REXX interpreters but they are no longer available. However, Quercus is selling a revised version of the OS/2 Mansfield interpreter that is compatible with its DOS REXX interpreter. CTC also offers an ISPF editor for OS/2 (called SPF2) that allows REXX execs to utilize ISREDIT commands and build their own ISPF/PDF EDIT macros. Former CTC employees began recently offering Tritus REXX that runs under both DOS and OS/2.
4. Note that the required comment statement containing the word REXX (e.g. /*REXX*/) **must** start in column 1, line 1. This restriction *does not apply* to the statements following the required comment statement in the program.

MS-DOS (Kilowatt Software's Portable REXX)

1. A useful extension of the REXX language is using pipes. This means that you can "pipe" the results of a first exec to serve as an input file to a second exec as in this example:

```
exec exec1 | exec exec2. (| is the pipe operator.)
```

MS-DOS (Quercus Systems's Personal REXX)

1. Before invoking Personal REXX for the first time, enter RXINTMGR. This loads the Interrupt Manager into memory.
2. The path name of the exec may be used when invoking the interpreter:
   ```
   rexx c:\myexecs\prog1
   ```
3. Note the REX file extension is not required; any valid file extension may instead be used:
   ```
   rexx c:\myexecs\prog1.dos
   ```
4. In Personal REXX 3.0, the /O option produces an object version of the REXX code. This code will run faster the next time it is executed.

TSO/E

1. Note that REXX execs may be invoked explicitly or implicitly—exec is part of SYSEXEC (REXX execs only) or SYSPROC (REXX execs and clist programs) concatenation.

2. The following shows the only conditions when the EXEC interpreter decides it is a REXX exec (Otherwise, it is assumed to be a clist program):

   Note: For some of these commands, it is *not necessary* for the exec's first line to have comment statement containing the word REXX (e.g. /* *REXX sample* */). However, this statement is strongly recommended to (a) have a common look across REXX programs, and (b) reduce the surprises when porting REXX programs across various platforms.

Explicit

a. If invoked EXEC *exec_name* EXEC and *exec_name* are fully qualified dataset names. It is *not necessary* for the exec's first line to have a comment statement containing the word REXX.
b. If invoked EXEC *exec_name* and *exec_name* are fully qualified dataset names. It *is necessary* for the exec's first line to have a comment statement containing the word REXX.
c. If invoked EXEC *exec_name* EXEC and *exec_name* are not fully qualified dataset names (first and EXEC qualifiers implied). It *is not necessary* for the exec's first line to have a comment statement containing the word REXX.
d. If invoked EXEC *exec_name* and *exec_name* are not fully qualified dataset names (first and EXEC qualifiers implied.) It *is necessary* for the exec's first line to have a comment statement containing the word REXX.

Implicit

a. If invoked *%exec_name* and *exec_name* are the names of a sequential dataset or member of a partitioned dataset that is part of the SYSEXEC concatenation. It *is not necessary* for the exec's first line to have a comment statement containing the word REXX.

b. If invoked *%exec_name* and *exec_name* are the names of a sequential dataset or member of a partitioned dataset that is part of the SYSPROC concatenation. It *is necessary* for the exec's first line to have a comment statement containing the word REXX.

UNIX (uni-REXX)

1. To quickly process a simple sequence (such as "say 'what is your name?';parse pull nm;say 'name is' nm") enter rxx -c *"sequence"*

Invoking a Background REXX Exec

CMS, OS/2 and TSO/E are the only environments that can invoke a REXX exec in background. Here is how to do this:

CMS

Use the CMSBATCH or VMBATCH commands to process the REXX compiler/interpreter in the background.

OS/2

1. Piping (|) and redirection (< or >) operators are allowed in a DETACH command or the program specified by the DETACH command.
2. Use DETACH to invoke a REXX exec in background. DETACH always returns a confirmation message similar to—*The process identification number is 88.*

```
Detach prog2 [Name of REXX exec that doesn't prompt for input.]
```

TSO/E

Under TSO/E you must submit a JCL (job control language) program to process a REXX program in background (see Chapter 3's section on invoking a list program in background for further information on JCL programs). Here is a sample skeleton for a JCL program to invoke a REXX exec in background.

```
//STEP1      EXEC PGM=IRXJCL,PARM='PROG1'
//STEPLIB    DD DSN=load dataset
//SYSTSIN    DD DSN=dataset,DISP=SHR (keyboard input)
             or
             DD DUMMY (not used)
//SYSTSOUT   DSN=dataset,DISP=OLD (EXEC output to a dataset)
//SYSEXEC    DSN=exec_dataset,DISP=SHR
             (SYSEXEC - - concatenated PDS datasets)
```

Tips and Traps:

1. Only one parm in PARM field but can have many tokens.
2. REXX exec cannot be in a sequential dataset.
3. STEP code contains exec return code.

THE FUTURE OF THE REXX LANGUAGE

The future of the REXX language looks bright. Here are some of the trends that I see:

1. *Continued porting of REXX to other machines and operating systems,* rumored to include the VSE and AIX operating systems. Having a widely available VMS REXX interpreter appears to be of some interest and the workstation group is rumored to be working on such an interpreter. Uni-REXX will also continued to be ported to other flavors of UNIX.

2. The forthcoming REXX ANSI standard *should ensure that REXX inter-preters/compilers are identical in the following areas:*
   - Interactive tracing
   - Input/output operations (especially with files)
   - Reserved words in REXX
   - The implementation limitations of an interpreter/compiler complying with the standard
   - Shared variable pools
   - Data used by REXX programs
   - The character set used
   - Built-in functions
   - Internal/external functions and subroutines
   - Error handling
   - REXX futures
   - REXX extensions and how to limit them
   - REXX portability
   - Parsing

   The result will eventually be greater similarity of REXX execs across operating systems. The initial emphasis of the REXX standard will be on making REXX more portable instead of extending the REXX language. See the Marks (1992) Reference for a good overview on the REXX Standards effort.

3. *Modest success is achieved by IBM as having REXX replace/supplement BASIC and batch language for DOS and OS/2.* Unfortunately, a good part of this depends on Microsoft—a company that to date has favored its own

BASIC interpreters and compilers over REXX. Here are some scenarios demonstrating how the preceding change can take place:

   a. Microsoft sees REXX instead of BASIC (i.e. Visual and Quick BASIC) as its high-level language of choice. It is unknown at this point if Microsoft is planning to include a REXX interpreter in the OS/2 module (API) for the forthcoming Windows NT product). Windows NT will be probably ported to RISC-based systems as part of the ACE (Advanced Computing Environment). Microsoft heavily supports BASIC and has released Visual BASIC as a high-level language for Windows. It is rumored that Microsoft will include a "macro language" in a later version of Windows, 4.0 or 4.1. It is highly unlikely that REXX will ever fully replace BASIC.

   b. A batch-file to REXX exec converter is included with OS/2 and ideally DOS.*

   c. OS/2 2.0 becomes a popular operating system and makes REXX a popular command language along with this rise.

4. Availability of *converters to REXX will increase the number of REXX users and ease of migration to REXX*. These could be:

   - CMS EXEC2 to REXX execs (It is rumoured that IBM had an internal XEDIT macro called REXXIFY that partially converted EXEC2 programs to REXX Execs. Also look at the Karpinski (1992) reference.)
   - DOS/OS/2 batch files to REXX execs
   - OS/400 CL to REXX execs
   - TSO CLIST programs to REXX execs
   - UNIX shells (probably Bourne, C, and Korn), awk and sed scripts to REXX execs
   - VMS DCL command procedures to REXX execs

   A converter called REXXTACY, now in beta test, converts OS/2 REXX code to Microsoft C. The company plans to port to other environments as well. Contact Anthony Green, RoboCo, 108 Madison Avenue, Toronto, Ontario M5R2S4; (416) 340-0887.

5. *An increase in the availability of REXX compilers.* IBM has promised release of a run-time TSO/E REXX compiler in spring 92 and no doubt others will follow in time. See the Pinter (1991) reference for the issues on developing a REXX compiler.

6. *The arrival of REXX interpreters and compilers that work with graphical user interfaces.* Both DOS REXX interpreters can or soon will support building MS Windows applications. IBM has announced its intent to add object-oriented extensions and 32-bit support to the REXX interpreter in a future OS/2 release.

---

* In fairness, Quercus has such an EXEC called REXXIFY.REX—but you have to buy Personal REXX to get a copy.

DEVELOPING REXX APPLICATIONS

Chapter 2 looked at three different types of common command language applications. The next three sections provide portable REXX sequences—unless otherwise stated—that are listed under the type of application where they are most commonly used. However, there is no reason why a particular REXX sequence could not be used by any type of application. The chapter's last section discusses some major concerns when developing REXX-based applications. It also looks at porting REXX programs across various operating systems and migrating to other command languages. Once the ANSI REXX standard is implemented by most REXX interpreters/compilers, portability of REXX programs across various operating systems should be less of a concern.

FRONT-END REXX APPLICATIONS

Two common tasks of REXX execs are to provide input ("housekeeping") for load modules (sometimes these REXX programs are called macros) and to provide startup tasks when logging in. The section reviews sequences to perform both of these.

How To Access Operating System Commands in a REXX Exec

REXX uses an unique approach in deciding what is a non-REXX command, sometimes called the REXX environment model. An **environment** is a non-REXX program or module with commands that can be executed within a REXX exec. The interpreter/compiler follows a sequence similar to the following:

1. Get the "instruction"
2. If it is REXX instruction, continue processing the instruction.
3. If part of an ADDRESS instruction—i.e. ADDRESS *instruction* such as (ADDRESS DOS 'time') or a clause in quotes (such as 'time') perform any necessary symbolic substitution and pass the character string to the command processor (or CP) for the operating system if no environment name is specified.
4. The CP for the operating system or some other environment processes the "instruction."
5. The return code from processing the "instruction" is stored in the system variable RC. It is passed back to the REXX interpreter/compiler and the exec continues to the next instruction. A zero return code means successful processing of the "instruction." Exception handling can be implemented with SIGNAL ON ERROR (All current REXX versions) or CALL ON ERROR (REXX 4.00 implementations).

Because the REXX interpreter/compiler does not have knowledge of the external environment instruction, this makes processing non-REXX commands operating-system independent. Table 4-1 lists the environments available for REXX interpreters.

Tips and Traps:

General

1. Use the ADDRESS function (available in most REXX interpreters/compilers) to process sequences only if a certain environment is active.

```
Select
  when address() = 'CMS' then do
    (ADDRESS CMS command)
    (ADDRESS CMS command)
    . . .
  end
  when address() = 'XEDIT' then do
   (ADDRESS XEDIT command)
   (ADDRESS XEDIT command)
   . . .
  end
  otherwise
    say 'environment is . . .' address()
end
```

2. Specifying ADDRESS by itself resets the environment to what it was before the last ADDRESS instruction was invoked. Therefore, to reduce surprises when porting programs and in everyday use of host commands, always prefix ADDRESS before each host and foreign command. Specifying ADDRESS *environment-name* resets the current environment to the one specified.

3. The *environment-name* may be the result of symbolic substitution or the value of a symbol such as:

```
x='DOS'
interpret address x 'TIME' /* Will not work with REXX compilers*/
```

Amiga (ARexx)

1. SHELL is an alias for ADDRESS. REXX is the default environment.
2. Using the ADDRESS command, AREXX has access to hundreds of programs (some include CygnusEd Text Editor, AmigaTeX, ProWrite, Art Department Pro, Buad Bandit, UltraCard Plus, Digi-Paint 3, CanDo, Deluxe Video III, The Director, MacroPaint, and ShowMaker).

CMS

1. COMMAND environment uses SVC 202 (CMS COMMAND processor interface). The command must be explicitly stated and *in uppercase.* Failure to do this may lead to problems that are hard to diagnose.

Table 4-1. Environments for REXX Interpreters.

Operating System	Environments
AMIGA (ARexx)	COMMAND
	[An address is really a message port. Pass command to AmigaDOS and continues processing]
	REXX
	[Default message port. Pass command to AREXX.]
CMS	COMMAND
	(Similar to CMS but places CP and EXEC in front of CMS commands and REXX instructions, respectively. Generally faster than CMS.)
	CMS
	(The default for operating system commands, execs, and load modules. Same as being entered at the terminal)
	ISPEXEC "SELECT service operands" (ISPF commands. May use any ISPF command once ISPF is invoked. Also used by Tso and Trident REXX.)
	ISREDIT "command operands" (ISPF/PDF EDIT macros). Also used by Tso and CTC's SPF/2 editor.
	XEDIT
	(Default environment for XEDIT macros)
DOS (Quercus Systems)	COMMAND
	(Executes a DOS command same as DOS but ignores searching for files with a .REX extension if a file extension is not specified.)
	DOS
	(Executes a DOS command same as COMMAND but searches for files with .BAT, .COM, .EXE, and .REX extensions if a file extension is not specified.)
	KEDIT
	(KEDIT—Mansfield's DOS and OS/2 version of XEDIT. See note below on invoking KEDIT.)
OS/2	CMD (default OS/2 environment)
TSO	ATTACH "*module*"\(Invokes module as a subtask and the exec waits for it to complete.)
	ISPEXEC "SELECT *service operands*"\(ISPF commands in TSO address space only. May use any ISPF command once ISPF is invoked.)
	ISREDIT "*command operands*"\(ISPF/PDF EDIT macro statements in TSO address space only.)
	LINK "*module value1..value*n"\(Loads load modules allocated to the link list and ISPPLIB.)
	MVS "*command value 1..value*n"\(The default if invoked from a MVS address space.)
	TSO "*command operand 1..operand*n"\(The default if invoked from the TSO address space whether in or out of ISPF.)
UNIX	UNIX (default)
	XEDIT (uni-XEDIT)
VMS	None (see below)

2. Some sites have MVS running as their CP. This means that MVS would be the default environment and the ATTACH and LINK environments would be supported.

MS-DOS (Kilowatt)

Many DOS commands can be implemented by non-portable built-in functions. A sample of the more than 25 functions available are: MS-DOS commands (dosver—returns DOS version); hardware functions (port—port input/output); and screen functions (clearscr—clears screen). See the section named "Portability of REXX Programs" for a list of these functions.

MS-DOS (Mansfield/Quercus)

1. KEXX is invoked by either REXX KEDIT *exec-name* (must have processed a SET RXCMD=YES from DOS to set the RXCMD environment variable) or REXX KEDITRX exec-name (REXX exec loads KEDIT, REXX interpreter is not resident, and have the environment RXCMD set to NO [the default].) The first line of the exec must include a comment statement with the word REXX in it (such as /* *REXX* */.) The ADDRESS KEDIT ' *KEDIT statement*' will not work but ADDRESS KEDIT will.

2. Many DOS commands can be implemented by non-portable Personal REXX built-in functions. A sample of the more than 70 functions available are: file operations (DOSDEL—delete a file, DOSMEM—returns free memory); hardware information (PCFLOPPY—how many floppy drives installed; PCTYPE—type of PC); hardware manipulation (CURSOR—sets cursor position, SOUND—sounds a beep at a specified frequency and duration); and RXWINDOW Functions (W_FIELD—sets a field's location and attributes in a window). See "Portability of REXX Programs" for a list of these functions.

OS/2

Rather than using ADDRESS, OS/2 uses the SQLDBS (starts/stops the Database Manager, enables/disables access to the particular database) and SQLEXEC (processes SQL requests to a particular database) calls to perform database operations. See Kong (1991) for a good introduction on this topic.

UNIX

1. Uni-REXX also includes a POPEN function, similar to the ADDRESS UNIX instruction but goes to an external data queue (stack) instead of standard output (or stdout—usually your terminal screen). This allows the output from the command to be retrieved and manipulated (see the next section for further information).

2. Also included are non-portable REXX functions. These include: CHDIR—reset current directory, CUSERID—retrieve current userid, GETCWD—

retrieve current directory, GETENV—get UNIX environment variable values, LOWER/UPPER—changes case of the argument, and PUTENV—modify a UNIX environment variable's value. See "Portability of DOS Functions" for more information on these functions.

VMS

The ADDRESS VMS instruction is not yet implemented. Also, you cannot currently have one process executing a REXX interpreter and the DCL interpreter.

How To Capture Output From a Command in a REXX Exec

Kelsey (1990, p. 176) discusses how command output capture differs for each operating system. This is not a limitation of the REXX language, but a dependency on the operating system the interpreter/compiler uses. Here is how various REXX implementations handle this:

1. *ARexx* can use the redirection command (found in MS-DOS and UNIX) to redirect output from an AmigaDOS command.

```
tempp = "work:tempp" /*Define directory*/
address command
"cd >nil:" tempp
/* This is different from DOS and UNIX which places the parameter
before the redirection operator*/
```

2. Most *CMS* commands can include a FIFO, LIFO, or STACK operand. This places the command output into the stack. (FIFO and STACK processes output in first-in-first-out order while LIFO denotes last-in-first-out order.) The following are skeletons of the two basic approaches:

```
"MAKEBUF"                              "MAKEBUF"
bufnum = rc                            bufnum=rc
lastq=queued()                         "CMS Command (STACK|FIFO|LIFO"
"CMS Command (STACK|FIFO|LIFO"         SENTRIES
Do until queued() - lastq=0            numlines= rc
  Parse logic (decrement lastq)        Parse logic (Usually part of a DO
                                       loop.)
End                                    "DROPBUF" bufnum
"DROPBUF" bufnum
```

The two approaches are similar because SENTRIES (a CMS command) and QUEUED (a REXX function) both return the same value of the total number of lines in the stack. However, using QUEUED is generally faster than SENTRIES. Note the second approach can be used by CMS, TSO, and both MS-DOS versions. (But no DROPBUF *buffer_number* is available for Kilowatt's REXX interpreter).

3. For *MS-DOS* (*Kilowatt*), there are two ways to capture output from a DOS command.

    a. Certain DOS functions (such as CHDIR, CHKDSK, DIRS, DOSVER, FILES, GETENV, INTDOS, INT86, and SETENV) simulate DOS commands and return command output if assigned to a symbol.

    b. Redirect any DOS command to a file such as *CHKDSK C:\>file1.* (Other devices such as com1, Ipt1, and prn (printers) are supported.)

4. For *MS-DOS* (*Quercus*), there are two ways to capture output from a DOS command.

    a. Certain DOS functions (such as DOSCD, DOSDIR, DOSDIRPOS, DOSDISK, DOSDRIVE, DOSENV, DOSMEM, DOSVERSION, and DOSVOLUME) simulate DOS commands and return command output if assigned to a symbol. See Portability of REXX Programs for more information on these functions.

```
A= dosdir('*.bat','nsdt') [lists the filename, size, modification
date and time for all .BAT files in the current directory.]
```

    b. Redirect any DOS command to the data queue by using the STK (stack) "device" such as *VER>STK.* To use it, a *DEVICE=C:\REXX\ STACKDRV.SYS* (or something similar) must be in your CONFIG.SYS file. Also, the Interrupt and Stack Managers must be loaded (*STACK-MGR /S60* creates a 60-kilobyte stack that can hold 30 kilobytes of characters. Other devices such as com1, Ipt1, and prn (printers) are supported.

5. For OS/2, redirect the OS/2 command to a file:

```
CHKDSK C: /V >LIST1 /*Puts a lists of all files on drive C into file*
```

6. For *TSO/E,* there are two ways you can do this:

If you have Session Manager installed at your site, you can use the TSO command SMCOPY to put all or part of your interactive session to a dataset for a later manipulation:

```
    ADDRESS TSO "SMFIND 'ALLOC' STREAM(TSOOUT)" /*Finds where first,
ALLOC is used*/
     LOCATE = RC /* Store this location in LOCATE*/
/*Copies from the ALLOCATE until line 999 and stores it in,
userid.SESSION.data*/
    "SMCOPY FROMSTREAM(TSOOUT) TODATASET(SESSION.DATA)
LINE('LOCATE':999)"
```

Notes:
1. Your entire TSO session is stored in a data "stream" named TSOOUT. By manipulating that stream, you can decide how much of your session to save.
2. If you are not going to copy the entire session, then using SMFIND to find the starting and ending lines to save is invaluable. Also consider using the various SMFIND operands such as ALL (all instances of a string. The

default is FIRST), ASIS (case-sensitive search), and FORWARD/BACK-WARD (direction of search in STREAM, default is backward).

The second approach is to use the OUTTRAP function (based on the CLIST control variable &SYSOUTTRAP).

```
    tr = OUTTRAP("capt.",100,NOCONCAT) /*Up to 100 lines store in,
    stem capt*/
/* TSO command listed below displays all cataloged datasets that have,
GROO as their first */
/* qualifier and TEXT as their third qualifier*/
    ADDRESS "TSO LISTC LVL('GROO.*.TEXT')"
    Do II = 1 until II = capt.trapped /* Move from compound symbol,
    to data queue */
     queue capt.II
    end
    do until queued() = 0 /*Parse lines in queue*/
     parsing sequence
    end
    OUTTRAP('OFF') /* Turns capturing off*/
```

Notes:
1. OUTTRAP may have up to three arguments in the following order:
   a. name of the compound symbol's stem including the period.
   b. The total number of lines that can be captured. The default is an adequate 999,999,999.
   c. Finally either CONCAT (the default, which appends to previously captured output) or NOCONCAT (which overwrites any previously captured output—beware!).

2. Once OUTTRAP has completed, the following can be used:
   compound_symbol.max (Total number of lines that can be captured)
   compound_symbol.trapped (Total number of captured lines. This is similar to the returncode from the CMS SENTRIES command or the QUEUED function for data queues.)
   compound_symbol.con (current setting of CONCAT/NOCONCAT arguments.)

7. For *UNIX,* the POPEN instruction saves the UNIX command output to a stack. Use a skeleton similar to the following:
```
call popen ('ls -l')
do while queued() > 0 [same as do until queued () = 0]
  (parse logic)
end
```

8. This cannot be done for *VMS;* Johnson (1990) suggests adding a /OUT-PUT=LIFO|FIFO qualifier to be used with most VMS commands when invoked in a REXX exec.

What To Include in a Startup REXX Exec

Each of the operating systems being discussed in this chapter have some type of startup or login procedure. Table 4-2 lists the different names and functions of each of these files which reside in the top directory (also called the root or home directory).

Check the user's guide or appropriate references for your operating system to learn more about creating or modifying your startup file. In most cases, the files mentioned previously would then invoke the REXX exec to do further processing. Only in CMS and TSO/E can a REXX exec be used directly as the startup file. Here are some ideas on what can be placed in a startup file regardless of your operating system:

1. *Welcome commands,* these personalize a session:
```
Say 'Good day Hal. It is' Date('w')',' Date(). The 'Day',
Date('D')'''th day of this year.'
```

Table 4-2. Functions of Files in Top or Root Directory

Operating System	Name of startup files
AREXX	startup-sequence
CMS	PROFILE (sets PF keys, link and access various disks, sets up TXTLIB and LOADLIB)
DOS	AUTOEXEC.BAT (sets path, prompt and other environment variables, initializes memory-resident programs, invokes desired application) CONFIG.SYS (sets device drivers, number of files, buffers, last drive, and so on)
OS/2	OS/2 1.0-1.2: STARTUP.CMD (the AUTOEXEC.BAT for OS/2) AUTOEXEC.BAT (same as for DOS but for DOS session[s] under OS/2) OS2INIT.CMD (when a protected mode session starts, not used in OS/2 1.2 and later) CONFIG.SYS (same as under DOS. Also specifies location of .DLL files, location of OS/2 shell, input/output privileges, enables DOS and configures the DOS session, and sets multitasking attributes) OS/2 1.3 and later: The START command specifies the initial application and reduces the need for a STARTUP.CMD file.
TSO/E	Site-dependent on name. Sets up PF keys, allocation of system and personal libraries and invokes initial application
UNIX	Varies from UNIX to UNIX implementations: System V: profile (sets terminal and characteristics, sets path, checks for mail, sets prompt) BSD: .login (sets environment variables such as prompt, path, shell)
VMS	LOGIN.COM (sets terminal characteristics, session symbols and logicals, invokes initial application)

```
Say ' It is' Time('C')
```
Sample output:
```
Good day Hal. It is Friday, 28 Dec 1990. Day 362 of this year.
It is 11:07am
```

2. *Menus,* if you find yourself accessing several programs on startup, perhaps a menu might be useful.
```
      Say 'Which would like to select?' /*On the Amiga, ECHO is an,
      alias for SAY*/
      Say 'A - - Execute an operating system command'
      Say 'B - - Execute another REXX exec'
      Say 'C - - Exit to operating system'
    Parse upper pull sel /*sets all input to upper case*/
  Select
     when sel = 'A' then do
        Say 'Enter Operating system command'
        Parse pull os_comm
        Interpret os_comm /* Not to be used with REXX compiler. Passed,
        to operating system*/
     end
     when sel= 'B' then do
       say "Enter what is the exec's name?"
       parse pull exec_name
       interpret 'call' exec_name
     end
     when sel='C' then do
        say 'Exiting to operating system'
        exit
     end
      Otherwise
        Say sel 'is an invalid choice' /*Could use a CALL ON or SIGNAL,
        instead */
        exit
     end
```

3. *Log datasets.* The following sequence appends the logon time and date of the current session to the end of the current dataset. Note there currently is no standard way to do this; each operating system is slightly different.
```
log_val.1= date() time('C')
      /* For ARexx*/
 open('logfile','rexx:temp','Write')
 writeln('logfile','date() time()')
 close('logfile')
      /* For CMS */
 "EXECIO 1 DISKW logfile * (STEM LOG_VAL."
 "FINIS" /* Closes at end of session anyway . FINIS could also be,
used as part of EXECIO*/
      /*For DOS (both versions)*/
 "EXECIO 1 DISKW C:\LOG.DAT (STEM LOG_VAL. FINIS"
      /*For TSO*/
 ADDRESS TSO
```

```
"ALLOC F(LOGD) DA('LOG.DATA') MOD"
"EXECIO 1 LOGD (STEM LOG_VAL. FINIS" /*No VAR option available*/
                       /* For UNIX */
/* Using CALL means return code stored in RESULT*/
call LINEOUT '/usr/hhg1/log.dat', 'DATE() TIME("C")' /*positions at,
end of file */
    if RESULT¬= 0 then say 'log data NOT updated'
```

SYSTEM/UTILITY REXX APPLICATIONS

System & Utility REXX applications are similar to front-end applications but emphasize performing system and general utility operations. By definition, this implies that this type of application is less portable. The section will discuss those aspects of system/utility REXX applications that apply to all platforms and focus on file operations.

How Do I Perform File Operations?

Those of you who glanced at the log dataset example in the section on startup REXX execs are already familiar with the idea that each REXX implementation does file input/operations slightly differently. However, there are two general approaches. The first is to use EXECIO, originally a CMS command. The AMIGA, CMS, TSO, and some MS-DOS versions (Kilowatt and Quercus) of REXX all support this approach but have slightly different syntax. EXECIO emphasizes the reading and writing of *records*. This is currently not part of the SAA REXX or REXX 4.00 specification. The second is to use Cowlishaw's file I/O model (1990a, pp. 139–145), which emphasizes the reading or writing of characters or lines from a *stream* of data (such as a file or from a host via a modem.) This approach is also part of the latest SAA Procedure Language specification, so it will eventually be incorporated in all the IBM-supported REXX interpreters. It is currently supported by the Amiga (with slightly different commands), MS-DOS, OS/2, and UNIX REXX interpreters. The commands include:

CHARS—function that tells the number of characters in the stream
CHARIN—instruction to read in so many characters from the stream
CHAROUT—instruction to write out so many characters to the stream
LINES—function that tells the number of lines in the stream
LINEIN—instruction to read in so many lines from a stream
LINEOUT—instruction to write out so many lines to a stream

REXX 4.00 specification includes the STREAM function. This returns the stream status which can be used in debugging problems (such as ERROR or NOT

READY). However, the stream name and stream commands depend on the operating system and REXX interpreter/compiler implementation.

Without doubt, this area will be clarified in the forthcoming REXX ANSI standard. The user-oriented choice would be to implement both and leave the choice to the user. Here are tips and traps regardless of which approach you use:

1. There are at least four approaches in using REXX to create new programs or reports in other languages:
    a. All the REXX interpreters that support EXECIO allow the use of the *STEM* option. You basically build a compound variable array containing all the records you want to write out to a file:

```
/* Write out a SAS program that tells all the system option set-
tings. */
     Line.=
     Line.1 "PROC OPTIONS;"
     Line.2 "RUN;"
```

For *CMS* (both)
```
'EXECIO 2 DISKW PROG1 SAS A 1 F 80 (FINIS STEM LINE.'
```

For *DOS* (both versions)
```
'execio 2 diskw c:\rexx\prog,sas (stem line. finis'
```

For *TSO*
```
address TSO
"allocate f(myfile) da(prog.sas) shr"
"execio 2 diskw myfile(stem Line. finis"
```
    b. For CMS and DOS, you can also use the *STRING* option to do the same thing.

CMS
```
'execio 1 disk1 prog1.sas a 1 f 80 (string' 'PROC OPTIONS;'
'execio 1 disk1 prog1.sas a 2 f 80 '(finis string 'RUN;'
```

DOS (Kilowatt and Quercus)
```
"execio 1 diskw c:\rexx\prog1.sas (string 'PROC OPTIONS;'"
"execio 1 diskw c:\rexx\prog1.sas (finis string 'RUN;'"
```
    c. For UNIX you must use LINEOUT (for DOS it is an option.)

DOS (Kilowatt and Quercus) and UNIX
```
     call LINEOUT '/usr/hhg1/prog1.sas','PROC OPTIONS;',1 /*last
argument is line number*/
     call LINEOUT '/usr/hhg1/prog1.sas','RUN;',2 /*Put in a DOS
file name for MS-DOS*/
     /* Quercus partially supports the line number argument Kilowatt
fully does.*/
```

> d. For ARexx, use WRITECH and WRITELN or purchase the accompanying WSHELL product (which includes an EXECIO command).

For *ARexx*

```
open('sasfile','rexx:temp','Write')
say writeln('sasfile',"Proc Options;")
say writeln(sasfile',"Run;") /*Appends after last line*/
close('sasfile') /*Now if only SAS was on the Amiga...*/
```

2. There are also several ways to update a line in a file. You should have a backup copy regardless of the approach you use.

   a. Use EXECIO DISKW to replace the line (for CMS and DOS).

```
/*To change line 1 in the above example to OPTIONS NOTEXT82;*/
   'execio 1 diskw prog1 sas a 1 f 80 (finis string' 'OPTIONS,
   NOTEXT82;'
```

   b. Use EXECIO DISKW (preferred for portability and ease of use) or DISKRU (read & update. Not available in other REXX interpreters) for TSO.

```
address tso
"allocate f(myfile) da(prog.sas) shr"
"execio 2 diskw myfile 1 (stem Line. finis" /*Line. array now,
has new lines*/
```

   c. Use LINEOUT.

```
call LINEOUT '/usr/hhg1/prog1.sas', 'OPTIONS NOTEXT82;',1
/*positions at line 1*/
```

3. To read a file use DISKR or LINEIN:

```
/* Execio. Note CMS has the LOCATE option to do the equivalent of,
the LINEIN example*/
/* Display first ten lines of a DOS file. Can be easily adopted for,
other operating systems*/
/* EXECIO )STEM - - Stores all lines in a compound symbol*/
      'EXECIO * DISKR c:\rexx\prog1.sas (finis stem line.'
        Do cnt=1 to 10
         say "Line number" cnt ':' line.cnt
        End

/*LINEIN example. Searches file for how many colons it has */
        file1 = 'c:\rexx.prog1.sas'
        cnt = 0
   Do while lines(file1) > 0
        line = linein(file1)
        if lastpos(':',line) <> 0 then do /*<> or \= is "not,
        equals"*/
            cnt = cnt + 1
        end
     end
        say 'There were' cnt 'occurences of : in file' file1
```

4. Under OS/2, you can use QUEUE (data stack), NULL (null device), and LPT1 parallel printer port instead of file names to redirect output:

```
LINEOUT("Queue:" ,"Sample Line") - - Redirect output to data stack
```

How Do I Parse A File Name?

There is no function that parses a file name, but with REXX's capabilities, it is very easy "to roll your own." Here are some simple ones for DOS, TSO, and UNIX:

```
/*DOS (BOTH VERSIONS)*/
/* Assume in symbol file_nm. Formats are c:\text.txt or text.txt.
Subdirectories not supported*/
     if pos(':',file_nm) > 0 then parse value file_nm with drive':\',
     base_nm '.' ftype
          else parse value file_nm with base_nm '.' ftype


/*TSO*/
/* Assume in symbol file_nm. Formats are HHG1.TEXT.TXT or,
HHG1.TEXT.TXT(MEM) */
     if pos('(',file_nm) > 0 then parse value file_nm with first '.',
     second '.' type'('member')'
          else parse value file_nm with first '.' second '.' third


/* UNIX */
/* Assume in symbol file_nm. Formats are /usr3/text.txt or text.txt,
Subdirectories not supported*/
     if pos('/',file_nm) > 0 then parse value file_nm with '/',
     directnum '/' first '.' second
          else parse value file_nm with first '.'second
```

Notes:
1. POS finds the first occurrence of a delimiter in a string. You could also use LASTPOS for the last position.
2. For a function or subroutine, use PARSE ARG instead.
3. Cowlishaw (1990a, pp. 118–126) gives a good overview on parsing capabilities. These have been enhanced under the REXX 4.00 specification. The preceding is only the simplest of parsing formats—parsing by literals. A later section (How to Capture User Input) will look at the more complicated aspects of parsing.

4. Personal REXX (MS-DOS) has a PARSEFN function that parses a complete file specification in its various parts.

How Do I Perform Data Queue Operations?

Besides writing data to a file, REXX execs can write to an external data queue, also called a buffer, data buffer, data queue, and queue. (For TSO and CMS it is called data stack, the stack, program stack, and the input stack.) In this book, stack and queue are synonymous and the term **data queue** will be used. Look at Hoernes 1989, pp. 284–8 for an excellent discussion on data queue operations especially for CMS and TSO.

Once they are in a data queue, the data elements can be written out to a file or another location. In some implementations, such as CMS, data elements can be captured from the keyboard. A **data element** is just a character string of variable length that takes up one "line or slot" in the data queue or data queue buffer. The maximum limit of a data element determined by the operating system/REXX implementation. For example, the maximum limit of a string *from the keyboard* under CMS is between 232 and 255 characters. This limit is dependent on your CMS account setup. A data queue has data elements stacked on top of each other as well as pointers marking the top and bottom of the data queue and between buffers (really just an allocated part of the buffer). Table 4-3 shows that REXX specifies three instructions to manipulate data elements in the data queue.

Table 4-4 lists the order in which two data elements will be pulled based on whether a PUSH or QUEUE instruction had placed the element on the data stack.

Table 4-3. REXX Instructions To Manipulate Elements in Data Queue

Instruction	Where in the Data Queue	Order in Which Retrieved
PUSH	On top of data queue	First element retrieved
QUEUE	On bottom of data queue	First element retrieved unless an element near the top of the data queue was PUSHed.
PULL	Does apply—retrieve only	Top element retrieved

Table 4-4. Order For Pulling Data Elements

First Element	Second	Element
	QUEUE	*PUSH*
PUSH	1,2	2,1
QUEUE	1,2	2,1

Data queue operations are very similar across various REXX platforms:

```
/*CMS, MS-DOS (Kilowatt and Quercus) & TSO */
    "MAKEBUF" /* For DOS & TSO: MAKEBUF not in quotes - - part of,
    interpreter*/
    BUFNO = RC
      queue /*null data element*/
      queue "second data element"
      push "third data element placed on top of queue"
/* Could use SENTRIES command for CMS and DOS (Quercus) and get the,
value from RC*/
    say "Number of data elements in the data queue: " QUEUED()
      pull x
    say "The top data element in the data queue is " x/* Third data,
element - - LIFO */
    "dropbuf buffno"
/* For DOS & TSO: DROPBUF not in quotes - - part of interpreter. Kilo-,
watt does not accept buffno argument*/


    /*UNIX - - Has no buffers so no MAKEBUF and DROPBUF needed.*/
queue /*null data element*/
queue "second data element"
push "third data element placed on top of queue"
say "Number of data elements in the data queue: " QUEUED()
pull x
say "The top data element in the data queue is " x/* Third data ele-,
ment - - LIFO*/
```

The following are tips and traps when dealing with data queues:

1. PULL converts all text to uppercase—use **PARSE PULL** for reading and retaining mixed case data. Remember the **QUEUED** function lists the current number of lines in the data queue.

2. Some data queue guidelines:
   a. Always use DROPBUF to clean up the buffers after you have completed all operations with that buffer.
   b. Having many data elements may slow down queue processing and lead to unpredictable results.
   c. Avoid pulling more data elements than you actually have in the data queue. PULL on an empty buffer removes the buffer (DROPBUF).

3. CMS, MS-DOS, and TSO uses the CMS data queue model (UNIX does not). This includes commands to set up buffers, which are user-allocated partitions of the data queue. **MAKEBUF** sets up buffers starting with a buffer number of 0, then 1, etc. (really sets up the buffer pointers). **DROPBUF** *buffer_number removes the specified buffer number and higher.* (The current buffer, the

one created by the last MAKEBUF, is removed if no *buffer_number* is specified. A *buffer_number* of 0 or **DESBUF** in CMS and MS DOS *removes all buffers*. Note a DROPBUF operation really removes a buffer's pointers.)

4. Data queue capabilities are available in the TSO and non-TSO address spaces. The concept of **primary** and **secondary** data queues was also added. Secondary queues allow multiple execs to access the same queue (if in the same environment). Only one secondary queue is active at a time. Two instructions were added: **NEWSTACK** (creates a secondary queue; RC is number of created stacks) and **DELSTACK** (removes secondary queue if one exists, or else it removes the current primary queue). Also three new functions were added for both primary and secondary data queues: **QBUF** (number of buffers in the queue and is stored in RC), **QELEM** (how many data elements exist in the primary stack and are stored in RC), and **QSTACK** (how many data queues exist).

5. For MS-DOS (Quercus), you can also use the PRESS instruction to place keystrokes in the data queue. There is also a DISABLE/ENABLE instruction to momentarily turn on or off the data queue. (Kilowatt provides a GETKEY function to simulate pressing keys by using their scan codes).

6. Although there is one queue in the CMS model, it is logically divided into a keyboard ("type-ahead") queue and a data (program) queue. (All stacks together are called the console queue but are sometimes synonymous with the keyboard queue.) Keyboard commands are processed in order (LIFO). Here are some tips in manipulating the keyboard queue:

    a. The EXTERNALS function—CMS, TSO, and MS-DOS—Quercus— returns the number of lines in the keyboard queue.

    b. If the keyboard queue is supported, the general search order of a PARSE PULL command is data (program) queue, keyboard queue, then the keyboard. PARSE PULL EXTERNAL—CMS, MS-DOS (Quercus) and UNIX searches the keyboard queue, then the keyboard.

    c. TSO supports its own version of the keyboard queue and it is often used to supply arguments to a command.
    ```
    pr_on = prompt("on")
    push "'hhg1.data.data'"
     address tso "list" /*lists hhg1.data.data*/
    ```

    d. TSO supports the following search logic: foreground—first retrieve from the data stack, then the keyboard, background—first retrieve from the data stack, read from the input file (if end of file is not detected). Otherwise, return null.

    e. PARSE LINEIN (or PARSE Value LINEIN) will parse the data and keyboard (on some REXX platforms) data elements.

7. OS/2 uses the RXQUEUE function to perform operations on private queues. Some examples are:

```
RXQUEUE('Create',q1)
/*Creates queue named q1. Once created, could use push,queue,and pull,
 to access queue.*/
RXQUEUE ('Delete',q2) /*Deletes queue if exists*/
```

Jay Tunkel of IBM created a shareware REXX OS/2 exec called SERVER.CMD that shows how you can use RXQUEUE to provide inter-process communication.

8. ARexx allows creation of a temporary file of commands on a RAM disk and then passes it directly to the shell.

SELF-CONTAINED REXX APPLICATIONS

Self-contained REXX applications are one or more REXX execs (and sometimes compiled programs) that are oriented to end-users instead of computer center staff. Sequences in this section will deal with some of the REXX language's more sophisticated features. These include (1) capturing, parsing, and validating user input, (2) communicating between a subprocedure/function, and the main exec and (3) miscellaneous operations (such as changing the case of a string).

How To Capture User Command Line Values

The major mechanism for capturing input from the command line is the ARG or PARSE ARG instruction. Note this instruction is also used to capture values from a subroutine or function. The example below shows the relationship between the command line and PARSE ARG.

```
                  From the command line:
     EXEC Exec1 1 (804) 555-1212
/*Or use the appropriate way to invoke your REXX interpreter or com-,
piler */
                    In EXEC1 exec:
     PARSE ARG VAR1 '(' AREA ')-' Exchange '-' Extension
     say 'var 1 is' var1 /* Displayed: var 1 is 1 */
     say 'area' area 'exchange' exchange 'extension' extension
/* Displayed: area 804 exchange 555 extension 1212*/
```

Parse ARG is followed by a template (or) pattern that contains the variables to contain the parsed values as well as the parsing "directions." These "directions" tell the interpreter to parse by *blanks* (usually for words), *character and substring delim-*

iters (for strings and substrings) or by *character position* (usually for variable strings). Here is a simple example of each type:

BY BLANKS

```
      PARSE ARG WORD1 WORD2
/* If entered Two Words then Word1 is Two and Word2 is Words*/
```

BY CHARACTER AND SUBSTRING DELIMITER

```
      PARSE value 'Parse by colon delimiter : it works !' with,
      part1 : part2
/* Displayed: Part1 Parse by colon delimiter. Part2 it works! */
```

BY ABSOLUTE (2) AND RELATIVE (+3) POSITION

```
      PARSE ARG ARG1 2 ARG2 + 3 ARG3
/*If string is three long words. Then arg1 is Thr and arg3 is ee long,
words*/
```

For greater detail on parsing input, see the later section on parsing command-line input. Keep in mind these tips and traps when capturing command-line input:

1. ARG is an alias for PARSE UPPER ARG, which translates all input to uppercase. Use PARSE ARG if you wish to retain the current case of command-line input. Leading blanks are always removed from input.
2. If there are more symbols than command-line values, then the extra symbols are assigned a null value. If user input does not match the PARSE ARG pattern (or template), then the string is assigned to the symbols to the left of the pattern and all else is assigned null values. If there are more words than symbols, then the last symbol is assigned the remainder of the command line.
3. One initial problem for TSO/E REXX users is the parsing of keyword operands [such as DATASET('USR1.DATA.S1990')] used by TSO commands and CLIST programs.* Use a procedure similar to the following:

```
/* Parse two keyword operands: PRINT DATASET('USR.DATA.S1990')*/
      parse arg I
      parse value I with p d '('dvalue')
      print = p;dv= dvalue;
      say 'p' p 'dvalue' dv 'd' d /* Displayed p PRINT dvalue,
      'USR.DATA.S1990' d DATASET*/
```

There is one shareware package available that emulates the CLIST PROC statement—XPROC created by Draper Labs. It is available from the MVS network server—service@mvsa.usc.edu. Read Hoernes (1992) for a good discussion of simulating the CLIST PROC statement in a REXX exec.

Possible enhancements may be using ABBREV to check for abbreviations of keyword and compound variables to scan longer command lines.

4. A period may be used to create a dummy or placeholder symbol. An application of this is trying to retrieve the third word in a command line but you are not interested in the first two:

```
                          command line
   EXEC exec1 The word 3
/*Or the appropriate way to invoke your REXX interpreter/compiler */


                              exec
   Parse arg..num /* num has a value of 3*/
```

5. A period at the end of a PARSE command, used as a "garbage collector," eliminates any additional input.

```
parse arg . wanit .
/*"Collects" only the second argument. The last period eliminates the.
remainder of input*/
```

How To Create Menus, User Prompts, and Confirmation Messages

This can all be done with the SAY statement optionally combined with built-in functions. Note under ARexx, ECHO is an alias for SAY.

```
                      SAY for Prompting input:
SAY "Enter your state of residence:"
pull st

SAY for Menus
Say '***********************************************'
Say '*                'TIME() '                   *'
Say '* Please Enter ONE of the following:          *'
Say '* 1 - 1990 Report                             *'
Say '* 2 - 1991 Report                             *'
Say '* 3 - 1992 Report                             *'
Say '***********************************************'
    pull choice
                   SAY for confirmation messages
    SAY 'Report for' ryear 'is queued to printer' prt
/*Displayed: Report for 1990 is queued to printer PRINTER1*/
```

Although the REXX language does not explicitly include commands that allow cursor manipulation and development of full-screen applications, a number of add-on products and commands do this:
AREXX—WSHELL
CMS—CMS/DMS,ISPF,XEDIT (not an add-on product), XMENU
DOS (Kilowatt)—screen access functions, part of portable REXX

DOS (Quercus)—RxWindow functions, part of Personal REXX*
OS/2—Easel, Dialog Manager
TSO—ISPF, Session Manager
UNIX—Curses
VMS—FMS, SMG, EasyEntry

The following are tips and traps when creating menus and other display text for REXX applications:

1. Under CMS and TSO, you can also use **immediate commands,** a two-letter command that temporarily or permanently stops an executing exec or command to perform another task. Some valid immediate commands are HI, which ends the program; HT, which stops displaying errors and messages; and RT, which resumes displaying errors and messages. HX (Halt Execution) is part of CMS not in TSO. Trace commands are mentioned in this chapter's section on debugging REXX execs.

   a. Under TSO, pressing PA1 or ATTN produces the message "ENTER HI TO END, A NULL LINE TO CONTINUE OR AN IMMEDIATE COMMAND." Entering HI ends the program, HT stops displaying errors and messages, RT resumes displaying errors and messages. HX (Halt Execution) is part of CMS not in TSO. Trace commands are mentioned later in this chapter.

The following *simulates* an immediate command and can be used for menus:

```
if answer = 'HT' | answer = 'HX' then exit /* If halt typing or execu-
tion*/
```

Under CMS, it is common to include immediate commands as part of the error sequences:

```
error1:
set cmstype rt /*Show error messages on error*/
signal on error
```

2. Use REXX built-in functions to enhance your menus and display text. Some suggestions include: DATE, ERRORTEXT (on error routines for menus), FORMAT (format numbers), TIME, TRANSLATE, and VALUE.

3. Programmers who recently switched from the CLIST to REXX language will be disappointed to find there is no equivalent of WRITENR (WRITE no return), which leaves the cursor at the end of the WRITENR text instead of

---

Both DOS REXX interpreters have or will soon have interfaces to MS Windows.

on the next line. There are ways to have similar functionality under various operating systems. (A TSO shareware version called XWRITENR was developed at Draper Labs. The syntax is CALL XWRITENR 'text'. It is available from the MVS Network Server service@mvsa.usc.edu.) It is likely that this will be in a future TSO release.

How to Capture User Input

A previous section already discussed most of the features of the PARSE PULL and PULL instructions (see the next section for learning more on building parsing template (or pattern) for PULL and other instructions). In most cases, a PARSE PULL or PULL followed by the symbol name(s) *optionally* followed by a parsing template (or pattern) is more than adequate.

```
Say 'what is the name of your lawyer?'
pull first last /*blank (word) is delimiter*/
```

The following are tips and traps using PARSE PULL and PULL:

1. PULL converts all text to uppercase—use **PARSE PULL** for reading and retaining mixed case data.
2. For more complicated user input, parsing by character delimiter(s)/substrings or by position may make more sense than parsing by blanks (words). A related topic, validating user input is covered in the section "How to Validate Command Line/User Input" later in this chapter.

How To Parse Command Line/User Input

One major strength of the REXX language is its parsing capabilities—the ability to break down a string into user-specified substrings. The most common REXX instructions to do this are ARG, and the many formats of PARSE, and PULL. Each of these instructions are followed by a template (or) pattern that contains the variables to contain the parsed values as well as the parsing "directions." These "directions" tell the interpreter to parse by *blanks* (usually for words), *character and substring delimiters* (for strings and substrings) and by *character position* (usually for variable strings). Most of this section will deal with the last method of parsing, including the minor changes made in this area by the REXX language 4.00 specification.

SIMPLE PARSING

```
Word (blank) delimited
    arg a,b,c
/* Takes a string and assigns the characters up to the first blank to,
the symbol A, the characters*/
```

```
/*between the first and second blanks to the symbol B, and the,
remainder to the symbol C.*/
/* Leading and trailing blanks are removed from the string*/

character delimiter
     parse value 'A : long string: with three colons:' with a ':' b,
     ':' c
/* Use of character delimiter A is A, b is long string and c is with,
three colons:*/

column position (absolute no plus or minus prefix)
     parse value 'This is a test' with a 8 b /* Splits into two sub-,
     strings at column 8*/
/* a is This is and b is a test (including blank.) Under REXX 4.00,
you can also prefix the column
/*number with an equals sign to tell REXX that the column position is,
 absolute.*/
```

ADVANCED PARSING

```
character delimiter from a symbol (place in parentheses)
/* Above example using symbols*/.
colons = ':'
parse value 'A : long string: with three colons:' with a (colons) b,
(colons) c
/* Use of character delimiter A is A, b is long string and c is with,
three colons:*/

relative position (adds based on last column position specified. Can
have plus or minus prefix.)
parse value ' You are experiencing just another day' with a 2 b + 3 c
/* Same as a 2 b 4 c/*
/* Result:b is Yo b is u c is are experiencing just another day*/

absolute/relative position from a symbol (symbol prefixed by plus,
minus, or equals signs and in parentheses. This is a 4.00 feature and
is also called the indirect column number.

pos1 = 2; pos2 = 3;
parse value ' You are experiencing just another day' with a = (pos1)
b = +(pos2) c
/* Same as previous example*/
```

These are other tips and traps when parsing strings:

1. The period can be used in a pattern to serve as a placeholder or dummy variable. Examples are shown in How to capture user command line values.

2. ARG A B C is not the same thing as ARG A,B,C. The first parses one string into three symbols. The second parses three strings. However, there is no reason you cannot combine the two.

```
    ARG A B, C , D
/* First string split between A and B, the remaining two strings are,
assigned to C and D*/
```

3. Combine parse with other functions (such as translate) and string operations (such as concatenation).

```
    say 'enter a single number'
        parse pull numa
    scramble=translate(numa,'9876543210','0123456789','.') /*Changes,
        a 0 to a 9 etc. */
/*Note if the output string is not as long as the input string, then
a pad character of period is used.*/
/* So 24680 becomes 75319 */
```

4. Parse or pull by position or column on records that are not delimited by blanks.

How to Validate Command Line/User Input

After you have obtained the input from the command line or the keyboard and it is parsed, then it is appropriate to check if the input is valid. Validations consist of four types.

1. *Checking the data type:**

```
    say 'Let me guess your data type'
    pull guess
    say 'Datatype is' datatype(guess) /*Returns either NUM or CHAR */
```

Or

```
    select
      when datatype(guess,'A') then say guess 'is alphanumeric'
      when datatype(guess,'B') then say guess 'is binary'
      .....
    end
```

2. *Checking for specific values:*

```
    pull numm
        if verify(numm,'0123456789','M') <1 then say 'invalid choice'
/*Greater than 1 implies a match*/
    ...
```

3. *Checking for a number range:*

```
    If num > 1 & num < 10 /* Selects between 2 and 9 - - or use,
    SELECT for multiple checks*/
```

---

*CMS/TSO supports C (mixed double byte characters) and Dbcs (double-byte characters) as an option under the Datatype function.

4. *Checking for blank/nonblank:*

```
        if numm = ' ' then do
/*Check if blank. Note that blank will return CHAR from the DATATYPE,
function.*/
        if numm <> ' ' then do /* Check if non-blank */
```

Date And Time Operations With REXX

DATE and TIME functions provide a means to display date and times in a variety of formats. Here are the most common ones:

```
Common DATE Formats                                 Example
Date('B') - Number of days since 1/1/0001.Added     3232565
in REXX 4.00
DATE('D') - Number of days so far this year.        5
DATE('E') - European format dd/mm/yy                05/01/91
DATE('N') - default format same as DATE()           05 Jan 1991 (maybe)
DATE('O') - yy/mm/dd for sorting                    91/01/05
DATE('S') - yyyymmd - good for date operations       19910105
DATE('W') - Capitalized day of the week             Saturday


Common TIME Formats                                 Example
TIME('C') -Time in 12 hour format (hh:mm:td         3:45pm
with td being am or pm)
TIME('E') -Returns the time elapsed from            5.012345 - -
the last                                            five seconds
TIME('E') or TIME('R') [resets timer to 0].
Elapsed time is in seconds and microseconds
TIME('H') - - current hour in 24 hour format        15
TIME('N') or TIME() - - default format              15:45:20 (maybe)
```

ARexx does not have a DATE function and its TIME function only supports the E, H, M, R, and S options.

To find the difference between two dates, put them both in yyyymmdd format and subtract the two. Another approach is to convert to the Julian format and subtract the two dates as in the following:

```
    date2= julian(01,05,91) /*Call function for first date*/
    date1 =julian(01,01,91) /*Call function for second date*/
    diff = date2 - date1
        exit
julian: arg m,d,y
    jdate=d-32075+1461*(y+4800+(m-14)/12)/4
    jdate=jdate+367*(m-2-(m-14)/12*12)/12
    jdate=jdate-3*((y+4900+(m-14)/12)/100)/4
return jdate
```

Most date and time algorithms can be converted to REXX functions and sub-procedures. A good introduction in the area including an overview of international date and time standards is Bemer (1979). Some REXX interpreters have functions to assist in date conversion. Personal REXX (MS-DOS) has a DATECONV function that will convert a date to the desired format, which is the same as the standard DATE function.

Text Case Operations With REXX

The following are tips and traps when dealing with text case operations:

1. Both the ARGS and PULL instructions translate strings to uppercase. Use PARSE ARG or PARSE PULL to retain the current case of a string.
2. Use DATATYPE to verify if a string is in lower-, upper-, or mixed case:

```
say 'what is your name?'
   pull nam
select
when datatype(nam,'L') then do
 (code for lower case processing)
end
when datatype(nam,'U') then do
 (code for upper case processing)
end
when datatype(nam,'M') then do /*Never gets to this, matches L,
and U first */
 (code for mixed case processing)
end
otherwise say 'case not applicable or unknown'
end
```

3. Use the TRANSLATE function to convert an entire string to uppercase:

```
TRANSLATE('hi') /*becomes HI */
```

4. MS-DOS (Quercus) and UNIX includes UPPER and LOWER functions to convert any string to a desired case. AREXX has an UPPER and ToUpper function (in system library).
5. Check if your operating system/keyboard allows lowercase and how it can be enabled.
6. Remember, ADDRESS CMS translates commands to uppercase but ADDRESS COMMAND does not.

String Operations With REXX

A major REXX strength is its string operations features. Also see the previous section and the later section on creating reports for additional ideas. This can be only a broad overview on what is available to help perform string operations in REXX execs:

1. REXX includes operators just for string operations. These include:
   a. blank between strings—concatenation with a blank between strings
   b. || –concatenation with no blank between strings
   c. no blank between strings—concatenation with no blank between strings
   d. = = –two strings are identical
   e. ¬= = or /= =–two strings are not equal and may use other symbols for "not equals" such as ^ or ~. Note that these comparisons are case sensitive and may also be dependent on the sorting order of the REXX implementation. There may be other differences as well (EBCDIC versus ASCII sort order or the various ASCII sort sequences, mainly for European users).

2. REXX has more than 60 standard functions, with half of these dedicated to performing operations on substrings, words, and sentences. In addition, various REXX interpreters have their own home-grown functions. String operation functions include:
   a. string justification (LEFT, RIGHT, CENTER)
   b. string/word search (POS, LASTPOS, SUBSTR, SUBWORD, WORD, WORDINDEX, WORDPOS)
   c. string/word length (LENGTH, WORDLENGTH)
   d. insert characters/words(COPIES, INSERT, OVERLAY, SPACE)
   e. remove characters/words (DELSTR, DELWORD, STRIP, TRUNC)
   f. verify strings (ABBREV, COMPARE, DATATYPE, VERIFY)
   g. other string operations (such as REVERSE, TRANSLATE, WORDS)

3. A point of confusion for some is that the ordering of the first two arguments of the POS/LASTPOS functions seems reversed (search string, string to search instead of the reverse).

4. Use ABBREV to validate if user input may include abbreviations.

What REXX Version Do I Have?

This chapter contains features of both the REXX 3.50 and 4.00 specifications. The following is a sequence to determine which REXX version you have:

```
parse version lang version vdate
say 'language is of course' lang /* displayed: language is of,
course REXX*/
say ' version is' version /* displayed: version is 4.0.0
say 'date version released is ' vdate /* date version released is,
10 Jan 1990*/
```

Notes:
1. This instruction may not be in all REXX interpreters/compilers and the format may be different than shown above. (For example the language value

may also have additional information—such as Personal REXX listing the version of the product and its release date). Here are some sample formats returned by a PARSE VERSION instruction:

```
                            AREXX

      ARexx V1.1 68020 NONE NTSC 60HZ
      /*1.1 is ARexx version followed by CPU chip, math coprocessor,
video type and clock frequency*/



                       CMS (COMPILER)

      REXXC370 3.46 1 Jul 89



                       DOS (KILOWATT)

      REXX Kilowatt Software Portable BV1.15 4.00 18 April 1991
      /*Kilowatt has both product and REXX version*/



                       DOS (QUERCUS)

      REXX Personal 4.0 August 1991



                            UNIX

      Uni-REXX 1.45 1 Apr 91 /* UNIX. 1.45 is uni-REXX Version*/
```

Personal REXX (Quercus) has a PRXVERSION function that returns the version level of the software.

What Global Options Can I Set?

The OPTIONS instruction allows a way to assign REXX interpreter/compiler settings that affect overall REXX processing. These settings, specific to that interpreter or compiler, are rarely portable to other operating systems. They are usually turned off by default. Some commonly used options are:

Option/Operating System   **Function**

DBCS (UNIX in a future release)   Enable double-byte characters

DEBUG (DOS—both)   Enables trace facility if enabled

ETMODE/NOETMODE (CMS, TSO, SAA). Enables/disables double-byte characters NOETMODE is the default. For CMS and TSO must be first option if used. This is not supported by ProREXX (Systems Center) on CMS.

EXMODE/NOEXMODE (CMS, TSO, SAA). Enables/disables double-byte character verification; NOEXMODE is the default.

FAILAT (ARexx) Set return code level to be recognized as an error

MIXEDCASE (UNIX in a future release) Leaves text in current case and not converted to upper case

NEWCOM/NONEWCOM(DOS—Personal REXX). Enables/disables running REXX from a batch (.BAT) file; NONEWCOM is the default.

PROMPT (ARexx) Assigns prompt string for PULL/PARSE PULL

RESULTS (ARexx) Asks for result when sending a command to an external environment

TRACE/NOTRACE (CMS, TSO) Enables/disables trace facility

Here are some tips and traps when dealing with the OPTIONS statement:

1. An invalid option is usually ignored rather than causing an error.
2. Place it near the top of your program so it can be easily removed or commented out if ported to other operating systems or is not needed.
3. There is no guarantee that an option will be enabled in a function or subroutine in the same program—set it there as well to avoid surprises.
4. ARexx also offers a PRAGMA function that allows further customization of the REXX session. The two values are directory (and directory name) and priority (and priority level).

How Do I Pass Information Between Execs?

Information (such as return codes and symbol values) are passed between REXX execs in a variety of ways:

1. When the REXX exec is invoked, also including parameters

2. Capturing the EXIT code from the exec by examining RC

3. The VALUE function under the REXX 4.00 specification now captures values from external variable pools (SAA supports a variable pool interface or VPI). Here is an example of how Cowlishaw would envision it implemented (variable pools are supported in some form under CMS, OS/2, and ARexx):

```
value('var1','newval,'shared')
/* assigns var1 a value of newval in the SHARED variable pool */
```

The OS/2 REXX interpreter allows access and modification of environment variables stored in the OS2ENVIRONMENT variable pool.

```
enx= 'OS2ENVIRONMENT' /*Assign OS2ENVIRONMENT to a variable*/
say value('path',,enx) /*display current value of path environment,
variable*/
```

4. Use of environment variables assigned values by a PUTENV (UNIX) or SETENV (DOS—Kilowatt) function and retrieved by GETENV (DOS— Kilowatt and UNIX) and DOSENV (DOS—Quercus) functions.

5. Both MS-DOS (Quercus) and CMS include a GLOBALV command that allows you to create, access, and modify global symbols that are accessible by all REXX execs. Here are some tips and traps when using GLOBALV:
   a. For MS-DOS (Quercus), you must invoke RXINTMGR and GLVMGR before invoking GLOBALV.
   b. GLOBALV operations include:

GET (subcommand of SELECT)   Access value of global symbol

LIST (subcommand of SELECT)   List values of variables

PUT (subcommand of SELECT)   Assigns REXX symbol values to global variables

PUTS(session) and PUTP (permanent) also available.

SELECT   Change name of global variable group

SET (subcommand of SELECT)   Create resident global symbol

SETP (subcommand of SELECT)   Create permanent global symbols or

SETS (subcommand of SELECT)   Create session global symbols

6. ARexx includes a clip list that can be used to pass values between programs, similar to the Clipboard in Macintosh, MS Windows and OS/2 environments. Values can be strings (any case) or numbers. Clip List functions include:

GETCLIP   Retrieve a value from the clip list

SETCLIP   Assign value to the clip list.

SHOW(CLIP)   Shows all values in the clip list.

How Do I Pass Information Between an Exec and Function/Subprocedure?

Information (such as return codes and symbol values) is passed between REXX functions/subprocedures and the "main" exec in a variety of ways:

1. When the function/subprocedure is invoked, up to 10 accompanying values are also included.

2. The RETURN instruction to pass a result from the function: A function must pass back a result via RETURN but a subroutine does not have to. If RETURN is used with a subroutine, the result is stored in the system (special) symbol named RESULT. Here is an example of the same sequence both as a function and subroutine:

/* function */	/*subroutine*/
a=2;b=2;	a=2;b=2;
X = addit(a,b) /* Result replaces,	call addit a,b
function */	
/*later in the same exec*/	Say a '+' b '=' result
EXIT /* Avoids reprocessing function */	exit /* Avoids reprocessing function */
ADDIT: ARG d,c	ADDIT: ARG d,c
return d+c	return d+c /* Placed in result */

Note that a subroutine can return multiple values using RESULT. However, these have to be parsed into individual values.

3. Making internal subprocedure and function symbols global (that is accessible and potentially changeable by the "main" exec). This is done by not including the desired symbol in a PROCEDURE EXPOSE instruction.
Note that PROCEDURE EXPOSE cannot be used with external subprocedures and functions.

4. Environment variables, and shared variable pools are explained in the previous section on passing information between execs.

Compound Symbol Operations Using REXX

This section gives an overview on using compound symbols including some of the new features included in the REXX 4.00 version. Here are some major points to remember when using compound symbols:

1. Compound symbols can be thought of as two or more symbols joined together by periods. The **stem** is the first symbol name and first period and the **tail** is the symbol name that resides between the first and second periods. The tail is not an indicator of the array size and may be composed of alphabetical, numeric, or null characters. The default value of a compound symbol is the symbol name in uppercase.

2. Compound-symbol operations examples:
   a. Assigning a value to the stem assigns the value to all compound symbols with that stem (regardless of their current value).
   ```
   x. = 20 /*So x.1 = 20 until reset*/
   ```

b. Assigning values from a compound symbol "array":

```
/* All REXX versions */
       val=0
       do cnt = 1 to 10
         a.cnt = val+10 /* a.1 = 10, a.2 = 20...*/
         val = val + 10
       end
```

```
/* REXX 4.00*/
       val=0
       do cnt = 1 to 10
         value('a.'cnt,(val+10))
         val = val + 10
       end
```

c. Retrieving values from an array:

```
/* All REXX versions */
       do cnt = 1 to 10
           say a.cnt /* or use say value('a.'cnt)*/
       end
```

d. Uninitializing compound symbols

```
/* All REXX versions */
       drop a. b.6.
/* REXX 4.00 */
     dalist = 'a.b.6' /* Create an indirect list of symbols to be,
     dropped*/
     drop (dalist)
/* Resets the value of compound symbols with an a. stem and the b.6,
compound variable*/
```

e. The values of internal subroutines or functions are *global*—that is, can be modified by the "main" exec—*beware!* You can make these symbols *local,* and free from the main exec, by using the PROCEDURE EXPOSE function and specifying only those simple or compound symbols that you wish to make accessible to the main exec.

```
/* All REXX versions */
       call subroot
       say a. b.6 c /*Displayed: a = 1, b.6=7,c=C (uninitialized),
       */
       exit
       subroot: Procedure expose a. b.6
       a=1;b.6=7;c=99;
       return
/* Exposes all compound symbols with a. as their stem and b.6. */
```

```
/* REXX 4.00 */
       dalist = 'a b.6' /* Create an indirect list of symbols to be,
       exposed
       subroot: Procedure Expose (dalist)
```

      f. Compound symbols can be used for File I/O, particularly with the EXE-CIO command and STEM option. This is covered in "How Do I Perform File Operations?"

3. The following are some of the common criticisms of compound symbols operations:

      a. There needs to be a way to access the entire array "subscripts" at once. This is somewhat limited (e.g. Clearing the stem eliminates associated values [DROP VAL.]. And you can initialize an entire array by initializing the stem [VAL. = 1]). This is in part because array "subscripts" are very flexible (a.hal is a valid compound symbol).

      b. The PROCEDURE EXPOSE mechanism is clumsy and another way is needed to control symbol scope (whether on compound or some other type of symbol).

      c. A real need exists to pass and receive stems and portions of arrays from subprocedures. This currently does not exist.

      d. The 1a.1 value only can be used as a counter variable by what immediately follows the first period of the compound symbol but not what follows the second period (e.g., you can loop through a.1 through a.10 but not a.1.1 to a.1.10).

These are valid criticisms that in the process of resolving may make some major changes in the REXX language. This may mean new instructions and formats.

How to Create Reports Using REXX

REXX is ideal to generate reports using a combination of its file operations and word/string handling capabilities. Combine this with KEDIT, XEDIT or ISPF/PDF EDIT commands and you can generate even very complicated reports. Here is an example of using REXX to generate a letter:

```
line.=
line.1=right(date('U'),80)
line.2=right("80 Radioactive Waste Lane",80)
line.3=right("Sludgeway,Mass 02138",80)
line.4 = "   "
line.5 = "   "
line.6 = center('25 Cutename Road',80)
line.7= center('Rexxville, Pa 01111',80)
line.8 = "   "
line.9 = "   "
line.10 = left('Dear mom:',80)
line.11 =right('I hope that all is well.',28)
line.12=left('All is fine here.',80)
line.13= '  '
line.14=left("  Love,",80)
```

```
line.15=left('  Herbert and Thelma Ruskins',80)
do cnt = 1 to 16
  say line.cnt
end
/* Send to a file using LINEOUT or EXECIO*/
```

The resulting letter:

```
                                        01/26/91
                            80 Radioactive Waste Lane
                              Sludgeway,Mass 02138

                  25 Cutename Road
                  Rexxville, Pa 01111

Dear mom:
  I hope that all is well.
All is fine here.

  Love,
  Herbert and Thelma Ruskins
```

The following are additional tips and traps when creating reports with REXX:

1. Set up a DO loop when printing the file to determine page breaks and to increment the page number.

2. These functions are especially useful in generating reports with REXX:
   a. DATE and TIME to add the current date and time in a report.
   b. CENTRE/CENTER, JUSTIFY (not in all platforms), LEFT, and RIGHT to justify text with or without user-specified padding and truncation.
   c. FORMAT to round and format numbers, SIGN to determine the current sign of a number, and TRUNC to parse and round numbers.
   d. INSERT, OVERLAY, SPACE, STRIP to insert/replace existing characters in a string.
   e. SUBWORD, WORD, WORDINDEX, WORDLENGTH, WORDPOS, and WORDS to perform subword and word operations. The following parses a sentence and assigns each word to a compound symbol:
      ```
      s = ('This has seven words in this sentence')
      cnt = words(s)
      do a= 1 to cnt /* Could instead have do a=1 to words(s)*/
         cv.a = word(s,a)
      end
      ```
   f. Length to determine the length of a sentence (if one string) or have a DO loop add up all the WORDLENGTHs.

3. Use the CC *code* DATA options of EXECIO PRINT to send carriage control characters to your printer. *Code* can be 0 (1 blank line printed) – (two blank lines printed), 1 (newpage), + (overprint on same line such as underline). This is currently supported by CMS, DOS (Kilowatt and Quercus). The DATA option specifies the control character will be in column 1 of each line. Note that the default without the CC invoked is a single space between lines.

```
EXECIO * PRINT (CC DATA
/*Specifies a carriage control character will be found in each line.,
*./
/*This statement may vary for your REXX interpreter or compiler.*/

EXECIO 1 PRINT (CC - STRING 'sample string'
/*Sends one line with the words "sample string" to the printer. The,
line is to be double spaced*./
/* (Specified by the CC - character.) This statement may vary for
your REXX interpreter or compiler*/
```

Subcoms, Packages, and REXX

External functions and subprograms (compiled programs not external execs) may be placed into libraries called **packages.** The advantage of this is faster execution time because the entire package is always available. Note that packages are not part of the REXX language or SAA procedure language specification. This means that the package developer must create the package (in assembler) as well as the supplemental REXX command to access it. Once created, these packages are transparently available as an extension of REXX language—i.e., the functions act and are called as any other REXX function.

Here is more information on REXX function packages:

1. Under **ARexx,** the ADDLIB function adds a function library to the function library list. Use the SHOW(FUNCTION) function to view the current function library list. You can create a function by passing message packets to the system. The packets contain the values defined in the RexxArg and REXXMsg structures. Part of the RexxMsg structure is the Rm_Action field. Valid values are RXADDLIB (Add to library list), RXADDFH (Add function host to the library list), and RXFUNC (Invokes a function), RXREMLIB (Remove from library list).

2. Under **CMS** and **TSO/E,** packages may be *private* (or user-level. These are searched first.), *local* (for workgroup and department packages) and *system* (usually for third-party and home-grown software and are searched through last). They are associated with the names RXSYSFN (system), RXLOCFN (local), and RXUSERFN (user). The section, Invoking a Foreground REXX Exec discussed how compiled programs can interface with REXX execs. CMS Function names are invoked by a call RX*name*FN LOAD RX*name*.

See the Shaw (1990) reference for a documented TSO/E function package example. Oppenheim (1992) has a documented CMS function package.

3. There are some non-commercial packages primarily available for **CMS** and **AMIGA** REXX interpreters. A list of the CMS sites can be accessed by sending a message to LISTSERV@host with a message SEND VM-UTIL FILELIST. (Hosts include DEARN, MARIST, TECMTYVM, UBVM, UTARLVM1, and UCF1VM.) A list of Amiga anonymous ftp sites can be found at hubcap.clemson.edu (130.127.8.1) in /pub/amiga/FTP-Sites.txt. Also check REXXLIB (REXXLIB@PSUVM).

4. The following are used in interfacing programs written in other languages with REXX for **CMS** users: EXECCOMM (allows other programs to access and manipulate REXX variables), EXECDROP (drop in virtual storage execs), EXECLOAD (loads an exec in virtual storage resulting in faster execution time), EXECMAP (lists in virtual storage execs), EXECSTAT (verifies if an exec is in virtual storage), REXX-GDDM (interface to GDDM calls using REXX execs), and RXSQL (embed SQL statements in a REXX exec).

5. The following function calls are available under **OS/2:**

REXXSaa   Used to (1) invoke REXX, (2) use in-storage execs, (3) create subcommands

RXFunctionRegister   Registers an external function that an exec can invoke using RxFuncAdd

RXMacroChange   Loads function into macro area

RXMacroSave   Saves macro area for later use

RxString   Structure for variable character strings of any case (Five pre-defined macros work with RxString.)

RxSubcomRegister   Creates a subcommand handler

RxVar   Allows manipulation of REXX variables and return codes

6. Under **MS-DOS** (Kilowatt), the following functions are available to interact with REXX execs:

xsexec   Executes an exec

xspull   Pulls element from the data buffer

xspush   Pushes element to the data buffer

xsqueue   Queues element to the data buffer

xsqueues   Shows number of elements in the data buffer

xsset   Assigns a value to a symbol

7. Under **MS-DOS** (Quercus), the FCNPKG(package) call returns a number indicating the package type. 0 is not loaded; 1 is loaded; 2 is a subcommand

environment. RXWINDOW (a windowing environment) is a built-in package. Functions include:

REXX_CALL   Accesses the call block, which invokes the REXX call

REXX_FCN   Invokes a REXX function package. Two subfunctions are also available.

REXX_SHV   Invokes shared variables interface

REXX SIGNAL   Sets signal for a condition

REXX_UNLOAD   Unloads the resident REXX interpreter

REXX_VERSION   Shows Personal REXX version

STK_BYPASS   Reads from keyboard buffer—not stack

STK_BUFFNO   Lists current buffer number

STK_DROPBUF   Drops a stack buffer

STK_FREE   Shows free space in a stack

STK_MAKEBUF   Creates a stack buffer

STK_READ   Same as STK_BYPASS but does not wait if no characters are available

STK_SENTRIES   Shows lines in a stack

STK_SET_STATUS   Turns on/off program stack

STK_STATUS   Is stack facility enabled?

STK_USED   Characters in keyboard and stack buffers

STK_WRITE   Writes to an exec's stack

8. The following REXX programming services are available for **TSO/E:**

These are available replaceable routines, which complement a system routine by doing pre-processing before the system routine is invoked (usually for assembly program). These include: GETFREER (tasks concerning storage); IRXINOUT (record I/O); IRXLOAD (load an exec into storage and later free it); IRXMSGID (allow displaying of message ID); IRXSTK (tasks concerning the data stack); and IRXUID (capture the userid).

Functions include: IRXEXCOM—creates, deletes, and passes the values of REXX variables to TSO/E and non-TSO/E address space. An alternative is IKJCT441 (TSO/E address space only and operations on REXX and CLIST variables); IRXEXEC (process an in-storage exec); and IRXIC (enables TRACE facility).

Two dummy package directories are included: IRXFLOC (local packages); IRXUSER (user packages).

9. The following program calls are available for uni-REXX (**UNIX**). Note these are similar to **TSO/E REXX** Programming Services:

IRXEXEC   Invokes a function, subroutine, or subcommand
IRXEXCOM   Creates, deletes, and passes the values of REXX variables
IRXJCL   Invokes REXX exec from a C program
IRXSTK   Data stack manipulation from a C program

10. For VMS REXX, two useful functions in this area are: VMREXX (list and modify REXX variable values); and KAGEM (invoke exec and a default environment).
11. If you are a creator of packages, decide on a scheme to set up your packages such as functions/subroutines in the same area, such as string, graphical, or mathematical functions. This reduces the chance of users loading a package when they will not use most of the functions.

Subcoms (Subcommand Environments)

Subcoms, subcommand environments, are a way for an ARexx CMS, MS-DOS, OS/2, TSO, UNIX and VMS application to become an environment under REXX. This allows the "environment" to receive commands from the operating system or to use the "environment" as part of the ADDRESS instruction (i.e., you can enter ADDRESS *environment* "*environment_command*" such as ADDRESS MYSUB "UP PERISCOPE"). Under CMS, there are two built-in subcoms—XEDIT and CMS. Again, note that this is not part of the REXX or SAA Language standards.
The following are tips and traps when using SUBCOMS:

1. A major strength of **ARexx** is interfacing with applications. You can create such an interface by passing message packets between the application and ARexx. (The packets contain the values defined in the RexxArg and REXXMsg structures. Part of the RexxMsg structure is the Rm_Action field, which must be set to RXCOMM for the application to send packets to ARexx).*
2. To test if a subcommand environment is active under **CMS** or **TSO** enter 'SUBCOM *environment*'. An RC of 0 will tell you if the subcommand was activated.
3. Under **MS-DOS** (Personal REXX), the FCNPKG(*package*) returns a number showing the package type with 2 indicating a subcommand environment is active. **REXX_FCN** is the call to enable or disable the subcommand environment. Use REXX_CALL to invoke REXX from an application.
4. Placing a ' RXSUBCOM' instruction in an exec to access a subcommand handler under **OS/2.**
5. **OS/2** provides a series of exits to make an application into an environment: These include RXFNC (external functions), RXCMD (operating system commands), and RXTRC (turn on trace). In **TSO/E,** these are called replaceable routines (such as IRXLOAD[load an exec], and IRXUID[checks userid]).

*Also look at ARexx Command Hosts by Eric Giguère in issue 4 of AmigaWorld Tech Journal.

6. For **UNIX** or **TSO/E,** IRXSUBCM is used to create and delete the subcommand environment.

7. FOR **VMS,** the SUBCOM function is the interface between REXX and the "environment."

OTHER REXX EXEC CONCERNS

This section is concerned with those topics appropriate for all types of REXX applications, including porting REXX to other platforms and other command languages.

How Do I Debug REXX Execs?

A command line, i.e. non-full-screen, trace facility is a standard part of the REXX language. It is more than adequate in resolving the inevitable programming problems that arise when developing REXX execs. Here is a brief overview of the trace facility:

The trace facility consists of two modes:

Non-interactive—the TRACE instruction or built-in function enables the trace facility. The user cannot enter additional TRACE commands while the exec is processing. Common TRACE operands include:

A—trace all clauses before execution

C—trace operating system commands with non-zero return codes before execution—a frequently used option

E—same as C but after execution—a frequently used option

I—traces all clauses before execution including intermediate symbolic substitution, usually the preferred option while debugging execs.

L—traces all labels processed during tracing.

N—same as E but operating system commands with negative return codes after execution.

O—disables all tracing

R—traces all clauses but only final symbolic substitution is shown.

Interactive—invoked by the TRACE ? instruction or TRACE("?") built-in function. All TRACE instructions/functions in the exec are disabled and all TRACE instructions entered at the keyboard are recognized. The display is paused at predetermined points during interactive tracing (called pause points). You may then enter:

null (not blank) to continue processing to the next pause point
equals sign to repeat the last instruction
Trace ? or *TRACE OFF* disables interactive tracing. *A REXX instruction*

The trace facility output does take some getting used to. Here is an example:

The exec:

```
trace i /*Intermediate steps shown as well */
s=('This has seven words in this sentence')
call separse s
  say 'Result is' Result
exit
separse: parse arg st
  cnt=words(s)
  do a=1 to cnt
    cv.a=word(s,a)
  end
  do a = 1 to cnt
    say cv.a
  end
return cnt


        With trace on (some repetitive loops are not shown)
2 *-* s=('This has seven words in this sentence') /*original,
line*/
 >L> "This has seven words in this sentence" /* line as a,
 literal*/
3 *-* call separse s
 >V> "This has seven words in this sentence" /*contents of s*/
6 *-* separse:
6 *-* parse arg st
 >>> "This has seven words in this sentence" /*value of st*/
7 *-* cnt=words(s)

 >V> "This has seven words in this sentence"
 >F> "7"
8 *-* do a=1 to cnt
 >L> "1"
 >V> "7" /* value of cnt*/
9 *-* cv.a=word(s,a)
 >V> "This has seven words in this sentence"
 >V> "1"
 >F> "This" /*Result of function*/
 >C> "CV.1" /*Name of compound symbol after substitution*/
10 *-* end /*cv.2 - - cv.6 left out*/
 9 *-* cv.a=word(s,a)
 >V> "This has seven words in this sentence"
 >V> "7"
 >F> "sentence"
 >C> "CV.7"
10 *-* end
10 *-* end
11 *-* do a = 1 to cnt
```

```
      >L> "1"
      >V> "7"
   12 *-* say cv.a
      >C> "CV.1"
      >V> "This"
This /* Final value of CV.1*/
   12 *-* say cv.a
      >C> "CV.7"
      >V> "sentence"
sentence /* Final value of CV.7*/
   13 *-* end
   13 *-* end
   14 *-* return cnt
      >V> "7"
    4 *-* say 'Result is' Result
      >L> "Result is"
      >V> "7"
      >O> "Result is 7" /*Result's value */
Result is 7 /* The final result of the SAY*/
    5 *-* exit
```

Here are some general debugging techniques using the following general approach:

What happened? Describe action (what happened, what was supposed to happen?) Record all error messages.

Gather more information about the problem: Where exactly is the error happening? On invocation, at a certain label, when invoking a subroutine, function, or another exec? Getting the problem to occur in a consistent fashion, makes it easier to resolve.

Make an educated guess on what caused the problem and a way to test it.

Perform the test. If it works, there is no need to go further. Otherwise return to the gather-more-information step.

- Use TRACE L (to see if the interpreter processed a certain label).
- Use TRACE I to see intermediate steps in symbolic substitution. If you do not see the intermediate symbolic substitution, use TRACE R (same as TRACE I but final symbolic substitution only).
- A and b can also be done by using SAY instructions: Check the value of a symbol before substitution (*SAY 'x is' x*). Check flow control (say *'got past this instruction'*).
- Examine system (special) symbols RC for general instructions, SIGL for the line number of the last CALL or SIGNAL and RESULT for values passed via a RETURN in a subroutine.
- Check the version of the REXX language (PARSE VERSION) to see if the problem is related to your REXX version. (Is something now a reserved word

that was not before or a function changed?) Also check the version of your interpreter or compiler and see if any updates are needed.

- Use the ERRORTEXT function to display the corresponding text message for a REXX error number.
- Write a subroutine that uses the SIGL system symbol and SOURCELINE function to redisplay the last instruction processed during an interactive trace (Mansfield, 1989).
- Using TRACE *symbol* or TRACE VALUE *symbol* will show the final result of a value.

You can also use SET EXECTRAC ON to enable the TRACE facility under CMS, ARexx, CMS, and TSO to both support immediate commands TS (TRACE Start) and TE (TRACE End). These are invoked by pressing ATTN/PA1 or from READY under TSO. Personal REXX (MS-DOS) does not indent trace output based on nesting level. It also supports TRACE $ to switch output between a printer or monitor. Also use the RXTRACE environment variable or the /TR option when invoking the interpreter to set the default REXX debugging settings for all REXX execs (until reset).

CMS and Personal REXX (MS-DOS) also support the ! command to disable processing operating system commands.

TRACE S was removed in the REXX 4.00 specification.

ProREXX (CMS) includes limited support for the TRACE function and statement.

The Elements of REXX Style

Once you have been writing REXX execs for a while, you begin to develop your own "fingerprint" or style. This section discusses some of the elements of good exec style. Read the Kernighan and Plauger (1978), Savile (1992) or the Dilorio (1989) references for further information. The following are general rules that apply to all types of REXX applications—use them based on your personal and site preferences:

1. *Make your REXX execs readable:*
   a. *Minimize the number of multiple clauses* appearing on the same line to enhance readability and ease of debugging.
   b. *Break your REXX execs into modules* that perform only one or two functions. Use label names to describe these functions and to mark their start.
   c. *Indent at least two or three spaces* for (1) code under a label, (2) The instructions contained within a THEN-DO-END or any DO structure; and (3) PULL after a SAY.
   d. *Line Up* all DOs and ENDs and SELECT and ENDs. Consider lining up equal signs in assignment statements.

e. Freely *use blank space* to separate modules (before lines to mark a new module) and flow control structures such as SELECT.

f. Some *commenting* to self-document the exec is necessary: However, they *do* affect the speed of the processing of the REXX exec. This is especially true for comments in iterative loops. Other things to watch out for are blanks ("whitespace") and variable name length. Consider using one of the "space crunchers" found on the Bitnet listservers in the next section that remove white space and comments to increase execution speed. Try to keep comments up to date. There are various styles of REXX commenting:

   (1) Comment only complicated—i.e. non-obvious—sequences.
   (2) Comment only non-portable REXX instructions.
   (3) Comment only the required first line containing the word REXX, not required for all REXX implementations.
   (4) Comment some type of header file that lists the exec name, what each label (module) does, any nested execs used, any global/shared variables used, and exec version history.
   (5) Comment next to each appropriate REXX instruction or environment command.
   (6) One or more comments before each label.
   (7) I prefer the "jump start" axiom—*write as much documentation to allow you or another person to quickly understand how the exec works.*
   (8) Full names for environment commands.

g. *Use various cases in your programs.* A common practice is to put environment commands in uppercase and in quotes, REXX instructions in lowercase, labels and host commands in uppercase, and REXX symbols in mixed case (Age). Although there are studies showing mixed case is easier to read, there are some people who vehemently oppose its use especially in long symbol names (AgeOfRespondent). An alternative may be to use underscores (Age_Of_Respondent). Whatever approach you use, make sure it is consistently applied for all execs.

h. *Use meaningful names* for REXX execs, labels, symbols, files, etc.

2. *Make your exec as effective as possible:*

   a. Leave things as you found them:
      (1) Close all buffers (DROPBUF) and files.
      (2) Remove all temporary files.
      (3) Remove all unneeded global/shared variables or reset those to be reused.
      (4) Purge the program stack.
      (5) Reset your editor/operating system settings if changed.
      (6) For UNIX and MS-DOS reset environment variables if changed.

   b. *Redo a flow control structure if it is not easy to understand*—i.e. too many nesting levels.

    c. *Don't use a SIGNAL as a GOTO* and try to prematurely exit a DO loop/flow control structure.

    d. Add parentheses to mathematical operations if you want an operation to be processed a certain way.

    e. Never assume user input is correct. Always check case, data type, if blank, if a valid value, and if in the valid range.

    f. If more than one exec is using a certain exec, then consider making it into an external function or subroutine. If the same exec is using a certain module heavily, then consider converting it to an internal function or subroutine.

How Can I Extend the REXX Language?

Although REXX is a full-featured language, it may not have all the components you need for a particular application. Here are some suggestions on how to extend the REXX language:

1. Build your own internal/external function and function libraries (packages). Or use the ones created by vendors or by other REXX users. This is discussed in the previous section on subcoms, packages, and REXX.
2. Combine REXX with an editor such as XEDIT or ISPF PDF EDIT to perform file operations.
3. Combine REXX with the following for a full-screen application:
   ARexx—WSHELL
   CMS—CMS/DMS, ISPF, XEDIT, XMENU
   DOS (Kilowatt)—screen access functions part of Portable/REXX*
   DOS (Quercus)—RXWindow functions part of Personal REXX*
   OS/2—Easel, Dialog Manager
   TSO—ISPF, Session Manager
   UNIX—Curses
   VMS—FMS, SMG, EasyEntry
4. Building your own subcommands. Subcoms, subcommand environments, are a way for a CMS, MS-DOS, OS/2, TSO, UNIX, and VMS application to become an environment. This allows the "environment" to receive commands from the operating system. See the subcom section for further information.

Where Can I Learn More About the REXX Language?

Here are some places where you can learn more about the REXX language and REXX applications. Sources include the semi-annual proceedings of the IBM user groups COMMON, SHARE, GUIDE, and SEAS (Share Europe):

Both MS-DOS REXX interpreters have or soon will have interfaces to MS Windows.

COMMON, 111 E. Wacker Drive, Chicago IL 60601; (312) 644-6610.

SHARE, 111 East Wacker Drive, Chicago, IL 60601; (312) 822-0932. Especially of interest is the MVS Group of the Operating Systems Support Division and the REXX project.

GUIDE, 111 East Wacker Drive, Chicago, IL 60601, (312) 644-6610.

For Europe, Middle East and Africa: Share Europe Association (**SEAS**), 17 rue Pierres Dulviton, 1207 Geneva, Switzerland; (41) 22 35 40 66.

For Australia and Asia: **Australasian SHARE/GUIDE,** P.O. 62, Turramurra, New South Wales 2074, Australia; (61) 2 449 6848.

The annual proceeding of the SAS User's Group International (SUGI) and the Northeast SAS Users Group have good examples of CLIST programs:

SUGI—c/o Publications Department, SAS Institute, SAS Campus Drive, Cary, NC 27513; (919) 677-8000.

NESUG—c/o Marge Scerbo, University of Maryland at Baltimore, 610 West Lombard Street, Baltimore, MD 21201; (301) 328-8424. Note that there are only a limited number of proceedings available to non-attendees.

Direct Access is a magazine about System Center's products including ProREXX; 1800 Alexander Bell Drive, Reston, VA 22091.

Enterprise Systems Journal (formerly *Mainframe Journal*) comes out monthly, is free to qualified readers and has good articles on CLIST, REXX, ISPF and much more:

Enterprise Systems Journal, Thomas Publications, 10935 Estate Lane, Suite 375, Dallas, TX 75238; (214) 343-3717.

VM/Update and *MVS/Update,* published monthly by Xephon Technology Limited, are filled with complete, production-quality REXX examples:

VM/Update and *MVS/Update,* Xephon Technology, c/o WPWS, P.O. Box 1059, Ovredo, FL 32765; (407) 366-8751; fax (407) 366-8751 or Xephon 27-35 London Road, Newbury, Berkshire RG13 1JL, England; 0 635 38342. Cost is $190 a year (VM), $250 (MVS), and more outside the U.S.

TSO Times is published on a periodic basis by Chicago-Soft with a mix of articles on REXX. This is a free publication.

TSO Times, Chicago-Soft, 738 North LaSalle Street, Suite 2, Chicago, IL 60610, (312) 525-6400.

At least four electronic bulletin boards are dedicated to REXX:

Blue Edge BBS in Maryland (301) 526-7243 (look in REXXLIB) has REXXLIB software (see below).

Mansfield Software in Connecticut, (203) 429-3784, 1200 8-N-1.

Quercus Systems in California (408) 867-7488 1200 or 2400 8-N-1 has REXXLIB software (see below).

REXXpert Systems Inc. in Rocklin, California (916) 783-4739, 7 am–7 pm Pacific time, Monday–Friday 2400-8-N-1.

Various REXX news discussion groups are available for BITNET users. Send a message to the LISTSERV@*host* (with *host* being listed below). The message should contain the words SUBSCRIBE *newsgroup* (with the *newsgroup* name listed in the table that follows).

Table 4-5. REXX News Discussion Groups

Newsgroup Name	Hosts	Topics
AREXX-L	UCF1VM	Amiga REXX
PC-REXX	UCF1VM	Personal REXX
REXXCOMP	UCF1VM	REXX Compiler
REXX-L	U1UCVMD	REXX General Language
REXXLIST	DEARN	REXX General Language
	EBOUB011	
	FINHUTC	
	HEARN	
	OHSTVMA	
	POLYGRAF	
	TWNMOE10	
	UALTAVM	
	UCF1VM	
	UGA	
TSO-REXX	UCF1VM	TSO/E-REXX
VM-REXX	MARIST	VM/SP REXX
	OHSTVMA	
	UCF1VM	
XEDIT-L	MARIST	XEDIT
	OHSTVMA	
	RUTVM1	
	TCSVM	
	UGA	
UREXX-L	UK.AC.LIVERPOOL (within UK)	Uni-REXX (UNIX)
	LIVERPOOL.AC.UK (out of UK)	

Mansfield Software has a quarterly newsletter on its XEDIT products:

Mansfield Software Group News, Mansfield Software, P.O. Box 532, Storrs, CT 06268.
Mansfield—GO PCVENA (this will be switched over to Quercus in 1992). GO IBMPRO (look at other languages).

Workstation Group

The **Workstation Group News** has a variety of information about Uni-REXX and Uni-Edit (XEDIT for UNX). The Workstation Group, 6300 North River Road, Rosemont, IL 60018; (800) 228-0255 and (708) 696-4800. Mail: news@wrkgrp.com.

REXXLIB

REXXLIB has a variety of REXX programs (with documentation) for all platforms. Send a message to REXXLIB@PSUVM to find out further information. REXXLIB is also available on Blue Edge BBS and Quercus Systems's BBS (see earlier in this section).

ARexxLib

ARexxLib is an anonymous ftp site specializing in ARexx programs. Its name is arexx.uwaterloo.ca. Look in /pub/arexx for the appropriate files between 6 pm and 8 am PST on weekdays.

Exception Handling in REXX Language

With the arrival of the REXX 4.00 specification, exception handling was greatly enhanced:

1. Before REXX 4.00, exception handling consisted of the following:
   a. SIGNAL ON *condition* turns on an error condition and SIGNAL OFF turns it off. Condition is either ERROR (non-zero return codes); FAILURE (non-zero return codes); HALT (on pressing attention/escape for environment commands); NOVALUE (uninitialized value); and SYNTAX (REXX syntax/symbolic substitution error). On encountering one of the preceding *conditions,* the subroutine *of the same name* is processed. System (special) variables RC (non-zero return code for SIGNAL ON ERROR│FAILURE│SYNTAX) and SIGL (line number with error on it) are set. The subroutine is processed—usually a message to the user about what happened. This is followed by an EXIT (exit exec) or RETURN (return to the line after the one causing the SIGNAL condition). Note that ERROR also acts on FAILURE conditions if SIGNAL ON FAILURE is not enabled.

b. Although not for errors, SIGNAL *label* and SIGNAL [VALUE] value will also interrupt normal processing and move to another location in the exec. (The VALUE keyword is required if *value* is a symbol or a character string.) This is not a GOTO and should not be used to break out of a SELECT or DO structure. SIGNAL VALUE is useful when the label to be selected is to be determined at run time (such as selected one of several possible CALLs). No return to the "main" exec is possible.

```
/* example of signal label */
      signal dude
/*later in the same exec*/
      dude: say 'hey dude where"s the party?'

/*example of signal value */
      name = 'hey_dude'
      signal value name
      hey_dude: say 'hey dude where"s the party?'

/* Useful for debugging errors*/
      signal on error
      |||| (mistake)
exit
(later in same exec)
ERROR:
      say 'The error was on line' sigl 'which is' sourceline(sigl)
      /*Lists number and text of line causing error - - The error was on,
line 3 which is ||||*/
      return
```

c. Consider using SIGNAL ON NOVALUE for large, complex applications that contain many subroutines.

2. REXX 4.00 exception handling consists of the preceding plus:

a. NOTREADY condition (error/failure condition for streams [file operations]).

b. CALL can now do error sequences as well as SIGNAL. The syntax is nearly identical (CALL ON SYNTAX). Here are the differences:

CALL ON	SIGNAL
REXX 4.00 and later, Kilowatt, OS/2, OS/400, TSO/E Version 2 Release 1 with APAR, and CMS REXX Compiler (VM/SP release 6 REXX and Apars VM36993 and 36944. Compiler version is 3.46 and later).	All REXX versions
Controlled exit	Abnormal error conditions
Can have CALL ON/OFF in subroutine and won't effect "main exec"	Can have SIGNAL ON/OFF in subroutine and won't effect "main exec"
Normal exec processing can resume on completion of subroutine	Normal exec processing cannot resume on completion of subroutine.

RESULT symbol ignored   Does not affect RESULT

Must be internal to exec   Must be internal to exec

Probably uses more resources than SIGNAL

   c. You can now use a label name that is different than the error condition. This is both for SIGNAL ON and CALL ON.

```
/* Use a different name*/
/* Use swab instead of syntax for labelname*/
      call on syntax name swab
(later in program)
      swab: /*for syntax - - document for others to know this */
        say 'you had a syntax problem on line' sigl
      return
```

3. Here is more exception-handling information:
   a. Printing out the error may be helpful in debugging a problem.

```
say 'The error was' errortext(rc)
```

   b. ARexx includes these additional (non-portable) signals: BREAK-C, BREAK-D, BREAK-E, BREAK-F, and IOERR.

Portability of REXX Programs

The forthcoming REXX standard should be released in 1993 or 1994. Its sole focus will be to standardize the REXX language where there currently are different ways of doing things. The following tables list the *major* non-portable REXX instructions and functions. A part of this is from Mason Kelsey's talk at the 1990 REXX Symposium and is reprinted with his permission: Kelsey (1990, p. 184).

Table 4-6. Non-portable Environmental Variables

PCPRJOUR (Kilowatt MS-DOS)	File transfer receive location
PCPRLOG (Kilowatt MS-DOS)	Execution log location
PCPRMEM (Kilowatt MS-DOS)	Specifies memory
PCPRTRCF (Kilowatt MS-DOS)	Defines trace log location
PCPRXSNO (Kilowatt MS-DOS)	Define Executor Services attributes
REXXLIB (UNIX)	Search path for REXX external functions
RXCMD (Quercus MS-DOS)	Search for .COM, .EXE, or .BAT files if the .REX file is not found
RXFLAGS (Quercus MS-DOS)	Set values of invocation options
RXINT (Quercus MS-DOS)	Specifies REXX interrupt
RXISA (Quercus MS-DOS)	Specifies REXX internal storage area
RXMEM (Quercus MS-DOS)	Specifies memory used for REXX program
RXNEWCOM (Quercus MS-DOS)	Use COMMAND.COM when accessing DOS?
RXSWAP (Quercus MS-DOS)	Enable disk and memory swapping
RXTRACE (Quercus MS-DOS)	Specifies REXX trace setting
XEDITPATH (UNIX)	Search for XEDIT REXX functions

Table 4-7. Non-portable Instructions

DELSTACK (TSO)	Delete stack
DESBUF (CMS, DOS [Quercus])	Clears buffer
DROPBUF (CMS, TSO)	Remove buffer
EXECIO (Amiga, CMS, MS-DOS—both versions—and TSO)	File I/O
GLOBALV (CMS and MS-DOS—Quercus)	Creates global variable area
LISTFILE (CMS and MS-DOS—Quercus)	List files and related information
MAKEBUF (CMS, DOS—both—TSO)	Create a new buffer
NEWSTACK (TSO)	Create new stack
PRESS (Quercus MS-DOS)	Takes input from keyboard and places onto the data stack
SENTRIES (CMS, MS-DOS [Quercus])	Like the Queue/function, gives the number of lines in the data stack

Other differences are:

- REXX filenames and file structure (ASCII vs. EBCDIC, fixed vs. variable length)
- How REXX interpreter/compiler is invoked
- Which environments are allowed in ADDRESS instruction
- Shared variable pool operation
- If packages and subcommands are supported and how they are invoked if they are
- Function keys on terminals (such as ESCAPE or ATTENTION)
- Buffer operation internals
- REXX-related environment variables (DOS/UNIX)
- Interpreter limitations on the length of strings, length of clauses, number of nodes in compound symbols, number of functions in arguments and so on

Migrating to Other Command Languages

There are few situations where one would consider migrating from REXX to other command language because of its portability, ease of use, flexibility, and power.

WHEN SHOULD I CONSIDER CONVERTING MY REXX EXEC?

When any of the following becomes a need:

- When more sophisticated file operations are needed (relational database, keyed records). Note that CMS, OS/2, and TSO can place SQL commands in a

Table 4-8. Non-portable Functions

	Hardware		
Instruction/Function	Operating System	Purpose	Equivalents
BEEP SOUND TONE	DOS OS/2	Emits a beep with specified frequency and duration.	BEEP for OS/2 SOUND for DOS (Quercus) TONE for DOS (Kilowatt)
GETKEY INKEY	DOS	Get keyboard input	GETKEY for DOS (Kilowatt) INKEY for DOS (Quercus)
INTDOS INT86	DOS (Kilowatt)	Perform a service through DOS interrupts	
INP OUTP PORT	DOS	Read/write hardware port	INP/OUTP (Quercus) PORT (Kilowatt)
MEMORY PEEK POKE	DOS	Check/modify memory	MEMORY (Kilowatt) PEEK (Quercus) POKE (Quercus)
PC Hardware Functions: PCDISK PCEQUIP PCFLOPPY PCRAM	DOS (Quercus)	PCDISK—information about PC drives. PCEQUIP—information about PC hardware. PCFLOPPY—number of floppy drives. PCRAM—information about memory	
PCPARALLEL PCSERIAL	DOS (Quercus)	PCPARALLEL—number of parallel ports PCSERIAL—number of serial ports	
PCTYPE PCVIDEO	DOS (Quercus)	PCTYPE—type of PC PCVIDEO—type of video card	

	Data Conversion/Bit Operations		
Instruction/Function	Operating System	Purpose	Equivalents
B2X	DOS (Kilowatt) and OS/2	Binary to hex string Part of REXX 4.00	

Table 4-8. *(Continued)*

		Data Conversion/Bit Operations	
Instruction/Function	Operating System	Purpose	Equivalents
BITCHG	AmigaDOS	Change bit state	
BITCLR	AmigaDOS	Clears bit	
BITCOMP	AmigaDOS	Compares bit	
BITSET	AmigaDOS	Sets bit	
BITTST	AmigaDOS	Shows state of bit.	
C2B	AmigaDOS	Character to binary string	
X2B	DOS (Kilowatt) and OS/2	Hex to binary string Part of REXX 4.00	

		File, Buffer and Stack Operations	
Instruction/Function	Operating System	Purpose	Equivalents
CHARS	DOS (Kilowatt) OS/2	Number of characters still in a stream	
CHARIN	DOS (both), OS/2, and UNIX	Characters read from a stream	EXECIO DISKR for CMS, TSO, and DOS (both)
CHAROUT	DOS (both), OS/2, and UNIX	Characters written to a stream	EXECIO DISKW for CMS, TSO, and DOS (both)
CLOSE	AmigaDOS	Close a file	Implied on CHAROUT, LINEOUT. FINIS on EXECIO.
DELSTACK	TSO	Delete a stack	
EOF	AmigaDOS	End of File	
EXECIO	AmigaDOS, CMS, DOS, (Personal REXX) TSO/E	Read/write to a file	CHARIN CHAROUT LINEIN LINEOUT for DOS (both), OS/2, and UNIX
EXISTS	AmigaDOS	Test if file exists	SYSDSN—TSO

Table 4-8. *(Continued)*

		File, Buffer and Stack Operations	
Instruction/Function	Operating System	Purpose	Equivalents
EXTERNALS	CMS, DOS (Quercus), TSO	The number of lines in the keyboard queue	
LINEIN	DOS (both), OS/2, and UNIX	Line read from a stream	EXECIO DISKR for Amiga, CMS, TSO, and DOS (both)
LINEOUT	DOS (both), OS/2, and UNIX	Lines written to a stream	EXECIO DISKW for Amiga, CMS, TSO, and DOS (both)
LINES	DOS (both), OS/2, and UNIX	Lines left in a stream	
LOWER	DOS(ARexx) UNIX	Translate to lowercase	
NEWSTACK	TSO	Create data stack	
OPEN	AmigaDOS	Opens file	Implied for LINEOUT and CHAROUT
OUTTRAP	TSO	Captures output from a command or instruction.	See, How to Capture Output from a Command in REXX exec
POPEN	UNIX	Execute a UNIX command and place in queue to later capture output.	ADDRESS, UNIX command in quotes
QBUF QELEM QSTACK	TSO	Number of buffers, buffer lines, and number of stacks.	
READCH	AmigaDOS	Read characters from a file	CHARIN EXECIO DISKR
READLN	AmigaDOS	Read line from a file	LINEIN EXECIO DISKR
STREAM	DOS (Kilowatt) OS/2	Stream status, part of REXX 4.00	
UPPER	DOS (Quercus) AmigaDOS UNIX	To upper (ARexx)	

Table 4-8. *(Continued)*

File, Buffer and Stack Operations			
Instruction/Function	Operating System	Purpose	Equivalents
WRITECH	AmigaDOS	Write characters to a file	EXECIO DISKW CHAROUT
WRITELN	AmigaDOS	Write lines to a file	EXECIO DISKW LINEOUT

Drive/Directory/File Operations			
Instruction/Function	Operating System	Purpose	Equivalents
CHDIR DOSCHDIR PRAGMA	AmigaDOS DOS (both) UNIX	Changes the current directory	CHDIR (Kilowatt, UNIX) DOSCHDIR (Quercus) PRAGMA (Amiga)
CHDSK DOSDISK DOSDRIVE	DOS (Quercus)	DOSDISK—lists information about current drive CHDSK, DOSDRIVE— change drive	CHDSK (Kilowatt) DOSDISK (Quercus) DOSDRIVE (Quercus)
DIRECTORY DOSCD GETCWD	DOS (Quercus), UNIX	Lists current directory	DIRECTORY (OS/2) DOSCD (Quercus) GETCWD (UNIX)
DIRS DOSDIR DOSDIRPOS SHOWDIR	AmigaDOS DOS (both)	Finds/lists directory	DIRS (Kilowatt) DOSDIR (Quercus) DOSDIRPOS (Quercus) SHOWDIR (Amiga)
DOSCHMOD	DOS (Quercus)	Change file attributes	
DOSCREAT DOSDEL DOSMKDIR DOSRMDIR	DOS (Quercus)	DOSCREAT (Quercus)— create file DOSMKDIR (Quercus)— create directory DOSDEL (Kilowatt)— delete file DOSRMDIR (Kilowatt)— delete directory	

Table 4-8.   *(Continued)*

		Drive/Directory/File Operations	
Instruction/Function	Operating System	Purpose	Equivalents
DOSMEM DOSRENAME DOSVERSION DOSVER	DOS (both)	DOSMEM (Quercus)—free RAM DOSCHMOD (Quercus)—change file attributes DOSRENAME [Quercus]—rename a file DOSVER (Kilowatt) ,DOSVERSION (Quercus)—current DOS version.	DOSVER (Kilowatt) DOSVERSION (Quercus)
DOSVOLUME	DOS (Quercus)	Returns volume label of drive	
EXISTS SYSDSN	AmigaDOS TSO	DATASET status	EXISTS (Amiga) SYSDSN (TSO)
VALIDNAME	DOS (Quercus)	Returns if valid filename	
FILES FILESPEC	DOS (Kilowatt) OS/2	Finds a file/drive	DOSDIR (Quercus) FILES (Kilowatt) FILESPEC (OS/2)
		Miscellaneous	
Instruction/Function	Operating System	Purpose	Equivalents
CMSFLAG	CMS	Show settings in CMS	
CONDITION	DOS (Kilowatt) OS/2	Return information about error condition (Part of REXX 4.00 specification)	
DIAG DIAGRC	CMS	DIAG—issue operating commands, perform file operations. DIAGRC—return from DIAG	ADDRESS, EXECIO

Table 4-8. *(Continued)*

	Operating		
Instruction/Function	System	Purpose	Equivalents
DOSENV GETENV PUTENV SETENV	DOS (both) UNIX	GETENV (Kilowatt and UNIX), DOSENV (Quercus)—retrieve environment variable value PUTENV (UNIX), SETENV (Kilowatt)—set environment variable	GETENV (Kilowatt and UNIX) and DOSENV (Quercus) PUTENV (UNIX) SETENV (Kilowatt)
DOSENVSIZE	DOS (Quercus)	Size of free environment area	
ENDLOCAL SETLOCAL	OS/2 DOS (Quercus)	ENDLOCAL—restores the environment SETLOCAL—saves the current environment	
FC	DOS (Kilowatt)	Edit a character string	
FIND	DOS (Quercus) CMS,TSO	Finds number of the word in a string	WORDPOS for DOS (both)
FREESPACE GETSPACE	AmigaDOS	Frees memory Allocates memory	
GETCLIP	AmigaDOS	Retrieves a clip list value	
HASH	AmigaDOS	Hash attribute of a string	
IMPORT	AmigaDOS	Create a string	
JUSTIFY	CMS, TSO,UNIX	Justifies string	CENTER,LEFT,RIGHT (Amiga, both DOS)
KAGEM	VMS	Execute a file	
LINESIZE	CMS, TSO	Retrieve size of line	
LISTDSI	TSO	Dataset attributes	
Mathematical functions: ACOS	DOS (Kilowatt)	16 mathematical functions	Third-party/shareware provides same functionality
MSG	TSO	Enables/disables error messages	

Miscellaneous

Table 4-8. *(Continued)*

		Miscellaneous	
Instruction/Function	Operating System	Purpose	Equivalents
PRAGMA	AmigaDOS	Change priority and current directory	
PROMPT	TSO	Enables/disables prompting for missing positional operands	
PRXVERSION	DOS (Quercus)	Version of Personal Rexx	
RXFUNCADD RXFUNCDROP RXFUNCQUERY	OS/2	Function operations	
SETCLIP	AmigaDOS	Add value to clip list	
SHOW	AmigaDOS	View clip list, files, libraries	
STORAGE	Amiga-DOS, CMS, TSO	Reads or writes data in virtual storage	
SUBCOM	CMS, TSO, VMS	Test if subcom is active Use to create and deactivate a sub command	
SYSVAR	TSO	Obtain status of system variables	
USERID/CUSERID	CMS, TSO, UNIX	Returns userid of user	CUSERID (UNIX)
VALUE	DOS (Kilowatt), OS/2	Obtain/set values in shared variable pool, part of REXX 4.00	
VMREXX	VMS	Create and modify REXX symbols.	
Window/screen functions ATTR CURSOR W_ATTR	DOS (Both)	Screen functions (Kilowatt) ATTR, (nine other functions) Screen functions (Quercus) CURSOR, (five other functions) Window functions (all pe): W_ATTR (eight other functions)	

REXX exec (also the REC option of EXECIO under CMS accesses the record directly).
- When faster processing is needed and a REXX compiler is not available
- If migrating to an environment that does not have REXX readily available (such as some UNIX platforms, VMS)
- When more sophisticated reports need to be produced

WHAT COMMAND LANGUAGE SHOULD I CONVERT TO?

1. A *compiled language program* remains a good possibility. A half-way step could be converting parts of an exec to external functions outlined in a previous section.
2. The *DOS Batch language* is only available for MS-DOS and would result in a serious loss of functionality. Various references in the suggested references section compare the DOS batch language and REXX.
3. *DCL* (Digital command language) is a choice if you are migrating to VMS. BOSTON Business Computing's VCL allows you to port DCL code to TSO, MS-DOS, and UNIX. There would be some loss of features moving to DCL.
4. *Perl* is a good alternative to REXX. Its strengths compared with REXX would be stronger array operations, stronger file operations, and availability of mathematical functions. One of Perl's drawbacks is that it is harder to learn. It is available only on four of the operating systems that REXX is—MS-DOS, Amiga, OS/2, and UNIX.
5. The *CLIST* language is available on TSO and MS-DOS (pclist). However, there are only a few minor tasks that it does better than REXX—its handling of subcommands, its ease of written ISPF and Session Manager commands, and ease of handling of keyword operations. Since the clist interpreter will not be supported at some future date, it makes little sense to develop new long-term programs using the clist language using REXX.

Based on the preceding, only a compiled language, DCL, and PERL are possibilities that would offer some or major improvement over the REXX language and would be available on some of the operating systems supported by the REXX interpreter/compiler. The rest of the chapter will discuss the major issues in converting from the REXX language to DCL and to Perl (Figure 2-2 and Chapter 8's section on comparing commands for equivalents in the various command languages.)

REXX TO DCL (DIGITAL COMMAND LANGUAGE)

1. These DCL concepts and commands have no equivalent in the REXX language:
   a. Learn to use **logicals** (an alias for a file, tape, disk device, or another logical). It may help you to substitute the word "location" when thinking

about logicals) and **symbols** (an alias for a command, character string, another symbol or lexical function). For MS-DOS and UNIX users, these are similar to using environment variables where you can assign an alias to the directory or file name. For other REXX users, these are similar to the idea of shared (global) REXX symbols.

b. These lexical functions: F$CONTEXT, F$DIRECTORY, F$FILE_ATTRIBUTES,F$GETDVI, F$GETQUI, F$GETSYI, F$LOGICAL, F$MESSAGE, FPID, FPRIVILEGE, F$SETPRV, F$USER

c. Global symbols $SEVERITY and $RESTART

d. STOP

2. Here are recommendations on REXX instructions and built-in functions that can easily be converted to DCL equivalents:

a. PARSE ARG to P1 to P8

b. SAY to INQUIRE and READ to READ/PROMPT

c. POS or LASTPOS to F$LOCATE

d. LENGTH to F$LENGTH

e. SUBSTR to F$EXTRACT, F$ELEMENT or F$EDIT

f. DATATYPE to F$TYPE

g. Subroutines (invoked by CALL) to subroutines (invoked by CALL or GOSUB)

h. TIME and DATE to F$TIME or F$CVTIME

i. RC to $STATUS

j. Statements that have the same name and perform similar functions (but not necessarily the same syntax): Assignment statement, CALL, EXIT, Labels, IF-THEN-ELSE, READ, RETURN, and WRITE.

k. REXX and VMS have some equivalent statements for exception handling:

REXX	VMS
CALL ON ERROR/SIGNAL ON ERROR	ON ERROR
CALL ON FAILURE/SIGNAL ON FAILURE	ON SEVERE_ERROR
CALL ON HALT/SIGNAL ON HALT	ON CONTROL_Y
CALL ON SYNTAX	No equivalent
CALL ON NOVALUE/SIGNAL ON NOVALUE	IF .not. var...
No equivalent	ON WARNING

l. TRACE instruction to SET VERIFY and TRACE function to F$VERIFY

m. Harder but not impossible to convert: SELECT to multiple IFs, DO to loop structure, file I/O

  n. TRANSLATE (case only) to F$TRNLNM
  o. ERRORTEXT to F$MESSAGE
  p. D2X,X2D to F$FAO
  q. SYMBOL to F$LOGICAL or SHOW LOGICAL or SHOW SYMBOL
  r. PARSE template to F$PARSE (parse filename only)

3. The following REXX instructions/concepts have no equivalent in REXX and probably should not be converted:
  a. Data buffer or stack operations (other than PULL or QUEUE)
  b. Compound symbols and related instructions
  c. PARSE VERSION
  d. ADDRESS
  e. Interactive tracing
  f. Parsing templates

REXX TO PERL

1. The following Perl concepts have no equivalent in the REXX language:
  a. Math functions (available from REXX list servers and third-party vendors)
  b. Directory functions (although many REXX interpreters/compilers include these)
  c. Networking functions (a REXX TCP/IP networking product is available from Bitnet based servers.
  d. DBM functions (system database)
  e. Environment variables (except for CMS—global variables—MS-DOS, and UNIX REXX interpreters)
  f. Awk to Perl, C header files to Perl, and sed to Perl converters
  g. Setuid and setgid scripts
  h. Associative arrays
  i. Character versions of operations (such as EQ for equals)
  j. Report variables
  k. File test (included in some REXX interpreters/compilers)
  l. Binary file mode.

2. Here are recommendations on REXX instructions/functions that can be easily converted to PERL equivalents
  a. IF-THEN-ELSE to if-elsif. DO-WHILE to do *block* WHILE, DO-UNTIL to do *block* until
  b. The following statements have the same names and perform similar functions (but may not necessarily have the same syntax): RETURN, some operators [+,−,*,/,%. However & and | have different meanings.],EXIT, LENGTH and SUBSTR functions
  c. INTERPRET to statement with backticks, eval, or s//ec.

    d. ADDRESS to exec or system functions
    e. TRACE to perl -d
    f. SUBSTR or POS to index and LASPOS to index
    g. CHARIN to getc
    h. SAY to print or printf or sprintf
    i. LINEIN to read or sysread
    j. LINEOUT to write or syswrite
    k. SAY 'Bad code' ;EXIT to die
    l. DATE and TIME to gmtime or localtime
    m. PROCEDURE EXPOSE to local (actually they are opposites of each other, but specifying all the symbols not included in a PROCEDURE EXPOSE instruction is equivalent to a local function)
    n. SYMBOL returning VAR to defined function
    o. DROP to undef function
    p. RANDOM to rand and RANDOM(,,*seed*) to srand
    q. RC to $? (system variable)
    r. PARSE VERSION to $] (system variable)
    s. PARSE ARG to @ARGV

3. The following REXX instructions/concepts have no equivalent in REXX and probably should not be converted:
    a. Data buffer or stack operations (other than PULL or QUEUE)
    b. Compound symbols and related instructions

SUGGESTED READINGS

Adesse Corporation, 1988. *Program Development Using REXX.*

Bemer, R.W., 1989. "Time and the Computer." *Interface Age,* February, pp. 75–79.

Brink, Edwin W., 1986. *An Assessment of the Restructured Extended Executor (REXX) with Respect to Certain Important Characteristics.* Unpublished paper.

Cowlishaw, M.F., 1990b. "REXX 4.00." *Proceedings of the REXX Symposium for Developers and Users,* pp. 1–32.

Cowlishaw, M.F., 1987. The Design of the REXX Language. *IBM Systems Journal.* 23(4), pp. 326–335.

Cowlishaw, M.F., 1990a. *The REXX Language: A Practical Approach to Programming.* 2d ed. Englewood Cliffs, N.J.: Prentice-Hall.

Daney, Charles, 1990. "REXX in Charge," *Byte,* August, pp. 245–253.

Daney, Charles, 1991. "Issues in the Specification of REXX." *Proceedings of the REXX Symposium for Developers and Users,* pp. 25–28.

Denney, Michael, "The SAS System Under CMS: Tricks of the Trade." *Proceedings of the Twelfth Annual SAS User's Group International Conference.* (Handout).

Dilorio, Frank, 1989. "Good Code, Bad Code: Strategies for Program Design." *NESUG 89: Conference Proceedings,* pp. 260–266.

Englebart, Doug, 1988. *The Future of Computing.* Notes from a talk given at GTE Laboratories on November 15.

German, Hallett, 1991. "The Adventure Continues: Using CLIST, DOS Batch Language DCL, and REXX Command Languages in the SAS Development Cycle." *NESUG 91 Proceedings.* (Forthcoming).

Giguère, Eric, 1991. "Platform-Specific Standards for REXX: Issues for Developers and Implementors." *Proceedings of the REXX Symposium for Developers and Users,* pp. 32–38.

Hawes, William, *ARexx User's Reference Manual Version 1.0.* 1987.

Hoernes, G.E., 1989. REXX on TSO/E. *IBM Systems Journal.* 28(2), pp. 274–293.

Hoernes, Gerhard E., 1992. "REXX for CLIST Programmers" in The REXX Handbook, Gabriel Goldberg & Philip H. Smith III (eds). New York: McGraw-Hill, pp. 557–586.

IBM Corporation, 1990. *CMS REXX Compiler: User's Guide and Reference.* SH19-8120.

IBM Corporation, 1990. *Operating System/2 Extended Edition 1.3 User's Guide: Volume 1: Base Operating System.*

IBM Corporation, 1990. *TSO/E Version 2 REXX User's Guide.* SC28-1882.

IBM Corporation, 1990. *TSO/E Version 2 REXX Reference.* SC28-1883.

IBM Corporation, 1988. *Using REXX in Practice: EXEC 2 to REXX Conversion Experiences.* GC24-1615.

Johnson, Tony, "SLAC Use of REXX on VM and VMS," *Proceedings of the REXX Symposium for Developers and Users,* pp. 133–150.

Karpinski, Jeff, 1992. "REXX for EXEC 2 Programmers" in The REXX Handbook, Gabriel Goldberg & Philip H. Smith III (eds). New York: McGraw-Hill, pp. 541–555.

Kong, Jerry Y., 1991. "The Bounty of OS/2 EE REXX," *Enterprise Systems Journal.* 8(9). September, pp. 112–115, 129.

Kelsey, Mason, 1990. "REXX in Three different environments," *Proceedings of the REXX Symposium for Developers and Users,* pp. 175–230.

Kerninghan, Brian W., and P.J. Plauger, 1978. *The Elements of Programming Style.* 2d ed. New York: McGraw-Hill.

Kilowatt Software, 1990. *Portable REXX Reference Guide.*

Kusnierz, Thomas E., 1989. REXX in MVS. *SEAS 89 Proceedings,* pp. 1–23. (Handout).

Lee, Han-li, 1990. "Using REXX to Build a Front-end User Interface," *NESUG '90 Conference Proceedings,* pp. 220–224.

Lovelace, Michael, 1986. "REXX Techniques." *Proceedings of the SEAS Spring Meeting,* pp. 1215–24.

Mansfield Software, 1988. *Personal REXX User's Guide Version 2.00.* Mansfield, Conn.

Mansfield Software, 1989. "Advanced String Handling in REXX." *Mansfield Software Group News,* pp. 15–19.

Marks, Brian, 1992. "Language Evaluation & Standards Activities" in The REXX Handbook, Gabriel Goldberg & Philip H. Smith III (eds). New York: McGraw-Hill, pp. 597–606.

McGuire, Rick, 1990. "IBM SAA REXX for OS/2." *Proceedings of the REXX Symposium for Developers and Users,* pp 101–111.

Milstead, Neil, 1991. "X3J18 REXX Standard Committee Discussion Notes."

Moser, Karen, 1990. "Buyers Say portable code is a Mixed Blessing." *PC Week.* June 11, p. 82.

Moser, Karen, 1990. "IBM to Draft REXX Spec to Foster SAA Language." 7(9), *PC Week,* p. 65.

Milstead, Neil, 1990. "REXX for UNIX." *Proceedings of the REXX Symposium for Developers and Users,* pp. 112–123.

Nielsen, Paul, 1991. "REXX,BASIC Vie for Macro Standard." *PC Week,* 8(15), pp. 101–102.

O'Hara, Robert, and David Gomberg, 1990. *Modern Programming Using REXX.* Englewood Cliffs, N.J.: Prentice-Hall.

O'Hara, Robert, 1990. "Why REXX Died (a Retrospective)," *Proceedings of the REXX Symposium for Developers and Users,* pp. 124–131.

Oppenheim, Larry, 1992. "Extending CMS REXX with Function Packages" in The REXX Handbook, Gabriel Goldberg & Philip H. Smith III. New York: McGraw-Hill, pp 597–606.

Pinter, R.Y., P. Vortman, and Z. Weiss, 1991. "Partial Compilation of REXX" *IBM System Journal* 30(3) pp. 312–331.

Pachl, Walter, 1990. "CMS REXX Compiler & Library," *Proceedings of the REXX Symposium for Developers and Users,* pp. 33–64.

Rutherford, John, 1987. "Utility Programming with REXX." *Online Review,* 11(6), pp. 369–80.

Savit, Jeffrey B., 1992. "REXX Programming Style" in The REXX Handbook, Gabriel Goldberg and Philip H. Smith III. New York: McGraw-Hill, pp 47–67.

Shaw, Michael, 1990. "Writing a REXX Function Package," *TSO Times,* 1(3), pp. 2–3.

Shammas, N.C., 1988. "Personal REXX," *Byte,* January, pp. 167–171.

Simon, Barry, 1986. "Living with DOS: Batch Environments." *Text file on Compuserve.* (Also published in Capital PC Monitor of January 1987).

Workstation Group, 1990. *uni-REXX Reference Manual.*

5

Command Language Advisor—DCL

DCL (stands for Digital command language) are the commands a user enters for communicating with the computer—to many users this *is* the operating system. DCL is found on computers sold by DEC (such as the VAX and ALPHA lines) that use the VMS operating system. (A flavor of DCL is also available on the RT-11, RSX-11, RSTS, and IAS operating systems.) However, since the late 1980s, Boston Business Computing has been selling a product called VCL that allows portability of DCL to other environments such as MS-DOS and UNIX (28 flavors). More than 2000 copies had been sold to date. Other VMS emulators exist as well but are not discussed here.

In this chapter, we are concerned with DCL as a general command language rather than as a means to access VMS. That is, placing a series of DCL commands and data in a file (called a **command procedure**) and sequentially processing them in either foreground or background. DCL is an interpreted language processed by the **command language interpreter** (CLI) going through three phases. The emphasis in the chapter is on VMS Version 5, under which DCL was greatly enhanced. So many things became far easier to do and new capabilities were added. The latest VCL release (3.0) includes some VMS 5.0 features.

Unless otherwise stated, all examples can be used by either the DCL or VCL interpreters. Information about operations on specific platforms will be highlighted by a change bar. Examples were tested under VMS and MS-DOS using an evaluation copy of VCL that Boston Business Computing provided.

WHEN TO USE THE DIGITAL COMMAND LANGUAGE

DCL is a good programming language that is especially useful when:

- You need to quickly develop a program for performing system support and maintenance tasks

- You need to quickly develop a prototype for an application. This can later be converted to a compiled language or be enhanced.
- You want to create "personal commands" that enhance existing VMS commands. By using these personal commands together, you can create a personal environment.
- Portability is a concern (if used with VCL or other DCL emulators).
- You need an alternative to the DOS batch language.

HOW TO INVOKE DCL COMMAND PROCEDURES

DCL command procedures are usually invoked in foreground but on VMS may be invoked in background (batch) as well.

Invoking a Foreground DCL Command Procedure

Invoking a DCL command procedure in foreground is different for each operating system. Listed below are some of the different formats used: These are all entered at the DOS (C:), UNIX (% or $), or VMS ($) prompt.

MSDOS/UNIX

```
vcl c:\dcl\prog1.cmd sunday ! full path name and one parameter (sun-
day) for DOS
vcl prog1 !Searches currently defined path if not full name. Assumes -
to be .CMD.
@prog1 !invokes PROG1.CMD. !Invoke from a command procedure or using -
VCL -c @prog1
```

VMS

```
@prog1 !executes prog1.com in the current directory
```

Tips and Traps:

GENERAL

1. All DCL/VCL interpreters may include operating system commands in the command procedure. Also, up to eight parameters may be supplied when the command procedure is invoked. These parameters are assigned to symbols P1 through P8 (P1–P8) and are converted to uppercase (regardless of the original case) *unless enclosed in double quotes.*

2. If the complete file specification is not used, then a file type of .COM (or .CMD for VCL) is used. This file specification cannot include wild card characters such as (* or ?).
3. The @ command allows a /OUTPUT=*file_name* qualifier. This sends all output from a command procedure to a file specified by *file_name.* or the SYS$OUTPUT logical.
4. A command procedure is processed sequentially.
5. Since Version 5, command procedures can now contain data and also DCL commands. The interpreter tells the difference by the first character in the command. If it is a $, then it is seen as a DCL command. Otherwise, it is assumed to be data. Use a DECK-EOD structure to pass data to an image.

VCL (DOS, UNIX)

1. The VCL command allows the following arguments:
   - **-c**—executes the accompanying command(s) and returns to the operating system on completion.
   - **-m**—runs command procedures with less memory and greater speed but at the cost of not displaying error message text (added in 3.0 for PC DOS only).
   - **-q**—turns off the VCL header that displays before the command procedure is processed.
   - **-v**—turns on the trace or debug facility. This is the same result as entering a SET VERIFY command before a command procedure is invoked.
2. To invoke VCL for DOS, you may want to use a batch file similar to the following:
   ```
   IF "%1"= ="" GOTO EXIT
   IF EXIST C:\VCL\%1.CMD VCL C:\VCL\%1.CMD %2
   :EXIT
   ```
   The preceding executes if the file exists (statement 2) and a file name is supplied when the batch file is invoked. Statement 1—%1 is assigned the first word after the command name—e.g. if the batch file is named RUNIT, then RUNIT PROG1 will have PROG1 assigned to %1. %2 is null unless you assign a parameter to invoke VCL with such as -m or -v. For DOS 3.3 and later users, place an @ECHO OFF to supress displaying the commands as they are processed.
3. If not using the complete file specification, then the current directory and directories defined by the PATH command (VCL interpreters only) is searched. In VCL 3.1, you can also set the environment variable VCL to a desired directory that contains the VCL executables and supporting files, such as SET VCL=C:\DCL. Avoid using APPEND to assign additional paths—it may create duplicate and unnecessary files.

Invoking a Background DCL Command Procedure

VMS is the only environment that allows a DCL command procedure in background. A batch job runs in a **job queue** with pre-assigned characteristics. The SUBMIT command accomplishes this from the DCL prompt ($):

```
$    SUBMIT prog1 /AFTER=6:00 -
     /NOTIFY /PARAMETERS=(MONDAY," a space")
!Returns JOB PROG (queue SYS$BATCH, entry 999) holding until 1-March--
1991 0:600
! Submits prog1.com to run after 6 am, notifies you when the job is -
done, and includes two parameters assigned to symbols P1 and P2.
```

Tips and Traps:

1. You may use wildcard characters (such as * and ?) to submit more than one file. Or you may explicitly include multiple file names separated by commas.
2. Use the /AFTER qualifier such as /AFTER=TOMORROW to run a job after 11:58 p.m. on that day.
3. There are 30 qualifiers that may be used with the SUBMIT command. Besides those listed above, these include:

   /CONFIRM—asks you to confirm SUBMIT.

   /HOLD—holds in a job queue until a SET ENTRY *number* /NOHOLD or SET ENTRY *number* /RELEASE is invoked. (*Number* is the entry number of the job you wish to perform an operation on.)

   /LOG_FILE=*file_name.* Specifies a different file to hold the job log in. The default name is the *name_of_the_job.*log in the default directory of the user that the batch job is run under.

   /NAME=*name.* Overrides the default file name with a specified name of up to 39 characters.

   /QUEUE=*queue_name.* To specify a different job queue than the current queue (usually, the default, SYS$BATCH).

4. If you are using certain qualifiers every time you submit a batch job, then consider creating a special command procedure to do this:

FROM DCL PROMPT

```
@RUNIT PROG1
```

IN RUNIT.COM

```
$ SUBMIT 'P1.COM /NOTIFY /QUEUE=FAST_QUEUE /LOG=RUN.LOG
```

5. During batch processing, output that usually goes to the screen (such as command output and error messages) is sent to a log file instead.
6. Any images or command procedures prompting for input when run interactively must be converted to use preassigned answers to run in batch.
7. If you have a sequence in a command procedure (such as LOGIN.COM) that you want to be executed only if running in batch mode, use the following sequence:

```
$ IF F$MODE() .EQS. "BATCH"! Other values are INTERACTIVE, NET-
WORK, OTHER
$ THEN
  (batch sequence)
$ ELSE
  (other sequence)
$ENDIF
```

Or

```
$ IF F$GETJPI(" ",MODE) .EQS. "BATCH"!VMS only.
```

Or

```
$ IF F$ENVIRONMENT("INTERACTIVE") .eqs. "FALSE"
$ THEN
  (sequence)
$ENDIF
```

Each time you invoke a command procedure in batch, your LOGIN.COM gets reexecuted. Thus, including a *$IF F$MODE() .EQS. "BATCH" THEN EXIT* command guarantees that your LOGIN.COM file is not processed and places you in the default directory. Also, note that above sequences for F$MODE and F$ENVIRONMENT work under VCL.

8. If using the INQUIRE command, place the user input on the next line. See the section named How to Capture User Input for further information.
9. Minimize use of SET VERIFY to keep output log small.

THE FUTURE OF DCL

DCL will continue to exist for some time. Here are some current trends:

1. *VCL will continue to be ported to other operating systems and UNIX flavors.* Three new platforms were planned for first quarter of 1991 alone.
2. *Starting with VMS 5.5. VMS will be compliant with the interface and calls specified in the IEEE POSIX [Portable Operating System X] standards.* These include POSIX 1003.1 [system interface], 1003.2 [shells and tools], and 1003.4 [real-time extensions]. This allows a POSIX application to run easily on other operating systems. See a later section for further information.
3. *VMS and DCL will be ported by DEC to RISC machines (such as the Alpha line and MIPS).* There are rumors of a port to MS-DOS as well.

4. *The DCL compiler* is of interest to many users but *is highly unlikely to be developed.* The reasons against this happening include:
- DEC appears to have no interest in doing this. Watson (1989) notes that it would have done so already if it was technically possible.
- Technically it may not be possible to do this. Creating the spawned images necessary for such a product are generally slower than the interpreter and are costly for system performance. Also, a compiler could not handle some of the ambiguity present in some symbol assignments. The presence of a GOTO means that the flow of the command procedure can be set to go anywhere such as into a loop.
- Barkes (1991) talks about an alternative—Using Channel Island's Software DCP product that takes DCL code and converts it to FORTRAN source, which later can be compiled. The address for the company making this product can be found in Appendix 1.

DEVELOPING DCL APPLICATIONS

Chapter 2 looked at three different types of common command language applications. The next three sections in this chapter provide portable DCL sequences— unless otherwise stated—that are listed under the type of application where they are most commonly used. However, there is no reason why a particular DCL sequence could not be used by any type of application. The last section discusses some of the major concerns when developing DCL-based applications. It also looks at porting DCL programs across various operating systems and migrating to other command languages.

FRONT-END DCL APPLICATIONS

Two common tasks of DCL command procedures are (1) to provide input ("housekeeping") for images (compiled programs) and (2) to run startup tasks when logging in. The section reviews sequences to perform both of these.

How To Access Operating System Commands In a DCL Command Procedure

DCL is the native environment for VMS, so no special interface is needed to access operating system commands. This is not the case for VCL interpreters. However, several ways are available to process an operating-system command in a VCL command procedure.

```
                    VCL (MS-DOS AND UNIX)
$ SET VCL/PASSTHRU !Passes command to operating system for pro- -
cessing
$ ver ! Shows version of DOS. Place any DOS or UNIX command here.-
Still checks if this a VCL
$!command so slows down processing. Look at EXECUTE as an alter-
nate.

$ EXECUTE ver !Sends command straight to the operating system
$ ! (or what executable specified by the SYS$SHELL symbol). Use -
if a command has the same
$ ! name for both the operating system and VCL (Actually the same
first four characters.)

$UNIX ls -l ! Same as EXECUTE but for UNIX only.


                              VMS
$ VMS_command !no specific interface is necessary.
```

Tips and Traps:
1. EXECUTE performs symbolic substitution only if the symbol is in single quotes.
2. The CD/CHDIR command will not work as expected using PASSTHRU—the current directory does not change. Creating a CD logical is a workaround.

How To Capture Output From a Command in a DCL Command Procedure

DCL provides a variety of ways to capture output from an operating system command or image (compiled program). These include:

1. DCL commands such as RUN (which executes an image), DIRECTORY /COLUMN=1 and SHOW SYSTEM include a /OUTPUT qualifier to send command/image output to a file. (Note that VCL supports this approach.)
2. DEFINE/USER_MODE SYS$OUTPUT OUT.TXT followed by a DCL command sends command output to a file regardless of whether the command has an /OUTPUT qualifier. The /USER_MODE qualifier means the symbol assignment is in effect until the next image (DCL command). However, the preceding DEFINE cannot be used by the more than 60 commands that are processed by the command language interpreter (CLI).

What To Include in a Startup DCL Command Procedure

The LOGIN.COM file is where users set up their own personal environment by defining logicals and symbols, setting terminal characteristics and DCL prompt, setting default file protections, defining libraries for their compiler, debugger, and editor, and much more. The focus will be on using DCL as a command language in startup files which means some of the above tasks may not be covered here. Use DCL for enhancing your LOGIN.COM files in the following ways: These examples will work under VCL unless otherwise stated—but they are stored in LOGIN.CMD. A sample LOGIN.CMD is supplied with the product.

1. *Welcome commands* personalize a session:

IN COMMAND PROCEDURE:

```
$    DATE = F$EXTRACT(0,8,F$TIME()) !VCL
$    DATE = F$EXTRACT(0,11,F$TIME()) !VMS
$    WRITE SYS$OUTPUT "Good day Hal. Today is ", DATE
```

DISPLAYED:

```
Good day Hal. Today is 02-03-91 !VCL
Good day Hal. Today is 03-FEB-1991 !VMS
```

---

2. *Menus.* If you find yourself accessing several programs on startup, perhaps a menu might be useful:

```
$ MENU100:
$       WRITE SYS$OUTPUT    "*******************************"
$       WRITE SYS$OUTPUT    "* 1-Reports                   *"
$       WRITE SYS$OUTPUT    "* 2 Spreadsheets              *"
$       WRITE SYS$OUTPUT    "* 3 Games                     *"
$       WRITE SYS$OUTPUT    "*******************************"
$       READ SYS$COMMAND/PROMPT="Enter your menu selection (1-3)" -
        choice
$       IF CHOICE .EQS. "" THEN GOTO INV
$       IF CHOICE .LT. 1 .OR. CHOICE .GT.3 THEN GOTO INV
$       IF CHOICE .EQ. 1 THEN GOTO REPORT
$       IF CHOICE .EQ. 2 THEN GOTO SPREAD
$       IF CHOICE .EQ. 3 THEN GOTO GAME
$       EXIT
$INV:
$       WRITE SYS$OUTPUT "Invalid choice. Please try again"
$       GOTO MENU100
$ REPORT:
```

```
            (Report logic)
$ SPREAD:
            (Spreadsheet logic).
$ GAME:
            (Game logic)
```

3. *Log file:*

    The following sequence appends to the end of the current file the login time and date of the current session.

```
$       LINE = F$TIME()
$       OPEN/APPEND FILE1 DISK10:[HAL]LOG.DAT ! Assigns file logical -
        name of FILE1
$       ! Change to UNIX or MS-DOS file name for VCL
$       WRITE FILE1 LINE
$       CLOSE FILE1
$       EXIT
```

4. Make sure that *batch mode does not execute LOGIN.COM:*

```
$ IF F$MODE() .EQS. "BATCH" THEN EXIT
```

5. Set up a "personal environment" using symbol and logical definitions:

```
$       ! Common examples of global symbols that can be used by any com-
        mand procedure.
$SYM:
$       DEL_C :== DELETE/CONFIRM
$       PSU*BMIT :== SUBMIT /NOTIFY /QUEUE=FAST
$       ! * means may enter PSU as an abbreviation for the command.-
$ LOGIC:
$       ! Some logicals:
$       DEFINE HOME$DIR                 SYS$LOGIN:
$       DEFINE COM$DIR          .       'P2:['P1.COM] !2nd quote optional
$       !Change above for VCL specify directory and device
$       DEFINE COM$DIR                  [usr.com] ! VCL for UNIX
$       DEFINE COM$DIR                  SYS$DISKC:[com] ! VCL for MS-DOS
$       ! SYS$DISKC refers to drive C
```

How To Issue UNIX (POSIX) Commands Within VMS

Starting with VMS 5.5, VMS will be compliant with the interface and calls specified in the IEEE POSIX [Portable Operating System X] standards. These include POSIX 1003.1 [system interface] 1003.2 [shells and tools—really a UNIX-based shell] and 1003.4 [real-time extensions]. This allows a POSIX application to run easily on other operating systems. Since this product is still under development at the time of publication, some of the following information may not apply to the final product:

1. A "VMS POSIX" kit will have to be additionally purchased and installed to have a fully POSIX-compliant operating system. It includes a POSIX kernel and shell for VMS, a POSIX run-time library, and various system administration components.

2. The location of the POSIX libraries will be assigned to the system logical posix$include.

3. The POSIX interface will be accessed in one of the following ways:
   a. "Run a POSIX command and then return to VMS" such as *POSIX POSIX$BIN:DATE* (POSIX$BIN refers to the location of the /bin directory which contains the executables for commands such as date (which lists the current date and time). Parameters are enclosed in double quotes.
   b. "Drop to POSIX" such as entering *POSIX POSIX$BIN:SH* to use the Bourne (sh) shell. Then enter whatever POSIX (UNIX-like) commands you wish and enter *Control-Z* to return to VMS.

4. Some of the qualifiers for the POSIX command include: /DEBUG—invoke the debugger and /OUT=*filename*—save output to a file.

5. A very powerful aspect of the POSIX shell is that you can issue DCL commands and even combine them with POSIX commands.
   ```
   psx> dcl "DIR *.COM"| grep LOGIN.COM
   ```
   (Does the user have a LOGIN.COM file?)

6. You can specify the POSIX shell as the default at the username prompt:
   ```
   Username: VELOSO/CLI=POSIX$CLI
   ```


SYSTEM/UTILITY DCL APPLICATIONS

System & utility DCL applications are similar to front-end applications but emphasize system and utility operations. By definition, this implies that this type of application is less portable. This section will discuss those aspects of system/utility DCL applications that apply to all platforms and focus on file operations. Information on any lexical function can be obtained by entering H LEXICAL F$*lexicalname*.

How Do I Perform File Operations?

Those of you who glanced at the log dataset example in a previous section on startup DCL command procedures have already had a look at file input/operations. The following shows the basic skeleton for sequential file operations:

```
                          ADD/APPEND
$    OPEN/WRITE FILE1 DISK8:[SUNDAY]LOG.TXT ! Add
$    !for VCL OPEN/WRITE FILE1 SYSDISK$C:[VCL]LOG.TXT ! Add
     Or
$    OPEN/APPEND FILE1 DISK8:[SUNDAY]LOG.TXT !Append
$LINE_IN:
```

```
$    READ SYS$COMMAND/PROMPT="ENTER THE LINE OR XX TO QUIT" LINE1
$      IF LINE1 .EQS. "XX" THEN GOTO CLOSE_IT
       (validate input sequence with loop)
$    WRITE FILE1 LINE1 !from user
$    WRITE FILE1 "Line from command procedure"
$      GOTO LINE_IN
$CLOSE_IT:
$    CLOSE FILE
$    EXIT
```

BROWSE

```
$    OPEN/READ FILE1 DISK8:[SUNDAY]LOG.TXT !If put below, keeps read-
     ing same line
$    CNT = 1
$READ_IT:
$      READ /END_OF_FILE = END_OF FILE1 LINE
$      L'CNT = LINE !Array for later display
$    WRITE SYS$OUTPUT L'CNT
$    CNT = CNT + 1
$    GOTO READ_IT
$END_OF:
$    CLOSE FILE1
$    EXIT
```

The following are tips and traps when performing file I/O operations:

1. If needing more complicated file operations, then consider using ISAM (indexed sequential access method) files. These are fixed or variable length records with primary and secondary key (index) fields such as employee id number or any unique record identifier field. Then use the CREATE/FDL command to create a new file and the OPEN and READ commands (with the qualifiers listed below) to provide indexed or random access to a file. These include:

   OPEN/SHARE=READ/WRITE—allows multiple user access to a file.

   READ/DELETE—deletes a record after an OPEN/READ/WRITE.

   READ/INDEX=number—the key for accessing a file. Default is the primary key with a value of zero.

   READ/KEY=string—used with /INDEX to randomly access a file.

   READ/MATCH=operator.—another way to match keys.

   ISAM files are not currently supported by VCL (although ISAM files are used by other software).

2. Use the following to control errors during file operations:
   a. Christiansen (1984) suggests having all file logicals in an OPEN command end with a colon such as OPEN/READ FILE1:DO1:[TEMP]DATA.DAT.

Then you can do a SHOW LOGICAL *: to see what files are still opened —since closed files no longer have symbols assigned to them.

b. Use F$SEARCH to see if a file exists:

```
$ DEFINE FILE1 file_specification
$    IF F$SEARCH("FILE1") .EQS "" THEN action ! if file does not
     exist then...
```

c. OPEN, READ, and WRITE have /CHECK=*label* qualifier, which means you can specify a label to transfer to if an error occurs. This label could include capturing the error message, noting which line in the file the error occurred on and close the file.

3. OPEN/READ is the default operation for OPEN so files will not be accidentally written over.

How Do I Parse a File Name?

DCL (and VCL) both support the F$PARSE lexical function, which makes it easy to parse such as in the examples that follow:

VCL (MS-DOS AND UNIX)

```
$ FI_NAME = "C:[DCL]SAMPLE.CMD" !Can't use DOS file name
$ dev     = F$PARSE(FI_NAME,,,"DEVICE") ! Assigned C:
$ dir     = F$PARSE(FI_NAME,,,"DIRECTORY") ! Assigned [DCL]
$ fn      =F$PARSE(FI_NAME,,,"NAME") ! Assigned SAMPLE
$ typ     =F$PARSE(FI_NAME,,,"TYPE") ! Assigned CMD
```

VMS

```
$FI_NAME  ="CHELSEA::DISK99:[CRUISERS]ALESUKI.TXT"
$nod      =F$PARSE(FI_NAME,,,"NODE") ! Assigned CHELSEA:
$dev      = F$PARSE(FI_NAME,,,"DEVICE") ! Assigned DISK99:
$dir      = F$PARSE(FI_NAME,,,"DIRECTORY") ! Assigned [CRUISERS]
$fn       =F$PARSE(FI_NAME,,,"NAME") !Assigned ALESUKI.
$typ      =F$PARSE(FI_NAME,,,"TYPE") !Assigned TXT
```

Tips and traps:

1. F$PARSE has an optional fifth argument with values of SYNTAX_ONLY (checks if file syntax is valid) and NO_CONCEAL (continues processing if a concealed logical is found.)

2. Combine F$SEARCH with F$PARSE to parse and check syntax of multiple files:

```
$F_CHECK:
$    PAT = F$SEARCH("*.COM")
$     IF PAT .EQS.""THEN EXIT 2
$    NM = F$PARSE("''PAT'",,"NAME")
$    CHECK= F$PARSE("''NM'",,,,"SYNTAX_ONLY")!Check if valid
$     IF CHECK .EQS. "" THEN WRITE SYS$OUTPUT "Invalid file name"
$    GOTO F_CHECK
```

3. Note in the preceding examples that commas are used as placeholders in order to specify the fourth or fifth argument.

How Do I Get Information About the System?

You can use lexical functions for creating your own DCL commands giving information about your system. Gomez (1988) provides a good introduction to this area. The following are tips and traps in using lexical functions to give information about the system that would be of interest to most users.

1. Many of these functions are unavailable under VCL. You can get the same information with DOS or UNIX commands and utilities.
2. The most useful lexical function in this area is F$GETSYI. It can retrieve information about a stand-alone VAX or one on a cluster. The following command procedure retrieves information about a "node at a glance" with information that may be of interest to the general user. (Do not specify a node name [second argument] for a stand-alone VAX.)

```
                                   VMS
$         CLUS= F$GETSYI("CLUSTER_MEMBER") !Returns TRUE or FALSE
$         IF CLUS .EQS. "TRUE" THEN!If a cluster then do
$            BOOT_TIME=F$GETSYI("BOOTTIME","DRAGON")
$! Time of last boot such as 23-Feb-1991 16:05:58:91
$            CPU_TYPE = F$GETSYI("CPU","DRAGON") !CPU type such as 0
$            VMS_VERSION = F$GETSYI("VERSION","DRAGON") !VMS Version
$            HW_MODEL = F$GETSYI("HWMODEL","DRAGON") ! VAX Model Number -
             such as 159
$            HW_NAME = F$GETSYI("HW_NAME","DRAGON")
$! VAX Model Name such as VAX 6000-410
$            NODE_NAME = F$GETSYI("NODENAME","DRAGON") !Node name such -
             as DRAGON
$            NODE_HTYPE = F$GETSYI("NODE_HWTYPE","DRAGON")
$! Hardware of Node such as 6410
$            NODE_HVER= F$GETSYI("NODE_HWVERS","DRAGON")
$! Hardware version such as 009F0000000000000B000005
$            NODE_NUM = F$GETSYI("NODE_NUMBER","DRAGON")
$! Node DECNET Number such as 1
$            NODE_SW = F$GETSYI("NODE_SWVERS","DRAGON")
$! Node software version such as V5.4
$            ! Place a WRITE $SYSOUTPUT for each of the above symbols -
             here
$         ENDIF
$         ! Could put an else if not in a cluster
```

VCL (MS-DOS/UNIX)

```
$       BOOT=F$GETSYI("BOOTTIME") !Time system booted. Always 12:00 -
        for DOS.
$       CPU=F$GETSYI("CPU") !Type of CPU (DOS only)
$       VERSION=F$GETSYI("VERSION")!VCL Version
$       WRITE SYS$OUTPUT "boot",boot,"cpu",cpu,"version",version
!Displayed boot 12:00:00:00 cpu 2 version 3.0.1 (CPU 0= 8088/86, -
2=286, 3=386, 4=486)
```

Also, The F$GETSYI can list a variety of SYSGEN and system parameters not of interest to most users. See the *VMS DCL Dictionary* for further information.

3. F$GETDVI tells various information about a specified device. The following retrieves information that can be used to generate a "device at a glance" report:

VMS

```
$   DEV_AVAIL = F$GETDVI("DISK3","AVL") ! Can I use this device now? -
    TRUE or FALSE
$   DEV_NAM = F$GETDVI("DISK3","DEVNAM") !Name of device such as -
HSC000000$DUA3
$   DEV_EX = F$GETDVI("DISK3","EXISTS") ! Does system see this -
    device? TRUE or FALSE
$   DEV_FOR = F$GETDVI("DISK3","FOR") ! A foreign disk? TRUE or FALSE
$   DEV_FNAM = F$GETDVI("DISK3","FULLDEVNAM") ! Full device
    name_1$DUA3:
$   DEV_LOG = F$GETDVI("DISK3","LOGVOLNAM") !Logical name of volume -
    UDISK3:
$   DEV_TTYP = F$GETDVI("DISK3","MEDIA_TYPE")
$! Type of Tape (if applicable) Returned DU (or device prefix)
$   DEV_TRM = F$GETDVI("DISK3","TRM") ! Is this device a terminal? -
    TRUE or FALSE
```

VCL

```
$   DEV_LOG = F$GETDVI("SYS$DISKC","ALL") !Does drive C exist? Or use -
    EXISTS instead of
$   !ALL. Returns TRUE or FALSE.
$   VL = F$GETDVI("SYS$DISKC","VOLNAM") !Name of disk (volume)
$   DEVNAM = $GETDVI("SYS$DISKC","DEVNAM") !Physical device name (C -
    in this case)
$   MNT = $GETDVI("SYS$DISKC","MNT") !Is drive available. Returns -
    TRUE or FALSE. Or
$   ! Use AVL instead of MNT.
```

This is just a small sample of what this function can give you about a device!

4. F$GETQUI displays information about one or more queues. Here is how to list the names of all available queues:

```
    $CNT = 1
$JOB_SHOW:
    $A = F$GETQUI("DISPLAY_QUEUE","QUEUE_NAME","*")
    $IF A .EQS. " " THEN EXIT
       $WRITE SYS$OUTPUT CNT,">",A
       $GOTO JOB_SHOW
```

This looks like a complicated function to learn, but it is worth the time if you wish to create customized versions of commonly used commands such as DISPLAY ENTRY, DISPLAY JOB, and DISPLAY QUEUE. Note this is a Version 5 feature.

How Do I Get Information About My Process?

Use DCL or VCL to give much useful information about your process with relatively little effort. The Davis and Owen (1988), Gomez (1988), and Watson (1989) references may be helpful in learning more about this area. Here are some tips and traps in using lexical functions in providing information about a process that would be of interest to most users:

1. F$GETJPI is the most useful function in this area. Here is how to use GETJPI in creating a command procedure that "shows a process at a glance:"

VCL (3.0 AND LATER)

```
$! First argument is current spawn level for MS-DOS.
$   GRP = F$GETJPI("","GRP") !Group of process such as 200
$   USET = F$GETJPI("","LOGINTIM") !Time used VCL such as 0 00:00:05
$   OWNER = F$GETJPI("","OWNER") !Owner of process such as 200
$   PID = F$GETJPI("","PID") ! Process id such as 0
$   UIC = F$GETJPI("","UIC") !Process UIC such as USER,USER.
$   UN = F$GETJPI("","USERNAME") ! Username of process such as USER
$   ! Note F$PID is supported
```

VMS

```
$   BLNK = "" ! Set to null
$   PID = F$PID(BLNK) !Obtain process id that is needed for F$GETJPI
$!    OR Both return a number such as 2020193F
$   PID = F$GETJPI(,PID) ! Can also set first argument to null below
$   ACT = F$GETJPI("PID","ACCOUNT") !Account name such as MORG088
$   PRIV = F$GETJPI("PID","CURPRIV") !Current privileges such as,
    NETMBX
```

```
$    IMAG = F$GETJPI("PID","IMAGNAME") !What is the current image name
$    GRP = F$GETJPI("PID","GRP") !UIC Group Name
$    MODE = F$GETJPI("PID","MODE") !Interactive, batch or network -
     mode?
$    OWNER = F$GETJPI("PID","OWNER") ! Owner of process
$    PROCESS = F$GETJPI("PID","PRCNAM") ! Name of process such as RAS6
$    UIC = F$GETJPI("PID","UIC") ! UIC of process MORGO88,RAS6
$    USER = F$GETJPI("PID","USERNAME") !User of process such as RAS6
```

Note that you may need the appropriate privileges to use these functions to access any processes besides your own. Watson (1989, p. 166) discusses the shortcomings of using this function. In short, if your system is already heavily swapping, then generally avoid using this function. He suggests obtaining the state of the process (the state argument of F$GETJPI) before invoking F$GETJPI.

2. F$MODE also will tell the mode of the current process. See the section on invoking a background DCL command procedure for further information.

3. F$ENVIRONMENT provides information about the DCL environment. Here are some examples of arguments.

VCL (3.0 AND LATER) AND VMS

```
$    F$ENVIRONMENT("DEFAULT")
$! Default directory name and device it resides on. Sample value VCL-
C:[VCL], VMS DISK1:[HHG1]
$    F$ENVIRONMENT("ON_CONTROL_Y")
$    ! Was ON_CONTROL_Y invoked? Returns TRUE or FALSE
$    F$ENVIRONMENT("ON_SEVERITY")
$    ! Invoke ON_SEVERITY on what level. Sample values: None, 0-4
$    F$ENVIRONMENT("PROTECTION")
$    ! Shows default file protection. Sample values -
     S=RWED,O:RWED,W:NO ACCESS
$    F$ENVIRONMENT("PROCEDURE")
$    ! Name of active command procedure. Sample value VCL-
     C:[DCL]PROG2.CMD
$    !VMS DISK1:[HHG1]PROG2.COM
$    F$ENVIRONMENT("VERIFY_IMAGE")
$    ! Is display data lines in trace mode on? Returns TRUE or FALSE
$    F$ENVIRONMENT("VERIFY_PROCEDURE")
$! Is display command procedure in trace mode on? Returns TRUE or -
FALSE
```

4. F$PROCESS() returns the current process name. For VCL, this process name includes the process id (UNIX) or spawn level (MSDOS).

5. Use F$PRIVILEGE to see if you are authorized to set a privilege. Then use F$SETPRV to set or reset a privilege (these are not supported by VCL). Here is an example of the two lexical functions in action:

```
$    ! Can you be granted READALL? (You can read all files with this
     privilege)
$    DREAM_PRIV = F$PRIVILEGE("READALL") ! Returns true or false
$    IF .DREAM_PRIV .EQS. "TRUE" THEN A = F$SETPRIV("READALL")
$    ! Do a show symbol to see if A was assigned the new privilege
```

SELF-CONTAINED DCL APPLICATIONS

Self-contained DCL applications are one or more DCL command procedures (and sometimes compiled programs) that are oriented to end-users instead of computer center staff. Sequences in this section will include (1) capturing, parsing, and validating user input; (2) communicating between a subprocedure and the main command procedure; and (3) miscellaneous operations (such as changing the case of a string).

How To Capture User Command Line Values

Up to eight parameters can be specified when invoking a command procedure. These are stored in local symbols P1 through P8 as character strings. (This means other command procedures cannot directly access these symbols). Parameters are separated by spaces. If there are more P symbols than command line parameters, then the extra parameters are assigned a value of null (this means that P symbols are never uninitialized).

Here are some tips and traps when capturing command line input:

1. Parameters must be in double quotes to preserve blanks and special characters and to retain lower- and mixed-case. Remember to use three double quotes to produce one, five to produce two, and so on. Here is an example of the difference a command line parameter can make.

FROM DCL PROMPT ($)

```
@TEST HAL GERMAN
```

```
                        IN TEST.COM
$    WRITE SYS$OUTPUT p1! Displayed: Hal
$    WRITE SYS$OUTPUT p2 !Displayed: German (on next line after Hal)


                    FROM DCL PROMPT ($)

@TEST "HAL GERMAN"


                        IN TEST.COM

$    WRITE SYS$OUTPUT p1! Displayed: Hal German
$    WRITE SYS$OUTPUT p2 ! Displayed: (null)
```

2. Use SHOW SYMBOL/LOCAL/ALL or a WRITE SYS$OUTPUT P*n* to display the value of a P*n* symbol (with *n* being from 1 to 8). This is invaluable in debugging command procedures.
3. All of the preceding also applies to the VCL and @ commands of VCL.
4. Use IFs to validate input and decide where to branch based on the parameter value.

```
             TEST FOR BLANKS AND PROMPT NEW VALUES.

$    IF P1 .EQS. "" THEN READ SYS$COMMAND/PROMPT="Enter a valid state" st


                            BRANCHING

$    IF P1.EQS. "DEL" THEN GOTO DEL100
$    (later in command procedure)
$ DEL100:
```

How To Create Menus, User Prompts, And Confirmation Messages

This can be done with the WRITE $SYSOUTPUT command (see the next section on how the INQUIRE and READ commands combine the prompt with capturing input.)

```
               WRITE SYS$OUTPUT for prompting input:
$    WRITE SYS$OUTPUT "Enter your state of residence:"
$    READ SYS$COMMAND ST
$    !Could be combined into command with READ/PROMPT. Default prompt -
     is DATA:
```

```
                    WRITE SYS$OUTPUT for Menus
$   WRITE SYS$OUTPUT"*******************************************"
$   WRITE SYS$OUTPUT"*      ",F$TIME() "                        *"
$   ! Displayed*     5-Mar-1991 10:25:11.18                     *
$   WRITE SYS$OUTPUT "* Please Enter ONE of the following:      *"
$   WRITE SYS$OUTPUT "* 1 - 1990 Report                         *"
$   WRITE SYS$OUTPUT "* 2 - 1991 Report                         *"
$   WRITE SYS$OUTPUT "* 3 - 1992 Report                         *"
$   WRITE SYS$OUTPUT "*******************************************"
$     READ SYS$COMMAND CHOICE


                 WRITE SYS$OUTPUT for confirmation messages
$    WRITE SYS$OUTPUT "Report for",ryear,"is queued to printer",prt
$!Displayed: Report for 1990 is queued to printer PRINTER1
```

1. Note above that commas and not blanks delimit strings and symbols in a WRITE command.
2. Although DCL does not directly include commands that allow cursor manipulation and development of full-screen applications, there are a number of add-on products and commands that do this, such as UNIX/MSDOS—Curses and VMS—FMS, SMG, EasyEntry.
3. For VMS and MS-DOS, you can use terminal escape sequences to enhance your display output. This is discussed in Using Escape Sequences with DCL.
4. Document at the start of your command procedure what each parameter is and valid/default values.

How To Capture User Input

Previous examples have used the two major ways to capture user input:

1. The INQUIRE command accompanied by a symbol to store the input and an optional display prompt string (the symbol name is displayed if there is no prompt string).
   ```
   $INQUIRE CLA "ENTER YOUR FAVORITE COMMAND LANGUAGE"
   ```
2. The READ command is followed by a logical specifying the input source and the symbol for assigning the input. The following is the equivalent of the preceding INQUIRE statement:
   ```
   $    READ SYS$COMMAND CLA -
        /PROMPT="ENTER YOUR FAVORITE COMMAND LANGUAGE"
   ```

The following are tips and traps when capturing user input:

1. Anagnostopoulos (1989), Kiefhaber (1988), and Watson (1991—both references) discourage use of INQUIRE because:

Input from INQUIRE is always converted to uppercase.

A single quote in the user's input performs symbolic substitution before being assigned to a symbol. This means the input may be unexpectedly invalid or be used by users to build a DCL virus (or a user can enter SET VERIFY or F$VERIFY(1) as input and see what your symbols mean) especially those used for passwords.

Only one blank is retained if two or more blank characters are encountered in the string.

Leading and trailing blanks are not assigned to the symbol.

User input is stored in the command history buffer, leading to potential confusion.

Prompt strings must be character strings and not the result of symbolic substitution.

2. Useful qualifiers include /GLOBAL—make the INQUIRE symbol into a global one. The default is /LOCAL—available to the current command procedure only and /PROMPT—assign a prompt (instead of the default DATA:) to be used with the READ.

3. VCL supports all the above commands and associated qualifiers.

4. Specify the default and valid values as part of your display prompt—to minimize surprises that you and the user have to go through.

How To Parse Command Line/User Input

Three major ways are used to parse generic strings:

1. If the delimiter is known but the length of the substring is not, use F$ELEMENT. You specify which substring (element) to obtain, the delimiter, and the string to use. The example below parses an input string into words that are assigned to array variables.

```
$   READ SYS$COMMAND LINE/PROMPT = "Enter the string to be parsed"
$   CNT = 0
$ STR_PARSE:
$   WORDS=F$ELEMENT(CNT," ",LINE) ! Loop through words in line
$   A'CNT=WORDS ! Assign to array variable A1..An
$   EL=A'CNT
$   WRITE SYS$OUTPUT EL ! Write out word
$   CNT = CNT + 1     ! Bump Counter
$   IF (F$LENGTH(WORDS) .GT. 1) THEN GOTO STR_PARSE!If not blank -
    reloop
$   EXIT
```

2. If the length and starting location of the substring is known, consider using F$EXTRACT instead. The simple example below parses a telephone number:

```
$   READ SYS$COMMAND LINE/PROMPT = "Enter the telephone number"
$   LEN = F$LENGTH(LINE)
```

```
$    IF LEN .EQ. 8 THEN ! such as 555-5555
$     EXCHANGE = F$EXTRACT(0,3,LINE)
$     NUMB=F$EXTRACT(4,4,LINE)
$     AREA = ""
$    ELSE ! Such as 617-555-5555
$     AREA = F$EXTRACT(0,3,LINE)
$     EXCHANGE = F$EXTRACT(4,3,LINE)
$     NUMB = F$EXTRACT(8,4,LINE)
$    ENDIF
$    WRITE SYS$OUTPUT AREA, " ", EXCHANGE,"",NUMB
```

3. If the length of the substring is known, but the starting location is unknown, then combine F$LOCATE with F$EXTRACT.

```
$    STR="A String with a , in the middle"
$    LOC = F$LOCATE(",",STR) ! Find comma
$    LEN = F$LENGTH(STR) ! Length of total string
$    SLEN = LEN - LOC ! Length of first string - - BEFORE_COMMA
$    BEFORE_COMMA = F$EXTRACT(0,SLEN,STR) ! Result: A String with a
$    AFTER_COMMA= F$EXTRACT(LOC+1,LEN,STR) !Result: in the middle
```

Other tips and traps when parsing strings are:

1. The preceding examples also work with VCL.
2. These approaches can be used whether the string is assigned to a symbol, the string is obtained from a READ or INQUIRE, or the string is obtained from the command line and assigned to a P*n* symbol.
3. Remember use F$PARSE to parse a file name as outlined in a previous section named How Do I Parse a File Name.

How To Validate Command Line/User Input

After you have obtained the input from the command line or the keyboard and it is parsed, then it is appropriate to check if the input is valid. Validations generally consist of four types (these work both for VCL and DCL interpreters):

1. *Checking the data type:*
```
$    WRITE SYS$OUTPUT"LET ME GUESS THE DATA TYPE OF YOUR INPUT"
$    READ SYS$COMMAND GUESS
$    WRITE SYS$OUTPUT "GUESS IS", F$TYPE(GUESS)
$! Returns INTEGER, STRING, or null string (if unknown)
```
2. *Checking for specific values:*
```
$    READ SYS$COMMAND CHOICE
$     VALID_VALS = CHOICE .EQS. "A" .OR . CHOICE .EQS. "D"
$    IF .NOT. VALID_VALS
$    THEN
$     WRITE SYS$OUTPUT "INVALID VALUE. MUST BE A OR D" !lowercase -
fails
```

```
$      GOTO ERR_LABEL: !Goes to invalid value label (not shown)
$      ENDIF
```

3. *Checking for a number range:*
```
$   IF NUM .GT. 1 .AND. NUM .LT.10 ! Selects between 2 and 9 but not -
    decimals (2.1)
```

4. *Checking for blank/nonblank:*
```
$   IF NUM .EQS. ""THEN ! Check if blank.
$   IF NUM .NES. ""THEN ! Check if non-blank */
```

Date And Time Operations With DCL

DCL is particularly strong in the area of date and time manipulations. Here are some tips and traps when using DCL lexical functions to perform date and time operations:

1. A good introduction in the area including an overview of international date and time standards is Bemer (1979). Watson (1989) provides good examples of date and time operations using DCL.

2. F$TIME returns the current date and time. Here is an example:
```
$   WRITE SYS$OUTPUT "Current Time is", f$time()
$   ! displayed 1-FEB-91 10:10:05 (VCL)
$   ! displayed 1-FEB-1991 10:10:05.53 (VMS)
```

3. Use F$LOCATE, F$ELEMENT and F$EXTRACT to extract a part of the F$TIME string. This also can be done with F$CVTIME.
```
$   A = F$TIME()
$   MONTH=F$ELEMENT(1,"-",A)
$ ! extract month part of F$TIME string - - Returns Feb
```
   or
```
$   A=F$TIME()
$   MONTH=F$CVTIME(A,,"MONTH") ! Returns 02
```

4. F$CVTIME is a powerful function that converts dates and times between various formats: ABSOLUTE—specific date or time; DELTA—relative time from the current date and time; and COMPARISON—date format to compare which of two dates is older. This is the default:
```
$   CURDATE= F$TIME()
$   F$CVTIME(CURDATE,"COMPARISON","DATETIME")
$!Converts from dd-mmm-yyyy to yy-mm-dd and hh:mm:ss to hh:mm:ss:cc
$!cc=hundreds of seconds
$! Sample: 1991-02-01 10:10:05.10
```
   F$CVTIME also extracts the desired substring from a date/time string:
```
$   A=F$TIME()
$   TIME=F$CVTIME(A,,"TIME") !Time part of date time string -
10:00:00:00
```
   Other values for the third argument are DATE (just date part), DATETIME (entire string), DAY, HOUR, HUNDREDTH (hundreds of a second), MINUTE, MONTH, SECOND, TIME (time part of string).

This function also compares which of two dates/times is older and other date/time operations, which is extremely useful for file operations:

```
$   DATE1 ="01-JAN-1991"
$   DATE2 ="05-JAN-1991"
$   D1 = F$CVTIME(DATE1,,"DATE")
$   D2 = F$CVTIME(DATE2,,"DATE")
$   IF D2 .EQS. D1 THEN WRITE SYS$OUTPUT "D1 and D2 are the same -
    dates"
$   IF D2 .GTS. D1 THEN WRITE SYS$OUTPUT "D2 is later than D1"
$   IF D2 .LTS. D1 THEN WRITE SYS$OUTPUT "D1 is later than D2"
```

5. The !%T (time) and !%D (Date and time) of F$FAO allow you to place the current date and time into a string.

6. Using substring replacement, you can change the format of a date (this was added in VCL 3.0).

```
$ a_date="12/12/90"
$ a_date[2,1] := "-" !change first slash to dash
$ a_date[5,1] :="-" !change second slash to dash
$ write sys$output a_date !Displayed 12-12-90 changed slashes to -
dashes!
```

Text Case Operations With DCL

The following are tips and traps when dealing with text case operations for both DCL and VCL:

1. Use F$EDIT for changing a string to upper- or lowercase.

```
$   READ SYS$COMMAND str/prompt="Enter your string to convert"
$   READ SYS$COMMAND sel /prompt="What is your choice UPPER or LOWER -
    (case)?"
$   IF SEL .EQS. "UPPER"
$     THEN
$   A=F$EDIT(STR,"UPCASE")
$   WRITE"STR IS NOW",A
$   GOTO STR_NOW
$   ENDIF
$   IF SEL .EQS. "LOWER"
$     THEN
$   A=F$EDIT(STR,"LOWERCASE")
$   ENDIF
$STR_NOW:
$   WRITE "STR IS NOW",A
$EXIT
```

2. The preceding sequence fails if entered in lowercase because it is being compared to an uppercase string. If in doubt on the case of user input, always use F$EDIT to convert first to uppercase.

3. DCL always converts symbol names to uppercase regardless of the case you enter them in.

4. F$TRNLNM translates a logical either CASE_BLIND (default) or CASE_SENSITIVE. The fourth argument determines which is used.

String Operations With DCL

The following are tips and guidelines when performing string operations with DCL/VCL commands and lexical functions:

1. When performing string operations on symbols, "+" indicates concatenation and "−" indicates truncation.
```
$   ONE = "NEW"
$   TWO = "YORK"
$   THREE = ONE + TWO + ", USA"
$! Concatenate two strings plus text Result:NEWYORK, USA
$   FOUR = THREE - ","
$! Removes comma if found, else nothing happens. Result: NEWYORK USA
```

2. F$EDIT also can be useful in manipulating character strings. TRIM removes leading/trailing blanks and COMPRESS removes multiple embedded blanks. The only exception is that embedded blanks within double quotes are retained.
```
$   A=" A STRING WITH MULTIPLE BLANKS AND LEADING/TRAILING BLANKS "
$   NEW_A = F$EDIT(A,"TRIM,COMPRESS")
$   WRITE SYS$OUTPUT "A is ", NEW_A
$! Displayed A string with multiple blanks and leading/trailing -
blanks
```

3. In addition to the parsing techniques discussed in a previous section, you can change substrings within character strings. This is also a way to add leading/trailing blanks to a string (added in VCL Version 3.0).
```
$   a_date="12/12/90"
$   a_date[2,1] := "-" !change first slash to dash
$   a_date[5,1] := "-" !change second slash to dash
$   write sys$output a_date !Displayed 12-12-90 changed slashes to -
dashes!
```

4. Bit field operators also may be used for manipulating character strings and is especially useful for using special characters (such as line feed) in a command procedure. Since each character takes up eight bits, you can use the substring operator shown in the last example to assign a special character (added in VCL Version 3.0).
```
$   spec="AA"
$   spec[8,8]=%x0A !The second character is now assigned a line field
$   ! (hexadecimal 0A)
```

5. Non-strings can be converted to character strings and the reverse in various ways, including:

F$CVSI—takes bit fields in a character string and converts them to a signed integer (added in VCL 3.0).

F$CVUI—takes bit fields in a character string and converts them to an unsigned integer (added in VCL 3.0).

F$FAO—converts data in various types to ASCII strings (added in VCL 3.0). This will be discussed in How can I create reports using DCL.

F$INTEGER—converts a string to an integer.

F$STRING—converts an integer to a string.

How Do I Pass Information Between Command Procedures?

Information (such as return codes and symbol values) is passed between DCL command procedures in a variety of ways.

1. By making a symbol global, a value is available to all command procedures. This is done by using two equal signs (i.e. ==) in a global symbol-assignment statement. Try to document in the command procedure any global symbols created or used. Unlike local symbols global symbols can be created at the DCL prompt or in a command procedure and last until you log off. SHOW SYMBOL/GLOBAL shows all currently defined global symbols.

```
$   A = = "22" ! Makes a a global symbol with the value the character-
    string of 22.
```

2. Passing parameters when invoking a second command procedure within the main command procedure:

```
    Within FIRST.COM command procedure
$   @SECOND 12 88 HELLO ! Passes three values on invocation
```

3. Define a logical to be added to the default process table. The assignment is in effect until you log off.

```
DEFINE VALDISK1:[HHG1]DATA.TXT
```

4. Accessing the four $GLOBAL symbols:

$ENTRY—entry number generated from last PRINT or SUBMIT (VMS 5.4 and later).

$STATUS—return code from the last DCL command. Between command procedures, this usually means passing a code from an EXIT command. Note $STATUS normally returns a 1 or 3. However, when a command does not work correctly, an even return code is given: 0—warning; 2—error; and 4—fatal error. Note that this will not work with CONTINUE, EOD, GOTO, IF, and several other VMS commands.

$SEVERITY—error level of $STATUS: 0—warning; 1—no error; 2—some error; 3—information (not an error); 4—fatal error.

$RESTART—did batch job start after the system went unexpectedly down (added in VMS 5.4)?

How Do I Pass Information Between a Command Procedure and Function/Subprocedure?

Information (such as return codes and symbol values) is passed between DCL/VCL subroutine and the "main" command procedure in a variety of ways:

1. Use of global symbols and logicals as outlined in the previous section. Local symbols are also used to pass values to subroutines invoked by a GOSUB. Remember that GOSUB does not have a direct way to pass parameters. Being on the same level as the "main" command procedure, local symbols are accessible by both.

```
$    parml = "A" ! Local symbol to be used by subroutine
$    gosub sample ! Invoke label named sample
$    write sys$output "parml " , parml
$! Next statement processed after gosub - - displays B
$      EXIT !so won't reinvoke subroutine
$sample: ! Start of subroutine
$    parml = "B"
$    return 1 ! Could also capture with $STATUS and $SEVERITY in the -
main command procedure
```

2. Using the CALL command to invoke a command procedure accompanied by parameters assigned to symbols P1 through P8. Because a new level is formed, only global symbols and logicals (not local symbols) can be used to pass values between the "main" command procedure and the subroutine. Note that CALL is a Version 5 feature.

```
$    B==88 !Global symbol
$    CALL SAMPLE "A" !invoke label named sample
$    WRITE SYS$OUTPUT "B", B !Next statement processed after call.
Returns B
$      EXIT !so won't reinvoke subroutine - - not really needed
$SAMPLE: !Start of subroutine
$    SUBROUTINE
$    WRITE SYS$OUTPUT "B", B !Returns 88
$    B=="B"
$      EXIT !Optional because subroutine also ends subroutine. RETURN
for GOSUB
$    ENDSUBROUTINE
```

You can have up to 32 nested CALLs and also may use the /OUTPUT qualifier to send output to a file.

3. Use of EXIT/RETURN and accompanying global symbols $STATUS and $SEVERITY, which is described in the previous section.

```
$    GOSUB TESTIT
$    IF $STATUS .NE. 1 THEN WRITE SYS$OUTPUT $STATUS, $SEVERITY
$    EXIT
$TESTIT:
$    ! Place your routine here
$    RETURN
```

How To Create Reports Using DCL

The following are tips and guidelines using DCL lexical functions to create reports:

1. Use the string manipulation techniques discussed in previous sections on parsing common line input and string operations to get a string or substring in a desired format.
2. Use F$FAO to generate your reports (available in VCL 3.0). F$FAO is similar to PRINTF in C or PERL or FORMAT in FORTRAN—converting data in various formats to ASCII strings. Here is a sample report showing many of the features of F$FAO:

```
$   FIRST = "HALLETT"
$   LAST = "GERMAN"
$   AGE = 19
$   A1 = F$FAO("!10*# !%D") ! 10 # followed by Time and Date
$   A2 = F$FAO("NAME is !2(AS)",FIRST,LAST)
$ !Note two arguments match two strings specified by AS
$   A3 = F$FAO("AGE is !SL",AGE) ! Substitution of age
$   A4=F$FAO("!/") ! Adds a carriage return and line feed
$LOOP:
$   IF CNT .GT 4 THEN GOTO BYEBYE ! Loop through array and write out -
values A1-A4.
$   LINE = A'CNT ! Line = A1
$   WRITE SYS$OUTPUT LINE !write value
$   CNT = CNT + 1
$   GO TO LOOP ! Continue through loop until greater than 4
$BYEBYE:
$   EXIT
  Displayed:
########## 30-JUN-1990 18:37:20.06
Name is HallettGerman
Age is 19
```

3. F$FAO is good for producing column-oriented reports and formatting records in a file. Here is a simple example:

```
$VALUES:
$   NAME = "HAL GERMAN" !Normally goes through a loop to read multi-
ple records
$   AGE = 19
$   SEX = "M"
```

```
$    SSN="555-55-1212"
$REPT:
$    WRITE SYS$OUTPUT F$FAO("!80AS","NAME    SEX AGE SSN")
$    WRITE SYS$OUTPUT F$FAO("!45*@")
$    WRITE SYS$OUTPUT -
$    F$FAO("!25AS!1AS!2AS!1AS!2SL!2AS!11AS",NAME," ",SEX," ",AGE."
     ",SSN)
     Displayed:
NAME          SEX   AGE   SSN
HAL GERMAN    M     19    555-55-1212
```

Which VMS Version Do I Have?

Knowing the VMS version is useful in discovering what DCL features and commands are available and in debugging command procedures. The following shows various ways of getting this information:

LOCAL NODE

```
$    VER=F$GETSYI("VERSION") ! Sample Output:V5.4-1A
     Or
$    VER= F$GETSYI("NODE_SWVERS") ! Sample Output:V5.4
```

ANY NODE ON A CLUSTER

```
$    RADIO_NODE=F$GETSYI("NODE_SWVERS","RADIO")
$! Gives version for a node named RADIO that is part of a cluster
```

VCL (DOS AND UNIX)

```
$    SHOW VERSION
     Displayed:
VCL00096CDO,Version 3.01 Copyright (c) Boston Business Computing,
Ltd. 1985-1990. All rights reserved.
     or
$    VER=F$GETSYI("VERSION") !Added in VCL 3.0 Sample Output:3.01
```

Using Escape Sequences With DCL

DEC (VT 100 and higher) terminals and third-party DEC terminal emulators use escape sequences to control various screen attributes. Using DCL, you can use escape sequences to enhance your menus and other screen output. To do this, here are some tips and guidelines:

1. For additional information see the Anagnostopoulos (1989), Christiansen (1988), Davis and Owen (1988) and Watson (1989) references.

2. Do not place the Escape character directly in a command—assign it first to a symbol, then use the symbol. Otherwise your screen may look strange or a print job may be illegible after the escape character is encountered.

```
$    WRITE SYS$OUTPUT"<ESC>[1m" ! WRONG - - may cause display/print
     problems


$    ESCAPE[0,8]=27 or $ESC[0,8] = %X1B
$    REVERSE = ESC +"[1m"
$    RESET=ESC + "[0m"
$    WRITE SYS$OUTPUT REVERSE, "This is in reverse"
$    WRITE SYS$OUTPUT RESET,"This is back to normal"
```

3. Table 5-1 lists common sequences for VT220 and higher terminals (some work on VT100s):

4. For multiple escape sequences, separate them with a semicolon:

```
$    ESC[0,8]=27 or $ ESC[0,8] = %X1B
$    BLINK = ESC +"[5;7m" !Blinking reverse
```

5. The following shows examples of manipulating the height and width:

```
$    ESC[0,8]=27 or $ ESC[0,8] = %X1B
$    DHT=ESC + "#3" - - ! double height top part
$    DHB=ESC + "#4" - - ! double height bottom part
$    SW=ESC + "#5" - - ! single width
$    DW=ESC + "#6" - - ! double width
$!YOU MUST SPECIFY THE SAME STRING for BOTH HALVES
$    WRITE SYS$OUTPUT DHT "A DOUBLE HEIGHT STRING"
$    WRITE SYS$OUTPUT DHB "A DOUBLE HEIGHT STRING"
```

6. A useful feature is using escape sequences to position where the cursor is to be located.

```
$    ESC[0,8]=27 or $ ESC[0,8] = %X1B
$    LOC = ESC + "[12;1H" !Place at line 12 and column 1 of screen.
$    WRITE SYS$OUTPUT LOC "STRING IN MIDDLE OF THE SCREEN"
```

7. There are additional functions that are used to make simple full-screen applications:

>   ESC +"(0" enables line drawing mode that can be used to make boxes.
>   ESC + "│1;│2 r" sets up a scroll region from line │1 to line │2.
>   ESC +"[r" turns off scroll region.

Table 5-1. Common Escape Sequences for VT220 Terminals

Mode	Enabled	Disabled
Normal	ESC +"[0m"	N/A
Intensity	ESC +"[1m"	ESC +"[22m"
Underscore	ESC +"[4m"	ESC +"[24m"
Blinking	ESC +"[5m"	ESC +"[25m"
Reverse	ESC +"[7m"	ESC +"[27m"

8. An undocumented feature of VCL is that you can use escape sequences in MS-DOS. You must have a DEVICE=C:\ANSI.SYS in your CONFIG.SYS file.

```
$   ESC[0,8]=27
$   REVERSE= ESC+"[0;7m"
$   WRITE SYS$OUTPUT REVERSE, "THIS IS IN REVERSE"
```

Some of the more common escape sequences are listed in Table 5-2. Microsoft's *DOS Technical Reference* and similar books have more escape sequences.

Table 5-2. Common Escape Sequences

ESC +"[0m"	Normal
ESC +"[1m"	Bold
ESC +"[5m"	Blink
ESC +"[7m"	Reverse
ESC +"[30m"	Black text (foreground)
ESC +"[31m"	Red text (foreground)
ESC +"[32m"	Green text (foreground)
ESC +"[33m"	Yellow text (foreground)
ESC +"[34m"	Blue text (foreground)
ESC +"[40m"	Black screen (background)
ESC +"[41m"	Red screen (background)
ESC +"[42m"	Green screen (background)
ESC +"[43m"	Yellow screen (background)
ESC +"[44m"	Blue screen (background)
ESC +"[x:yH"	Place cursor at line x and column y.

OTHER DCL COMMAND PROCEDURE CONCERNS

This section is concerned with topics appropriate for all types of DCL applications. This includes porting DCL to other platforms and converting to command languages.

How To Debug DCL Command Procedures

The following are tips and guidelines in debugging DCL command procedures:

1. A simple debugger, available for DCL, is enabled two different ways:
   a. By issuing a SET VERIFY, SETVERIFY=IMAGE, or SET VERIFY=PROCEDURE. A set VERIFY shows all command and

images after symbolic substitution while using a value of IMAGE or PROCEDURE turns on the trace facility just for that image or command procedure. Issuing a SET NOVERIFY disables the trace facility.

b. By assigning to a symbol a F$VERIFY(1,1) to turn on both command procedure (the first argument) and image (the second argument) tracing. Assigning a value of zero disables tracing for the specified argument. Once the symbol is created, it can be used to either issue a SET VERIFY or SET NOVERIFY or to restore a previous F$VERIFY value.

```
$     TRACE_BEFORE= 0 ! Generally place your F$VERIFY near the start -
      of the command procedure
$! If parameter turned on, then enable tracing
$     TRACE_NOW =""
$     IF P1 .EQS "DBUG" THEN TRACE_NOW=F$VERIFY(1)
$     IF TRACE_NOW .NES.""
$       THEN
$         SET VERIFY !otherwise set noverify
$       ELSE
$         SET NOVERIFY
$ENDIF
$     (later in the command procedure)
$     RESET = F$VERIFY(TRACE_BEFORE,TRACE_BEFORE) !Disable tracing
```

2. Use F$ENVIRONMENT ("VERIFY_IMAGE") and F$ENVIRON-MENT("VERIFY PROCEDURE") to obtain or reset the current F$VER-IFY settings.

3. The following tips may help in debugging a problem:

   a. Issue WRITE statements to see if a certain line was processed, or to inspect the value of a symbol/logical.

   b. Use SHOW SYMBOL, SHOW LOGICAL, and SHOW TRANSLA-TION to see the currently assigned values for a symbol or logical. Also use F$LOGICAL, F$TYPE, and F$TRNLNM.

   c. Examine $STATUS and $SEVERITY to see how successful a command procedure or subprocedure was.

   d. Use F$MESSAGE to learn more about any errors found.

   e. F$GETJPI (current process) and F$ENVIRONMENT (DCL interpreter settings) give useful information that may be invaluable in debugging a problem.

   f. In VCL 3.0, SET VCL/OVERFLOW_WARN lets you know if a symbol resulted in a numeric overflow (note VMS does not warn if this happens).

4. Use the following general approach in debugging problems:

   What happened? Describe action—(what happened, what was supposed to happen)? Record all error messages and their severity level.

Gather more information about the problem: Where exactly is the error happening? On invocation, at a certain label, when invoking a subroutine, image, or another command procedure? Getting the problem to occur in a consistent fashion makes it easier to resolve. Use the techniques mentioned in point 3 above.

Make an educated guess on what caused the problem and a way to test it. Perform the test. If it works, there is no need to go further. Otherwise return to the gather-more-information step.

5. VCL -v is the equivalent of enabling SET VERIFY before running a program.

The Elements of DCL Style

Once you have been writing DCL command procedures for a while, you begin to develop your own "fingerprint" or style. This section discusses some of the elements of good command procedure style. Of all the command languages discussed in this book, DCL has the most references on this topic. These include Anagnostopolous (1989), Flowers (1988), Kiefhaber (1989), Watson (1989), and Wischow (1988).

The following are general rules that apply to all types of DCL applications—use them based on your personal and site preferences:

1. *Make your DCL command procedures readable:*
   a. *Minimize use of abbreviating commands and qualifiers.* This can lead to confusion as to what the program's creator meant to do. This abbreviation may apply to more than one command in a later VMS release.
   b. *Break your DCL command procedures into modules* performing *only one or two functions.* Use label names to describe these functions and to mark their start.
   c. *Indent at least two or three spaces* for (1) code under a label—left justify; (2) the instructions contained within an IF-THEN-ENDIF structure; or (3) commands after a dollar sign (DCL prompt); and (4) data for an image (left justify).
   d. *Line Up* all SUBROUTINEs and ENDSUBROUTINEs, IFs and ENDIFs. All labels should be capitalized and not indented. GOTO statements should go to a capitalized label.
   e. *Use blank space freely* to separate modules (before labels marking a new module), between symbol and logical assignments and flow control structures such as IF.
   f. Some *commenting* to self-document the command procedure is necessary: Since they are scanned up to the exclamation point, comments may have some effect on the speed of processing of the command procedure. Exclamation points (or bangs) should be placed immediately after the dollar

signs in column two. A little known fact is that lexical functions placed in comments will be evaluated!

Try to keep comments up to date. There are various styles of DCL commenting:

(1) Comment only complicated (i.e. non-obvious) sequences.

(2) Comment only non-portable DCL commands.

(3) Place comments at the end after the EXIT command to speed up processing (so, it never gets read).

(4) Comment some type of header file that lists the command procedure name, what each parameter (P1–P8) is, what each label (module) does, any nested command procedures used, any global symbols used, and command procedure version history (creator, revisor, date and modification).

(5) Comment next to each appropriate DCL command, but not highly used commands (such as in a loop).

(6) One or more comments before each label.

(7) My own preference is the "jump start" axiom—*write as much documentation to allow you or another person to quickly understand how the command procedure works.*

g. *Use various cases in your programs.* A common practice is to put DCL commands in uppercase and comments in lowercase. Note that the command line interpreter converts all commands to uppercase anyway. Avoiding this conversion makes larger command procedures run faster. Whatever approach you use, make sure it is consistently applied for all command procedures.

h. *Use meaningful names* for DCL command procedures, labels, symbols, logicals, files, and so on.

2. *Make your command procedure as effective as possible:*

a. Leave things as you found them:

(1) Close all files.

(2) Remove all temporary files.

(3) Remove all unneeded global symbols and logicals or reset those to be reused.

(4) Reset your editor/operating system settings, privileges, and protections if changed.

(5) For UNIX and MS-DOS, reset environment variables if changed.

(6) Do all of the above if an error is encountered and you are about to exit from the command procedure.

b. Add parentheses to mathematical operations if you want an operation to be processed in a certain order.

c. Never assume user input is correct. Always check case, data type (F$TYPE), if blank, if a valid value, and if in the valid range.

d. If the same command procedure heavily uses a certain module, then consider converting it to a subroutine. If several command procedures use a certain command procedure, then extract the pertinent part to be used as a nested command procedure.

e. Consider doing the following at the start of a command procedure: (1) issue a SET VERIFY or SET NOVERIFY; (2) initialize all variables; (3) provide a way to capture input for P1–P8 if parameters are not supplied; and (4) clear the screen before displaying output.

f. Depending on the type of users you have using a command procedure, consider having different sequences for different types of use.

g. Create a library of command procedures to perform heavily used tasks such as file operations, exception handling, and prompting for input.

How Can I Extend the DCL Language?

It is possible that DCL may not have all the components that you need for a particular application. Here are some suggestions on how to extend the DCL language:

1. Build your own subroutine and command procedure "libraries." The next section will give you ideas on where to look for these.

2. If you have knowledge of a compiled language, you can use this to build your own DCL command that can be used by any command procedure. This is done by using the VMS Command Language Utility (CLU). Pyron (1989) has a good overview on this topic.

3. Combine DCL with the following for full-screen applications, UNIX—Curses; VMS—FMS, SMG, EasyEntry; and DOS PC Curses.

Where Can I Learn More About DCL?

Here are some places where you can learn more about DCL language and DCL applications:

- The semi-annual proceedings of the DEC user group (DECUS, DECUS Canada, DECUS Europe):
  DECUS, 333 South Street SHR1-4/D31, Shrewsbury, Mass. 01545-4112; (508) 841-3389. Especially of interest is the VAX System SIG, which has at least two or three sessions on DCL at each DECUS symposium, sponsors a two-hour DCL course before the symposium, and produces the session notes for its section at each symposium. Also a DCL clinic is sometimes given by one or more DCL "masters." This is well worth attending. DECUS also make useful contributions to the tape library. For information on tapes call (508) 841-3389 and to order (508) 841-3500.

- The annual proceeding of the SAS User's Group International (SUGI) and the Northeast SAS Users Group has good examples of DCL command procedures:

  SUGI, c/o Publications Department, SAS Institute Inc., SAS Campus Drive, Cary, NC 27513; (919) 677-8000.

  NESUG, c/o Marge Scerbo, University of Maryland at Baltimore, 610 West Lombard Street, Baltimore, MD, 21201; (301) 328-8424. Note that there are only a limited number of proceedings available to non-attendees.

- *DEC Professional* and *VAX Professional* (especially the issues in the 1980s) come out monthly, are free to qualified readers (*DEC Professional* only), and have good articles on DCL. Monthly columns of interest in *DEC Professional* are ULTRIX™ and DCL Dialogue.

  Kevin Barkes, the regular DCL columnist, will be glad to send you a "I Love DCL sticker" and a list of all FidoNet electronic bulletin boards—the catch is that you have to send a self-addressed, stamped #10 envelope to KGB Consulting, 4107 Overlook Street, Library, PA 15129. Or call his BBS at (412) 854-0511 at 1200 or 2400 baud for the list.

  DEC and VAX Professional, Professional Press, 101 Witmer Road, Horsham, Pa., 19044; (215) 957-4269.

- *Connections* is published periodically by Boston Business Computing with a mix of articles on the company's products, including VCL. This is a free publication.

  Connections, Boston Business Computing, 3 Dundee Park, Andover, Mass. 01810; (508) 470-0444.

- The *comp.os.vms* deals with a variety of VMS questions including DCL. Sources are occasionally posted. Also look at vmsnet.misc and vmsnet.sources.

  DEC Professional—GO VAXFORUM. Free other than Compuserve and phone charges. Programs from the monthly columns (including DCL) are available here for downloading.

- *DECUServe*

Call (800) 521-8950 with a username of INFORMATION to learn about accessing this service.

- *Anonymous ftp* for programs:

Anonymous ftp sites include:

amarna.gsfc.nasa.gov   128.183.112.2

lyman.pppl.gov   192.55.106.129

rigel.efd.lth.se   130.235.48.3

rml2.sri.com   128.18.22.20

sphunix.sph.jhu.edu   128.220.51.103

vms1.ucc.okstate.edu   192.31.83.2

watsun.cc.columbia.edu   128.59.39.2

- *Digital Review.* Allen Watson has a semi-regular column in *Digital Review* called VMS Views. Many of these articles are on DCL. The address for a free subscription to qualified readers is **Digital Review,** Cahners Publications, 44 Cook Street, Denver, Colo. 80206-5800.
- *Hardcopy.* Although now defunct, *Hardcopy* had a regular column called VAX/VMS Toolbox by Steve Davis and Matthew Owen. The columns have many good examples of DCL command procedures. Check libraries for back issues.

Exception Handling in DCL

The following are tips and traps in dealing with error handling in DCL command procedures:

1. Placing a SET NOON (no-on not the time of day) command in a command procedure disables error checking but still preserves the values of $STATUS and $SEVERITY for your exception-handling sequences. As a result, you, rather than the command procedure, determine when to exit the command procedure. However, a SET NOON will have no effect if another command procedure level is created, for example, by an @ or CALL command.
2. The alternative to SET NOON is SET ON, which exits a command procedure on most errors but saves the value of $STATUS and $SEVERITY.
3. The ON command is used to detect many of the errors. These include:

```
$    ON WARNING THEN GOTO ERR_WARN ! $SEVERITY of WARNING
$    ON ERROR THEN EXIT 2 !$SEVERITY of ERROR
$    ON SEVERE_ERROR THEN EXIT $STATUS
$!SEVERITY of SEVERE_ERROR
$    ON CONTROL_Y THEN GOTO CTRLY
(sequence with possible errors goes here)
$    EXIT
$CTRLY:
$!Not available for MS-DOS version of VCL. Detects if user tries to
escape from !program. Use
$SET NOCONTROL to disable CTRL Y
$    WRITE SYS$OUTPUT "DO YOU WISH TO EXIT Y/N?"
$    READ SYS$COMMAND ANS
$    IF ANS.EQS. "Y" THEN EXIT
$      ELSE GOTO LAST_LAB !Return to the last label
$    ENDIF
```

4. A common way to check $STATUS is as follows:

```
Command
   $IF .NOT. $STATUS
```

The reason why this works is $STATUS usually returns a 1 or 3. However, when a command does not work correctly, an even return code is given (0—warning; 2—error; and 4—fatal error). Note that this will not work with CONTINUE, EOD, GOTO, IF, and several other VMS commands.

5. Try to have error-handling routines take the flow away from the main part of the command procedure, clean up as outlined in the previous section, and then exit.

```
$IF $SEVERITY GE 2 THEN GOTO ERROR_SEQ
(later in the command procedure)
$ERROR_SEQ:
     $set val= $status
     $write sys$output "An error was found. Now exiting program"
     $close file99 ! Close all files
     $del temp.tmp;* ! Delete all temporary files
     exit val
```

6. For DCL (not VCL), you can place in an error routine the text of an error by using F$MESSAGE.

WITH SET VERIFY

```
$    SET NOON
$    DIO /PPP !bad command
%DCL-W-IVVERB, unrecognized command verb - check validity and -
spelling \DIO\
$    A = $STATUS
$    WRITE SYS$OUTPUT F$MESSAGE(%XA)
%SYSTEM-E-ACCVIO, access violation, reason mask=!XB, virtual
address=!XL PC=!XL
```

Portability of DCL Programs

With the availability of VCL, many DCL programs can be ported without difficulty. However, some commands cannot be converted. This section covers these and other porting concerns:

The following is available in VCL (DOS and UNIX) but not under DCL (VMS):

1. Commands:

DECRYPT   Decrypts a file (Version 3.0)
ENCRYPT   Encrypts a file (Version 3.0)
EXECUTE   Executes command by native command shell
SET VCL   Sets VCL session attributes
SHOW VCL   Shows VCL session attributes
SHOW VERSION   Shows VCL version
SUSPEND   Stops VCL (UNIX only).

TEACH   Shows DOS or UNIX equivalent of a command or file name.

UNIX   Issues a UNIX command.

VCL   Invokes VCL.

2. Logicals/symbols:

SYS$EDITOR   Default VCL editor

SYS$EDITOR_COMPAT   Does editor support EDT+ ?

SYS$SHELL   DOS (command.com) or UNIX (csh or sh) shell.

SYS$VCL   VCL default directory.

SYS$VCLHELP   VCL help directory.

3. Note that many VCL commands have subtle differences and generally fewer qualifiers than their DCL counterparts.

4. Other differences:
   - VMS filenames vs DOS and UNIX (length, case, and version numbers).
   - VMS versus UNIX groups and file protections.
   - Function keys on terminals (such as CTRL Y or CTRL T).
   - VCL-related environment variables.

The following features are available for DCL (VMS) but not in VCL (MS-DOS and UNIX):

1. Commands: There may be UNIX or PC-DOS equivalents for the commands listed below. These are functions that concern accounting, job queue operations, RMS, network operations, device operations, and access control lists (ACLs):

ACCOUNTING, ALLOCATE, ANALYZE, ATTACH, BACKUP, CANCEL, CONVERT, DEALLOCATE, DEBUG, DEPOSIT, DISCONNECT, EXAMINE, EXCHANGE, INITIALIZE, INSTALL, JOB, LINK, MACRO, MAIL, MESSAGE, MONITOR, NCS, PASSWORD, PATCH, PHONE, REQUEST, RUNOFF, SET ACCOUNTING, SET ACL, SET AUDIT, SET BROADCAST, SET CARD_READER, SET CLUSTER, SET COMMAND, SET DAY, SET DEVICE, SET ENTRY, SET FILE, SET KEY, SET LOGINS, SET MAGTAPE, SET OUTPUT_RATE, SET PRINTER, SET PROCESS, SET QUEUE, SET RESTART_VALUE, SET RIGHTS_LIST, SET RMS_DEFAULT, SET SYMBOL, SET TIME, SET UIC, SET VOLUME, SET WORKING_SET, SHOW ACCOUNTING, SHOW ACL, SHOW AUDIT, SHOW BROADCAST, SHOW CLUSTER, SHOW CPU, SHOW ENTRY, SHOW ERROR, SHOW INTRUSION, SHOW

KEY, SHOW MAGTAPE, SHOW MEMORY, SHOW PRINTER, SHOW QUEUE, SHOW QUOTA, SHOW RMS_DEFAULT, SHOW WORKING_SET, START, SUBMIT, SYNCHRONIZE, UNLOCK.

2. The following lists the VMS commands that are available only for some versions of VCL. The operating systems where the commands are available are also listed:

LIBRARY (UNIX), SET PASSWORD (UNIX), SHOW DEVICES (MS-DOS), SHOW MEMORY (MS-DOS), SHOW NETWORK (UNIX), SHOW SYSTEM (UNIX), SHOW USERS (UNIX), SUSPEND (BSD UNIX).

3. Logicals/Symbols that are available for VMS but not for VCI:

Global symbols: $ENTRY, and $RESTART

Logicals: DBG$INPUT, DBG$OUTPUT, LMN$DIRECTORIES, LMN$FILE_DEV, LMN$PERMANENT_MAILBOX, LMN$PROCESS_DIRECTORY, LMN$SYSTEM_DIRECTORY, LMN$SYSTEM_TABLE, LMN$TEMPORARY_MAILBOX, SYS$COMMON, SYS$ERROR_LOG, SYS$EXAMPLES, SYS$HELP (equivalent - - SYS$VCLHELP), SYS$INSTRUCTION, SYS$LIBRARY, SYS$MAINTENANCE, SYS$MESSAGE, SYS$NODE, SYS$SHARE, SYS$SPECIFIC, SYS$SYSDEVICE (equivalent - - SYS$DISK), SYS$TEST, SYS$UPDATE

4. Lexical functions available under VMS not available under VCL: F$GETQUI, F$IDENTIFIER, F$MESSAGE, F$PRIVILEGE, F$SETPRV

5. Other differences:

- Filenames on DOS and UNIX (length, case, and version numbers) versus VMS.
- Groups and file protections versus VMS.
- Function keys on terminals (such as CTRL Y or CTRL T).

Migrating to Other Command Languages

Watson (1989) and others mention that heavily used DCL programs will affect your VAXs' performance. Therefore, you will highly likely need to convert your programs to something else.

When Should I Consider Converting My DCL Command Procedure?

When any of the following becomes a need:

When more sophisticated file operations are needed (relational database.)

When faster processing is needed or your command procedures become quite large.

If migrating to an environment that does not have DCL readily available (such as MVS, CMS, and non-MS-DOS microcomputer environments [such as the Macintosh or the Amiga]).

What Command Language Should I Convert To?

1. A *compiled language program* remains a good possibility. VMS supports a variety of language compilers such as Macro, C, and Pascal. Barkes (1991) talks about an alternative—using Channel Island's Software DCP product that takes DCL code and converts it to FORTRAN source (which later can be compiled). The address of this product's manufacturer can be found in Appendix 1.

2. The *DOS batch language* is only available for MS-DOS and would result in a serious loss of functionality. There are no known references comparing the DOS batch language and DCL.

3. *Perl* is a good alternative to DCL. Compared with DCL, it has stronger array and file operations and availability of mathematical functions. Perl's drawbacks include difficulty of learning, and it is available only on two of the operating systems that DCL is—PC DOS and UNIX. (There are VMS versions floating around, but none that are supported). Although not covered here, a comparison of shell programming and DCL can be found in Lazarus (1991).

4. The *CLIST* language is available on TSO and MS-DOS (pCLIST). It offers marginal improvements over DCI, including more flow control structures, more flexibility in parameter passing, and more sophisticated subroutine structure. However, a CLIST interpreter is available on only one of the operating systems that DCL is—MS-DOS.

Based on the preceding, a compiled language, CLIST, Perl, and REXX are the only possibilities that would offer some or major improvement over the DCL language and would be available on some of the operating systems supported by the DCL interpreter. The rest of the chapter will discuss the major issues in converting DCL command procedures to scripts in those languages.

CLIST LANGUAGE TO DCL (DIGITAL COMMAND LANGUAGE)

Look at Figure 2-2 in Chapter 2 for equivalent commands in DCL. The following are tips and traps in converting from DCL command procedures to CLIST programs:

1. These useful DCL concepts and commands have no equivalent in the CLIST language:
   a. **Logicals,** an alias for a file, tape or disk device, or another logical. It may help you to substitute the word "location" when thinking about logicals

and symbols, Alias for a command, character string, another symbol, or lexical function. It may help you to substitute the word "action" when thinking about symbols. For TSO/E, a logical is similar to the FILE() operand of TSO commands such as ALLOCATE and FREE—an alias for one or more files. (But the life of the logical can be for the whole session while the life of the FILE() operand is just while the command is being processed.) For MS-DOS, it is similar to using environment variables or the SUBST command, where you can assign an alias to be a directory or file name. Symbols are similar to the idea of regular and global CLIST symbolic variables.

  b. These lexical functions: F$CONTEXT, F$CVSI, F$CVUI, F$DIRECTORY, FFAO, FFILE_ATTRIBUTES, F$GETQUI, F$GETDVI, F$GETSYI, F$LOGICAL, F$MESSAGE, F$PARSE, FPID, FPRIVILEGE, F$SETPRV, F$TRNLNM (some), and F$TYPE.

  c. Global symbols: $SEVERITY and $RESTART.

  d. STOP

  e. Severity of error messages into three types: warning, error, and severe error

2. The following VMS commands and lexical functions can be easily converted to TSO equivalents:

  a. P1–P8 to PROC positional operands

  b. INQUIRE or READ/PROMPT to WRITE and READ

  c. F$LOCATE to &SYSINDEX

  d. F$LENGTH to &LENGTH

  e. F$EXTRACT or F$ELEMENT or F$EDIT to &SUBSTR

  f. F$TYPE to &DATATYPE

  g. F$INTEGER to &EVAL and F$STRING to &STR

  h. F$TIME or F$CVTIME to &SYSSTIME and &SYSDATE

  i. Subroutines (invoked by CALL or in simple cases GOSUB) to subprocedures (invoked by SYSCALL)

  j. $STATUS to &LASTCC

  k. Statements that have the same names and perform similar functions (but not necessarily the same syntax): EXIT, GOTO, Labels, IF-THEN-ELSE, READ, RETURN, and WRITE.

  l. The attention (ATTN) key is the CLIST equivalent of CTRL Y. You can use *ATTN sequences* to handle when the attention key is pressed.

  m. F$ENVIRONMENT to CONTROL

  n. SET VERIFY to CONTROL CONLIST etc and F$VERIFY to &SYSCONLIST etc.

  o. OPEN to OPENFILE and CLOSE to CLOSFILE

  p. Harder but not impossible to convert: multiple IFs to SELECT, a loop sequence to DO statements

q. F$SEARCH and F$GETDVI(EXISTS) to &SYSDSN

r. F$TRNLNM and SET TERMINAL/UPPERCASE or /NOUPPER-
CASE to &SYSCAPS and &SYSLC

s. Assignment statement to SET

t. F$GETDVI("TT","DEVBUFSIZ") to &SYSWTERM

3. The following CLIST statements have no equivalent in DCL and will have to
be added after the command procedure is converted:

a. DATA-ENDDATA and DATA-PROMPT-ENDDATA

b. LISTDSI

c. NGLOBAL, SYSREF.

d. &NRSTR, &SYSNSUB, &SYSONENBYTE, &SYSTWOBYTE,
&SYSCLENGTH, &SYSCSUBSTR

e. All the control variables not listed above

DCL TO REXX

1. These DCL concepts and commands have no equivalent in the REXX language:

a. **Logicals,** an alias for a file, tape, or disk device, or another logical. It may
help you to substitute the word "location" when thinking about logicals
and **symbols,** an alias for a command, character string, another symbol or
lexical function. For MS-DOS and UNIX users, these are similar to using
environment variables where you can assign an alias to the directory or
file name. For other REXX users, these are similar to the idea of shared
(global) REXX symbols.

b. These lexical functions: F$CONTEXT, F$DIRECTORY,
F$FILE_ATTRIBUTES, F$GETDVI, F$GETQUI, F$GETSYI,
F$LOGICAL, F$MESSAGE, FPID, FPRIVILEGE, F$SETPRV, and
F$USER.

c. Global symbols $SEVERITY and $RESTART.

d. STOP.

2. Here are recommendations on DCL commands and functions that can be easily converted to REXX instructions and built-in functions:

a. P1–P8 to PARSE ARG

b. INQUIRE to SAY and READ/PROMPT to READ

c. F$LOCATE to POS or LASTPOS

d. F$LENGTH to LENGTH

e. F$EXTRACT, F$ELEMENT or F$EDIT to SUBSTR

f. F$TYPE to DATATYPE

g. Subroutines (invoked by CALL or GOSUB) to subroutines (invoked by
CALL)

  h. F$TIME or F$CVTIME to TIME and DATE

  i. $STATUS to RC

  j. Statements that have the same name and perform similar functions (but not necessarily the same syntax):

    Assignment statement, CALL, EXIT, Labels, IF-THEN-ELSE, READ, RETURN, and WRITE

  k. VMS and REXX have some equivalent statements for exception handling:

VMS	REXX
ON ERROR	CALL ON ERROR/SIGNAL ON ERROR
ON SEVERE_ERROR	CALL ON FAILURE/SIGNAL ON FAILURE
ON CONTROL_Y	CALL ON HALT/SIGNAL ON HALT
No equivalent	CALL ON SYNTAX
IF .not. var..	CALL ON NOVALUE/SIGNAL ON NOVALUE
ON WARNING	No equivalent

  l. SET VERIFY to TRACE instruction and F$VERIFY to TRACE function

  m. Harder but not impossible to convert: multiple IFs to SELECT, loop structure to DO to, file I/O

  n. F$TRNLNM to TRANSLATE (case only)

  o. F$MESSAGE to ERRORTEXT

  p. F$FAO to D2X,X2D

  q. F$LOGICAL or SHOW LOGICAL or SHOW SYMBOL to SYMBOL

  r. F$PARSE (parse filename only) to PARSE template

3. The following REXX instructions/concepts have no equivalent in DCL and will have to be added after the command procedure is converted:

  a. Data buffer or stack operations (other than PULL or QUEUE)

  b. Compound symbols and related instructions

  c. PARSE VERSION

  d. ADDRESS

  e. Interactive tracing

  f. Parsing templates

DCL TO PERL

1. The following PERL concepts have no equivalent in the DCL language:

  a. Math functions

  b. Networking functions

    c. DBM functions (system database)

    d. Environment variables (except for MS-DOS and UNIX VCL interpreters)

    e. Awk to Perl, C header files to Perl, and sed to Perl converters

    f. Setuid and setgid scripts

    g. Associative arrays

    h. Report variables

    i. Binary file mode

2. Here are recommendations on DCL commands/functions that can be easily converted to Perl equivalents:

    a. IF-THEN-ELSE to if-elsif, loop structure to do *block* while and do *block* until.

    b. The following statements have the same names and perform similar functions (but may not necessarily have the same syntax): some operators [+,–,*], CLOSE, DUMP, EXIT, GOTO, OPEN, READ, RENAME, RETURN, and WRITE.

    c. EXECUTE and UNIX (both VCL) to exec or system functions

    d. SET VERIFY to perl -d

    e. F$LOCATE to index and F$EXTRACT to substr, F$LENGTH to length, and F$ELEMENT to split

    f. WRITE and F$FAO to print or printf or sprintf

    g. READ to read or sysread and WRITE to print or printf or write or syswrite

    h. WRITE SYS$OUTPUT "Bad code" and EXIT to die or warn

    i. F$CVTIME and F$TIME to gmtime or localtime

    j. $STATUS to $? (system variable)

    k. SHOW VERSION (VCL) and F$FGETSYI("NODE_SWVERS") to $] (system variable)

    l. SET PROTECTION to chmod, SET DEFAULT to chdir, SET FILE /OWNER= to chown, STOP to kill, CREATE/DIRECTORY to mkdir and DEL file.dir to rmdir(file), SET PROCESS/PRIORITY to setpriority

    m. READ/END_OF_FILE to eof, F$FILE_ATTRIBUTES to stat

    n. F$PID to getppid, F$GETSYI("NODE_NUMBER") to gethostbyaddr, F$GETSYI("NODENAME") to gethostbyname, F$SEARCH to readdir

    o. F$INTEGER to int, %O to oct

    p. @ and VCL to require, eval etc.

    q. P1–P8 to @ARGV[]

3. These DCL concepts and commands have no equivalent in the Perl language and probably should not be converted:

    a. **Logicals,** an alias for a file, tape, or disk device, or another logical. It may help you to substitute the word "location" when thinking about logicals;

and **symbols,** an alias for a command, character string, another symbol or lexical function. For MS-DOS and UNIX users, these are similar to using environment variables where you can assign an alias to the directory or file name. For Perl users, these are similar to the idea of global variables.

b. These lexical functions: F$CONTEXT, F$DIRECTORY, F$FILE_ATTRIBUTES, F$GETDVI, F$GETQUI, F$GETSYI, F$LOGICAL, and F$MESSAGE

c. Global symbols $SEVERITY and $RESTART

SUGGESTED READINGS

Anagnostopoulos, Paul C., 1989. *Writing Real Programs in DCL.* New York: Digital Press.

Barkes, Kevin G., 1991. Compiled DCL, *DEC Professional.* 10(9), September, pp. 114–116.

Barkes, Kevin G., 1986. DCL Lexical Functions: Some Practical Uses—Part 1, *VAX Professional,* August, pp. 44–48.

Bemer, R. W., 1989. Time and the Computer, *Interface Age,* February, pp. 75–89.

Blaylock, Dewey A., and Larry E. Salvo, 1985. An Environmental Data System using SAS Software on the VAX 11/780, *Proceeding of the Twelfth Annual SAS Users Group International Conference,* pp. 675–678.

Boston Business Computing, 1990. *VCL Reference Guide.*

Boston Business Computing, 1990. *VCL Version 3.0 Supplement.*

Christiansen, Eric, 1984. Better DCL Programming under VMS, *The Proceedings of the Digital Equipment Computers Users Society Fall 1984 Symposium,* pp. 647–651.

Davis and Owen, 1988. Making VMS Say Hello, *Hardcopy,* March, pp. 83–7.

Davis and Owen, 1988. Creating Another System Tool, *Hardcopy,* April, pp. 83–5.

Denning, Bill, 1990. Error Handling in DCL Procedures, *The Proceedings of the Digital Equipment Computers Users Society Fall 1990 Symposium,* pp. 85–101.

Denning, Bill, 1991. Obtaining User Input in DCL Procedures, *VAX Systems SIG Session Notes 1991 Spring DECUS Symposium,* pp. 153–159.

Digital Equipment Corporation, 1988. *Guide to using VMS Command Procedures,* Maynard, Mass.

Digital Equipment Corporation, 1988. *VMS DCL Concepts.* Maynard, Mass.

Digital Equipment Corporation, 1988. *VMS DCL Dictionary.* Maynard, Mass.

Digital Equipment Corporation, 1990. *VMS Version 5.4 Release Notes.* Maynard, Mass.

Dilorio, Frank, 1989. Good Code, Bad Code: Strategies for Program Design, *NESUG 89 Conference Proceedings,* pp. 260–266.

Forster, Robert W., 1988. DCL Menu Shell: Eliminating Calls for the Same Menu Syntax, *VAX Professional,* February 10(1), pp. 15–17.

Flowers, Harry E., 1988. Programming in DCL: Techniques and Standards, *VAX Systems SIG Session Notes 1988 Fall DECUS Symposium,* pp. 207–218.

Gomez, Stephen C., 1988. DCL Lexical Functions for System Management, *VAX Systems SIG Session Notes 1988 Fall DECUS Symposium,* pp. 196–206.

Gezelter, Robert, 1990. Introduction to DCL programming using lexical functions, *The Proceedings of the Digital Equipment Computers Users Society Fall 1990 Symposium,* pp. 79–83.

Gezelter, Robert, 1991. Keeping Error Messages on VMS, DCL Consistent, *Digital News,* February 4, (6:3), p. 30.

Gomez, Stephen C., 1988. DCL Lexical Functions for System Management, *VAX Systems SIG Session Notes 1988 Fall DECUS Symposium,* pp. 196–206.

Haigh, David, 1982. RSTS/E V7.1 Using DCL, *The Proceedings of the Digital Equipment Computers Users Society Canada 1982 Symposium,* pp. 921–924.

Harrison, Brad, 1990. Digital Opens VAX/VMS to Compete with UNIX. *Lan Computing,* December 1(4), pp. 1, 7.

Kiefhaber, Nikolaus. An In-depth look at the f$verify() DCL Lexical function, *DECUS Fall Symposium,* 1989. (Handout). pp. 1–3.

Khoury, Philip, and Peter Laskarzewski, 1985. Converting CLINFO Data Sets into SAS Data Sets, *Proceeding of the Twelfth Annual SAS Users Group International Conference,* pp. 679–683.

Kerninghan, Brian W., and P.J. Plauger, 1978. *The Elements of Programming Style,* 2d ed. New York: McGraw-Hill.

Lazarus, Brian, 1991. Shell Programming and DCL, *UNIX SIG Session Notes 1991 Spring DECUS Symposium,* pp. 541–563.

McClinton Jr., Arthur T., 1988. "Introduction to Command Procedures" *Fall 1988 DECUS Symposium,* pp. 1–7. (Handout).

Pyron, Dillion, 1989. "Modifying and Extending DCL with the VMS Command Language Utility," *VAX Systems SIG Session Notes 1989 Spring DECUS Symposium,* pp. 197–202.

Rubel, Andy, "RSX-11M Speaks DCL," 1980 *The Proceedings of the Digital Equipment Computers Users Society Spring 1980 Symposium,* pp. 1125–1127.

VMS POSIX, *1991 Spring DECUS Symposium.* (Handout).

Vizard, John. DCL Standards for SAS® Applications Running on VMS Host Computers, *NESUG 90 Conference Proceedings,* pp. 210–212.

Warner, Richard S., 1985 Advanced DCL Programming, *The Proceedings of the Digital Equipment Computers Users Society Spring 1985 Symposium,* pp. 445–457.

Watson, Allen A., 1991. A Grab Bag Chock-full of DCL Tricks, *Digital Review,* July 8, p. 28.

Watson, Allen A., 1991. More Tricks Out of the DCL Grab Bag, *Digital Review,* August 5, p. 30.

Watson, Allen A. Nifty things to do with VMS DCL, *VAX Systems SIG Session Notes 1989 Spring DECUS Symposium,* pp. 154–172.

Watson, Allen A., 1989. Some Suggestions on Improving DCL Performance, *Digital Review,* April 17, 1989.

Wischow, Paul. DCL Standards: Reliability and Flexibility, *DECUS Spring 1988.* (Handout), pp. 1–21.

6

Command Language Advisor— DOS & OS/2 Batch Language

Because it is included with every PC DOS, MS-DOS and OS/2 operating system sold, the **batch language,** (or sometimes just "batch" or "bat language"—after the .bat file extension—is one of the more popular command languages available today. The DOS or OS/2 batch language contains most of the command language components discussed in Chapter 2. However, it is a limited language and cannot do some of the operations that the other command languages presented in this book can. This does not mean the batch language is useless—far from it. For those wishing to extend the language, there are many third-party and shareware extensions available to do this. Batch files also work with popular graphical user interfaces (or GUIs) such as MS Windows or OS/2's Presentation Manager. Unless otherwise stated, all examples can be used by MS-DOS, PC DOS, and OS/2. Examples in this chapter have been tested under DOS 3.3, DOS 5.0 (the current release), and OS/2 1.21.

Examples and information specific to one platform or environment are highlighted by a change bar. Most examples have comments in brackets explaining what various statements in the batch program are doing. *Do not enter these bracketed comments if running any of these programs under DOS or OS/2!*

WHEN TO USE THE DOS or OS/2 BATCH LANGUAGE

The DOS or OS/2 batch language is especially useful for the following situations:

- Your in-house expertise is mainly in the DOS or OS/2 batch language and you need to create a program relatively fast.
- When the emphasis is on manipulating operating system commands instead of text or files.

- When file operations are simple (i.e. browsing a file, searching for a specific record, sorting a file, and adding/deleting/updating records to a file).
- When you need to provide some "housekeeping tasks" before processing an executable (i.e. .exe or .com files).
- When data types (strings or numbers) and flow control (IF, FOR-IN-DO, GOTO) structures are simple.
- When you want to create "personal commands" that enhance existing DOS or OS/2 commands. By using these "personal commands" together, you can create your own "personal environment."
- When portability is not a concern (unless porting to another PC-DOS/MS-DOS or OS/2)

HOW TO INVOKE DOS or OS/2 BATCH FILES

DOS batch files are usually invoked in foreground but in MS-Windows and OS/2 may be invoked in background (batch) as well.

Invoking Foreground DOS or OS/2 Batch Files

Listed below are some of the various ways to invoke a DOS or OS/2 batch file in foreground (*again, do not type in the descriptive text in brackets*):

DOS & OS/2

```
    prog1.bat
[The full batch file name. If invoking a second batch file, it does
not return to the main batch file on completion. For OS/2 sessions,
the batch file would be PROG1.CMD.]
    prog1 [Bat extension does not need to be specified.]
    call prog2
[Available in DOS 3.3 (and later) and OS/2, CALL invokes a second
batch file within the main batch file. This avoids starting a second
command processor and retains the values set by the second batch file
when returning to the first one. Note CALL can be used at the DOS or
OS/2 command prompt.]
    cmd /c dir c:\
[For OS/2 only, starts a new command processor and processes the
specified command.]
    command /c prog2
[Available in DOS 3.0 (and later) and OS/2, COMMAND/C invokes a sec-
ond command processor to process a second batch file within the main
batch file. The values set in the second batch file are lost on
returning to the first one. Note COMMAND can be used at the DOS or
OS/2 command prompt.]
```

WINDOWS—From File Manager

1. Once in Windows, select the File Manager.
2. Using the directory tree, find the appropriate batch file and double-click on it.

Or

2. Click on the file once (or Tab-Enter to select the file), then select RUN option under FILE on the menu. Enter the name of the file in the *command line* field.

WINDOWS—From Program Manager

1. If already added as an icon, then just double click on the icon. Use the NEW option under FILE on the menu to do this.

Or

2. Click on the file once (or Tab-Enter to select the file), then select RUN option under FILE on the menu.

Tips and Traps:

General

1. A batch program is a text file that is processed sequentially.
2. You may invoke a batch file along with nine parameters stored in %1–%9. (%0 is the partial or full filename of the batch file in UPPERCASE). This can be done with any of the preceding ways:
   ```
   CALL PROG2 A B C [%0 is PROG2.BAT,%1 is A, %2 is B, %3 is C]
   ```
3. The default file extension for DOS batch files is .BAT and for OS/2 is .CMD. The .CMD extension is also used by OS/2 REXX execs.
4. One possible trap is not specifying the .BAT or .CMD extension when an executable exists with the same name as the batch file (e.g. if PROG1.COM or PROG1.EXE *and* PROG1.BAT or PROG1.CMD all exist). DOS's or OS/2's default process order is first to invoke PROG1.COM, then PROG1.EXE, *then* PROG1.BAT (DOS) or PROG1.CMD (OS/2). Thus entering PROG1 may invoke PROG1.EXE not PROG1.BAT.
5. For OS/2 and DOS, CALL statements cannot include pipe ($|$) and redirection (>) operators.
6. The name of the command processor for DOS is COMMAND.COM and for OS/2 is CMD.EXE.

MS Windows

1. To customize a batch file to run under Windows, create a *PIF* Program interface file that has a .PIF extension. Customizing areas include memory, fore-

ground, and background processing. The batch file would usually then invoke a Windows or DOS application. You create a PIF file by invoking the PIF Editor in the Accessories window of the Program Manager. Two later sections on environment variables and extending the batch language have more information about Windows.

2. Note that the BAT extension under Windows's File Manager is "associated" by default as being a program file. This makes batch files "ready-to-run" when they are clicked. The icon looks like the following:

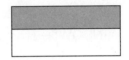

3. When using Windows, consider using WINSTART.BAT, a special batch file only for the 386 mode of Windows. An application invoked by this file is accessible only to all Windows applications.

OS/2

1. Under OS/2, a batch file invoked by either CALL or the batch file name may include a /Q qualifier. This is the equivalent of ECHO OFF—no displaying of the command as it is processed.

2. The START command can be used instead of/in addition to batch files for invoking an application, (whether or not it is a Presentation Manager application). Useful options include:

   /C or /K—executes program without invoking a new command processor (called CMD). How these two options differ is whether they close the window or application when processing is completed. /C closes the window or application while /K (the default) does not.

   /I—when the new command process (CMD) is invoked, it contains the environment variables set in CONFIG.SYS. Do not use /I with /C.

   /WIN—invokes as a windowed application while /PM invokes as a Presentation Manager application.

   Here is an example using the START command:
```
START /C "DIRECTORY LISTING" DIR/W [Creates a new window called
"directory listing." The directory is then listed and the new window
is closed on completion.]
```

3. The CMD command will create a second command processor and has qualifiers similar to the START command.

Invoking Background DOS or OS/2 Batch Files

There are currently two ways to process a DOS or OS/2 batch file in background—either using Windows or OS/2. Examples of how to do this are listed below.

OS/2

```
Detach prog2 [Name of batch file that doesn't prompt for input.
Returns the Process Identification Number is 29.]
```

MS Windows (386 mode only)

1. Invoke windows in 386 mode (*win /3*).
2. Invoke (click on) the PIF editor in the Accessories window of Program Manger.
3. Click on the *Execution: Background* box so it is checked (x).
4. Click on the *Advanced box* near the bottom of the screen.
5. Once on the advanced options screen, you may wish to change the foreground or background priority to make it run faster or slower. Look under multitasking options. (The default value is 50 for background and 100 for foreground and ranges from 0 to 10000.). By selecting settings from an application's menu, you can modify these values.
6. After saving the PIF file, reenter the Program Manager and select File from the menu and the NEW option. Click OK you want to create a new program item. Then enter a description (when the icon is displayed—this is optional) and the line to invoke the batch file with accompanying parameters.) The complete path is needed if the batch file is in a directory not in the search path specified by the PATH environment variable.

Tips and Traps:

General

1. Do not run batch files in background that prompt for input. Instead convert these files to include "pre-set" values.

OS/2

1. Piping (|) and redirection (< or >) operators are allowed in a DETACH command or the program specified by the DETACH command.
2. DETACH always returns a confirmation message similar to—*The process identification number is 88.*

THE FUTURE OF THE DOS or OS/2 BATCH LANGUAGE

From reading the trade journal headlines, one gets the impression that future direction of DOS, Windows, and OS/2 is changing weekly. Here are some current trends:

1. *DOS and the DOS batch language will continue to exist and be enhanced.* DOS 5.0 recently came out and later releases are planned by Microsoft and IBM. However, DOS is likely to be DOS in name only. Future releases may replace the file allocation table structure (or FAT) with a new approach, and the DOS command prompt being replaced by a graphical user interface. It is rumored that a future DOS release will contain Microsoft Windows as part of the product. How users will react to this remains to be seen.

2. *OS/2 looks like a niche product at best and has an uncertain future.* OS/2 appears best for client-server applications such as databases, local area networks, and real-time applications. With Microsoft recently reversing itself and promising to incorporate many OS/2 features (such as a high performance file system and multithreading) into a high-end version of Windows (called Windows NT), the advantage of going with OS/2 is becoming less apparent. Some feel that OS/2 2.0 (developed by IBM to support 16/32-bit OS/2 applications and multitasking of DOS and Windows applications) is OS/2's last chance. It appears clear that IBM will do their own development of OS2 3.0 (OS/2 running on non-Intel RISC computers) including MIPS now that Microsoft will be attempting to port Windows NT to these same machines including DEC. The short-term future is the simultaneous existence of several environments: Microsoft pushing DOS for the low-end, Windows for DOS for intermediate to advanced users, and Windows NT for high-end use. IBM is countering by actively promoting DR DOS on the low end and OS/2 2.0 as the platform that integrates DOS, Windows, and OS/2 applications seamlessly for intermediate and advanced users. See McLachan (1991) for a good description of the entire situation. Where can this all leave the user and developer communities but confused and frustrated!

3. *Microsoft will be pushing its "Visual Basic" as a replacement for DOS or OS/2 batch language. While IBM is countering with REXX.* With OS/2 and DOS becoming more graphical user interface (GUI) oriented, a new command language is needed to manipulate them. IBM has included REXX in both the standard and extended editions of OS/2 1.3 (REXX, which stands for REstructured eXtended eXecutor, is discussed in Chapter 4. It has been part of OS/2 Extended Edition since Version 1.2.) However, Microsoft has expressed no interest in REXX but instead is promoting its "Visual Basic" for Windows and in time for OS/2. It is rumored that a basic-like command language will be added to a future release of Windows beyond Version 3.1.

4. *In time, DOS or OS/2 will be compliant with the interface and calls specified in the IEEE POSIX [Portable Operating System X] standards.* These include POSIX 1003.1 [system interface], 1003.2 [shells and tools], and 1003.4 [real-time extensions]. This allows a POSIX application to run easily on other operating systems. At this time, only Microsoft has expressed support for POSIX for Windows NT (components of POSIX have not been specified). In addition, IBM has indicated that future releases of OS/2 will support key elements

of the Open Software's Foundation operating systems (OSF/1 and OSF/2). IBM's stand on POSIX support should be announced by publication of this book.

5. *OS/2 and Windows (NT) will be ported by Microsoft/IBM to RISC machines.* This was mentioned above. Rumors consistently mention DEC, IBM RISC, MIPS, and SPARC workstations.

6. *A DOS batch compiler* is of interest to many users but *is highly unlikely to be developed.* The reasons against this happening include:
   - IBM/Microsoft have expressed no interest in doing this.
   - Technically it is not easy to do this. Also, a compiler could not handle some of the ambiguity present in some variable assignments. The presence of a GOTO means that the flow of the batch file can be set to go anywhere such as into a loop.
   - There are some third-party products that already do something like this. These include: Pro Command and Extended Batch Language.
   - Even if a compiler was available with either DOS or OS/2, the batch language still has many limitations that make it worth considering using other command and programming languages.

7. *Scripting languages will emerge as an alternative to the DOS batch language.* Scripting languages like Claris's Hypercard for the Macintosh (and some day for PCs?) and Asymetrix's Toolbook for Windows use OOP (object-oriented programming) where you manipulate objects such as buttons (which you click on) or fields (where you enter text). Lamont Wood's article in *Byte* (April 1991) gives a good overview of this area.

DEVELOPING DOS or OS/2 BATCH LANGUAGE APPLICATIONS

Chapter 2 looked at three different common types of command language applications. The next three sections provide portable batch language sequences (unless otherwise stated) that are listed under the type of application where they are most commonly used. However, there is no reason why a particular batch language sequence could not be used by any type of application. The last section discusses some of the major concerns when developing batch language-based applications. It also looks at porting batch-language programs between DOS and OS/2 and migrating to other command languages.

FRONT-END DOS or OS/2 BATCH LANGUAGE APPLICATIONS

Two common tasks of DOS and OS/2 batch files are to provide input ("housekeeping") for executables (i.e. those files with .COM and .EXE extensions) and to run tasks on booting up a machine. The next section reviews sequences to perform both of these tasks.

How To Access Operating System Commands in a DOS or OS/2 Batch File

DOS and OS/2 are native environments, so no special interface is needed to access operating system commands from a batch file—just include the command that you want in the batch file. This is also true if running a DOS batch file from a DOS session within Windows or OS/2. However, the following DOS commands are not permitted or may not work correctly in these compatibility box environments:

1. Under Windows: Using APPEND, CHKDSK/F, COMPRESS and similar file optimization/undelete utilities, JOIN, SUBST, UNDELETE and UNFORMAT.
2. Under OS/2: Most file/directory commands will accept only one file or a directory as an argument (such as DIR and MKDIR). When you have more than one serial port in your PC and DEVICE=COM02.SYS is part of your CONFIG.SYS file, then include a SETCOM40 COM2=ON or something similar (in a DOS session under OS/2) to allow your DOS application to use the serial port.
3. For a few DOS or OS/2 commands, you can capture an ERRORLEVEL to see if it processed correctly. Note that only the following DOS or OS/2 commands return an ERRORLEVEL. (This is the same as an exit code or a return code.) Listed below are the DOS commands that give ERRORLEVELs as of DOS 5.0. Note that DOS 3.3 included only BACKUP, GRAFTABL, KEYB, REPLACE, RESTORE, and XCOPY.

BACKUP   0 (Worked) 1 (Can't find files) 3 (Ctrl-C pressed) 4 (Unknown error)

DISKCOMP   0 (Disks are the same), 1 (disks are not the same) 2 (Ctrl-C pressed), 3–4 (Errors)

DISKCOPY   0 (successful), 1 (Read/write error), 2 (Ctrl-C pressed) 3–4 (Errors)

FORMAT   0 (Worked), 3–4 (Error), 5 (Ctrl-C pressed)

GRAFTABL   0 (Worked) 1 (Replaced existing table), 2–3 (Error) 4 (Need DOS 5.0 and later)

KEYB   0 (Worked) 1–2 & 4–5 (Various errors)

REPLACE   0 (Worked), 2–3 (Invalid from files) 5,8,11 (Miscellaneous errors)

RESTORE   0 (Worked), 1–4 (Miscellaneous errors)

SETVER   0 (Worked), 1–5 (Invalid entry), 6–12 (Generally system file errors), 13–14 (Table operation errors)

XCOPY   0 (worked), 1 (invalid files) 2 (Ctrl-C pressed) 4–5 (Miscellaneous errors)

In all cases, having the following code detects an error:

```
IF ERRORLEVEL = 1 GOTO BADCOM [If non-zero ERRORLEVEL, then do]
```

4. Note you can execute a BASIC command line with a batch program: (DOS only). The following command displays the current time or date:

PC DOS or MS DOS (Versions 1–4)

```
if "%1"=="" goto exit [goes to exit label]
if "%1"=="DATE" goto runit
if "%1"=="TIME" goto runit
goto exit
:runit
    echo print %1$:system|gwbasic [MS-DOS Becomes PRINT DATE$ or
PRINT TIME$]
    echo print %1$:system|basica [PC DOS. Could also use BASIC
instead of BASICA.]

:exit
[Note colon to separate multiple BASIC commands.]
```

The following example works for DOS 5.0 and later, since QBASIC is a full-screen interpreter, which briefly displays when processing DATE.BAS or TIME.BAS. Note that QBASIC must be invoked with the /RUN qualifier and the invoked BASIC program must contain SYSTEM as its last statement for this to work.

DOS 5 and later

```
if "%1"=="" goto exit [goes to exit label]
if "%1"=="DATE" goto dateit
if "%1"=="TIME" goto timeit
goto exit
:dateit
    QBASIC /RUN DATE.BAS [DATE.BAS contains PRINT DATE$:SYSTEM]
goto exit
:timeit
    QBASIC /RUN TIME.BAS [TIME.BAS contains PRINT TIME$:SYSTEM]
goto exit
:exit
```

How To Capture Output From a Command in a DOS or OS/2 Batch File

Both DOS and OS/2 can capture output from an operating system command or executable, i.e. files ending with .exe or .com. These include:

1. For DOS, and OS/2, capturing output from a system command or an executable is done using redirection operators: Do not use redirection operators with the CALL command for either operating system. These manipulate the three types of input/output: STDIN or standard input—normally your keyboard—for application/command input, STDOUT or standard output—usually your monitor's screen for a command's or application's normal output, and STDERR (or standard error—normally your monitor's screen) for error messages encountered during the processing of a command or application.

   Redirection operators include:

   command> name—where *command* is a DOS command or executable and *name* is a file or device name such as NUL (null device), COMn (serial port) and LPTn (parallel port) that standard output is being redirected to *If the file already exists, it is overwritten.* If the file doesn't exist, then it is created.

   ```
   DIR/W>DIRLIST.TXT [Places the output from listing the current direc-
   tory in "wide" format into the file DIRLIST.TXT.]
   ```

   command>>name—where *command* is a DOS command or executable and *name* is a file or device name that standard output is being redirected to. *If the file already exists, then the redirected output is appended to the end of the file.* If the file doesn't exist, then it is created.

   ```
   DIR/W>>DIRLIST.TXT [Appends the output from listing the current
   directory in "wide" format to the end of the file DIRLIST.TXT.]
   ```

   command< name—where *command* is a DOS command or executable and *name* is a file or device name that standard input (or stdin) is being redirected to. *This allows a command to read input from a file instead of the keyboard.*

   Standard input redirection is used with the FIND (DOS's grep or search—finds text in a file), MORE (like its UNIX counterpart, displays output from a command/file by breaking it down to sections that each fits one screen and pauses when each screen "section" is displayed), and SORT (sorts a file in ascending or descending order or by using specified columns). These three commands are called *filters* because they process files in a specified way and "filter out" unnecessary information.

   ```
   more<a.txt [Displays the file a.txt a screen at a time]
   ```

2. OS/2 enhanced redirection allows identification of multiple files and the three types of input/output. This is done through the use of file handles—0 for STDIN, 1 for STDOUT and 2 for STDERR, and 3—9 for files used by appli-

cations. If used on the *right side of a redirection operator,* an ampersand must prefix the file handle. If used on the *left side of a redirection operator,* then the file handle requires no ampersand prefix.

```
dir/w>&2 OR dir/w>^&2
[Sends a directory listing (and errors) of the current directory in
"wide" format to standard error - - the monitor screen. If run under
DOS, this creates a file named &2.]
dir/w>dir.txt 2>&1
[Hard to understand at first but the above means: Send a listing of
the current directory in "wide" format to dir.txt. And also redirect
to dir.txt any error messages encountered - - redirection of STDERR
and STDOUT.
Note also the space between dir.txt and the 2 file handle.]
```

3. To further refine a command's output, it may make sense to first "pipe" the output from one command into another.

MS/PC DOS

```
DIR C:\DOS|FIND "TXT">TEXTLIST [List of TXT files]
DIR C:\DOS|FIND /C "TXT">>TEXTLIST [How many TXT files]
MORE<TEXTLIST [Display TEXTLIST]
  Displayed:
PROG1 TXT 32 3-08-84 1:18am
1
[Pipes output from DIR to FIND and redirects to the file named
TEXTLIST. Then displays to the screen the number of .TXT files in the
current directory which is one.]
```

OS/2

```
DIR|FIND /C "BAT" 2>&1 [Pipes output and errors from DIR to FIND and
redirects to standard output. Displays to the screen the number of
BAT files in the current directory. Beware- -also includes other
files containing the string "BAT" !]
DIR|(FIND ".DOC" & VER) 2>&1 [Pipes output and errors from DIR to
FIND and redirects to standard output. Displays to the screen the
number of .DOC files in the current directory and the current OS/2
version. Note the parentheses to place commands together and the & to
separate multiple commands.]
DIR *.TXT||DIR*.DOC 2>&1 (Displays names of .TXT files if there are
any (left-side task first). If none, then display names of .DOC files
if there any. (right-side task second). Redirect the output to stan-
dard output.
DIR *.TXT && DIR*.DOC 2>&1 (Use of double ampersand (AND). Displays
names of .TXT files if there are any (left-side task first). If there
are .TXT files, then display names of .DOC files if any (right-side
task second). Redirect the output to standard output.
```

What To Include in an AUTOEXEC.BAT File

The AUTOEXEC.BAT file is where users set up their own "personal environment." This is done by defining environment variables, paths to search for application and data files, setting function keys with ANSI escape sequences, and defining the default prompt. Use the DOS batch language to enhance your AUTOEXEC.BAT files in the following ways:

1. *Welcome commands* personalize a session:

In AUTOEXEC.BAT:

```
PROMPT Hello Hal. The date is $d and the time is $t$g
[No quotes are needed for strings, $d (current date), $t (current
time), and $g (greater than >)]


  Displayed:
Hello Hal. The date is Tues 3-08-1989 and the time is 12:15:16.38>
```

In AUTOEXEC.BAT:

```
PROMPT $p$g
[Display the current directory and the greater than sign. This is the
most commonly used prompt.]


  Displayed:
C:\BAT> [Or whatever the current directory is.]
```

Other useful prompts include $b (the | symbol), $e (escape—used with ANSI escape sequences. See a later section for more information), $g (greater than sign —>), $l (less than sign —<), $n, (current drive), $q (equals sign — =), $v (DOS version), and $_ (places the cursor on the next line).

Also use the ECHO command to display messages to the screen—these display if echo is on or off:

In AUTOEXEC.BAT

```
  echo WELCOME TO JOES PC
```

---

2. *Menus.* If you find yourself accessing several programs on startup, perhaps a menu might be useful:

```
     echo off [to display correctly]
:MENU100
     echo      ******************************
     echo      *1-Reports                   *
     echo      *2 Spreadsheets              *
     echo      *3 Games                     *
     echo      ******************************
     echo Enter your menu selection (1-3)
     READ CHOICE
[You must create/get a copy of a program to read input. ERRORLEVEL
will contain the number entered.]
     FOR %%A in (1 2 3) do if errorlevel %%A GOTO CHOICE%%A
[FOR counter must in ascending order if using ERRORLEVEL. Go to the
label based on choice selected—i.e choice 1 goes to label CHOICE1.
Note %%A instead of %A% is used. Would be %A if entered from the DOS
prompt in DOS 5.0.]
:BADCHOICE
     ECHO "Invalid choice. Please try again"
     CLS [Clears screen]
     GOTO MENU100
:CHOICE1
     (Report logic)
:CHOICE2
     (Spreadsheet logic)
:CHOICE3
     (Game logic)
```

Notes:
- With DOS 5.0, you can use a FOR statement from the DOS prompt. If used, only *one* % (such as %p) is needed for the counter variable that appears immediately after the FOR keyword in the statement. However, *two* %% (such as %%p) are required for the counter variable in a FOR statement within a batch file.
- Another approach is using secondary batch files matching the possible choices. So entering 1 invokes 1.bat, etc. The tradeoff in doing this is having more batch files that are harder to maintain.

3. Set up a "personal environment" using environment variables:
```
     SET BATDIR = C:\BAT
     [Set up aliases for directory. USE SUBST to assign to a logical
drive a specified directory]
     SET MONITOR = MONO
```

```
[Used for networks to determine which batch file to use]
SET USER = HAL
SET PATH = C:\;C:\123;C:\BATDIR
```
```
[Assigns search path for applications (really .BAT, .COM, .EXE
files.) Delimited by semicolons]
```

4. In addition to PATH, APPEND (DOS 3.3 and later) can be used to search for data files—that is, those files not having an extension of .BAT, .CMD, .COM, and .EXE. Note, many applications do not recognize APPEND settings. Use DPATH instead for OS/2.

```
APPEND /E
```
```
[Places the APPEND path values in an APPEND environment variable.]
```

```
APPEND C:\DATAFILE
```
```
[Searches the DATAFILE directory in the C drive when looking for
datafiles.]
```

What To Include in a STARTUP.CMD File

OS/2's equivalent of AUTOEXEC.BAT is STARTUP.CMD. Besides the preceding, the following are usually found in STARTUP.CMD:

1. Prompt has additional arguments under OS/2:
   $a—ampersand
   $c—left parenthesis and $f - right parenthesis
   $v—OS/2 (not DOS) version
2. Under OS/2, PATH also searches for .CMD files in the specified directories. DPATH can be used to search for data files (that is, those files not having an extension of .BAT, .CMD, .COM, and .EXE). Note, many applications do not recognize DPATH settings.
3. Enhanced redirection as shown in the section on capturing output from a command in a DOS or OS/2 batch file.
4. Using SETLOCAL, you can temporarily assign local environment variables yet still retain the current drive, directory, and environment variable values. These are in effect until the batch file ends and is recognized by any CALLed batch files.
   ```
   SETLOCAL
   SET ID=TEST [Temporarily overrides the current value of ID]
   ENDLOCAL
   [ID is reset when the batch file completes processing.]
   ```
5. Placing EXTPROC *program_name options* in a batch file allows use of another command processor (for example, the Perl command language interpreter) in processing that file.

SYSTEM/UTILITY DOS or OS/2 BATCH LANGUAGE APPLICATIONS

System & utility DOS or OS/2 batch language applications are similar to front-end applications but emphasize performing system and general utility operations.

Unfortunately, DOS does not include any built-in function library to obtain system information—type of machine, how much memory and type, video display, type of keyboard, and so on. Rubenking (1990) documents a program named BATCH-MAN that can be used in a batch file to provide this information. Chapters 4 and 5 show how REXX and DCL interpreters can easily obtain this information while running under DOS. Many similar shareware and commercial programs exist as well.

How Do I Perform File Operations?

File operations using DOS or OS/2 batch files are limited but are useful for simple flat file "database" tasks. The following shows the basic skeleton for DOS or OS/2 sequential file operations:

Add/Append

```
ECHO %1 %2 %3 %4>>FILE.DAT
[If the name of the batch file was FILEADD.BAT, then the user could
enter FILEADD PATRICK EWING 212-555-4290 28 at the DOS prompt. Since
the parsing is blank delimited, %1 is assigned PATRICK, %2 - - EWING,
%3 - - 212-555-4290, and %4 - - 28. This "record" is appended to the
end of FILE.DAT.]
```

Browse

```
FIND/N/I"%1"FILE.DAT
[Finds the "record(s)" matching the string in any case (because of
the /I) and their line number in FILE.DAT. If the name of the batch
file was FILEREC.BAT, then the user could enter FINDREC PATRICK. This
displays: [10] PATRICK EWING 212-366-4290 28. Note that /I is in DOS
5.0 and later only.
```

Delete

```
[Find all lines NOT matching a string (/v) in either upper or lower-
case (/I -DOS 5.0 and later). Write them out to autoZ.bat. Delete the
old autoexec.bat and rename autoz.bat to autoexec.bat]
FIND /V/I "%1" AUTOEXEC.BAT>AUTOZ.BAT
DEL AUTOEXEC.BAT
RENAME AUTOZ.BAT AUTOEXEC.BAT
[Note you will have to manually delete the first line that will look
like - - - - - AUTOEXEC.BAT - - - - .]
```

Sort

```
TYPE FILE.DAT|SORT /R/+26
[Sorts in descending order starting with column 26. SORT will work
with files up to 64K
```

How Can I Learn if a File Exists?

There are various ways to determine if a DOS or OS/2 file exists:

IF EXIST

```
IF EXIST C:\AUTOEXEC.BAT RENAME C:\AUTOEXEC.BAT AUTOEXEC.OLD
[Renames AUTOEXEC.BAT to AUTOEXEC.OLD if it exists]
```

IF NOT EXIST

```
IF NOT EXIST C:\LOG.LOG COPY A:\LOG.LOG C:
[IF LOG.LOG doesn't exist, then copy the LOG.LOG on A :\(floppy
drive) to C:\(the current directory on the hard drive)]
```

CHKDSK and FIND

```
CHKDSK/V |FIND "%1" [Before DOS 5.0, FIND is case sensitive- -BEWARE]
[Searches through a list of all files (including system and hidden
files) for a specified file.]
```

DIR and FIND

```
DIR%1|FIND"%2"
[If the above command was in a file named IFTHERE.BAT, someone could
enter IFTHERE C:\ AUTOEXEC.BAT. %1 is assigned to C:\ and %2 to
AUTOEXEC.BAT. The batch file would "pipe" a directory listing of the
C root directory to the FIND command that then displays the specified
file name (AUTOEXEC.BAT).]

[For large directories, the search could be made faster by sorting
first. Here are two ways to do this:]
                        DOS 4.01 and earlier
DIR %1|SORT/+1|FIND"%2" [Sorts the directory by file name. Before DOS
5.0, FIND is case sensitive- -BEWARE. This also finds strings match-
ing the file name.]
                        DOS 5.0 and later
DIR %1 /o:n|FIND/i"%2" [Sort the directory by file name- -no SORT
command needed]
```

Performing System Maintenance Using DOS or OS/2 Batch Files

A very common use of DOS and OS/2 batch files is performing system maintenance on your PC. Here are six common system maintenance tasks that a batch file can perform:

Add to the PATH list

```
SET PATH=%PATH%;%1
```
[Appends a new path to the old one (stored in the environment variable PATH.) Always issue a SET or ECHO %PATH% or PATH to display the current path. The above approach will not work with DOS 3.0. Or you can assign the current path to an environment variable and restore later:]

```
SET CURPATH=%PATH%
SET NEWPATH=C:\TEMPDIR
COPY A:\*.*C:\TEMPDIR
SET PATH=%CURPATH%
SET CURPATH=
```

Backup your hard drive

```
BACKUP C:\D:/S/A
ECHO BACKUP DONE
```
[Does an incremental backup (/A) to the D: drive (Probably a tape device or network) including all subdirectories. Could use replaceable parameters (%1) or environment variables to further customize the batch file.]

Clean up your file allocation table

```
ECHO N|CHKDSK C: /F
```
[Echo passes answer (N) to the prompt *"Recover lost data into files?""* Don't use this in a DOS session under Windows or under OS/2 (especially if something is running in background).]

Compress unneeded files

```
PKZIP %1 %2
```
[Compresses specified files %1 in a file named *the_value_of %2*.ZIP. This allows a simple way to archive unneeded files. Replace the above line with your favorite file compression command.]

Create a new directory

```
MKDIR %1 [creates the directory]
CD %1 [moves to it]
DIR [confirms in right directory]
```

Move files

```
XCOPY %1 %2/S /E
IF ERRORLEVEL 1 GOTO EXIT
IF ERRORLEVEL 0 DEL %1
[Copies the specified files (%1) to the new location (%2) including
subdirectories (/S) even if they are empty (/E). Then if successful,
delete the original files. You can add sequences for the nonzero
error level codes if desired.]
```

Using Environment Variables with DOS or OS/2 Batch Files

One of the more important components of the DOS or OS/2 batch language is the availability of environmental variables. There are many good references just on this topic. These include: Jaeschke (1990), Shaw (1987), and Vallino (1987). The following are tips and guidelines when using DOS or OS/2 batch files:

1. By entering SET, you can see what environment variables are defined and the corresponding values. The following are the default environment variables:

```
C:\>set
APPEND=C:\DATAFILE
[IN DOS 3.3 and later, search path for data files if APPEND
=C:\DATAFILE/E was issued. Use DPATH for OS/2.]

BOOKSHELF=C:\OS2\BOOK
[Since OS/2 1.2, location of the OS/2 on-line command reference]

COMSPEC=C:\COMMAND.COM
[Location and name of current command processor. For OS/2 is CMD.EXE]

DIRCMD /O:E/W
[In DOS 5.0 and later, sets the default qualifiers when using the DIR
command. This saves you typing DIR/O:E/W every time you run the DIR
command.]

DPATH=C:\DATAFILE
[Search path of data files if DPATH=C:\DATAFILE/E was issued. Use
APPEND instead for DOS.]

HELP=C:\OS2\HELP
[Location of HELP information]

PATH=C:\DOS;C:\BATDIR;C:\
[Search directory of all .BAT, .CMD, .COM, and .EXE files set by PATH
command.]

PROMPT=$p$g
[Prompt value defined by PROMPT command.]

TEMP=C:\TEMP
[In DOS 5.0 and later, the location of "work in progress" files while
```

performing operations. If you are using a RAM drive (such as RAM-DRIVE.SYS supplied with DOS 5.0 and later and also MS Windows), make sure that TEMP points to the RAM drive. (e.g. *set temp=D:\tmp*) Must always be a subdirectory that is not the root (C:\) directory.]

2. The name of the environment variable is always converted to uppercase.

3. A common problem is "environment variable rot." This is usually caused by gradually increasing the size of your PATH statement and adding SET commands, or adding applications that add their own SET commands to AUTOEXEC.BAT. Then one day the message "out of environment space" is on the screen and the memory-resident applications and other programs that depend on these variables fail. You have exceeded the default environment size of 127 or 160 characters. This depends on the DOS version. Also, PATH and COMSPEC use no less than 29 characters. To resolve this problem:

1. First, remove any unnecessary SET commands and reduce the size of your PATH command.

2. Add the following to your CONFIG.SYS, based on your DOS version:

DOS 2.1 and 3.0

In AUTOEXEC.BAT, SET DUMMY1=AAAAAAAAAAAAAAAAAAAAAAAAA.
Then once at the C prompt, SET DUMMY1=
[DUMMY1 sets the environment size and SET DUMMY1 = frees the space so you can use it. There are patches that you can add to COMMAND.COM to increase environment size as well.]

For DOS 3.1

SHELL=C:\COMMAND.COM /E:12 /P
[The value of /E is not bytes but a multiple of 16 and ranges from 11 (176 characters) to 62 (992 characters). Therefore, the above command specifies an environment size of 192 characters. Note this is NOT documented in the DOS manual.]

DOS 3.2 and later

SHELL=C:\COMMAND.COM /E:512 /P
[This sets command.com with a 512 character environment space. The value of /E can be from 160 to 32768. /P means keep the COMMAND.COM in memory and then execute AUTOEXEC.BAT. It also prevents you booting from a floppy so don't forget it!]
  Or
COMMAND /E:200 /P [Creates a secondary command processor whose values are lost upon completion. The value of /E can be from 160 to 32,768 characters.]

4. The following summarizes basic operations with environment variables:

Create/Update an environment variable

```
SET MONITOR=VGA
[Creates or updates the environment variable MONITOR and assigns a
value of VGA. Note no percentages around MONITOR. Having a space
between MONITOR and the equals signs will include the blank in the
environment name and may cause problems.]
```

Display the setting of an environment variable

```
SET
[Display values of all currently set environment variables]
  Or
ECHO %var_name%
[Such as echo %VGA%. Note the use of % as found with replacement
parameters. (such as %1.) Under DOS, this will only work correctly
from a batch file and not from the DOS prompt. With OS/2, it will
work from either location.]
```

Clears the setting of an environment variable

```
SET MONITOR=
[Sets MONITOR to null and no longer exists.]
```

Using the environment variable in other statements

```
ECHO %MONITOR% [Display value of monitor]

IF %MONITOR% = VGA goto VGA [Use value of MONITOR to determine which
label to go to.]
```

5. For C programmers, included in the library <stdlib.h> are usually two functions to obtain the current value of an environment variable (getenv) and to modify an environment variable (putenv—not part of ANSI C).

   Unfortunately, you cannot easily pass an environment variable value to a C program:

```
#include <stdio.h>
#include <stdlib.h>
char *estring;/* Getenv and Putenv both return a pointer to char.*/
main()
{
```

```
estring =getenv("PROMPT");/*Get prompt value if it exists*/

/* IF getenv is not NULL (If a value for PROMPT exists, then*/
/*display it.)*/
if (estring != NULL) printf("The value of PROMPT is %s",estring);
else {/*If no PROMPT value, then set one and later display it*/
        putenv("PROMPT=$P$G");/*Define new value for*/
        /*PROMPT*/
        estring =getenv("PROMPT");/*Get new PROMPT value */
        printf("The value of PROMPT is %s",estring);/*Then*/
        /*display it*/
    }
}
```

Petzold (1987), Jaeschke (1990), and Vallino (1987) all have C examples on what you can do with environment variables. The code is no longer than the preceding but produces powerful results.

6. The following is reprinted with permission of Tom Haapanen and comes from his very useful document on frequently asked questions in the comp.windows.ms Usenet newsgroup:

Why do I run out of environment space when I run a batch file in a DOS session?

When Windows starts up a DOS session, by default it gives the session an environment of 224 bytes or the space required to hold your current environment, whichever is larger. If you need more space, there are two methods of circumventing this. In order of desirability:

```
1. Use a .pif file file for each DOS application you run. In this you
can specify the environment size by using the /e:nnn option (Author's
note: see earlier in this section.) You need a separate DOS file for
each program. (You can, however, just create a command.pif with a
suitable /e:nnn, and then specify in win.ini a line such as:
[Extensions]
bat=command.pif ^.bat //for DOS users
ksh=sh.exe ^.ksh     //for MKS users
With this, you can create batch file icons freely, and still get the
options specified in command.pif.
                            Or
2. Specify a dummy variable such as DUMMY1=xxxxx..../ before starting
up Windows. Then, as the first thing in each DOS session, do
 set DUMMY1=
to reclaim the space used by DUMMY1 for other environment variables.
```

7. With GWBASIC and IBM BASIC 3.0 and later, (packaged with DOS 3.0 and later), you can now set and display environment values. These were undocumented commands in earlier BASIC versions. Here are examples on how to do this:

Assign a value to an environment variable

```
ENVIRON "NAME=JORGE" [Assigns Jorge to the environment variable
NAME.]
```

Display an environment variable's value:

```
PRINT ENVIRON $("PROMPT")
```

Remove an environment variable

```
ENVIRON "PROMPT=" or ENVIRON "PROMPT=;"
```

---

8. The following are some tips when debugging environment variables:
   a. If an environment variable called name is not displayed or shown as % name, then you did not enter the environment name correctly. Check if the name is mispelled or missing a beginning or closing percent sign. Especially in a FOR statement.
   b. You have assigned a value to an environment variable but it is not displaying. A SET command will quickly reveal if a blank was included when you created the environment variable. If this is the case, delete the environment variable and reassign it to a variable name without a blank or change all appropriate commands to include a blank when using that environment variable.
   c. There are many useful shareware software in debugging environment variables. Two of these are:
      ENVREP, environment variable reporter, created by Barry Simon and Richard Wilson and posted on Compuserve. It displays the total available environment size, the environment size used, and the total amount used by each environment variable.
      ENVSIZE also displays the environment size but also allows you to change it for PCs with DOS 3.0 and earlier. It is available from Compuserve at the following address: Charles P Scott/Team Alpha, 519 Garden Springs Drive, Mount Sterling, Kentucky, 40353. There appears to be no requirement other than registering the software.

SELF-CONTAINED DOS or OS/2 BATCH LANGUAGE APPLICATIONS

Self-contained DOS or OS/2 applications are one or more batch files (and sometimes compiled programs) oriented to end-users instead of Computer Center staff. Sequences in this section include (1) capturing, parsing, and validating user input, (2) communicating between a nested batch file and the main batch file, and (3) miscellaneous operations (such as changing the case of a string).

How To Capture User Command Line Values

Up to ten **replaceable parameters** can be specified when invoking a command procedure. These are stored in local symbols %1 through %9 as character strings. Note that %0 stores the file name of the batch file. Parameters, when entered on the command line, are separated by spaces. The cumulative length of the replaceable parameters can be no more than 127 characters. If there are more command line values than replaceable parameters specified in a batch file, then the extra values are not assigned.

Here are some tips and traps when capturing command line input:

1. Use the SHIFT command if you wish to input more than nine parameters. Note that you cannot recall past parameters once the "shift" has taken place.

From DOS or OS/2 prompt:

```
DLOOP A.LOG B.LOG C.LOG D.LOG E.LOG F.LOG G.LOG H.LOG I.LOG J.LOG
```

In DLOOP.BAT

```
LOOP1:
    IF "%1" == ""GOTO EXIT
    DIR %1
    SHIFT
    GOTO LOOP1
:EXIT
    ECHO completed
[A label cannot be the last line in some versions of OS/2 if a GOTO
refering to that label is used.]
```

---

2. Since % always has a special meaning in a batch file, you must specify two %s, so it is viewed as a % character rather than as indicating a replaceable parameter.

3. Use IFs to validate input and decide where to branch based on the parameter value. (Do note that DOS versions through 2.1 have problems if the replaceable parameter (i.e. %1) is on the left side. *Note that* two *equals signs are used for string comparisons and that there is no space between the replaceable parameter (%1 for the example below) and the blank string test character ($ for the example below).*

Test for blanks

```
IF %1$==$ goto noval
```
Or

```
IF "%1"=="" goto noval
```
[If the user does not enter a value when invoked, this translates to if $= $ which is a true condition. Other characters could be used instead of $ such as double or single quotes.]

Branching

```
IF "%1"=="DEL" GOTO DEL100
(later in command procedure)
:DEL100
```

---

4. It is recommended to put both sides of an IF string comparison command in quotes so zero-length strings don't unexpectedly stop the batch file from processing and to compare strings with embedded blanks and special characters.

Good

```
IF %1==DEL
```
[If blank may give a "syntax" error" or "DELETE was unexpected at this time".]

Better

```
IF "%1"=="DEL"
```

How To Create Menus, User Prompts, and Confirmation Messages

This can be done with the ECHO command (see the section on how to capture input).

ECHO for prompting input:

```
Echo Enter your state of residence:
READ ST [Shareware/third-party command]
```

ECHO for Menus

```
ECHO*********************************************
ECHO*Please Enter ONE of the following:          *
ECHO* 1 - 1990 Report                            *
ECHO* 2 - 1991 Report                            *
ECHO* 3 - 1992 Report                            *
ECHO ********************************************
   PAUSE [Pause to allow user to read choices.]
   READ CHOICE [Shareware/third-party command]

 ECHO for confirmation messages
set prt=
set ryear=
set ryear=1991
[No spaces between = and value]
set prt=prt1
echo Report for %ryear% is queued to %prt% [Displayed: Report for
1991 is queued to prt1]
```

The following are tips and guidelines in creating display output:

1. You can use terminal escape sequences to enhance your display output. This is discussed in a later section on using escape sequences with DOS or OS/2 batch language.
2. Document at the start of your batch file each replaceable parameter and valid/default values.
3. ECHO ON enables displaying of ECHO text, ECHO OFF disables displaying ECHO text starting the next message. With DOS 3.3 and later or OS/2 1.2 and later: (1) @ECHO OFF disables displaying of ECHO text starting with this command and (2) @ in front of any DOS or OS/2 command disables displaying just that command.
4. Putting a CLS to clear the screen before the menu will always guarantee that the complete menu appears on the screen.

How To Capture User Input

Unfortunately, DOS or OS/2 files can accept parameters only through the command line. There is no command that accepts input from within a batch file.

However, there are various approaches you can use to build your own command to do this:

1. Create a DEBUG script. See Axelson and Hughes (1989), and Mason (1990) on how to do this.
2. Create an Assembler program. See Volkstorf (1987).
3. Create a BASIC program that generates a COM file. See Axelson and Hughes (1989) on how to do this.
4. Create a BASIC program to capture input. Since BASIC is included with DOS, this will be for many the easiest way to do this. A routine can be found in Jourdain (1986, p. 96).
5. Create a C program. A variety of public domain and C compilers are available for DOS such as Small C and DSMET C. Here is a program that captures input and then returns to the batch file the decimal ASCII value:

TESTIT.C

```
#include <stdio.h> /*Needed for printf*/
#include <stdlib.h> /*Needed for getchar*/
main()
{/*main function*/
        int c; /*needed to capture*/
        printf("Enter your input character");
        /*Could change the program so value is passed by batch*/
        /*file*/
        c = getchar(); /* Capture one character and assign to*/
        /*c.*/
        exit(c); /* exit program and pass to batch file (via the DOS*/
        /*ERRORLEVEL command)*/
```

Regardless what approach you adopt, you then use an IF ERRORLEVEL or FOR loop to process the input. A common "gotcha" with IF ERRORLEVEL is that the IF ERRORLEVEL is true if the value is equal *or greater than* the test condition. Hence you will probably have to have multiple IF ERRORLEVELs (with the highest ERRORLEVEL first) or a FOR (with the lowest ERRORLEVEL first) statements. Here are some common ERRORLEVELs:

Decimal Value	Translates to
48–57	Numbers 0–9 (such as decimal 48 is 0, decimal 1 is 49).
65–90	Uppercase A–Z (such as decimal 65 is uppercase A, decimal 66 is uppercase B).

97–122 Lowercase a–z (such as decimal 97 is lowercase a, decimal 98 is lowercase b).

The following program checks if the user inputs upper- or lowercase A. Because an errorlevel is true for a value equal or greater than a condition, it takes 4 IF ERRORLEVEL commands instead of 2 to handle all cases:

```
echo on
testit [The compiled input program shown earlier.]
[98 = lowercase b-z, decimal 98 and higher]
[97 = lowercase a]
[66 = uppercase b-z and decimal 66 through 96]
[65 lowercase a]
if errorlevel 98 goto loth
if errorlevel 97 goto la
if errorlevel 66 goto uoth
if errorlevel 65 goto ua
goto exit
:la
    echo lowercase a
    goto exit
:ua
    echo uppercase a
    goto exit
:loth
    echo other lowercase letter
    goto exit
:uoth
    echo other uppercase letter
    goto exit
:exit
echo completed
[A label cannot be the last line in some versions of OS/2 if a GOTO
refering to that label is used.]
```

If possible, try to specify the default and valid values as part of your display prompt—to minimize the surprises to you and the user.

How To Parse Command Line/User Input

The DOS or OS/2 batch language has very limited parsing capabilities. Values entered on a command line are parsed by blanks into the appropriate replaceable parameter. (So a value up to the first blank goes into %1 and so on.) If you need to parse into substrings, consider the following:

1. Look at shareware/commercial alternatives, including "batch language extenders."

2. Combine batch files with those from another command language such as CLIST, DCL, REXX, or Perl.

3. Write a program in another programming language that you can call in a batch file.

How To Validate Command Line/User Input

A previous section discussed some of the validations you can do on command line values. And another section showed that you can create a program to capture user input from within a batch file and validate for selected values using IF ERRORLEVEL. This section shows other validations you can do on user input captured from within a batch file:

1. The following are additional IF ERRORLEVEL statements to consider:
```
IF ERRORLEVEL 12 [Form Feed]
IF ERRORLEVEL 32 [Blank or Space]
```

2. One way to set up data type validation:
```
set dtype=
testit [Compiled input program shown in How to Capture User Input.]
for %%p in (65 90 97 122) do if errorlevel %%p set dtype=CHAR
    if "%dtype%"=="CHAR" goto ctype
for %%p in (48 57) do if errorlevel %%p set dtype=NUM
    if "%dtype%"=="NUM" go to vtype
:ctype
    echo "%dtype%" is valid
    goto exit
:vtype
    echo "%dtype%" is invalid
    go to loopit [not shown]
:exit
[A label cannot be the last line in some versions of OS/2 if a GOTO
refering to that label is used.]
```

3. Using IF EXIST to see if a file exists:
```
if exist goto label_name:
if not exist goto label_name
```

Date and Time Operations With DOS or OS/2 Batch Language

Although DOS includes DATE and TIME commands, batch files have no direct way to capture the current date and time. For example, there are no environment variables called %TIME% and %DATE%. Options include the following:

1. Writing a batch file that captures the current date from the DATE command. Sources include at *PC World,* September 1989, p. 215, *LAN* magazine, May 1990, p. 14, or *LAN Technology,* October 1990, p. 65. The following is a com-

mon approach to do this: Note that it varies from DOS versions, on how to pass a blank line. This is discussed in a later section.

```
ECHO:|DATE>>log.log
```

Note that OS/2 will do the same thing but puts an extra DATE prompt in log.log.

2. Using a BASIC program that writes the value of DATE$ or TIME$ to a file which a batch file could read and capture. *PC World,* July 1990, p. 202 has further information.) The following displays the current date or time:

```
    IF "%1"=="" goto exit [goes to exit label]
    IF "%1"=="DATE" goto runit
    IF "%1"=="TIME" goto runit
:runit
    ECHO PRINT %val%$:system|gwbasic
:exit
[Note colon to separate basic commands. See the notes in the section
on Operating System Commands on using this batch file.] .
```

3. Using an assembly program that uses function 2AH of DOS interrupt 21H to get the date. CX holds offset from a base year such as 10 from 1990 being 10 years after base year 1990, DH holds the month, and DL holds the day. See Jourdain (1986, p. 52) on how to do this. Or use function 2CH of Interrupt 21H.

4. Write a C program that outputs a date and time (perhaps using the asctime function to capture the date or time).

5. Write a program in another command or programming language.

6. Terber (1990) describes an interesting way to assign today's date to an environment variable. This is done by "touching" the file with the COPY command to get today's date which does a FIND until the value is obtained.

Here are some tips on date and time operations with DOS or OS/2 batch language:

1. By changing the *COUNTRY* = command, you can change the default date time, and currency format. For example, the default date format for US is mmddy, but for much of Europe it is ddmmyy.

2. Swan (1988, p. 271) created a .COM using DEBUG that returns the day of the week (0 equals Sunday, 1 = Monday, 6 = Saturday). He then uses IF ERROR-LEVEL commands to see if a utility such as CHKDSK, file optimizer, etc.) should run that day. Or you can use function 2CH of Interrupt 21H and get the day of the week from AL.

Text Case Operations With DOS or OS/2 Batch Language

The following are tips and traps when dealing with text case operations for both DOS or OS/2 batch language:

1. When dealing with command line input, you will need at least two IF statements to test upper- and lowercase for a string (because IF is case-sensitive):

```
IF "%1"=="at" goto runit
IF "%1"=="AT" goto runit
IF "%1"=="aT" goto runit
IF "%1"=="At" goto runit
```
Or

```
for %%p in (at AT aT At) do if "%1"=="%%p" goto runit
[Note that a FOR still checks all conditions so it isn't necessarily
more efficient, but does take less space.]
```

2. Another common technique to convert a string is assigning it to a path or PATH (APPEND or DPATH) environment variable. This does not work under OS/2:

```
SET VAR = lc
SET HOLDER=%PATH% [holds path]
SET PATH=%VAR% [assigned value to change]
SET NEWVAR=%PATH% [assigned in upper case. Use this instead of VAR
here on.]
SET PATH=%HOLDER% [reassigned old path]
SET HOLDER=
SET VAR=
```

3. Other ways would be to write a sequence in another program or command language (with OS/2, REXX is included with the operating system). This could include using VCL's F$EDIT function, REXX's ARG and TRANS-LATE function, Perl's tr, and C's toupper/tolower functions.

String Operations With DOS or OS/2 Batch Language

Without any built-in functions, string operations for batch files are limited. Here are some tips and guidelines when performing string operations with DOS or OS/2 batch language:

1. Consider using another command language such as CLIST, VCL, REXX (included with OS/2), or Perl. All of these have adequate string handling capabilities, but REXX is especially strong in this area.

2. Write a BASIC or GWBASIC program that does the string operation. The program below returns a substring starting from the middle of the string continuing to the end (substitute BASIC or BASICA for PC DOS users. This will not work with OS/2 and Quick Basic included in DOS 5.0).

```
IF "%1"=="" GOTO EXIT [The statement below doesn't work with blanks.]
ECHO X$="%1":B=INT(LEN(X$)/2):PRINT MID$(X$,B):SYSTEM|GWBASIC
:EXIT [Print half of a string.]
```

3. Write a program in another programming language.

How Do I Pass Information Between Batch Files?

Information (such as return codes and variable values) are passed between DOS or OS/2 batch files in a variety of ways.

1. All environment variables (except %0-%9) are global wherever they are created:

Main batch file

```
SET X=21
CALL BAT2
ECHO %X% %Y% [Returns 21 B. B was set in BAT2.BAT or BAT2.CMD]
```

BAT2.BAT or BAT2.CMD

```
ECHO %X% [Returns 21. This was set in the main batch file.]
SET Y=B
EXIT
```

---

2. Passing parameters when invoking a second batch file within the main batch file: (In OS/2, variables in a SETLOCAL-ENDLOCAL structure can be used by CALLed batch files.)

Within FIRST.BAT command procedure

```
    CALL12 88 HELLO
[Passes three values on invocation 12 to %1, 88 to %2, HELLO to %3]
```

---

3. Neither DOS nor OS/2 has an EXIT or RETURN statement to pass ERROR-LEVELS (exit) so you can use (IF ERRORLEVEL). However, it is easy to create such a command. The source is included in the upcoming section on extending the DOS or OS/2 batch language. In addition, you can't redirect output—the following is **invalid** for DOS and OS/2:
   ```
   CALL BAT2>OUT.OUT [Where bat2 has an echo statement passing a string.
   Under DOS, the file is created but is blank.]
   ```
4. However, COMMAND/C allows redirection and piping, so it can pass the results of a batch file processing. The tradeoff is that you are invoking a second command processor, which uses more memory. Also, environment variables created this way are not retained by the main batch program.
5. Although you can run DOS batch files under OS/2 and the reverse as well, the command processor will "fail" on any statements not supported under that operating system. These are discussed in an upcoming section on portability of DOS or OS/2 batch files.

Subroutines and Batch Files

For both the DOS and OS/2 batch languages, subroutines or functions are not directly supported—that is, calling a routine in the same file. However, Rubenking (1989, pp. 369–370) lists two ways to simulate subroutines for the DOS batch language. In addition, all the other command languages that run under DOS or OS/2 to support subroutines and functions. These include CLIST, DCL, REXX, and Perl. If this is a desired feature, then consider porting to one of these command languages.

How to Create Reports Using DOS or OS/2 Batch Language

The DOS or OS/2 batch language was not designed to generate reports, so only the simplest of reports are possible. Here are some tips and guidelines to do this:

1. Use environment variables to customize your report:
   ```
   @ECHO OFF [So report is displayed correctly]
   SET DATE=10-10-91
   SET COMP=POETRY BY DAY
   ECHO————————————%DATE%————————
   ECHO————————REPORT FOR %COMP% COMPANY————————————
   TYPE REPT1.TXT|MORE [display report pausing at each screen of infor-
   mation]
   ```
2. Combine batch output with another command language such as CLIST, DCL, REXX (included in OS/2), or another programming language to produce a desired report.

Which Version of DOS or OS/2 Do I Have?

Knowing the DOS or OS/2 version is useful in discovering what DOS features and commands are available and in debugging batch files. For example, DOS 2.0 added redirection, piping, and many batch file commands; 3.3 added @ to suppress command display; and CALL to cleanly nest batch files. The following shows one way of getting this information:

```
VER>>LOG.LOG
```

Using Escape Sequences With DOS or OS/2 Batch Language

By placing DEVICE=ANSI.SYS in your CONFIG.SYS, you can use escape sequences to control various screen attributes. These are nearly identical to those found in DEC—VT 100 and higher—terminals and third-party DEC terminal emulators. Here are some tips and guidelines to do this:

1. See the BCS (1988), Liebing (1990), Microsoft (1983) and Winer (1987) references for additional information.
2. As an alternative, the Norton Utilities and other software allow you to enter commands in the batch file that easily enable colors using ANSI.SYS.
3. You can place escape sequences in a batch file in various ways.

TO ENHANCE A PROMPT

```
ANSI [OS/2 only - - allows use of ANSI escape sequences]
prompt $e[31;44m [Gives the prompt a red foreground and a blue back-
ground.]

prompt $e[31;44m $e[1m
[Same as above but in bold. Note you can set multiple escape
sequences with the same prompt.
Note multiple escape sequences in the same $e are separated by semi-
colons and you must have an ECHO ON before issuing any PROMPT $E com-
mand. Save your prompt and later restore it before doing the above.]
See macros and the DOS batch files on how in DOS 5.0 and later using
DOSKEY to save prompts as a macro.
```

USING DEBUG

```
e 200 1B "[31;44m"
```

IN A FILE

```
ECHO ←[31;44m
[To get escape, press ALT-27 from the numeric keypad. The ← should
then appear.]
```

4. Some of the common escape sequences are listed below. Microsoft's *DOS Technical Reference* and similar books have more escape sequences.

PROMPT $e[0m   Normal

PROMPT $e[1m   Bold

PROMPT $e[4m   Underscore

PROMPT $e[5m   Blink

PROMPT $e[7m   Reverse

PROMPT $e[30m   Black text (foreground)

PROMPT $e[31m	Red text (foreground)
PROMPT $e[32m	Green text (foreground)
PROMPT $e[33m	Yellow text (foreground)
PROMPT $e[34m	Blue text (foreground)
PROMPT $e[40m	Black screen (background)
PROMPT $e[41m	Red screen (background)
PROMPT $e[42m	Green screen (background)
PROMPT $e[43m	Yellow screen (background)
PROMPT $e[44m	Blue screen (background)
PROMPT $e[x:yH	Place cursor at line x and column y.

5. A common technique is using ANSI escape sequences to remap function keys. This can be done by having the AUTOEXEC.BAT include *prompt $e* commands to customize your environment and the last prompt being the prompt for your session:

```
ECHO ON [Needed by ANSI.SYS]
PROMPT $e[0;62;"FORMAT A:";13p
[Pressing F4 which has a scan code of 62 will issue a FORMAT A: com-
mand. The 13 simulates an ENTER key being pushed and the p means that
it is a key remapping. This does not work under OS/2.]
```

Here are commonly used scan codes—the complete list can be found in the Microsoft BASIC manual:

1 (ESC), 57 (Space Bar), 59 (F1), 60(F2), 61(F3), 62(F4), 63(F5), 64(F6), 65(F7), 66(F8), 67(F9), 68(F10), 84(Shift-F1), 93(Shift-F10), 94 (Ctrl-F1), 103(Ctrl-F10), 104(Alt-F1), 113(Alt-F10), 133(F11), 134(F12), 135(Shift-F11), 136(Shift-F12), 137(Ctrl-F11), 138(Ctrl-F12), 139(Alt-F11), and 140(Alt-F12)

6. You can use this technique to send escape sequences to a printer:

```
ECHO (ALT-15)>LPT1:
[Press 15 from numeric keypad. Sends escape sequence for condensed
print]
PRINT TEXT.TXT LPT1 or COPY TEXT.TXT>LPT1:
[Print file in condensed print]
ECHO (ALT-18)>LPT1
 [Press 18 from numeric keypad. Resets condensed print.]
```

7. Under OS/2, ANSI ON (the default) or ANSI OFF enables/disables escape sequences being processed.

Batch Files and LANs

Many of the DOS or OS/2-based local area networks (or LANs) use a script language that is similar to the DOS or OS/2 batch language. These scripts can interact with batch files. *LAN* magazine has a monthly column called Patches and Fixes that has many examples in this area. See Hiners (1990, 1991) and Stone (1990) for more ideas. Some ideas of generic batch files that can be used with LANs are listed below:

LOGIN SCRIPTS

```
SET STATION=1
SET ID=DAVE
SET PRINTER=PRT2
SET DATE=%1
SET MONTH=NOV
echo %ID% LOGIN %DATE%>>%ID%%MONTH%.DAT
[Writes to DAVENOV.DAT - - DAVE LOGIN 10-10-91]
LOGIN %STATION% %ID% %PRINTER% [or the appropriate login command]
```

LOGOUT SCRIPTS

```
DEL*.TMP
COPY %ID LOGOUT %DATE%>>%ID%%MONTH%.DAT
logout [or the appropriate logout command]
```

ACCOUNTING

```
FIND /C "DAVE LOGIN" %ID%%MONTH%.DAT
[how many times Dave logged in this month? Returns -----DAVENOV.DAT: 1]
```

Cropsey (1991) mentions that the DOS SET command in Novell scripts cannot have environment variables with underscores in them. This works correctly under DOS.

Macros and DOS Batch Files

DOS 5.0 added a new dimension to the DOS batch language with the ability to recreate macros. **Macros** are "mini-DOS batch files" stored in memory that can store and recall up to 127 characters that perform a sequence (such as accessing an application.) This macro can be invoked by the *doskey* command followed by the macro name. You should consider using keyboard macros when:

- You have more than adequate RAM to run the macro.
- There is a repetitive task(s) that you use moderately to heavily on a daily basis.
- You need faster performance than batch files.
- You need to group a series of commands together as one unit.

- The sequence is up to 127 characters.
- The sequence is not dependent on environment variables.

CREATING MACROS

```
doskey viewit=type autoexec.bat$bmore$t type config.sys$bmore
```

```
[$b or $B=same as piping, $t or $T= command separator. Note that
macros can only be created but not used in a batch file.]
```

DELETING MACROS

```
doskey viewit =
```

LIST ALL MACROS

```
doskey /macros or doskey /m
[Returns a blank line if there are no defined macros. If viewit was
defined, would return viewit=type autoexec.bat$bmore$t type
config.sys$bmore.]
```

RUNNING A MACRO

```
viewit
[May enter up to nine parameters after the macro name such as viewit
1 2]
```

SAVE A MACRO IN A BATCH FILE
(OR HOW TO KEEP A PARTIAL SESSION LOG)

```
doskey /history>viewit.mac or doskey/h>viewit.mac
```

The following are tips and guidelines when using macros with batch files:

1. We already listed above some of the special operators that can be used in a macro. Here is the complete list:

$*　　　　　A replaceable parameter that captures everything entered after the macro name (same as all the values of $1–$9 together).

$1–$9　　　Replaceable parameters that correspond the nine parameters that may be entered after the macro name upon invocation.

$$	Translates to $.
$B or $b	Translates to | (piping).
$G or $g	Translates to > (redirect output).
$L or $l	Translates to < (redirect input).
$T or $t	Use to separate multiple commands.

2. For OS/2, you can simulate macro commands by using special operators: ^ allows you to use an operator as a character; () places commands as one unit, & separates multiple commands, && performs a second task if the first task is successfully completed, || performs the first task if true, else performs the second task.

3. To eliminate the problem of not having a large enough buffer to store the macro, enter *doskey /bufsize=2048* or a size larger than the default 512 bytes. If DOSKEY is already enabled, enter *doskey /reinstall /bufsize=2048*.

4. $0 is undefined and is not the name of the macro.

5. Spaces before or after the equal signs in the macro creation have no effect on processing.

6. Environment variables can be defined but cannot otherwise be used in macros.

7. Macros can be used to invoke batch files. Batch files can only create but not invoke macros. You also cannot nest macros.

Blank Lines And DOS Batch Files

When using some DOS and OS/2 commands in a batch file, you often have to simulate pressing an enter key, such as using the DATE and TIME commands. The following are just some of the characters that can generate blank lines within batch files (others are also available). *Note the ALT-space-(255) is the only method that works on all DOS versions.*

DOS 3.0 AND LATER/OS/2

```
ECHO. or ECHO+ or ECHO: or ECHO (Alt-space-255) — pressing 255 on
numeric keypad
```

BEFORE DOS 3.0

```
ECHO= or ECHO; or ECHO: or ECHO (Alt-space-255) — pressing 255 on
numeric keypad
```

OTHER DOS or OS/2 BATCH LANGUAGE CONCERNS

This section is concerned with those topics that are appropriate for all types of DOS or OS/2 batch language applications. This includes porting batch language programs between DOS and OS/2 and converting to command languages.

How Do I Debug DOS or OS/2 Batch Files?

The following are tips and guidelines in debugging DOS or OS/2 batch files:

1. A simple debugger available for DOS or OS/2 is enabled by entering ECHO ON. Entering just ECHO shows if the current setting is ON or OFF. This displays each command processed including symbolic substitution of replaceable parameters. Note that the default is to leave this on. In DOS 3.3 and later plus OS/2, this can be turned off by placing an ECHO off at the start of your batch file or @ to suppress messages/output from one command. In earlier releases, patches are available to make the default ECHO OFF for all releases DOS 3.0 and later. These are listed in a note that Jon Wright posted on the Usenet MS-DOS groups in late 1989 that is reposted from time to time. These are also stored in the simtel anonymous ftp site (26.2.0.74) and simtel echo servers in PD1:<MSDOS.BATUTL> ECHOOFF.PAT.

2. The following tips may help in debugging a problem:
   a. Entering just SET or ECHO %*var*% shows the current value of environment variable *var*. Knowing the current value can explain why an IF or FOR command is being ignored.
   b. Entering ECHO goto *label xxx* can be useful in understanding how a batch file is branching.
   c. Examining ERRORLEVEL to see how successful an executable was.

3. Use the following general approach in debugging problems:
   What happened? Describe action—what happened, what was supposed to happen?
   Record all error messages.
   Gather more information about the problem:
   Where exactly is the error happening—on invocation, at a certain label, when invoking another batch file, or invoking an executable?
   Getting the problem to occur in a consistent fashion makes it easier to resolve.
   Use the techniques mentioned in point 3.
   Make an educated guess about what caused the problem and a way to test it.

Perform the test. If it works, there is no need to go further. Otherwise return to the gather-more-information step.

4. An earlier section discusses how to debug common environment variables problems. The ECHO and SET are helpful in this process.

The Elements of DOS or OS/2 Batch Language Style

In spite of its limitations, there are several styles for developing easy-to-follow and efficient batch language programs. This section discusses some of the elements of good batch language style. For those seeking further information on this topic, consult these references—Val Wolverton (1991) and Lante Corporation (1987).

The following are general rules that apply to all types of batch language applications—use them based on your personal and site preferences:

1. *Make your DOS or OS/2 batch files readable:*
   a. *Minimize use of abbreviating commands and qualifiers.* This can lead to confusion about what the creator meant to do. This abbreviation may apply to more than one command in a later DOS or OS/2 release.
   b. *Break your DOS or OS/2 batch files into modules* performing only one or two functions. Use label names to describe these functions and to mark their start.
   c. *Indent at least two or three spaces for* (1) code under a label (left justify), (2) the commands contained within an IF or FOR structure, and (3) data for an executable.
   d. *Line Up* all IFs and FORs.
   e. Freely *use blank space* to separate modules (before labels marking a new module), between environment variable assignments and flow control structures such as IF.
   f. Some *commenting* to self-document the command procedure is necessary:
       Using the REM command, you can have comments (or remarks) up to 123 characters (same limit both for DOS and OS/2). Note: to issue an @ECHO OFF or place a @ before the REM command to suppress displaying the comment. You can also use redirection (<, >) piping (|), and special (in quotes) characters in a REM command. In DOS 4.0 (and later) and OS/2, you can use REM commands in CONFIG.SYS without error messages appearing. (Earlier releases allowed you to use REM but an error message would appear on processing it.)
       Comments have no effect on the speed of processing of the batch file.
       Try to keep comments up to date. There are various styles of batch file commenting:
       (1) Comment only complicated (i.e. non-obvious) sequences.
       (2) Comment only non-portable DOS or OS/2 commands.

(3) Comment some type of header "record" that lists the command procedure name, what each parameter (%1–%9) is, what each label (module) does, any nested batch files used, any environment variables used, any features that may not work in earlier releases, and batch file version history [e.g. creator, revisor, date, and modification].

(4) One or more comments before each label

(5) My own preference is the "jump start" axiom—*write as much documentation to allow you or another person to understand quickly how the command procedure works.*

g. *Use various cases in your programs.* A common practice is to put SET commands in uppercase and comments in lowercase. Whatever approach you use, make sure it is consistently applied for all command procedures.

h. *Use meaningful names* for DOS or OS/2 batch files, labels, environment variables, files, and so on.

2. *Make your command procedure as effective as possible:*

a. Leave things as you found them.

(1) Close all files.

(2) Return to the original directory.

(3) Remove all temporary files.

(4) Remove all unneeded environment variables or reset those to be reused.

(5) Reset your editor/operating system settings, privileges (LANs), and protections (Lans) if changed.

(6) Do all of the above if an error is encountered and you are about to exit from the command procedure.

b. Never assume user input is correct. Always check case, data type, if blank, if a valid value, and if in the valid range.

c. If the same batch file uses a certain module heavily, then consider converting it to a pseudo-subroutine. If several batch files use a certain batch file, then extract the pertinent part to be used as a nested batch file.

d. Do the following at the start of a command procedure: (1) Issue an @ECHO OFF or ECHO ON; (2) initialize appropriate environment variables; (3) provide a way to capture input for %1–%9 if parameters are not supplied; and (4) clear the screen before displaying output (probably using CLS).

e. Depending on the type of users you have using a batch file, consider having different sequences for different types of use.

f. Create a library of batch files and accompanying BASIC, C, PASCAL, other command language and assembly programs to perform heavily used tasks such as file operations, exception handling, and prompting for input.

g. Minimize what gets displayed to the user: @ECHO OFF and @ before a command will help tremendously. Some of these are usually disabled during debugging a batch file.

h. Have one common exit point that takes errors away from the main part of a program.

How Can I Extend the DOS or OS/2 Batch Language?

Throughout the chapter, we presented various places where the DOS language could be enhanced or supplemented with a programming or command language. These include when any of the following are needed:

- Capturing input within a batch file.
- Date and time operations
- More complicated file operations
- True subroutines
- String and substring operations
- More powerful flow control structures
- Processing of integers, decimals, and exponents
- Access to system hardware and software information
- Faster execution speed

If you need any of the preceding, then consider any of the following ways to extend the DOS or OS/2 batch language:

1. Build your own subroutine and command procedure "libraries." The next section will give you ideas where to look for these.

2. If you have knowledge of a programming language, you can use this to build your own DOS command that can be used by any batch file. Also consider using another command language such as CLIST, DCL, REXX (included with OS/2), and Perl.

3. Combine batch files with a programming language using full-screen application libraries such as the following: Greenleaf Functions, Hi Screen XL, PC Curses, SoftCode, and Window Boss.

4. Consider purchasing any of the batch file "extenders," which allow you to use BAT files but add additional commands. These are just a small sample of what is available for DOS machines. Note that the author does not make any recommendation about any of the software mentioned in this section:

Extended Batch Language (Seaware); $79, Seaware Corporation, P.O. 1656, Delray Beach, FL 33444; (800) 634-4070. EXEC2 like. Demos available on many bulletin boards.

Pro Command (Innovative Technology); $89, Innovative Technology, 2710 Lancaster Road, Unit 101, Ottawa, Ontario CANADA K1B 4W8; (613) 738-3375. Can run batch files without modifications.

Builder (Hyperkinetix); $149.95, Hyperkinetix Inc, 666 Baker Street, Suite 405, Costa Mesa, CA, 92626; (800) 873-9993: batch file compiler.

Batcom (Wenham Software); $59.95, Wenham Software Company, 5 Burley Street, Wenham, MA 011984; (508) 774-7036. Batch file compiler.

Many programs execute like DOS commands and enhance batch file processing. Some of these include:

Good monthly programs from *PC Magazine* including BATCHman (returns information for batch files), KEY-FAKE (easily sends scan codes to the console), PUSHDIR/POPDIR (saves and restores directories).

Owen Baker, 5 Parkhill Drive, Ringwood, Victoria, Australia, 3134: (061) 3 879-5013, has written ERRORLVL (returns errorlevel from a batch file) and CHECKTD (is the entered time later than the PC's date and time). He charges $20 (Australian).

Bill Davidsen wrote an Errorlevel that he released in the public domain called ERR. Here is the simple C program he created. I include it to show that it doesn't take a long program to greatly enhance your batch file processing:

```
#include <stdlib.h> /* may be needed*/main(argc,argv)
/*Example: user enters ERR 22.22 (the errorlevel) is assigned to*/
/*argv[1].*/
   int argc; /* necessary declarations*/
   char *argv[];
{
exit(argc>1?atoi(argv[1]):0);
/* This looks tricky but really isn't - - if the user-entered error-*/
/*level is greater than one, then convert it from a string to an*/
/*integer. Else assign it a value of zero.*/
}
```

Copyright © 1990, Bill Davidsen, All Rights Reserved. (Comments by author.)

Timo Salmi has released a whole series of batch file helpers into the public domain. These can be found at the anonymous ftp site 128.214.12.37 (garbo.uwasa.fi) in a series of files called TSBATxx.ZIP (xx is the version number). He has also written other collections of new DOS "commands" and compiled a list of frequently asked questions about DOS.

5. Look at any of the alternatives to ANSI.SYS that provide additional escape sequences.

Where Can I Learn More About DOS or OS/2 Batch Language?

The following is a list of some places where you can learn more about DOS or OS/2 batch language and DOS or OS/2 applications:

The semi-annual proceedings of the DEC user group (DECUS, DECUS Canada, DECUS Europe) does have a strong PC section with some talks on batch language.

DECUS, 333 South Street SHR1-4/D31, Shrewsbury, Mass. 01545-4112; (508) 841-3389. Especially of interest is the PC SIG which has at least two or three sessions on batch language at each DECUS symposium and produces the session notes for their section at each symposium. DECUS also make useful contributions to the tape library. For information on tapes call (508) 841-3389, and to order (508) 841-3500.

The annual proceedings of the SAS User's Group International (SUGI) and the Northeast SAS Users Group have good examples of DCL command procedures.

SUGI—c/o Publications Department, SAS Institute Inc., SAS Campus Drive, Cary, NC 27513; (919) 677-8000.

NESUG—c/o Marge Scerbo, University of Maryland at Baltimore, 610 West Lombard Street, Baltimore, MD 21201; (301) 328-8424. Note that there only a limited number of proceedings available to non-attendees.

PC Magazine has monthly columns on DOS, OS/2, and Windows. Of special interest are the PC Lab Notes, PC Tutor (or Tutor), Environments, and User to User columns. Each issue usually contains at least one utility that enhances DOS, OS/2, or Windows.

PC Magazine, Ziff-Davis Publications, 1 Park Avenue, New York, N.Y. 10016, (212) 503-5255. Call 800-346-3247 with your modem to get the number of the PC MAGNET nearest you. Once connected, enter PHONES at the HOST name prompt. Or call customer service at (800) 848-8990. Cost is $13 an hour. Magazine subscription $45 a year, non-U.S. orders add an additional $31 a year.

PC World is published monthly. Two regular columns filled with batch file examples are the help screen and star-dot-star.

PC World, World Communications, P.O. 55029, Boulder, CO 80322-5029, (800) 825-7595. Cost is $30 a year and an additional $18–$46 for non-U.S. orders.

The *comp.os.ibmpc* deals with a variety of DOS questions including batch files. Also try comp.windows.ms (MS-Windows), and comp.os2. Sources are occasionally posted. Also look at comp.binaries.ibm.pc and comp.binaries.os2 for software to try out.

GO PCMAG (subscription), GO IBMSYS. Free other than Compuserve and phone charges. Many batch files are available here for downloading.

Anonymous ftp for programs.
Anonymous ftp sites include:

WINDOWS

cica.cica.indiana.edu (in pub/pc/win3)   129.79.20.22
clvaxl.cl.msu.edu   35.8.2.1
gandalf.umcs.main.edu   130.111.112.21
lan_stuff.ucs.indiana.edu   129.79.16.96

DOS

cc.sfu.ca   128.189.32.250
csc2.anu.edu.au   130.56.4.25
doc.cso.uiuc.ed   128.174.33.105
f.ms.uky.edu   128.163.128.6
garbo.uwasa.fi (& windows)   128.214.12.37
grape.ecs.clarkson.edu   128.153.28.129
iesd.auc.dk   130.225.48.4
mars.ee.msstate.edu   130.18.64.3
msdos.archive.umich.edu   141.211.165.34
nic.funet.fi   128.214.6.100
peace.waikato.ac.nz   130.217.64.62
plains.nodak.edu   134.129.111.64
quiche.cs.mcgill.ca   132.206.51.1
vmtecmex.cem.itesm.mx   132.254.1.4
wsmr-simtel20.army.mil   26.2.0.74
wuarchive.wustl.edu   128.252.135.4

OS/2

funic.funet.fi   128.214.6.100

luga.latrobe.edu.au   131.179.2.2

mims-iris.waterloo.edu   129.97.129.116

mtsg.ubc.ca (CD OS2:) & DOS   137.82.27.1

novell.com (limited hours)   130.57.4.1

vega.hut.fi   130.233.200.42

Byte has covered DOS from the beginning and has many good articles on OS/2, Windows, and PC UNIX. Columns of interest are: The UNIX /bin, Networks, Beyond DOS, and OS/2 Notebook. Subscriptions are $30 a year; Canada or Mexico, $35 a year; Europe $50–$70; elsewhere $150. Contact (800) 257-9402 (U.S.); (609) 426-7676 (non-US); or **Byte** Subscription Department. P.O. 555, Hightstown, N.J. 08520. Program listings are on Bytenet: (617) 861-9764.

Inside DOS presents basic and advanced tutorials on enhancing DOS and batch files. Subscriptions are $30 a year and non-US $79 a year. Contact (800) 223-8720 (U.S.), (502) 491-1900 (non-U.S.) or **Inside DOS** Customer Relations, 9420 Bunsen Parkway, Suite 300, Louisville, Ky. 40220.

PC Resource and PC Tech Journal: Although now defunct, these magazines have many good many articles on the batch language—including letters to the editor and the pullout pages. Check a library for back issues.

Electronic bulletin boards. Here is a of bulletin boards oriented to *OS/2*. They are presented as is and are untested by the author—including how virus free they are.

203-483-0348   Fernwood [Connecticut]

213-494-6168   Blue BBS [California]

215-879-3310   Optical Illusion [Pennsylvania]

301-680-7792   Medlantic BBS [Maryland]

404-835-6000   **IBM BBS**

503-759-3811   Comu-Plane BBS [Oregon]

514-374-9422   Logistique LMM [Montreal, Canada]

703-385-4325   OS/2 Shareware BBS [Virginia]

703-560-5616   Life's like that [Virginia]

714-963-8517   Omega-Point BBS [California]

805-582-9306   Magnum BBS [California]

805-684-0589   OS/2 Magazine [California]

901-386-4712   WSI BBS [Tennessee]

904-682-1620   Wizard's Opus [Florida]

919-226-6984   Programmer's Oasis [North Carolina]

33-1-6409-0460   OS/2 Mania [France]

The following is a list of bulletin boards oriented to *MS Windows*. They are presented as is and are untested by the author—including how virus free they are.

203-345-2111   Big Byte [Connecticut]

209-732-7192   Colossus Programmer's Net [California]

212-889-6438   RamNet Software Concepts Design (NY)

303-494-0533   OKY BBS [Colorado]

415-284-9151   ComOne [California]

617-742-9194   Linchpin [Massachusetts]

703-548-7849   Max's Doghouse [Virginia]

OS/2 & Windows Magazine covers OS/2 (mainly) and Windows. There have been rumors that these are splitting into a magazine devoted to each environment.

> **OS/2 and Windows Magazine** is published monthly by The Silicon Beach Operation, 1101B Eugenia Place, Carpinteria, Calif. 93013; (805) 566-1282. Cost is $35.95 a year (U.S.).

Programmer's Journal and *TECH Specialist* are rare birds—technical PC magazines that are easy to understand and cover a variety of topics. (Gone are *PC Tech Journal, Micro Cornucopia,* and others)

> **Programmer's Journal** is published bi-monthly by Oakley Publishing Company, 150 North 4th Street, Springfield, Oreg. 97477; (503) 747-0800. Subscriptions cost $24 a year (U.S.).

> **TECH Specialist** is published monthly by R&D Publications, 2601 Iowa, Lawrence, Kans. 66046; (913) 841-1631. Subscriptions cost $29 U.S., $38 Canada and Mexico, and $48 overseas.

Exception Handling in DOS or OS/2 Batch Language

The following are tips and traps in dealing with error handling in DOS or OS/2 batch files:

1. BREAK can be issued at the DOS prompt, from a batch file, or from CONFIG.SYS. This means that you can turn BREAK ON or OFF before processing a command that reads/writes a lot to a screen, printer, or a file. Entering just BREAK returns the current setting of ON or OFF.

2. Placing a BREAK ON command in the CONFIG.SYS file in either DOS or OS/2 (but affects DOS sessions only) and pressing CTRL-BREAK or Ctrl-C interrupts processing for batch files and DOS commands if you are performing file operations, reading from the keyboard, printing, and displaying to the screen.

3. BREAK OFF, contrary to popular belief, does not disable CTRL-BREAK /Ctrl-C recognition but interrupts processing for fewer circumstances. These are reading from the keyboard, printing, and displaying to the screen. This is the default so it does not have to be set. Note that any change to CONFIG.SYS takes place the next time you boot your PC.

4. OS/2 does not have a BREAK command because CTRL-BREAK/Ctrl C is automatically detected for reading from the keyboard, printing, and displaying to the screen.

5. If a CTRL-BREAK/CTRL-C is recognized while a batch file is running, the following message appears on the screen: *Terminate batch job (Y/N)?* Answering Y stops the current batch command processing and moves onto the next command in the batch file. If CTRL-BREAK/CTRL-C is issued from a DOS command, a ^C and then the DOS prompt are displayed on the screen.

6. Although DOS does not have a IF BREAK structure, under DOS 5.0, several commands will give an ERRORLEVEL if CTRL-C is pressed.

Errorlevel 2   DISKCOMP, DISKCOPY, and XCOPY
Errorlevel 3   FORMAT, RESTORE
Errorlevels but not for Ctrl-C   REPLACE, SETVER

7. If you need a more technical understanding of how batch file exception handling works or which interrupts to use for extended exception handling, then read the Rollins (1987) article in *PC Tech Journal.*

Portability of DOS or OS/2 Batch Files

This section will discuss concerns when porting batch files between DOS and OS/2. The following commands are available in DOS (if PROTECTONLY=NO is in CONFIG.SYS) but not under OS/2 full-screen or windowed mode:

CONFIG.SYS COMMANDS

BREAK   Detects CTRL-Break/Ctrl-C is pressed
DRIVPARM   In DOS 5.0, sets parameters of drives
FCBS   Sets the number of file control blocks

FILES   Sets the number of files that can be opened at once

LASTDRIVE   Number of drives to recognize

SHELL   Loads a specified command processor

DOS COMMANDS

APPEND   Search directory for data files. OS/2 uses DPATH instead.

ASSIGN   Reassigns drive letter. OS/2 uses SUBST instead.

CTTY   Uses another input device.

COMMAND   Invokes a new DOS command processor. OS/2 instead uses START or CMD.

DOS   In DOS 5.0 to load DOS into high memory area of extended memory.

DOSKEY   In DOS 5.0, serves both as a command history and a way to build and use keyboard macros.

DOSSHELL   In DOS 5.0, invokes a DOS shell. Invoking OS/2 directly invokes a shell.

EXIT   In DOS 5.0, exits the current command processor and returns to the initial one. OS/2 does the same thing but the command processor is OS/2.

EDLIN/EDIT   OS/2 uses a full-screen editor also invoked by E. DOS 5.0. It also has an EDIT command that invokes a full-screen editor.

FASTOPEN   Disk caching. Not needed under OS/2.

FC   In DOS, compares two files. O/2 equivalent is COMP.

/?or HELP *command*   DOS 5.0 includes a help on commands. A /? qualifier after any *command* or help *command* statement will give more information about that command. OS/2 has HELP *messagenum* that tells you what error occurred and how to resolve it and CMDHELP to give help on an OS/2 command.

JOIN   Access network drives. (IN OS/2 1.2)

PROMPT/VER $v displays DOS version. In OS/2 $v displays the OS/2 version

QBASIC   In DOS 5.0, invokes Quick Basic interpreter

SETVER   In DOS 5.0, sets an executable to a certain DOS version

VER   Displays DOS version. In OS/2 displays the OS/2 version.

Other differences are that since OS/2 Version 1.2, you can use a HPFS (high performance file system). This allows file names of up to 254 characters, extended attributes. Unfortunately, DOS recognizes only the first eight characters of the extended file name. It is rumored that DOS 6.0 will contain something similar to High Performance File System. Another difference is that DOS batch files end with .BAT, OS/2's end with .CMD. Also, DOS differs from OS/2 in use of pre-defined environment variables. OS/2 has several more listed in the prior section on using environment variables with DOS or OS/2 batch files.

The following features are available for OS/2 but not DOS:

Because OS/2 has a graphical user interface, users enter fewer commands. Not all these commands are in each OS/2 version.

ANSI   Allows escape sequence support under OS/2

CACHE   Enables/Disables HPFS cache

CALL   Same as OS/2 but has CALL/Q (echo off)

CONFIG   Edit and modify CONFIG.SYS

CMD/C, START   Start a second command processor. Equivalent is COMMAND.

CMDHELP, HELP   CMDHELP is help on an OS/2 command. HELP is on an OS/2 message. DOS 5.0 includes command help by using the /? qualifier or invoking the HELP *command* statement.

CREATEDD   Creates dump of memory

DDINSTAL   Installs a new device driver

DETACH   Starts a background process

DPATH   Sets search path for data files. DOS equivalent is APPEND.

E   Invokes system editor. DOS equivalents are EDIT (full-screen in DOS 5.0) and EDLIN.

EAUTIL   Puts extended attributes into another file

ENDLOCAL/SETLOCAL   Sets/restores previous directory settings

EXTPROC   Uses an external command processor

Labels   For some OS/2 releases, a label cannot be the last name in a batch file if referred to in a GOTO.

MOVE   Moves a file or directory to another location

PATCH   Patches an executable with a fix

PMREXX   Invokes REXX in a window

PROMPT   Added $a (ampersand), $c (left parenthesis), $f (right parenthesis), $i (HELP), $v (OS/2 version)

PSTAT   Gives information about one or more processes

SETCOM40   Really a DOS under OS/2 command that allows running DOS communications program under OS/2

SPOOL   Starts printer spooler

SYSLOG   Enables/disables logging of commands

TRACE   Turns on trace facility

TRACEFMT   Sends TRACE output to the screen

VER   Displays OS/2 version

- More batch file operators—^ allows you to use an operator as a character, () places commands as one unit, & separates multiple commands, && performs a second task if the first task is successfully completed, | | performs the first task if true, else performs the second task.
- More control over file handles and redirection. These are discussed in a previous section on capturing output from a command in a DOS or OS/2 batch file.
- A greatly enhanced CONFIG.SYS. Duncan (1989) in the September 12 *PC Magazine* does a great job in summarizing these changes.
- Among other differences, since OS/2 1.2, you can use a HPFS (high performance file system). This allows file names of up to 254 characters, extended attributes. Unfortunately, DOS recognizes only the first eight characters of the extended file name. It is rumored that DOS 6.0 will contain something similar to a High Performance File System. Another difference is that DOS batch files end with .BAT; OS/2's end with .CMD. DOS versus OS/2 environment variables.

Migrating to Other Command Languages

As pointed out in a previous section in discussing how to extend the batch language, the batch language is very limited. So, there will be a good many occasions when you will need to convert to other command languages. Fortunately, all the command languages are available under DOS and most under OS/2 (except for pCLIST and VCL), so there is some variety on what to choose.

When Should I Consider Converting My DOS Batch File?

When any of the following becomes a need:

- Capturing input within a batch file
- Date and time operations
- More complicated file operations
- True subroutines
- String and substring operations
- More powerful flow control structures
- Processing of integers, decimals, and exponents
- Access to system hardware and software information
- Faster processing

What Command Language Should I Convert To?

1. A *compiled language program* remains a good possibility. DOS and OS/2 are rich in the number of compilers supported such as Assembly, BASIC, C, FORTRAN, and Pascal.
2. *Perl* offers a major improvement to batch language. Its strengths over the batch language are stronger flow control structures, ability to capture input,

true functions/subroutines, mathematical operators, a rich function library, stronger array operations, and stronger directory/file operations. It is available for DOS and OS/2 so a high degree of portability is allowed. Perl's drawbacks include ease of learning for people not familiar with C or UNIX, and no support yet for networking and database functions under MS-DOS and OS/2.

3. The *CLIST* language is available for MS DOS (pCLIST). It offers some improvements over the batch language including more flow control structures, a good function library, ability to capture system information, subroutines, and more flexibility in parameter passing. However, a CLIST interpreter is available only on one of the operating systems that the batch language is—MS DOS. CLIST code is also portable to the TSO environment found on IBM mainframes.

4. A *DCL* interpreter is available for DOS and OS/2. It would offer some improvements over the batch language, including ability to retrieve system and hardware information, a good function library, subroutines and functions, and report generation. DCL code is also portable to VMS and UNIX.

5. REXX interpreters are available for DOS (Kilowatt, Quercus and Tritus) and OS/2 (since 1.2 for extended edition and 1.3 for standard edition). REXX offers major improvements to the batch language including the ability to capture system and hardware information (non-portable to other REXX interpreters/compilers), a rich function library, string and function capabilities, a variety of data types, and report generation. REXX code is also portable to the AMIGA, UNIX, and VMS.

Any of the preceding choices would be an improvement over the batch language with REXX and Perl being the best choices. The rest of the chapter will discuss the major issues in converting batch language files to scripts for all four command languages.

BATCH LANGUAGE TO CLIST

Look at Figure 2-2 in Chapter 2 for "equivalent" commands in batch language.

The following are tips and traps in converting from DOS or OS/2 batch language files to CLIST programs:

1. These useful batch language concepts and commands have no direct equivalent in the CLIST language:
   a. Environment variables. These are similar to global symbolic variables.
   b. Converting DOS commands to TSO.

2. The following batch language commands can be easily converted to CLIST equivalents:
   a. %1–%9 to PROC positional operands

   b. Environment variables to local and global symbolic variables
   c. Multiple IFs to SELECT
   d. FOR to DO-WHILE, DO UNTIL or iterative DO
   e. DOS commands to DOS and the command (pCLIST only)
   f. CALL, COMMAND, CMD, and START to EXEC CLIST, or *CLIST_name*
   g. A heavily used module in a batch file to a subprocedure (SYSCALL)
   h. ERRORLEVEL to &LASTCC
   i. ECHO to WRITE
   j. IF %1 to PROC
   k. ECHO.│DATE│FIND "1990" to &SYSDATE
   l. ECHO.│TIME│FIND ":" to &SYSTIME
   m. Statements that have the same names and perform similar functions (but not necessarily the same syntax): GOTO, Labels, IF, SET
   n. CTRL-Break/Ctr-C is the equivalent of the attention (ATTN) key being pressed. You can use *ATTN sequences* to handle when the attention key is pressed.
   o. ECHO ON to CONTROL CONLIST and so on
   p. IF EXIST to &SYSDSN
   q. VER to &SYSTSOE
   r. SET PATH to &SYSCAPS and &SYSLC

3. The following CLIST statements have no equivalent in batch language and will have to be added after the command procedure is converted:
   a. DATA-ENDDATA and DATA-PROMPT-ENDDATA
   b. LISTDSI
   c. NGLOBAL, SYSREF
   d. All functions and control variables not listed above
   e. Double ampersand symbolic variables.

BATCH LANGUAGE TO DCL

Here are recommendations on DOS batch language commands that can be easily converted to DCL commands:

1. These useful batch language concepts and commands have no direct equivalent in DCL:
   a. Environment variables—these are similar to global symbolic variables
   b. Converting DOS commands to VMS

2. The following batch language commands can be easily converted to DCL equivalents:
   a. %1–%9 to P1–P8
   b. Environment variables to local and global symbols

  c. SET to assignment statement

  d. FOR to a loop sequence

  e. DOS commands to DOS *command* (or VMS equivalent)

  f. CALL, COMMAND, CMD, and START to CALL

  g. A heavily used module in a batch file to a subprocedure (GOSUB or CALL)

  h. ERRORLEVEL to $STATUS

  i. ECHO to WRITE.SYS$OUTPUT

  j. IF %1 to IF P1

  k. ECHO.│DATE│FIND "1990" to F$TIME

  l. ECHO.│TIME│FIND ":" to F$TIME

  m. Statements that have the same names and perform similar functions (but not necessarily the same syntax): GOTO, Labels, IF, Multiple IFs.

  n. Ctrl-Break/Ctrl-C is the equivalent of the attention (CTR-Y) key being pressed. You can use *ON CONTROL_Y sequences* to handle when the Control-Y is pressed.

  o. ECHO ON to SET VERIFY

  p. IF EXIST to IF F$SEARCH

  q. VER to F$GETSYI("VERSION")

  r. SET PATH to F$EDIT

  s. PROMPT $e to REVERSE = ESC+"[..."; WRITE SYS$OUTPUT REVERSE

3. These DCL concepts and commands have no equivalent in the batch language:

  a. **Logicals**—an alias for a file, tape, or disk device, or another logical. It may help you to substitute the word "location" when thinking about logicals and **symbols,** an alias for a command, character string, another symbol or lexical function. For PC DOS/MS-DOS users, these are similar to using environment variables where you can assign an alias to the directory or file name.

  b. All lexical functions not mentioned above.

  c. File protections and system privileges (except for DOS or OS/2-based LANs)

  d. Global symbols SEVERITY and RESTART

  e. STOP

BATCH LANGUAGE TO PERL

1. The following Perl concepts have no equivalent in the batch language:

  a. Math functions

  b. Networking functions

    c. DBM functions (system database)

    d. Awk to Perl, C header files to Perl, and sed to Perl converters

    e. Setuid and setgid scripts

    f. Associative arrays

    g. Report variables

    h. Binary file mode

2. Here are recommendations on batch language commands that can be easily converted to Perl equivalents:

    a. %1–%9 to @ARGV for main scripts and @_for subroutines

    b. Environment variables to environment variables or scalar variables

    c. SET to assignment statement

    d. FOR to FOR. (more powerful in Perl)

    e. DOS or OS/2 commands to exec or sys and DOS or OS/2 *command*

    f. CALL, COMMAND, CMD, and START to eval, perl *name* and syscall function

    g. A heavily used module in a batch file to a subprocedure (sub). With return is a function, otherwise is a subprocedure.

    h. ERRORLEVEL to $?.

    i. ECHO to print.

    j. IF %1 to if $ARGV[1].

    k. ECHO.|DATE|FIND "1990" to gmtime or localtime

    l. ECHO.|TIME|FIND":"to gmtime or localtime

    m. Statements that have the same names and perform similar functions (but not necessarily the same syntax): GOTO, Labels, IF, Multiple IFs, FOR, piping, redirection.

    n. CTRL-Break/Ctr-C is the equivalent of signals sequences as indicated by the $SIG array. These include ABRT (abnormal script terminal), ILL (illegal command), INT (equivalent to CTRL/C and CTRL Break), QUIT (quit script), and TERM (termination request).

    o. ECHO ON to perl -d.

    p. IF EXIST to -e *filename.*

    q. VER to perl-v.

    r. SET PATH to tr.

    s. IF to if-elsif, FOR to do *block* while and do *block* until.

BATCH LANGUAGE TO REXX

1. Here are recommendations on Batch commands and functions that can be easily converted to REXX instructions and built-in functions:

    a. %1–%9 to PARSE ARG (more powerful)

    b. Environment variables to local and global symbols

    c. SET to assignment statement

    d. FOR to SELECT, Iterative DO, DO WHILE, DO UNTIL

    e. DOS or OS/2 commands under REXX would be ADDRESS DOS "*command*" or ADDRESS CMD "*command*"

    f. CALL, COMMAND, CMD, and START to cmd *execname* (OS/2), rexx *execname* (DOS—Quercus Systems), ex *execname* (DOS—Kilowatt Software)

    g. A heavily used module in a batch file to a subprocedure (CALL)

    h. ERRORLEVEL to RC

    i. ECHO to SAY

    j. IF %1 to PARSE ARG val1;IF val1 (no predefined command-line variables)

    k. ECHO.|DATE|FIND "1990" to DATE()

    l. ECHO.|TIME|FIND ":" to TIME()

    m. Statements that have the same names and perform similar functions (but not necessarily the same syntax): Labels, IF, Multiple IFs

    n. CTRL-Break/Ctr-C is the equivalent of a SIGNAL sequence that can be detected by a CALL ON HALT/SIGNAL ON HALT

    o. ECHO ON to TRACE command and function

    p. VER to PARSE VERSION

    q. SET PATH to DATATYPE (to detect) and TRANSLATE (to convert)

    r. FIND.|VER to PARSE VERSION

2. The following REXX instructions/concepts have no equivalent in batch language and will have to be added after the command procedure is converted:

    a. Data buffer or stack operations (other than PULL or QUEUE)

    b. Compound symbols and related instructions

    c. ADDRESS

    d. Interactive tracing

    e. Parsing templates

SUGGESTED READINGS

Alperson, Burton L., Andrew Fluegalman, and Lawrence J. Magid. 1985 The Fully Powered PC, *PC World.* 3(7), pp. 228–232.

Alperson, Burton L., Andrew Fluegalman, and Lawrence J. Magid. 1985 Designer Screens, *PC World.* 3(11), pp. 244–251.

Anderson, Julie, 1984. Irresistible DOS 3.0, *PC Tech Journal.* December, pp. 74–80.

Archer, Rowland, Jr. 1983. The IBM PC XT and DOS 2.00, *Byte.* November, pp. 294–304.

Arnold, David, 1984. DOS for Beginners, *PC World.* 2(4) pp. 44–51.

Axelson, Jan, and Jim Hughes, 1989. Make your Batch Files Stop, Look, and Listen, *PC Resource.* October, pp. 65–69.

Bemer, R.W., 1979. Time and the Computer, *Interface Age.* February, pp. 74–79.

BCS, 1988. Using Batch Files, *Boston Computer Society.* Course handout.

Cropsey, Sam, 1991. Dos Environment Variables, Underscores Not Allowed, *LanStreet Journal,* p. 8.

Dagget, Richard and Nancy Woolford. 1989 Newsletter Exchange. *PC Report.* 8(8) pp. 43–45.

DeVoney, Chris, 1990. How Not to Get Lost When you Change PATHs, *PC Computing,* June p. 264.

DeVoney, Chris, *MS-DOS Users Guide,* 1988. (3d ed). Revised by Allen I. Wyatt. Que: Carmel, Indiana.

Dilorio, Frank, 1989. Good Code, Bad Code: Strategies for Program Design, *NESUG 89 Conference Proceedings,* pp. 260–266.

Duncan, Ray, 1989. Configuring OS/2 for your system, *PC Magazine.* September 12.

Fernandez, Judi, and Ruth Ashley, 1989. *The Power of OS/2: A Comprehensive User's Manual.* Windcrest Books: Blue Ridge Summit, Pa.

Gibson, Steve, 1990. 7½ years Later, MS-DOS Configuration Files are Outdated, *InfoWord.* 12(45), p. 47.

Haapenen, Tom, 1991. *Frequently Asked Questions, Comp.Windows.Ms Edition.* Electronic document.

Heller, Martin, 1987. An Architecture for the Future. *PC Tech Journal.* November, pp. 67–83.

Hellewell, Rick, 1989 PROMPTing Around the Clock, *PC World.* 7(1), pp. 232–236.

Higgins, Mike, 1987. Advanced MS-DOS Batch procedures, *Computer Language,* pp. 45–49.

Hinners, Bonnie, 1990. Patches and Fixes, *Lan Magazine.* 6(11), pp. 14–16.

Hinners, Bonnie, 1990. Patches and Fixes, *Lan Magazine.* 6(5), pp. 12–14.

Hinners, Bonnie, 1991. Patches and Fixes, *Lan Magazine.* 7(1) p. 12.

Holtzman, Jeff, 1987. Batch File Basics, *PC Resource,* pp. 61–65.

IBM Corporation, 1983. *Disk Operating System 2.10 Reference.*

IBM Corporation, 1983. *Disk Operating System 2.10 Technical Reference.*

IBM Corporation, 1987. *Disk Operating System 3.30 Reference.*

IBM Corporation, 1991. *OS/2 2.0 Considerations: White Paper Revision 0.65.*

IBM Corporation, 1990. *Operating System/2 Version 1.3 Getting Started.*

IBM Corporation, 1990. *Operating System/2 Version 1.3 User's Guide:Base Operating System.*

Inside DOS, 1990. Creating Batch Commands that Operate on Variable Data. *Inside DOS,* 1(3), pp. 8–9.

Inside DOS, 1990. Displaying a Blank Line in a Batch File, *Inside DOS,* 1(8) p. 11.

Inside DOS, 1990. Redefining your Function Keys with ANSI.SYS, *Inside DOS,* 1(7), pp. 1, 12.

Inside DOS, 1990. "Using the FOR Command to Issue Several Commands at Once," *Inside DOS,* 1(6), pp. 9–12.

Kerninghan, Brian W., and P.J. Plauger, 1978. *The Elements of Programming Style* (2d ed). New York: McGraw-Hill.

Koessel, Karl, 1990. "The Help Screen/Why Upgrade DOS?" *PC World,* 8(11), pp. 49, 52.

Knorr, Eric, 1988. Getting the Feel of OS/2, *PC World.* 6(4), pp. 188–193.

Jaeschke, Rex, 1990. Environment Control, *The C Users Journal.* 8(11) pp. 25–34.

Jourdain, Robert. 1986 *Programmer's Problem Solver for the IBM PC, XT, and AT.* Prentice Hall: New York.

Landgrave, Tim, 1991. Dealing with the IF Command's Case Sensitivity, *Inside DOS.* 2(1), pp. 10–11.

Lante Corporation, 1987. Batch File Programming Methods Ease Use of Applications, *PC Week.* September 8, p. 42.

Lante Corporation, 1987. How to Build Powerful, Efficient Batch-File Menu Systems, *PC Week.* September 1, p. 51.

Lante Corporation, 1987. Shifting the PC into High Gear with AUTOEXEC.BAT Files, *PC Week.* August 25, p. 48.

Lante Corporation, 1987. Warm Up Work with a Customized CONFIG.SYS, *PC Week.* August 18, p. 40.

Liebing, Edward A., 1990. "How to Add Color to Your DOS Prompt," *Lan Times.* July pp. 88–89.

Lieberman, Phil, 1990. *OS/2: A Comprehensive Hands-On Introduction Course.* Notes.

McLachlan, Gordon, 1991. IBM, MS Prepare for OS/2 Fallout, *Lan Computing.* 2(15), September, pp. 1, 9.

Mason, Marco, 1990. Soliciting Input in a Batch File. *Inside DOS.* 1(5), pp. 1, 10–12.

McGowan, William T., 1991. "Star-Dot-Star/Insensitive Batch File Arguments," *PC World,* 10(1), pp. 207–211.

Minamsi, Mark, 1989. Figuring Out Config.Sys, *Byte,* July, pp. 129–132.

Mirecki, Ted, 1987. Enter OS/2, *PC Tech Journal.* November, pp. 52–65.

Microsoft Corporation, 1989. *BASIC 3.0 Reference.*

Microsoft Corporation, 1991. *Microsoft MS-DOS Users Guide and Reference Version 5.0.*

Microsoft Corporation, 1990. *Various .TXT Files on Windows 3.0.*

Norton, Peter, 1987. Power your PC with BatchFiles, *PC World.* 5(2), pp. 316–323.

O'Conner, Vincent D., 1989. Star-Dot-Star/Day In, Day Out, *PC World.* 7(2), pp. 215–216.

Paterson, Tim, 1983. An Inside Look at MS-DOS, *Byte.* June, pp. 230–232.

Petzold, Charles, 1987. PC Tutor, *PC Magazine.* April 28, p. 342–348.

Piper, Dan. 1989 Star-Dot-Star/Hickory Dickory DOS, *PC World.* 7(7), p. 202–206.

Roberts, Tony, 1990. Getting started with batch files, *Compute.* May, pp. 32–36.

Rollins, Dan. 1987 DOS Exception Handling, *PC Tech Journal,* pp. 130–140.

Roshfeld, Larry, 1987. Journey Through DOS, Part 3, Lotus. 3(12), pp. 82–88.

Rizzo, Tony, and Richard Hale Shaw, 1989. OS/2-A New Perspective, *PC Magazine.* July 1989, 8(10) pp. 293–317.

Rubenking, Neil J., 1990. Enhance your Batch File Processing with BATCHMAN, *PC Magazine.*

Rubenking, Neil J., 1991. User-to-User/Blank Lines in Batch Files, *PC Magazine.* 10(12), p. 377–378.

Rubenking, Neil J., 1989. "User-to-User/Echo Off," *PC Magazine.* 9(6), p. 359–364.

Rubenking, Neil J., 1989. User-to-User/Simulating Subroutines, *PC Magazine.* 9(9), pp. 369–370.

Shaw, Richard Hale, 1987. "Expanding the DOS Environment," *PC Magazine.* April 14, pp. 295–311.

Sheldon, Tom, 1986. DOS Tips, Tricks, and Techniques, *PC Magazine.* March 25, p. 237–248.

Siever, Ellen, 1990. "Using Function Keys to Issue Commands, *PC Report.* 9(12), pp. 15–16.

Spanbauer, Scott, 1990. Do-It-Yourself Menus with Norton Utilities, *PC World.* 8(1), pp. 146–148.

Stone, Mike, 1990. An OS for every Workstation, *LAN Technology.* 6(10), pp. 61–75.

Swan, Tom, 1988. Star-Dot-Star/Batch of the Day, *PC World.* May, pp. 271–272.

Terber, Victor V., 1990. User-to-User/Do it Today. *PC Magazine.* 9(22), pp. 445–446.

Vallino, Jim, 1986. Environment Expansion, *PC Tech Journal.* 4(11), p. 49.

Vallino, Jim, 1987. Environment Variables, *PC Tech Journal.* 5(5), p. 51.

Volkstorf, Ed, 1987. Batch File Interaction, *PC Tech Journal.* 5(6), p. 51.

Wachtel, Alan. 1989 Star-Dot-Star/Finding the Date and Time, *PC World.* 7(9), pp. 215–220.

Welch, Bill, 1991. The Other DCL—The DOS Command Language, *DECUS Spring '91 Symposium.* (Handout).

Winer, Ethan, 1987. "Digging Deeper Into DOS," *PC Magazine.* March 10, pp. 331–347.

Wolverton, Van, 1991. "Checking the Errorlevel," *Inside DOS.* 2(3), pp. 4–5.

Wolverton, Van, 1991. Dress up the Appearance of Your Batch Files, *Inside DOS.*

Wolverton, Van, 1990. Getting to Know a Handy Batch File Tool: The IF Command, *Inside DOS.* 1(8), pp. 6–7.

7

Command Language
Advisor—Perl

Available since the late 1980s, Perl, standing for *p*ractical *e*xtraction and *r*eport *l*anguage, or the lesser known, *p*athologically *e*clectic *r*ubbish *l*ister has become a very popular command language on UNIX, MS-DOS/PC-DOS, OS/2, ATARI ST, and AmigaDOS and Macintosh ("minimum stand alone application" & MPW under MAC OS). Its uses include system management, text file manipulation, report generation, and generating code that also can pass as poetry. Until recently, Perl users had to resort to learning about the language through the **man** (or help) pages supplied with Perl for creating their **scripts** (what a Perl program is called). (If man is operating on your system, enter *man perl* to browse the 90 plus help pages. Or use ftp to obtain a formatted version of the man pages from chem.bu.edu—IP number 128.197.30.18). But 1991 brought the publication of the book *Programming Perl* by Larry Wall (Perl's creator and maintainer) and Randall Schwartz that is a combination reference, tutorial, and program idea sourcebook. The availability of their book should spur the popularity of this command language. Another reason for its popularity is that Perl is available free (as part of the GNU general license) and with source code.

Perl supports a variety of data types each with a unique identifier. *This identifier also determines how a statement is processed.* The basic data types include:

Scalars (*Variable names are prefixed by a $*) that contain numbers (including decimals), characters, or Boolean (1,0). Jumping slightly ahead, scalars are also used to represent elements of Perl's simple and associative arrays.

Simple arrays (*Array names are prefixed by a @.*) Simple arrays can contain elements that have numbers or characters. The **key** (also called index or

After this text was initially written, several MS-DOS and OS/2 Perl interpreters became available. DOS refers to the Lin Reed/Tom Dinger version. OS/2 refers to the Raymond Chin/Kai Rommel version. These other interpreters will be included in future editions.

element number) is a unique number representing the position of the element in the array and is used to access the array element. The key is placed in parentheses. Beware that the first element of an array has a default key of 0 *not* 1.

Associative arrays *(Array names are prefixed by a %.)* Associative arrays can have one or more keys (which can include any valid scalar variable value) used to obtain the values associated with that key.

The emphasis on this chapter will be on using Perl for applications and on how Perl operates under each operating system. Space does not allow showing the many alternative ways of doing these examples in Perl. *(And make no mistake, there are many different ways to do the same thing in Perl.)* A change bar will highlight aspects of Perl that are non-portable (applying to one or more operating systems). Examples have been tested under MS-/PC-DOS, OS/2, and UNIX and should run on most operating systems unless otherwise noted.

Why Select Perl?

There are a good many shells (**shell** is another name for command languages with which users interact with the UNIX operating system) available for the UNIX operating system such as sh (Bourne), csh (C-shell), and ksh (Korn). There are also general programming languages such as Icon, TCL, and Python. Why is Perl excluded from these?

1. *For an increasing number of users. Perl has become the shell/command language of choice.* Although the other shells have their supporters, none has emerged as a de facto shell standard because of various limitations. Perl appears to be heading in this direction. Perl tutorials are now regularly given at DECUS, USENIX, and Sun (SUGfest) user group conferences.

2. *Perl interpreters on various platforms have some input from Perl's creator, Larry Wall.* This means some control over the quality of the interpreter's implementation. There is little such control over some of the other UNIX shells on other platforms. A standard set of tests is included with the Perl source code that can help in determining how compliant a Perl interpreter is.

3. *Perl is available on a variety of UNIX and non-UNIX platforms.* Not all of the above UNIX shells are available on other platforms. Three exceptions to this are Python, Icon, and TCL which are also free. A future edition of this book could include chapters on all three command languages.

   Python is a general-purpose command language ideal for prototyping. It is available on all Perl platforms, including the Macintosh. Python is not included in this book because it still is in beta test. Even the documentation of current release 0.9 is far from complete.

Icon is a general-purpose command language especially useful for manipulating text. There are two books on Icon and it has its own Usenet users group (comp.lang.icon.) It is not included here because the author thinks that Perl is becoming a more popular language.

TCL (tool command language) is an embedded general-purpose command language. TCL interpreters are available for UNIX, MS-DOS, and Macintosh. It has its own Usenet users group (comp.lang,tcl,). It is not included here because of the same reason why Icon is not.

4. *Many UNIX commands can be simulated by Perl commands and functions.* With its over 90 functions, Perl is fairly complete and very flexible language. The language includes the capabilities of awk (text formatting language), sed (stream editor and text manipulator), and egrep (finding patterns in files). This means generally you will have less need to include costly (in terms of time and resources) system calls to perform UNIX functions. It also saves you the time learning a UNIX shell language and UNIX commands because almost all of what you need is in Perl! This is not true for other UNIX shell languages.

For further information, look at Ryan(1990) and Morin(1991). These articles both mention Perl and compare it to another script language. Mannheimer (1991) compares and contrasts the Bourne & C-shell languages.

WHEN TO USE PERL

Perl is especially good to use in the following situations when:

- Your in-house expertise is mainly in Perl and you need to create a program relatively fast.
- The emphasis is on manipulating *text files* rather than on *words* in text files.
- UNIX system administration tasks have to be performed (including the need of writing secure scripts).
- Directories need to be processed and manipulated.
- Data can be processed as scalars (such as numeric, character, integer, scientific notation, and an element in an array), lists, and arrays.
- You need to produce reports that include merged data from a file.
- Performing operations on a dbm/ndbm/gdbm (data base routines) or binary file(s).
- You want to create "personal commands" that enhance existing commands for your operating system. By using these "personal commands" together, you can create your own "personal environment."
- Portability is a concern

HOW TO INVOKE PERL SCRIPTS

Perl scripts may be executed in foreground (using the *perl* command or as a self-executing program) or in background.

Invoking Foreground Perl Scripts

Listed below are some of the various ways to invoke a Perl script in foreground (*if trying out these programs, do not enter the descriptive text in brackets*):

Using the Perl command

```
perl prog1
```
[Executes a program named PROG1 that resides in the default search directories. (Note PL is the conventional Perl script file extension but is not required. Also, for DOS and OS/2, and UNIX, the drive (DOS and OS/2) and directory (all three) can be specified along with the file name.)]

Perl one liners (UNIX) and Macintosh

```
perl -e 'print STDOUT "Here is how to run a one line script\n";'
```
[A major strength of Perl is to issue one line commands. This is done by using the -e option. It is good for trying out code. You enter multiple *Perl -e* commands to build a script. This script prints *Here is how to run a one line script* to the screen. The STDOUT is optional since it the default file handle (location) for print (standard output - - usually the screen). Note the \n issues a new line (return) to make sure that the next line of text sent to the screen is displayed on the following line.] NOTE: **The above cannot be used for AmigaDOS, DOS or OS/2. Use the following instead:** (The major difference is entering the entire command in double quotes and then using \" to represent a double quote within a pair of double quotes.]

Perl one liners (AmigaDOS/Atari DOS or OS/2)

```
Perl -e "print STDOUT \" Here is how to run a one line script\n\";"
```

Executing PERL commands in a text file

```
perl -x [from the command line]

#! perl [buried in a text file]
print "another self-running program"
```

[The -x qualifier (available for all Perl interpreters) says to ignore everything before the *#! perl*
Then place your script to be executed after this point. This is useful if you have a Perl script enclosed in a mail message.]

Self-executing Perl scripts (DOS, OS/2, UNIX)

DOS

Place in a batch (.BAT) file and enter the first part of the batch file name.

```
@SC=("
@perl -S %0.bat %1 %2
@goto exit ") if 0;
print STDOUT "hello world\n";[or any valid Perl command(s)]
@SC=("
:exit") if 0;
```

[The -S option tells Perl to look for the script in the directory search list specified by the PATH environment variable. To make this work, place the current directory as part of your PATH. %0 is the first part of the filename such as run if the file is named RUN.BAT]

OS/2 (Place this in a .CMD File)

```
EXTPROC C:\PERL\PERL.EXE -S
(place your PERL commands here)
```

[Use the EXTPROC command to define Perl as an external command processor. The -S qualifier tells Perl to look for the script in the directory search list specified by the PATH environment variable.]

UNIX

```
#!/usr/bin/perl
```

[Put this as the first line in your Perl script then just enter the **script name** at the UNIX shell prompt. Issue a CHMOD for the script so it has the **execute** permission (CHMOD 755 *perlscript_name* - - will change the script named to *perlscript_name* to have read, write, and execute permission for the owner and read and execute permission for other (anybody). Change the above to point to the directory where the Perl interpreter resides if in a different location.]

Tips and Traps:

General

1. Perl is rich with command line options. These include the following: (*Do pay attention to the case of the option.*)

-c Checks syntax only. Returns errors (if found) or syntax OK (if ok).

-d Perl debugger. Covered in a later section, on debugging Perl scripts. (Doesn't work under AmigaDOS.)

-D flagnumber Enables various debugging flags (if installed correctly). Covered in the section on debugging Perl scripts.

-e As shown earlier, executes a Perl "mini-program" that is one line long.

-i extension This allows modification of a file by using in-place editing. If an extension is specified, then a backup can be created. Note for DOS and OS/2 that creating only a backup is supported—so you must specify an extension different than that of the original.

-s Sets up simple parsing of command line arguments by creating a scalar variable and assigning it a value of 1. See the later section on capturing user command line values for further information.

-S Looks for a script using the directory search path assigned to the PATH environment variable. On the Amiga, the PATH list must be delimited by commas.

-u One way to create an executable— -u creates a core dump that an UNDUMP command can then process. The executable may run faster than the interpreted version but at the expense of disk space. On some systems (such as DOS), an undumped executable is generally slower than creating a new executable of a Perl script. UNDUMP may not be available for your operating system—such as the Amiga. The DUMP function is used to generate a core dump within a Perl program.

-v Prints version of PERL. Here is a sample output: (from MS-DOS)

```
This is perl, version 3.0

$Header: perly.c,v 3.0.1.9 90/11/10 01:53:26 lwall Locked $
Patch level: 44

Copyright (c) 1989, 1990, Larry Wall
MS-DOS port Copyright (c) 1989, 1990, Diomidis Spinellis
MS-DOS enhancements Copyright (c) 1990, Leonard Reed

Perl may be copied only under the terms of the GNU General Public
License, a copy of which can be found with the Perl 3.0 distribu-
tion kit.
```

The contents of this text changed in later releases.

-w Enables warnings for various conditions such as uninitialized variables and file handles. This may save you from using the debugger. But it may flag variable names that are perfectly valid.

-x   Tells Perl to execute everything after a #!*Perl* as a script until an end of the file (such as Control-Z) is encountered. Useful if you want to execute a Perl script embedded in a text file or mail message. Note the #! statement can contain any text as long as it contains the word Perl.

7. If invoking Perl in the foreground under MS Windows, add a line under the [Extensions] label of WIN.INI that is similar to the following:
```
pl=perl -w ^.pl
[Under File Manager, clicking on a file with a pl extension automati-
cally invokes the Perl interpreter. Make sure that PERL.EXE resides
in a directory specified by a PATH command.]
```
8. Perl works well under 4DOS. To make your scripts self-executable, issue a *set .pl=c:\perl\perl.exe* statement. (Replace with the directory where PERL.EXE resides on your PC or LAN.)
9. Perl invocation options not listed above (-a,-l,-p,-U) are not portable across all operating systems. For example under AmigaDOS, -u and -U are not meaningful or do not work.

Invoking Background Perl Scripts

Perl can be run in the background on most operating systems. Here is how to do it:

OS/2

```
detach perl -s prog2 [Name of Perl script that doesn't prompt for
input. Returns the Process Identification Number is 29.]
```

MS Windows (386 Mode only)

```
1. Invoke Windows in 386 mode (win /3).
2. Invoke (click) on the PIF editor under the Accessories window of
   Program Manager.
3. Click on the Execution: Background box so it is checked (x).
4. Click on the Advanced box near the bottom of the screen.
5. Once on the Advanced Options screen, you may wish to change the
   foreground or background priority to make it run faster or slower.
   These are under Multitasking options. (The default value is 50 for
   background and 100 for foreground and ranges from 0 to 10000.) By
   selecting settings from an application's menu, you can modify these
   values.
6. After saving the PIF file, reenter the Program Manager. Then select
   File from the menu and the NEW option. Click OK that you want to
   create a new program item. Then enter a description (this is shown
   when displaying the icon and is optional) and the name/path of the
   Perl executable with accompanying parameters.) The complete path is
```

```
      needed only if the Perl executable is not on the PATH variable's
      directory search list.
    Note that Perl works well as a full-screen or windowed application.


                               UNIX

    At the $ or %, enter Perl -e 'print STDOUT "A test";'>out.out &
    [& places the job in background and redirects the output to file
    out.out so you can view it later. A message similar to the following
    is then issued [1] 19006.]
```

Tips and Traps:

General

1. Do not run Perl scripts in background that prompt for input. Instead convert these files to use pre-determined values.
2. Don't change a file in foreground that a Perl script is accessing in background or unpredictable results may occur.

OS/2

1. Piping (|) and redirection (< or >) operators are allowed in a DETACH command or a program specified in a DETACH command.
2. DETACH always returns a confirmation message similar to—*The process identification number is 88.*

UNIX

1. The job number is displayed after the command with the & is issued.
   ```
   [1] 19066
   (then followed by.)
   [1] Done
   ```

THE FUTURE OF PERL

The following are some of the trends that will likely occur with Perl:

1. *Awareness about Perl will continue to grow especially among UNIX users.* With all of the following advertising the availability of PERL, it can't help but continue to grow: Overview articles have been appearing about Perl in UNIX trade journals. As mentioned earlier, PERL tutorials are now regular staples at DECUS, Sun (SUGfest), and USENIX user group meetings. A comp.lang.perl Usenet newsgroup is filled daily with a healthy number of

articles. Perl is now part of the popular GNU distribution and comes bundled with Convex and Dell UNIX machines.

2. *Porting of Perl to non-UNIX environments should continue.* There is at least one question each week on is Perl available under non-UNIX environments such as the Macintosh, VMS, and MVS. In time, some enterprising C programmer should develop ports to these environments. A port of Perl to MacMinix was being developed but not released at the time of this book. A release for the Macintosh under MPW is now available.

3. *Interfaces of Perl to various "environments" will continue to grow.* Many users love Perl enough to try to build interfaces with other UNIX tools, databases (such as Oracle, Sybase, and Ingres), and environments (such as Curses and X windows). These efforts will continue to grow.

4. *In time, Perl will be compliant with the interface and calls specified in the IEEE POSIX [Portable Operating System X] standards.* These include POSIX 1003.1 [system interface], 1003.2 [shells and tools], and 1003.4 [real-time extensions]. This allows a POSIX application to run easily on other operating systems.

5. *A Perl compiler* is of interest to many users but *is highly unlikely to be developed.* The reasons against this happening include: Perl's maintainers have no interest in doing this. And technically it is not easy to do this. Also, a compiler could not handle some of the ambiguity present in some variable assignments.

DEVELOPING PERL APPLICATIONS

Chapter 2 looked at three different types of common command language applications. The next two sections provide portable Perl sequences (unless otherwise stated) listed under the type of application where they are most commonly used. However, there is no reason why a particular Perl sequence could not be used by any type of application. The last section discusses some of the major concerns when developing Perl-based applications. It also looks at porting Perl scripts between various platforms and migrating to other command languages.

FRONT-END PERL APPLICATIONS

Two common tasks for Perl scripts are (1) to provide input ("housekeeping") for executables and (2) to run tasks on booting up a computer. The section reviews sequences to perform both of these tasks.

How to Access Operating System Commands in a Perl Script

As mentioned earlier, Perl has over 90 built-in functions included with the language. This reduces the need to invoke the operating system and generate unnecessary subprocesses. The following are tips and guidelines in using operating system commands in Perl scripts:

The following table lists Perl functions/commands and their operating system equivalents. Use this list in deciding if you need to use an operating system command in a script.

Note:

The following is from the README.OS2 file prepared in part by Kai Rommel and reprinted with his permission: (SETPRIORITY, GETPRIORITY, and KILL are Perl functions that simulate OS/2 system calls.)

- SETPRIORITY is now: SETPRIORITY(*class,pid,val*). See Description of DOSSETPRTY () for class and *val* meanings.

   Author's note: Italics added. An OS/2 process (or program) has one or more threads each of which is assigned a priority and a *pid* (thread or process identification number). For DOSSETPRTY, a *pid* of 0 indicates the current thread or process. *Class is* either 0 (Do not change), 1 (Idle Time), 2 (Regular), or 3 (Critical of time). *Val* is the priority level between −31 and +31. A typical use is *setpriority(0,0,+2)*—change priority of current thread or process by 2 (but does not change the current class.)

- GETPRIORITY is now: GETPRIORITY(*dummy,pid*). See description of DOSGETPRTY.

   Author's note: Italics added. An OS/2 process (or program) has one or more threads each of which is assigned a priority and a *pid* (thread or process identifica-

Table 7.1. Perl Functions and OS Equivalents

Perl/function	DOS equivalent	OS/2 equivalent	UNIX equivalent
chdir	chdir or cd	chdir or cd	chdir or cd
chmod	attrib (somewhat)	attrib/eautil (somewhat)	chmod
chown	none	eautil (somewhat)	chown
fcntl	none	none	fcntl
flock	none	none	flock
grep	find (limited)	find (limited)	grep,egrep,fgrep
ioctl	none	none	ioctl
kill	none	none (SEE NOTE ABOVE)	kill
mkdir	mkdir or md	mkdir or md	mkdir or md
readdir	dir	dir	ls
rename	rename	rename	mv
rmdir	rmdir or rd	rmdir or rd	rmdir or rm
setpriority	none	No command—system call (SEE NOTE ABOVE)	nice

tion number.) For DOSGETPRTY, a *pid* of 0 indicates the current thread or process. Typically used as *getpriority(0,0)*.

- KILL is now: Kill(*pid,sig*) where *SIG* can be 0 (kill process),1–3(Send process flag A-C See DOSFLAGPROCESS()). If *PID* is less than zero, the signal is sent to the whole process tree originating at -PID.)

  Author's note: Italics added.

If you wish to process a second script after terminating the first script, then consider using EXEC. Piping/Redirecting of output is allowed.

```
exec ("cat text.txt|more"); #Displays text.txt a screenful at a
time.
```

Under AmigaDOS, the EXEC function is set up in such a way that only the file handles (really an alias associated with a file) for STDIN (standard input) and STDOUT (standard output) are inherited when the function is invoked. This means that various file operations may not work under EXEC. *The following is from the README.AMIGA file created by David G. Grubbs and reprinted with his permission:* The effects of "dup," "fdopen," and the like are lost across an Execute. In particular, the hack of combining stderr with stdout doesn't work. Beware.

The following is from the README.DOS (for PC-DOS and MS-DOS) file created by Len Reed. and reprinted with his permission: The perl exec command (not system, but exec) needs work. It is not MKS compatible.

Author's note: MKS is a UNIX-like toolkit that runs under MS-DOS and OS/.2 (See Appendix 1 for more information.) and may not work at under some systems. It may leave temporary files stranded.

If you wish to process a second script while temporarily stopping processing on a first script, consider using the SYSTEM function. Use the WAIT function and examine $? to learn if the SYSTEM function executed correctly (and divide this number by 256). For UNIX, if calling another script using SYSTEM, use an EXIT *code* statement to pass an exit code with a value of *code* to the main script.

```
system ("cat text.txt|more'); #Displays text.txt a screenful at a
time.
wait (); #Not for Amiga DOS, MS-DOS, and OS/2 versions.
```

Piping/Redirecting of output is allowed in a SYSTEM function.

The following is from the README.ST (for Atari) file created by Jwahar R. Bammi and used with his permission. The command passed to system, etc. can contain redirections of stdin/out, but system does not understand fancy pipelines etc.

How To Capture Output From a Command In a Perl Script

In Perl, there are many ways to capture output from an executable or operating system command:

1. Perl can use the following redirection operators:

<   Read from standard input (STDIN—usually the keyboard) or specified file.

>   Copy to standard output (STDOUT—usually the screen) or specified file (that gets overwritten if it already exists).

>>   Append to standard output (STDOUT—usually the screen) or specified file (if it already exists).

2. Use the above redirection operators when invoking Perl to save output and errors from the processing of a Perl script.
   ```
   Perl prog 1.pl>log.log #Sends all output and errors from Perl to
   #log.log.
   ```
3. Use the above redirection operators in an EXEC or SYSTEM function to capture output. For AmigaDOS, place the redirection argument before other parameters and do not have any spaces between the file name and the redirection operator.
4. Perl supports the advanced redirection features found in OS/2. These include identification of multiple files and the three types of input/output. This is done through the use of file handles—0 for STDIN, 1 for STDOUT and 2 for STDERR, and 3–9 for files used by applications. If used on the *right side of a redirection operator* an ampersand must prefix the file handle. If used on the *left side of a redirection operator,* then the file handle requires no ampersand prefix.
   ```
   system("dir/w>dir.txt 2>&1");
   #Hard to understand at first but the above means: Send a directory
   #listing of the current directory in "wide"
   #format to dir.txt. And also redirect to dir.txt any error messages
   #encountered - - redirection of STDERR and
   #STDOUT. Note the space between dir.txt and the 2 file handle.

   #Note the same syntax can be used on invoking a single Perl
   #command.in AmigaDOS.
   Perl -e 'print "hello world\n" 2>&1';
   ```
5. Under MS-DOS, you have to invoke COMMAND.COM if using an internal DOS command that *does not* contain special characters such as (>,<, and | — these are defined by the METACHAR environment variable) or using another command processor. Examples of internal DOS commands built into

COMMAND.COM and not needing other ("external") files include (MS-DOS 5.0 and later):

> CALL, CHCP, CHDIR, CLS, COMMAND, COPY, CTTY, DATE, DEL (ERASE), DIR, ECHO, EXIT, FOR, GOTO, IF, LOAD-HIGH, MKDIR, PATH, PAUSE, PROMPT, RENAME, RMDIR, SET, TIME, TYPE, VER, VERIFY, and VOL).

```
system "echo.|date>version.txt"; #No need to invoke command.com
#because > is used.
system "command /c date"
#The above statement has an external command and no special charac-
#ters, so you need
#command /c. Note this not needed for OS/2 - - which can also use
CMD/C.]
```

6. Read a later section on performing file functions to learn how to use redirection with file operations.

What To Include in a Startup File

The startup file is where users set up their own "personal environment." This is done by defining environment variables, paths to search for application and data files, and the default prompt. The following is a list of startup files under the various environments where Perl is found:

AmigaDos   Startup-sequence

DOS   AUTOEXEC.BAT/CONFIG.SYS

OS/2   STARTUP.CMD/CONFIG.SYS

UNIX   The . files especially .login (BSD- only read once on login), .cshrc (setup file for the c shell), and .profile (System V - only read once on login)

Early in a startup file, a command could call a Perl script. Here are some things that you can put in this script:

1. "*Welcome commands*" These personalize a session:
```
($sec,$min,$hour)=localtime;
print "Hiya guy, its $hour:$min:$sec\n";
```
2. Seeing the *current values of environment variables* (or use SET instead for DOS, OS/2, and UNIX).
```
#Use the sequence below to capture all current Perl environment vari-
#ables and
#assign them to read-only scalar (string) variables.
require "importenv.pl";
#A GOTCHA under DOS and OS/2 (FAT version). The name is importen.pl.

print "Your search path is is $PATH\n";
```

These will not work on the Amiga because environment variables aren't supported by the default shell. See a later section on using environment variables with Perl for further information.

3. Also use the PRINT command *to display messages to the screen.*

```
              In startup script
    print STDOUT "This machine is Perl-driven\n";
```

4. *Menus.* If you find yourself accessing several programs on startup, perhaps a menu might be useful. Note that only one GOTO is used.

```
#Poor person's object-oriented programming. A menu is defined as a
#subroutine named DMENU.
sub DMENU{ #Start of subroutine
    print STDOUT "*******************************\n";
    print STDOUT "* 1 Reports                   *\n";
    print STDOUT "* 2 Spreadsheets              *\n";
    print STDOUT "* 3 Games                     *\n";
    print STDOUT "*******************************\n";
    print STDOUT "Enter your menu selection (1-3)\n";
    menu100:
      &DMENU;
      $choice=substr(<STDIN>,0,1);
    badchoice:
      if (($choice <1) || ($choice >3))
        {
        #Invalid choice logic goes here.
        print STDOUT "Invalid choice. Please try again\n";
        goto menu100;
        }
      $elsif ($choice == 1) {
      #Report logic goes here
        }
      $elsif ($choice == 2) {
      #Spreadsheet logic goes here
        }
      $elsif ($choice == 3) {
      #Game logic goes here
        }
```

5. Append to a log file that keeps a record when you last logged in:
```
open(LOGFILE,">>log.log");
#Opens the file log.log and associates it with the file handle LOG-
#FILE.
#All output is appended to the end of the file.
@tma=localtime(time);
#Reads the current time and assigns nine values to an array
#Logic to add am or pm.
```

```
if ($tma[2] > 12) {$ampm="a.m.";}
else {$ampm="p.m.";}
$part1 = $tma[4]."/".$tma[3]."/".$tma[5];
$part2 = $tma[2].":".$tma[1].":".$tma[0]." ".$ampm,"\n";
#Writes the concatenated (by .) month and date values out to log.log.
#Could use JOIN instead.
#Printed 10:10:10 a.m. 10/10/91
print $part1," ",$part2; #To screen.
print LOGFILE $part1," ",$part2; #To file.
close(LOGFILE);
```

SYSTEM/UTILITY PERL APPLICATIONS

Despite that its name emphasizes reports and extracts, Perl can more than adequately be used for developing system and utility applications (especially for UNIX sites). The focus of this section is reviewing the components used to develop this type of application on whatever operating system you use with Perl. Please look at the Wall and Schwartz book for further examples of ready-to-run system and utility applications.

How Do I Perform File Operations?

A major strength of Perl is its file operation capabilities, including processing text, binary, and dbm files. DBM files are special files that Perl processes by using associative arrays. These is not available on the the Amiga. A simplified version of a dbm file is a two field "record" with the first field being the "key" or "index" that uniquely identifies the record such as *88888 Rico* with 88888 being the key. This section discusses basic operations on text files. (This is by no means all that you can perform for file operations.)

Here is the basic skeleton of these operations:

Read records from a file

```
    open(FILE1,"</usr/gaj1/temp.txt");
#Read is the default operation so < is not required.
#Opens /usr/gaj1/temp.txt to be read. (Actually redirects input from STDIN
#(keyboard) to
#temp.txt). [The file name is associated with an alias or file handle that is
#conventionally entered
#in upper case.]

    while (<FILE1>){
#While there are records, read them.
        print STDOUT "Record number $. - - $_ \n";
```

```
#This looks more confusing than it is because of the use of special (system)
#variables. $. returns
#the current line (record) number being read. $_ contains the result of many
#operations. In this
#context, $_is the current line being read. So a typical record could look like
#the following:
#Record number 1 - - 88200 Chris Reo 12000
      }
    close(FILE1)
#Explicitly close the file so $. is correct for the next file opened.
```

Write records to a new file

```
    open(FILE1,">/usr/gaj1/temp.txt");
#Opens /usr/gaj1/temp.txt for writing. (An existing file with this name would
#be written over.)
#(Actually redirects output from STDOUT (screen) to temp.txt). The file name is
#associated with an
#alias or file handle that is conventionally entered in upper case.]
        print FILE1 "$id $fname $lname $income \n";
#Writes out one record that has the current value of scalar (string or number
#value) variables.
#Usually, this is in some sort of loop for writing out multiple records.
        close(FILE1)
#Explicitly close file so $. (The special variable containing the current line
#number processed) is
#correct for the next file opened.
```

Write records to an existing file (append)

```
    open(FILE1,">>/usr/gaj1/temp.txt");
#Opens /usr/gaj1/temp.txt to be written. An existing file with this name would
#be appended to
#the end of the file. (Actually redirects output from STDOUT (screen) to
#temp.txt). The file name is
#associated with an alias or file handle that is conventionally entered in
#upper case.]
#Remember to use >> to append to an existing file. The rest is the same as
#writing records to a
#new file is shown in the previous example.
```

The following are additional tips and guidelines when performing file operations with Perl:

1. *The following is from the README.AMIGA file created by David G. Grubbs and reprinted with his permission:*

   Author's Note: The following file operation features on the Amiga are not portable to some platforms where the Perl interpreter is available:

- The parent directory is "/", not ".." and the current directory is " " ..., not ".".
- File names are case *insensitive* . As a result, some of the Perl test scripts ('t' subdirectory) use a capitalized name of the Perl script as a temporary file and write over the script. It also means that Amiga Perl should probably have a "case insensitive compare" operator. Currently it doesn't.
- Temporary files are placed in "ram:"
- Open files are special on the Amiga. You may not move them. If open for writing, you may not read them.

  Author's Note: This means the + operator to both read and write to a file will not work.

  And you must close them before deleting them, even if they are open only for reading.
- The file system doesn't provide Creation or Access times on files.
- The default Amiga shell requires the I/O redirection operators to be *first* on the command line before the arguments. There must be no space between the > or < and the file name.

  Author's Note: redirection operators

2. To make your programs more flexible, create scalar variables to hold file names. Then refer to the scalar variable during file operations:
   ```
   $fnm = "/usr/hjg7/loan.txt";
   open (FILE1,"<$fnm");
   ```
   This makes it easy to change a file name in a program or port a program to another operating system since a change will have to be made in only one place.
   ```
   # $os is defined earlier in the program. [not shown]
   If (($os eq "DOS") || ($os eq "OS2")) {$fnm="c:\perl\loan.txt";}
   #If scalar variable $os is equal to DOS or (||) OS2 then use the
   #appropriate filename
   elsif ($os eq "UNIX") {$fnm="/usr/hjg7/loan.txt";}
   ```
3. There are various special (system) variables that you can use when performing file operations:

$.   Current line read. By closing a file, this value stays accurate.

$/   The delimiter to mark the end of a record. Usually a newline (carriage return or Control-J for the Amiga.)

**$?**   Value of last close. (0 is normal). *if ($?)* to handle abnormal closes.

4. OPEN returns a 1 if successful; use a DIE command to handle unsuccessful file openings. DIE issues a message and an error number and terminates the script.
   ```
   (open(TEMPX,"temp.txt")) || (die "Can't open temp.txt Damn! $!\n");
   # $! says print the error message (such as no such file or
   #directory) and \n says issue a new line
   # (carriage return).
   ```

Or

```
if (open(TEMPX, "temp.txt") !=1)
{die "Can't open temp.txt Damn! $!\n";}
# If open is not equal to 1 then issue the DIE command.
```

5. Use the EOF function for operations on the last record in a file:

```
if (eof(FILE1) ) {print "last record is $. - $_\n";}
#If the next record is the end of the file, print the last record
#number ($.) and the last record ($_).
```

6. Piping output into/from a file is supported. An | placed *before* a file name means the output from a command will be piped *to* that file. An | at the *end* of a file name means that output *from* the file is piped *to* a command. You can use - to pipe to/from STDIN and >- to/from STDOUT.

7. Binary files can be used to store data in a more compact format. Use the following functions to process a binary file using Perl. Note you must close and reopen a file to reset the current mode from binary to text.]

BINMODE   After an OPEN to tell to process a file as a binary file. Only argument is file handle. *This is needed only for ATARI, DOS and OS/2, not UNIX.*

PACK   Packs a string to be used in a binary file.

READ   Reads in a record of x bytes (the third argument) into a scalar variable, the second argument for a certain filehandle (the first argument).

SEEK   Randomly resets the file position.

SYSREAD   Reads a specified number of bytes into a scalar variable.

SYSWRITE   Writes a specified number of bytes from a scalar variable.

TELL   Displays the current position in the file. The only argument is the file handle.

TRUNCATE   Truncates a file to a specified length.

UNPACK   Unpacks a string from a binary file.

WRITE   Write a formatted record to a file. The argument is the file handle or an expression that translates to a file handle.

8. Here are the functions associated with dbm files. AmigaDOS will, in time, support Gnu dbm also called gdbm. Gdbm support was added to the ATARI, MS-DOS 4.10 and OS/2 3.38 perl releases.

DELETE   Deletes a record from a dbm file or an associative array.

DBOPEN   Opens a dbm file.

DBCLOSE   Closes a dbm file.

EACH   Retrieves the key and associated value for a DBM record or associative array.

KEYS   Returns keys (indices) from a dbm file or associative array.

VALUES   Returns all values from a dbm file or associative array.

9. Here are some other functions that are useful for file operations: CHOP removes a newline from a record in a file; SPLIT allows a record to be parsed.

```
open(FILE1,"temp.txt");
while (<FILE1>) {
    chop;
#strip newline from end of record. Assumes record looks like TOM
#SMITH 23
    ($first_name,$last_name,$age) =split(/ /,$_,3);
#Splits the current line into three scalar variables delimited by
#blanks. The result is assigned to
#three scalar variables. Using regular expressions (a combination of
#string and operators that in
#case provide parsing directions to the split function), a record
#could be parsed a variety of ways.
#See String Operations with Perl for more information.) Note that
#new values are assigned to these scalar
#variables when the next record in the file is processed.
```

Or

```
    @array1 = split(/ /,$_);
#Splits the current line into three fields delimited by blanks. The
#result is assigned to an array and
#each array element is assigned one of the three substrings. Thus,
#element 0 (the first element of
#the array NOT element 1) is assigned the first name, element 1 is
#assigned the last name and
#element 2 is assigned the age.

    $first_name = $array1[0];
#Retrieves the value of the first element of the array and assigns
#it to the scalar variable $first_name. AN IMPORTANT POINT - - ele-
#ments in an array are scalar variables such as ($array1[0] and
#@array1 refers to the entire array. (Unless used as an array slice
#such as @array1[0..2] referring to elements zero, one and two in
#the array1 array.]

    $last_name = $array1[1];
    $age = $array1[2]
    print STDOUT "$first_name $last_name $age\n";
#print the values of the parsed record
}
close(FILE1);
```

10. All files that are specified when Perl is invoked are stored in the @ARGV, and $ARGV is the name of the current file being processed or the current

element of the @ARGV array being processed. Doing a WHILE (<>) allows you to process a specified dataset at run-time.

11. The following is from the README.ST (for ATARI) file created by Jwahar R. Bammi and used with his permission.

- Avoid using the back tick ('command'). Use 'open(FOO, "command1")' and use the file handle FOO as appropriate.
- Pipes are a little flakey, but mostly work fine. Pipes, 'prog' etc. are much more efficient. If you have set the environment variable TEMP to point to a ramdisk. Note, when you set TEMP, it should contain *no* trailing back-slash or slash.
- Watch out for redirections. TOS blows up if you try to re-direct a re-directed handle. Atari has greatly improved this situation. Hopefully the next general release of TOS will contain these fixes.
- Files opened for write now correctly contain CR/LF unless they are removed.

How Can I Learn If a File Exists?

Most UNIX shells include a series of test operators that check for the existence of a file and other attributes. Perl is no exception to this. The following subroutine shows the use of the more common file test operators:

```
sub FILETEST {
local($fnm,$han) = @_;
print "here's what I can tell you about $fnm\n";
if (-e $fnm) {print "Yup the file sure exists\n";}
  else {print "Shame on you, giving me a non-existent file \n";}
if (-T $fnm) {print "Ooh a text file\n";}
  else {print "Its not a text file. The plot thickens \n";}
if (-B $fnm) {print "Oy a binary file\n";}
  else {print "Its not a binary file. We must look further \n";}
if (-d $fnm) {print "This ain't no file..Its a directory\n";}
  else {print "This file is many things but not a directory \n";}
if (-z $fnm)
{print "This is a malnourished file with a size of zero\n";}
  else {print "Its a bouncing healthy non-zero size file \n";}
if (-s $fnm) {print "Amazing, a non-zero file\n";}
  else {print "What we have here is a file with a size of zero \n";}
if (-W $fnm) {print "You have WRITE permission on a file. Lucky\n";}
  else
{print "Go to bed and no WRITE permission on the file young man \n";}
if (-X $fnm)
{print "You have EXECUTE permission on a file. Oh boy\n";}
  else
{print "EXECUTE permission on this file - - not for you dude \n";}
if (-R $fnm)
{print "You have READ permission on this file - - foiled again!\n";}
```

```
     else {print "READ permission on this file? - - next! \n";}
  if (-O $fnm) {print "You OWN the file and \$50,000 in taxes !\n";}
     else
  {print "You don't OWN or rent this file. A lease is available.! \n";}
  if (-t $han) {print "The file is OPEN. Oh my!\n";}
     else {print "This file ain't OPEN and neither is the bar! \n";}
  }
  open(FILEX,"log.log");
  &FILETEST("log.log","FILEX");
```

Note that directories for DOS and OS/2 will always be seen by the preceding tests as zero-size files. DOS text files will have read and write permission while executable files will have read, write, and execute permission.

These additional file test operators return values that can be of use. Most file test operators return 1 if processed successfully. These will not work correctly for operating systems that don't have creation or access times such as AmigaDOS and MS-DOS.

```
  $mdays = -M $fnm;
  #Number of days including parts of days (such as .25 being a quarter
  #of a day) since the file was
  #last modified.
  $adays = -A $fnm; #Meaningless for DOS and Amiga DOS.
  #Number of days including parts of days (such as .25 being a quarter
  #of a day) since the file was
  #last accessed.
  print "The file was modified $mdays ago and accessed $adays ago\n";
  #Returns a number like 8.03764339. Use the INT function to display
  #this as a whole number.
```

Here is some additional information about file test operators for various operating systems:

1. Most file test operators can have either the file handle or file name as arguments. For AmigaDOS Perl users, only file names can be used except for -t.
2. Additional test operators (such as -C, -M, -S, -b, -c, -g, -k, -l, -p, -u) not discussed here are not portable across Perl interpreters on various operating systems or will have meaningless results if run.
3. The Perl library has the validate sequence to perform multiple file tests.
   ```
   require "validate.pl";
   ```
   ```
   # Require is Perl's equivalent of C's #include - -can access any sub-
   #routine in the included Perl
   #script when invoked. By using the VALIDATE subroutine, you can per-
   #form multiple tests on
   #the same file. You can use the DIE or WARN functions to notify you
   #if a test fails or use the
   #default error messages.
   ```

```
&validate('
    /usr/test.txt -s || warn "file is zero size\n"
    /usr/ghi.gab -TB
```

Directory Operations With Perl

Perl can manipulate directories as well as files with relative ease. This is done by assigning the files in the directory to an array and then manipulating the array. To learn more about manipulating files using Perl, see a later section on learning if a file exists.

The following are the functions commonly used to perform directory operations: (A *directoryhandle* is an alias for a *directoryname.*)

chdir *directoryname*   Changes the current directory to *directoryname*

closedir *directoryhandle*   Closes a directory

mkdir *directoryname*   Creates a directory

opendir *directoryhandle directoryname*   Opens a directory using *directoryhandle* as an alias

readdir *directoryhandle*   Retrieves a directory listing (to be assigned to an array)

rewindir *directoryhandle*   Points the directory to the start of the listing

rmdir *directoryname*   Deletes a directory if containing no files

seekdir *directoryhandle*   Sets the directory listing pointer

telldir *directoryhandle*   Shows the position of the directory listing pointer

The following is a simple program that lists the sizes of files in a specified directory (note that it does not do a recursive descent):

```
sub dirlist{
    local($ddir) = @_; #Assign the directory argument to $ddir.
    chdir("$ddir")||(die "can't change to $ddir $!\n");
#The above makes the directory specified by $ddir the current direc-
#tory.
    opendir(DIR1,".")||(die "Can't open DIR1 $!\n"); #Then open it.
    @dalist =readdir(DIR1);
#The above gets a list of files in the directory and assigns them to
#the @dalist array.
    foreach $cnt (@dalist) { #Loop through array.
        $size = -s $cnt; #Get size using -s.
        print "$cnt has a size of $size K\n"; #Then print it.
    }
    closedir(DIR1);
}
&dirlist("."); #current directory
```

These are additional tips and guidelines when performing directory operations:

1. Use the *-d* test operator to test if a file is a directory.
   ```
   if (-d $fnm) {print STDOUT "File is a directory!\n";}
       else {print STDOUT "File is not a directory.\n";}
   ```

2. Keep this in mind when performing directory operations with AmigaDos Perl interpreter. a. CHDIR affects all processes — beware! b. RM (RMDIR) allows wildcard characters. MKDIR does not.

3. The Perl library has the PWD subroutine that can be used to assign the current directory to an environment variable named PWD.

4. The OS/2 Perl interpreter has the following differences when performing directory operations.
   a. OPENDIR actually stores the entire directory and releases it in parts for READDIR and other directory commands.
   b. CHDIR can include the drive letters in the *directoryname* argument and can switch to a particular drive. This is also true for DOS. So the following are valid:
   ```
   #chdir("A:"); #Switches to the A (floppy) drive.
   #chdir("A:\TEMP"); #Switches to the temp subdirectory on the A
   #drive.
   ```

Using Environment Variables With Perl

All Perl interpreters allow some form of **environment or shell variables.** (For example under MS-DOS, PC-DOS, and OS/2, these include %PATH — the current path, and the UNIX equivalent is $PATH. Also see Chapter 6 for more on the environment variables under MS-DOS and OS/2.) The following are tips and guidelines for using environment variables under Perl.

1. The Perl library includes an *importenv* script that copies the values of the currently defined environment variables and assigns them to Perl scalar variables of the same name. Note these scalar variables cannot be modified.
   ```
   require "importenv.pl" #This is importen.pl for DOS or OS/2.
   #All current defined environment variables are now Perl scalar vari-
   #ables of the same name.
   #later in the script.
   print "My current path is $PATH\n";
   ```

2. %ENV is a special (system) variable that contains all your currently defined environment variables. Because %ENV is an associative array, you can use the EACH, KEYS, or VALUES functions to display the currently defined values.

Assigning an environment variable value to a Perl variable

```
$VAR1 = $ENV{'PATH'};
```

Retrieve all currently defined environment variables

```
foreach $cnt(%ENV) {
    print $cnt, "\n";
}
```

Set an environment variable

```
$ENV{'TERMINAL'} = "VT100";
#This is inherited by all child processes such as SYSTEM or EXEC.
```

3. Keep this in mind when using environment variables with the AmigaDOS Perl interpreter: *The following appears in the README.Amiga file created by David G. Grubbs and is reproduced with his permission:*

> The default shell has no variables and doesn't evaluate environment variables. (e.g. $HOME) in any way. You can use $ENV() inside PERL, or use 'getenv VAR', if you have installed the "getenv" command, but "system 'echo $HOME' " will echo '$HOME'.

> Environment variables exist in two forms: AmigaDOS and Manx/Rokicki. I chose to use the AmigaDOS form, so I had to write a non-Manx pair of getenv/setenv functions. I also wrote simple user programs to get at these, though the Amiga-DOS versions should work fine. I provide source to a bunch of small tools: env (walks through ENV: and prints your environment variables), getenv (prints an environment variable), setenv (sets an environment variable).

> Author's note: parentheses added.

4. The DOS Perl interpreter will use the values of certain environment variables if they are defined. These include the following: (*This is from the README..ENV file created by Len Reed and is reprinted with his permission.*)

$COMSPEC   All pathnames can have forward or back slashes. Full path name of DOS command interpreter, e.g., "c:\\command.com." Used only if $SHELL is not defined. If not found, "\\command.com" is used. (It is bad practice to allow $COMSPEC to default or to have anything other than a full drive and path name. You don't want your programs to look for command.com on alternate drives.)

$METACHAR List of characters that are metacharacters to the $SHELL or $COMSPEC. Used to determine if command can run directly or if a subshell is invoked/ if undefined, |<> is used for COMSPEC and * " ?<>|()&] [$# ' \ for SHELL.

$PERLLIB Directory containing perl library. Defaults to /usr/local/lib/perl. Should be applicable even in UNIX.

> *Author's note:* The specified directory is appended to the @INC special (system)variable. @INC tells Perl where to search for a subroutine that resides in a file specified by a REQUIRE command. (The other directory searched is the current directory.)

$TMP First choice for temporary files, e.g. "h:\\tmp". If not set, uses $TMPDIR, if that's not set, the current directory is used. Swapping also goes here unless $EXESWP is defined. Temp files are pseudo-pipes, the swap file, and the -e file.

Here is an example of how to define these environment variables:
```
SET TMP=C:\TEMP
SET PERLLIB=C:\PERL\LIB
```

5. The following are some tips for using environment variables with the ATARI Perl interpreter: This is from the README.ST (ATARI) file created by Jwahar Bammi and used with his permission
   • Setenv PERLLIB to point to the subdirectory containing lib/*

   > *Author's note:* the Perl system library.

   (If you want PERLLIB to contain more than one path, separate them with commas)
   • ....Pipes, 'prog' etc are much more efficient if you have set the environment var TEMP to point to a ramdisk. Note when you set TEMP, it should contain *no* tailing backslash (or slash).
   • Put all these executables (perl.ttpperlglob.ttp, and echo.ttp) in your $PATH....
6. The Macintosh Perl version appears to have a large number of unique environment variables but these are not documented at the time of publication.

SELF-CONTAINED PERL APPLICATIONS

Self-contained Perl applications are one or more Perl scripts that are oriented to end-users instead of system administrators. Sequences in this section include (1) capturing, parsing, and validating user input, (2) communicating between a Perl subroutine and the main script and (3) miscellaneous operations (such as changing the case of a string).

How To Capture User Command Line Values

If any parameters are supplied when Perl is invoked, they are stored in the @ARGV array. Array elements range from $ARGV[0] to $ARGV[$#ARGV]. Here is a simple example:

```
#The Perl script expects two filenames as parameters. Exit if there
#are more than two arguments.
    if ($#ARGV <1) {die "Syntax: Perl copyit fromfile tofile \n";}
    if (-e $argv[0]) {$fromfile=$argv[0];}
        else {
            die "$fromfile doesn't exist\n";
        }
#If a "from file" is specified, then check if it exists. Exit the
#script if it does not.
```

Here are some tips and traps when capturing command line input:

1. $0 always will contain the currently executing Perl script. All files that are specified when Perl is invoked are stored in the @ARGV. And $ARGV is the name of the current file being processed or the current element of the @ARGV array being processed.
2. If you use command line switches (such as -t or /t) in your script and wish to have an easy means of processing them, consider using the *getopts* library sequence (or the *getopt* library sequence) to process just those switches requiring an argument.
```
require "getopts.pl"
#later in the script
&Getopts('f:h') #Note the mixed case
#Both f and h are valid options. But only f (because of the colon)
#takes an argument that is stored
#in $opt_f if present.
```
3. Or consider using the -s switch when invoking Perl. Additional switches if found are assigned to scalar variables of the same name.
```
Perl -s tellit.pl -u
if ($u) {#some sequence} #This is processed if -u is entered when
#Perl is invoked.
```

How To Create Menus, User Prompts, and Confirmation Messages

This can be done with the PRINT (more efficient) or PRINTF command. See the next section on how to capture input.

PRINT for prompting input

```
print STDOUT "Enter the abbreviation of your state of resi-
dence:\n ";
    $choice=substr(<STDIN>,0,2); #Takes only the first two characters.
```

PRINT for menus

```
print STDOUT "************************************************\n";
print STDOUT "* Please Enter ONE of the following:        *\n";
print STDOUT "* 1 - 1990 Report                           *\n";
print STDOUT "* 2 - 1991 Report                           *\n";
print STDOUT "* 3 - 1992 Report                           *\n";
print STDOUT "************************************************\n";
    sleep(2) ;[Pause to allow user to read choices.]
$choice=substr(<STDIN>,0,1);
```

PRINT for confirmation messages

```
$ryear=1991;
$prt=prt1;
print STDOUT " Report for $ryear is queued to $prt\n";
```

The following are tips and guidelines in creating display output:

1. You can use terminal escape sequences to enhance your display output.
2. Document near the start of your Perl script what each command-line parameter/flags are.
3. Putting a series of *print STDOUT " |n"*; to clear the screen before the menu always guarantees that the complete menu appears on the screen.

How To Capture User Input

Using Perl just to capture user input and process "conversational" scripts vastly underutilizes this command language. However, Perl can easily capture user input within a script. Here are some tips and guidelines for doing this:

1. Use the predefined file handle STDIN (file alias) to capture input from the command line:
   ```
   $a = substr(<STDIN>,0); #Captures all entered characters
   ```
2. Use the following to capture just one character:
   ```
   $a = substr(<STDIN>,0,1);
   #Captures the first character entered.
   ```

Or
```
$a = $getc(STDIN); #Slower performance than the first approach.
```
3. Here's one way to capture input into a file:
```
open(FILE1,">/usr/ten.txt");
    while (<STDIN>) { #Process until end of file. (Ctrl-D - -UNIX,
#Ctrl-Z - - DOS or OS/2)
        print FILE1 "$_\n";
    }
close(FILE1);
```

How To Parse Command Line/User Input

One of the major strengths of Perl is its string handling capabilities. This section reviews the major concepts of using Perl and string parsing:

The following are the functions/commands used for parsing strings:

1. **Split** (/substring/,string,variable limit) is the general-purpose function for parsing. *Substring* is composed of **regular expressions** or **regexp.** These are a combination of substrings and special operators used to select valid strings for parsing. This is discussed in a previous section on string operations with DOS or OS/2 batch language. The *string* is parsed by blanks if no *substring* is specified. *String* can be a string or scalar variable with $_ as the default. *Variable limit* specifies the maximum number of scalar variables that a *string* can be parsed into (very likely it will use fewer variables):
```
@a=split(/ /,$_,);
#Split string on blanks for the current line and assign it to the
#array @a. For example, if $_ was a
#string . Then $a[0] has a value of a and $a[1] has a value of
#string. Note // would split it by
#characters.

($one,$two,$three,$four) = split(/ /,$_,4);
#The third argument says that the string can be parsed up to four
#strings. For example, if $_ was a
#string. Then $first has a value of a and $second has a value of
#string and $three/$four are
#undefined. If the third argument is not supplied, the variable limit
#for the above list of scalar
#variables is 5 (This is always one more than the number of scalar
#variables on the left side of the equals signs.)
```
2. **Unpack** is used to unpack binary files and assign it to an array.
3. **Substr** can be used to parse a substring if the location of the substring in the string is known or can be derived using the INDEX (position of *first* appearance of a substring in a string) or RINDEX (position of *last* appearance of a substring in a string) functions. Note the value of the special (system) variable

$[determines the starting position (usually zero) if the starting position argument is not supplied:

```
#Retrieves a substring par that starts in position 13. (Remember that
#0 is the first position in a
#substring.)

$a = "A string to parse.";
$b=substr($a,12,3);
```
Or
```
$location=index($a,"par");
#Location has a value of 12.
$b=substr($a,$location,3);
```

4. SPLICE removes elements in an array and replaces it with a specified list.
```
@a= {'0', '1', '2', '3', '4'};
@b=splice(@a,0,2,'a','b','c'};
#discards 0,1,2 and replaces them with a,b,c so the array @a becomes
#a,b,c, 3,4. Note that @b
#holds the discarded elements (0,1,2). You can also mix and match
#pairs of backquotes (') and
#single quotes(`) in specifying array elements.
```

How To Validate Command Line/User Input

A previous section on capturing user command line values discussed some of the possible validations of command line values. Another earlier section showed validations you can do on files and directories. And a previous section on capturing user input showed you how to create a script to capture user input. This section shows other validations you can do on user input captured from within a Perl script:

Substring matching

```
#Here is a sample of regular expressions. Slashes (/) mark the start and end of
#the pattern (
#Two useful operators to place before strings are caret (^) [that matches the
#specified substring if
#at the start of the line] and $ [that matches the specified substring if at
#the end of the line. See String Operation with Perl.
#for more information on regular expressions.
#Note the default string to operate for most functions is $_. (Usually the cur-
#rent line.)

if (/^wednesday/i|/$wednesday/i) {sequence...}
#The | (vertical bar) allows you to match one of a series of multiple patterns.
#(In this case, if
#wednesday is either at the start or end of a string.) The i says to match
Wednesday if the string is found in any case.
```

Or
```
if (index($str,"wednesday") >=0) {sequence...}
#If wednesday is found in the first position (0) or higher in variable $str
#then do.
```
Or
```
if (substr($str,0,9) eq "Wednesday") {sequence...}
#If wednesday is found in the first position (0) or higher in variable $str
#then do.
```

Test for blanks\non-blanks

```
if (/^\s/) {sequence...}
#Regular expression tests if a string starts with a blank (\s is the character
#that specifies white
#space). An equivalent is if (!/^/S/)... . [! is a negation operator.]
```

```
if (/^\S/) {sequence...} or if (!/^s/) {sequence}
#Regular expression tests if a string starts with a non-blank character. (\S is
#the character that specifies a non-white space character (or blank).
```

```
if (/./) {sequence...}
#Regular expression (period) that matches on any character that is not newline.
```

Test if a number

```
if (/^\d/) {sequence...}
```
Or
```
if (/^[0-9]/){sequence...}
#Regular expression tests if a string starts with a number. (\d is the charac-
#ter that specifies a
#number or specify a range of numbers using brackets in this case 0-9.)
```

Test if a letter

```
if (/^\D/) {sequence...}
```
Or
```
if (/^[a-z|A-Z]/){sequence...}
#Regular expression tests if a string starts with a letter. (\D is the charac-
#ter that specifies a
#non-number or specify a range of letters using brackets. In this case any
#uppercase or lowercase
#letter.
```

Test for a word

```
if (/\btape\b/)
#Matches any occurrence of the word tape in the string $_. Without the \b, the
#command
#matches on any substring tape. (\b says match on the word not the string.)
```

Date And Time Operations With Perl

Perl is more than adequate in performing date and time operations. Here are some tips and guidelines in developing date/and time-oriented scripts.

1. $^T is the time that the current executing script started executing. Some of the file test operators use this result to determine the last time a file was modified (-M) or accessed (-A).
   ```
   #See how long since the current script started executing.
   $a = $^T; #Gets the time since the current script started executing
   print $a, "\n"; #Prints a number like 32617798
     ($sec,$min,$hour) = localtime($a);
   #Now convert the value into something more understandable.
     print "This script has been executing for $hour: $min: $sec\n";
   #Displayed: This script has been executing for 0:1:10
   ```

2. The Perl library includes two time-oriented sequences. Ctime.pl creates a date from a date-time value. Timelocal "unparses" a time/date array into a standard time format (number of seconds since 1/1/70 Greenwich Mean Time).

3. TIME returns the current time as the number of seconds since 1/1/70 Greenwich Mean Time. This is the default argument for GMTIME (parses current time) that generates a time/date structure based on Greenwich mean time. LOCALTIME is similar but generates a time/date structure that is based on your local time instead of Greenwich Mean Time. Note that you do not need to declare all nine fields, just the ones up to and including a desired field.
   ```
   ($seconds,$minutes,$hour,$day_of_the_month,$month_number,$year,
   $weekday,$yday,$dst) = localtime;
   print "$hour:$minutes:$seconds\n";
   print "$month_number/$day_of_the_month/$year\n";
   print "$weekday,$yday,$dst\n";
   #displayed 11:43:27 4/24/91 5,143,1 Read below to see what some values mean
   ```
   This summarizes *in order* the fields generated using a GMTIME or LOCALTIME function: *Value* refers to the argument provided to GMTIME or LOCALTIME (such as GMTIME(*value*).

Seconds   0–59 (seconds part of *value*)

Minutes   0–59 (minutes part of *value*)

Hour   0–23 (hour part of *value* in 24-hour format with 0 being midnight)

Day of the month   1–31 (day of the month for *value*)

Month   0–11 (month of *value* with 0 being January)

Year   xxxx (year of *value*)

Day of the week   0–6 (day of the week of *value* with 0 being Sunday)

Day of the year   0–365 (day of the year of *value* with 0 as January 1)

Daylight saving time indicator   0–1 (1 if daylight savings, 0 if no daylight savings)

4. You can also reformat values:

```
#this transforms hour values 0 (12 midnight) -23 (11 pm)
$hour1 = ("12am","1am", "2am", "3am", "4am","5am","6am","7am","8am",
    "9am","10am","11am","12pm","1pm","2pm","3pm","4pm","5pm",
    "6pm", "7pm", "8pm", "9pm", "10pm", "11pm")
[(localtime) [2] ]; #Remember that fields start with an index of 0
#not 1 so this is the third field.
print $hour1,"\n";
```

5. The UTIME function changes the access and modification date of a file. Its arguments in order are access time, modification time, file names.
6. The TIMES function gives the various elapsed times of the current process and related subprocesses.
7. Note you will have to set the TZ environment variable to use GMTIME under Amiga DOS.

Text Case Operations With Perl

The following are tips and traps when dealing with text case operations with Perl scripts:

1. See the previous section on validating command line/user input for validating input for upper-/lowercase including using the i operand in the m or // function.
2. Use the TR or Y function to translate all lowercase characters to uppercase or the reverse.

```
($str2 = $str) =~ y/A-Z/a-z/;
#Translates $str to lowercase and then copies to $str2.
#Note the =~ is used for pattern matching and be used with the m or /
#/.s, and tr functions.

($str = $_) =~ y/a-z/A-Z/;
#Translates $_to uppercase and then assign to $str.
```

String Operations With Perl

A major strength of Perl is its string-handling capabilities. Also see the early sections of Chapter 7 for ideas. Here is an overview of just some of Perl's string capabilities:

1. Many Perl functions (m or //, s, y or tr) use regular expressions to determine what strings to match or not match on. A regular expression usually consists of one or more of the following format. See the Carrato (1991) reference for further information.

/ prefix string frequency/

Prefix consists of:

   ^   (Match the start of the string)

   $ (Match the end of the string)

   \b   (Match on the word)

   \B   (Match on other things besides word)

String consists of a string with or without these special characters:

   ▪ (match all characters except newline [carriage return])

   [0–9] (match all numbers)

   [a–z] (match any lowercase character)

   [A–Z] (match any lowercase character)

   \n,\r [newline, carriage return]

   \d   [a number character (0–9)]

   \D   [a non-number character]

   \w   [any number or letter character]

   \W   [all non-number and non-letter characters]

   \s   [blank or white space]

Frequency consists of:

   +   (Match string one or more times. Same as {1,}.)

   *   (Match a string zero or more times. Same as {0,})

2. Placing one or more expressions in *parentheses* will allow you to perform further manipulation once the match is made:

  a. A very useful operator is | (vertical bar) allowing multiple strings to be tested from left to right.

  b. You can use special (system) variables to manipulate the result of a string operation. These are always local to the current command or block of commands.

     $& (returns the matched substring)

     $` (returns everything *up to* the matched substring)

     $+ (returns which multiple string (if using the | operator) was matched)

     $´ (returns the characters in a string *after* the matched substring)

     Also $1 through $9 contain, in order, each multiple string (if using the | operator) matched. $1–$9 are available only in the current block (structure).

3. To concatenate string, use the ▪ operator or the JOIN function (if using the same delimiter between substrings). However, using JOIN is a more efficient approach. Or use the .= operator to append one variable to another.

```
#Join three strings together with "/" between them.
$str1="usr";
$str2="jwh1";
```

```
$str3="lib";
$a=join('/',$str1,$str2,$str3);
print $a,"\n"; #Dsplayed /usr/jwh1/lib
```
Or
```
$a="/".$str1."/".$str2."/".$str3;
print $a,"\n";#Displayed /usr/jwh1/lib

#Concatenate two strings together.
$b=1;
$b .=$str1; #Using the .= to append the value of $str1 to $b.
print $b,"\n"; #Displayed 1usr
```

4. The x operator allows you to repeat a character or string a specified number:
```
$a = "*"; #Could also be a string like $a= "eggplant".
print $a x 40;
# This repeats the * character 40 times. A space is required between
#the x and the 40.
```

5. SUBSTR can be used to parse a substring if the location of the substring in the string is known or can be derived using the INDEX (position of *first* appearance of a substring in a string) or RINDEX (position of *last* appearance of a substring in a string) functions. CHOP deletes the last character chopped. (If on the *right side* of an equals signs, the scalar variable is assigned the character chopped.) And LENGTH returns the length of a string.
```
#Parses a string to parse and returns par.
$a = "A string to parse";
$b=substr($a, 12,3);
#Retrieves a substring par that starts in position 12. (Remember that
#0 is the first position in a
#substring.)
print $b,"\n"; #Displayed par.
```
Or
```
$location=index($a,"par");
#Location has a value of 12.
$b=substr($a,$location,3);
print $b; #Displayed par.
#An example that takes a string like /usr/local/lib and assigns it to
#two variables. So $last has a
#value of lib and $first has a value of usr.local.
$a = "usr/local/lib";
($a2=$a) =~ s/\//\./g;                   #Substitutes all / to ..
$len=length($a2);                        #Length of entire string.
$off=rindex($a2,".");                    #Position of last period plus
                                         #one
                                         #(start of substring lib).
$len2=($len-($len-$off));                #Length needed to find
                                         #usr.local.
$last=substr($a2,$off,($len-$off)+1);    #Assigned lib.
```

```
$first=substr($a2,0,$len2);          #Assigned usr.local.
print $first,"\n";                   #Print usr.local.
print $last,"\n";                    #Print lib.
```

6. SPLIT allows a record to be parsed. Regular expressions (listed earlier in this section) may be used.

```
($str1,$str2)=split(/ /,$str,2);
#Splits a string using the default delimiter of whitespace (blank)
#into scalar variable.
```

Array Operations With Perl

Besides its text operations, Perl has very strong array-processing capabilities. These include both simple arrays or associated (indexed) arrays.

1. Array and array subsets (slices) are prefixed by the @. However, a specific array element is prefixed by a $. (*Remember that array elements always start with zero not one.*) $#arrayname is the number of elements of the array and the number of the last element in the array. An array can mix and match decimals, strings, and whole numbers.

```
@array 1 =('0','1','2','3','4'); #define the array.
print @array1,"\n"; #Prints the entire array.
print @array1[0,1],"\n";#Refers to an array subset(slice), the first
#two elements on array (0,1).
print @array1[0..1],"\n"; #Same as previous example. Uses the range
#operator (..).
print $array1[0],"\n"; #Refers to the first element (0).
print $array1[$#array1],"\n"; #Refers to the last element in the
#array (4).
```

2. Once an array is created, various operators can manipulate them:

GREP   Find a regular expression in an array (like the UNIX command). You have to write your own sequence to grep on a file.

JOIN   Concatenates scalar variables or an array

POP   Deletes the *last* element of array

PUSH   Places a value at the *end* of an array

REVERSE   Rearranges an array with the last element now first

SHIFT   Deletes the *first* element of an array

SORT   Sorts an array in ascending order. (Note: sort does not sort numerically. You have to write a sequence to do that).

SPLICE   Remove and replace array elements.

UNSHIFT   Places a value at the *end* of an array.

Here are some examples:

Array Definition

```
@array1=(18,1.1,forecast,late,daddy,2.888);
```

Sort Array

```
@a=sort(@array1); #Returns 1.1, 18, 2,888, daddy, forecast, late.
#Note order.
print @a,"- -sorted - -\n";
```

Replace Element in an Array

```
splice(@array1,2,1,"rain");
#SPLICE substitutes forecast (starting with element 2 for only 1 ele-
#ment) with rain.
print @array1,"- -splice\n";
```

Find Elements Containing a Specified String

```
@array1=(18,1.1,forecast,late,daddy,2.888); #Restore original array.
@a=grep(/cast/,@array1); #Find elements with string "cast". Returns
#forecast.
print @a,"\n";
```

Reverse an Array

```
@a=reverse(@array1); #Reverses returns array 2.88, daddy, late, fore-
#cast, 1.1, 18
print @a,"\n";
```

Add a New Last Element to an Array

```
@a=push(@array1,"end"); #Puts the string "end" as the last element of
#the array.
print @array1,"\n";
```

Remove the Last Element of an Array

```
pop(@array1); #Then removes "end" as the last element in the array.
print @array1,"\n";
```

Add a new first element to an array

```
unshift(@array1,"start"); #Puts "start" as the first element of the
#array.
print @array1,"\n";
```

Remove the first element of an array

```
shift(@array1); #Then removes "start" as the first element in the
#array.
print @array1,"\n";
```

3. The following are some of the functions used with associative arrays and records from DBM files (available to all Perl interpreters except the AMIGA.):

delete   Deletes an associated array record

each   Retrieves the key and associated value for a DBM record or associative array. EACH, KEYS, and VALUES display associative array values in no discernible order.

keys   Return keys (indices) from a dbm file or associative array

values   Return all values from a dbm file or associative array. These are in the same order as the values returned by the KEYS function.

The following are some examples using these functions. Note that the % prefix designates an associative array.

```
#Simplified associative array with software and version
```

Define an Associative Array

```
%arrayx = (
'DBASE4',        '1.3',
'Perl',          '4.0',
'Scribe',        '8.1',
'Lotus 1-2-3',   '3.2'
);
```

List all the Values of an Associative Array

```
foreach $cnt (%arrayx) { #Lists all the records in an associative
#array.
```

```
($index,$asvalue)=each %arrayx;
print "INDEX $index ASVALUE $asvalue\n"; #Prints all records.
$a=delete $arrayx{'DBASE4'}; #Delete DBASE4 record.
```

Sort an Associative Array by its Keys

```
@index =sort keys(%arrayx); #Sort by keys
print @index,"SORT\n"; #Displayed:Lotus 1-2-3, Perl,Scribe
```

Display Just the Values of an Associative Array

```
@avalues=values(%arrayx);
print @avalues, "VALUES\n"; #Displayed: 8.1, 4.0, 3.2
```

How Do I Pass Information Between Perl Scripts?

You can pass information a variety of ways between Perl scripts:

1. Assigning a value to an environment variable. A child process inherits the environment variables available to the parent process. However, an environment variable created or modified by a child is not recognized by the parent process.

Main Perl Script

```
$ENV{'VALUE'} ="88";
eval ("exec(\"perl c:\env3.pl \")");        #DOS and OS/2 only
eval 'exec("/usr/bin/perl env3.pl")';       #UNIX
```

Second (nested) Perl Script

```
print %ENV,"\n";
#The above lists VALUE and its value 88 and all other currently
#defined environment variables.
```

2. Explicitly passing exit codes (whole number not characters) using the EXIT command. (Note the default value is zero.) On receiving the EXIT code, have your program divide the number by 256 to get the real exit code. Currently, this works only for UNIX.

Second Perl Script (Invoked by SYSTEM Command)

```
EXIT 1
```

First Perl Script

```
if ($? eq 256) {print "script failed";}
```

---

3. *For subroutines only,* either using the RETURN command (slower of the two) or a command that evaluates to a desired expression as the last statement in a subroutine:

```perl
#Simple calculator
sub CALC {
    local($a,$b,$op)=@_;
    $c=eval("$a $op $b");
    return $c;
}
#Later in the script...
&CALC(2,2,"*");
```

4. When invoking a subroutine, you may pass either values or names of arrays and filehandles.

Passing a Value

```perl
&CALC(2,2,"*")
#Passing two parameters trapped by the special (system) variable @_.
#From the above example.
```

Passing an Array Name

```perl
sub CALC2 {
    local(*aq) = @_;
    $c=eval("$aq[0] $aq[2] $aq[1]");
    return $c;
}
@array1=(2,4,'*'); #Here the array we will use
&CALC2(*array1);
#The above invokes the CALC2 subroutine. Note the * to pass the array
name.
#The * allows you to pass an array or filehandle name to a subrou-
#tine. That name is then
#substituted for the name used in the subroutine. In our example,
#array1 is substituted for arrayx.
```

Subroutines and Perl

Perl supports both *subroutines* and *functions*. The only difference between the two is that functions are used with other Perl commands:

```
#CALC is shown in the previous section and is a simple calculator.


                    Subroutine Invocation

&CALC(2,2,"*");


                     Function Invocation

if (&CALC(2,2,"*") eq 4) {sequence..}
    Also
print &CALC(2,2,"*"), "\n";
```

Here are some basic tips and guidelines when using subroutines and Perl:

1. This is the skeleton of a Perl subroutine definition:
   ```
   sub NAME {
   #Start of the subroutine structure. The subroutine NAME is usually in
   #UPPER case.
   local($a,$b...) =@_;
   #Capture the parameters supplied when invoking the subroutine. And
   #assign them to local
   #variables. @_ is a special (system) array that contains the parame-
   #ters passed when the
   #subroutine was invoked.
   sequence
   $c = operation;
   #Last variable that is returned to the main program. Or use the less
   efficient RETURN function
   } #end of subroutine
   ```
2. Subroutine definitions can be placed anywhere in a Perl script. However, placing them near the start of a Perl script makes them easier to find.
3. Note that by default, variables in a subroutine are *global* so it is easy to modify variables in the "main" script. Use the LOCAL function to limit the scope of a variable to just that function/subroutine. An alternative is to create new variables that are accessible by the "main" script (and don't overwrite any existing variables).
4. When invoking a subroutine, you may pass either values, or names of arrays and filehandles.

Passing a Value

```
&CALC(2,2,"*");
#Passing three parameters trapped by the special (system) array @_.
#From the example in the previous section
```

Passing an Array name

```
sub CALC2 {
    local(*aq) = @_;
    $c=eval("$aq[0] $aq[2] $aq[1]");
    return $c;
}
@array1=(2,4,'*'); #Here the array we will use
&CALC2(*array1);
#The above invokes the CALC2 subroutine. Note the * to pass the array
#name.
#The * allows you to pass an array or filehandle name to a subrou-
#tine. That name is then
#substituted for the name used in the subroutine. In our example,
#array1 is substituted for arrayx.
```

5. Because @_ is an array, you can perform normal operations on it including accessing array element $_[0]..$_[$#_]. (last element). This allows you to easily manipulate subroutine user-supplied parameters.

6. By using eval, you can trap errors from a subroutine (*eval "$addit";*). Special (system) variable $@ has a null value if the eval (subroutine) worked correctly. Otherwise it contains the error message from processing.

Packages and Perl

The previous section discussed how the LOCAL function allows variables to be local only for that function. However, suppose you have a *whole set* of variables and file handles that you want to make unknown to Perl scripts unless explicitly accessed. What's a Perl coder to do? The solution is to use **packages**—a special environment where all variables, arrays, and subroutine names are "not known" by other packages. Here are some tips and guidelines in using Perl and packages:

1. The default Perl package is called *main* (like the major function in C). It contains filehandles (such as STDIN and STDOUT). To switch a subroutine to be in the main environment, prefix it with main' (such as *sub main'addit*).

2. Placing a PACKAGE *package_name* command in a subroutine will have that subroutine associated with the specified package. *This is the only way to make a subroutine or file handle part of a package.*

```
sub halpack'addit { #Part of a subroutine.
    package halpack; #Associated with the package named halpack.
    $a = @_;
    $a="10";
```

3. An associative array called *%_package_name* (with *package_name* being the name of the package) stores the values of a package. The output is listed under point 4.

```
while (($k,$v) = each %_halpack) {
print $k,"= ",$v,"\n";
}
```

4. The Perl library provides the DUMPVAR routine to list all the variables and the values in a specified package.

```
#The following is a simple example using dumpvar and the sample out-
put.
require "dumpvar.pl";
$h ="halpack";
&dumpvar($h);
```

Sample output

```
addit= *halpack'addit          #Subroutine
a= *halpack'addit              #Variable
```

5. Once in the Perl debugger, use V (main or any package) and X (main) to list the variables for a package.

How Can I Create Reports Using Perl?

Perl has some special variables and commands that can easily produce formatted reports while including "merged" data. Here is a simple report that shows the major features:

```
#Record collection report.
```

Data File

```
Perl After Dark*CLs*Good*10.95
In a Loop*DO-WHILES*Bad*5.50
Wasted Wax*In for the $*Fair*0.00
```

Perl Script

```
#The format output header record that the WRITE command uses. The
#form follows:
```

```
format HEAD1=
#report record


        Tommy Jack's CD Collection
CD Name      Group        Condition       Cost
. #end of form


# the format output record that the WRITE record uses for the data.
format FILE2=
~ #The tilde operator hides blank lines.
@>>>>>>>>>>>>>>>  @<<<<<<<<<<<<<  @|||||||  @###.##
$cd              $group           $condition, $cost
     #blank line on purpose
. #end of form
# The above format record looks more mysterious than it actually is.
#Each field in the
#report is designated by an @ (single-line field) or ^ (multiple-line
#field). Within each field
#are dummy operators that each hold one place (character) of the
#field and also the place's
#justification. (So the $cd field is right justified a maximum of
#fifteen characters. Note the variable
#associated with a field is always found on the next line.) Place-
#holder operators include < (left
#justify),>(right justify) , | (center), #.## (numeric and decimal)

open(FILE1, "text.txt") || (die "cant open text.txt $!\n"); #Raw
#data.
open(FILE2, ">rept.txt") || (die "cant open rept.txt $!\n"); #Output
#report.
select (FILE2); $^ = "HEAD1";$~ = "FILE2";
#The above statement is where the header and data forms are defined.
while (<FILE1>) { #Loop through raw data.
chop;
($cd,$group,$condition,$cost) = split(/\*/,$_); #Split on *.
write(FILE2);
}
close(FILE1);
close(FILE2);
```

Report

	Tommy Jack's CD Collection		
CD Name	Group	Condition	Cost
Perl After Dark	CLs	Good	10.95
In a Loop	DO-WHILES	Bad	5.50
Wasted Wax	In for the $	Fair	0.00

Here are some tips and guidelines in reproducing reports with Perl:

1. Perl includes special (system) variables to be used just with formatted reports. These include:

$%	Current page number
$=	Current page length (60 is the default)
$-	Number of lines left to print on the current page
$~	The current report format
$^	The current format for top of page (if used)

2. Comments starting with an # are allowed in a format form.

Which Version of Perl Do I Have?

Knowing the Perl version is useful in discovering what features and commands are available and in debugging Perl scripts. (For example, later versions of Perl have the alarm function.) The following shows one way of getting this information:

```
perl -v #The OS/2 version lists invocation options as well (not
#shown)
   Or
print "$]"; #System version containing Perl version and patch number
```

Output (This is from OS/2)

```
This is perl, version 3.0

$Header: perly.c,v 3.0.1.9 90/11/10 01:53:26 |wall Locked $
Patch level: 41
#Only the above two lines are displayed with the print "$]";
Copyright (c) 1989, 1990, Larry Wall
MS-DOS port Copyright (c) 1989, 1990, Diomidis Spinellis
OS/2 port Copyright (c) 1990, Raymond Chen, Kai Uwe Rommel

Perl may be copied only under the terms of the GNU General Public
License, a copy of which can be found with the Perl 3.0 distribution
kit.
```

The contents changed under version 4.

OTHER PERL CONCERNS

This section is concerned with those topics appropriate for all types of Perl applications. This includes porting Perl scripts between various operating systems and converting to other command languages.

How Do I Debug Perl Scripts?

The following are tips and guidelines in debugging Perl scripts:

1. The Perl debugger (Perl -d) is not available for the Amiga environment.

2. Make sure the debugger is in the search path specified by the @INC special (system) variable. For DOS, this is done by placing the perldb.pl library script in a directory specified by the environment variable PERLLIB.

3. Perl does include a debugger that is invoked by a *Perl-d* statement (which is really a Perl script called perldb.pl. (Under OS/2 there is a file called perldb.dif that must be patched to perldb.pl so the debugger can run.) Using the debugger, you examine the value of variables, see where a program is branching to, establish breakpoints, and execute any Perl command(s)—and not just the current program. Here are the more commonly used debugger commands.

b *test* Establishes a breakpoint if *test is* true

d *line* Clear breakpoint

h Help

I *start+n* List n+1 number of lines starting with *start.* Alternate forms include | *line ,* | *start-finish, and* | *subroutine.*

q Quit the debugger

s Step through program one command at a time

T Trace

V package List variables in a package. X lists all the variables for the main (default) package.

! line ! by itself reexecutes the previous command. A line number can be specified.

Perl command Execute any Perl command

Here is a sample session:

4. The following tips may help in debugging a problem:
   a. Create a sequence like the following:

```
#Invoke this with perl -s scriptname -d. This creates a scalar vari-
#able called $d.
if ($d) {$dflag=1;} #enable debugging flag
sub DEBUGIT {
   local($line) = @ _;
   if ($dflag eq 1) {print STDOUT "$line";}
}
#Sample use of DEBUGIT subroutine.
$cnt=1;
&DEBUGIT("CNT is $cnt\n");
```

The preceding sequence is useful for those who do not wish to use the debugger or have the debugger unavailable to them. It can check the following: (a) values at a certain point in a script or (b) if a certain flow control structure is executed and branching correctly.

b. Entering *print "%ENV\n";* shows what is the current value of all environment variables. Knowing the current value can explain why an IF or FOR command is being ignored.

c. Check your version number of Perl as outlined in a previous section on Perl versions: Later versions may have fixed your problem. Run the tests supplied with Perl to see if your interpreter is running correctly.

d. By invoking a subroutine with an EVAL command you can capture any errors by examining the $@ special (system) variable.

e. Using DIE statements with $! will usually give you an error message (or in UNIX, errno associated with an action.)

f. Examining $? to see the result of a code passed in an EXIT command from a script invoked by a SYSTEM or EVAL SYSTEM statement. (UNIX only).

The following is from the README.ST (ATARI) file created by Jwahar Bammi and is printed here with his permission.

$! still doesn't contain the correct value when there is no error.

5. Use the following general approach in debugging problems: What happened? Describe action—what happened and what was supposed to happen? Record all error messages. Gather more information about the problem: Where exactly is the error happening? (On invocation, at a certain label, when invoking another script, executing a subprocess, or invoking an executable?) Get the problem to occur in a consistent fashion. This makes it easier to resolve. Use the techniques mentioned in point 4 above.

Make an educated guess on what caused the problem and a way to test it. Perform the test. If it works, there is no need to go further. Otherwise return to the gather-more-information step.

6. Running the following script may be useful in debugging Perl problems. It detects if you are missing one or more of special characters used with Perl. This is especially useful if you are getting a "syntax error" message and you

can't run the debugger on a script. Usually the culprit is that you are missing a bracket.

7. If your Perl interpreter was installed correctly, you are able to use debugging flags to to enhance your debugging capabilities. These are passed when Perl is

```
#Check.pl invoked by perl check.pl script-to-check (name of the script to
#check)
$lb=0;$rb=0;$sm=0;$lp=0;$rp=0;$pn=0;$c=0;$dq=0;$sq=0; #initialize variables
while (<>) { #Loop through Perl script specified (script-to-check).
if (^{/) {$lb++;}
if (^}/) {$rb++;}
if (^;/) {$sm++;}
if (^(/) {$lp++;}
if (/\)/) {$rp++;}
if (/\#/) {$pn++;}
if (^"/) {$dq++;}
if (^'/) {$sq++;}
}
print"              Report on $ARGV\n";
print '*' x 78,"\n";
print " Number of lines in file       $.\n";
print " Left Brackets                 $lb\n";
print " Right Brackets                $rb\n";
print " Semicolons                    $sm\n";
print " Left Parenthesis              $lp\n";
print " Right Parenthesis             $rp\n";
print " Comments                      $pn\n";
print " Double quotes                 $dq\n";
print " Single quotes                 $sq\n";
print '*' x 78,"\n";
if ($lb > $rb)
    {print "Possible syntax error: Need a RIGHT BRACKET\n";$c++;}
if ($rb > $lb)
    {print "Possible syntax error: NEED a LEFT BRACKET\n";$c++;}
if ($lp > $rp)
    {print "Possible syntax error: Need a RIGHT PARENTHESIS\n";$c++;}
if ($rp > $lp)
    {print "Possible syntax error: Need a LEFT PARENTHESIS\n";$c++;}
if ($sm < $.)
    {print "Possible syntax error: May be missing a SEMICOLON\n";$c++;}
if (($dq % 2) == 1)
    {print "Possible Syntax Error. Need a DOUBLE QUOTE\n"$c++;}
if (($sq % 2) == 1)
    {print "Possible Syntax Error. Need a SINGLE QUOTE\n";$c++;}
if ($c eq 0) {print "No potential problems with this script\n";}
else
    {print "There are at least $c possible errors. Check your script\n";}
```

invoked using the -D*number* option. With *number* being the debugging flag number such as 14 (trace script), 256 (display formats), and 512 (displays regular expressions after processing).

The Elements of Perl Style

Because of its versatility and flexibility, Perl has many different scripting styles. These general rules apply to all types of Perl applications—use them based on your personal and site preferences:

1. *Make your Perl scripts readable:*
   a. *Break your Perl scripts into modules* performing only one or two functions. Use label names to describe these functions and to mark their start.
   b. *Indent at least two or three spaces* for (1) code under a label (left justify), (2) the commands contained within an IF, FOREACH, FOR and WHILE structures, and (3) between arguments in a function.
   d. *Line Up* all structures IFs, FORs, FOREACHs, and WHILEs and equal signs in an assignment statement.
   e. Freely use *blank* space to separate modules (before labels marking a new module) and flow control structures such as IF.
   f. Some *commenting* to self-document the scripts is necessary: Comments, prefixed by a #, have no effect on the speed of processing of Perl scripts.
      Try to keep comments up to date. There are various styles of Perl script commenting:
   (1) Comment only complicated (i.e. non-obvious) sequences.
   (2) Comment only non-portable commands.
   (3) Place blank lines between blocks of comments.
   (4) Comment some type of header "record" that lists the script name, what each command line parameter (@ARGV) is, what each label (module) does, any nested scripts used, any subroutines/functions used, any environment variables used, any features that may not work in earlier releases, and script version history (creator, revisor, date and modification).
   (5) One or more comments before each label.
   (6) My own preference is the "jump start" axiom—*write as much documentation to allow you (after some period of time) or another person to understand quickly how a Perl script works.*
   g. *Use various cases in your programs.* A common practice is to put filehandles, subroutine and function names in *uppercase* and comments/commands in *lowercase.* Whatever approach you use, make sure it is consistently applied for all scripts.
   h. *Use meaningful names* for script names, labels, file handles, environment variables, variable names, array names, and so on.

2. *Make your script as effective as possible:*
   a. Leave things as you found them.
      (1) Close all files.
      (2) Return to the original directory.
      (3) Remove all temporary files.
      (4) Remove all unneeded environment variables or reset those to be reused.
      (5) Reset your editor/operating system settings, privileges, and protections if changed.
      (6) Do all of the preceding steps if an error is encountered and you are about to exit from the script.
   b. Never assume user input is correct. Always check case, date type, for blanks, for a valid value, and if in the valid range.
   c. If the same script, is using a certain module heavily, then consider converting it to a subroutine or function. If several scripts are using a certain script, then convert the pertinent part to a nested script.
   d. Do the following at the start of a command procedure: (1) Issue a #!/usr/bin/perl, (2) Initialize appropriate variables, (3) Provide a way to capture input if important command line parameters are not supplied, and (4) Clear the screen before displaying output.
   e. Depending on the type of users you have using a script, consider having different sequences for different types of users.
   f. Link a library of accompanying C subroutines to Perl to perform heavily used tasks such as file operations, exception handling, and prompting for input. See the next section to learn more about this.
   g. Minimize what gets displayed to the user: Some of these are usually disabled when debugging a Perl script.
   h. Have one common exit point that takes errors away from the main part of a program.

How Can I Extend the Perl Language?

Many user-created programs enhance Perl, including interfaces with other command languages and interfaces with window packages (look at the usub directory of the Perl general distribution).

Examples of doing this are available in the eg directory that is part of the Perl general distribution. If you need any of these enhancements, consider any of the following ways to extend Perl:

1. Build your own subroutine and function "libraries." The next section will give you ideas on where to look for these.
2. If you have knowledge of C, you can link it to create a customized Perl version. This is done by linking uperl.o and using the userinit subroutine.

3. Perl includes several convert programs. These may not be available on all operating systems (such as the Amiga):

a2p   Convert from awk to Perl
s2p   Convert from sed to Perl
h2ph   Convert C header files to Perl header files (not always transparent).

The preceding gets you started, but some further conversion may be necessary to run efficiently (faster) under Perl.
4. Use the syscall function to invoke operating system calls to further extend your Perl scripts.

Where Can I Learn More About Perl?

Here is a list of some places where you can learn more about Perl applications:

- There is currently no magazine column(s) dedicated to Perl. Articles have appeared from time to time in *UNIX Review, UNIX World, Byte,* and *Sun Expert* on Perl.
- The *Usenix* users group has Perl tutorials, as do the *Sun*'s user group (SUGfest) and the *DEC Users Group* (DECUS).
  - **DECUS,** 333 South Street SHR1-4/D31, Shrewsbury, Mass. 01545-4112; (508) 841-3389.
  - **SUN User Group** Suite 315, 1330 Beacon St, Brookline, Mass. 02416; (617) 232-0514, fax (617) 232-1347.
  - **Usenix Association** 2560 Ninth St, Suite 215, Berkeley, CA 94710; (415) 528-8649, Email: office@usenix.org.
- The *comp.lang.perl* is the most likely place to find information. Both Larry Wall and Randal Schwartz post answers to common problems. Availability of Perl updates, frequently asked question listings, and source (including examples from the Wall and Schwartz book) are posted. For non-Usenet users, mail messages to usersrequest@fuggles.acc.virginia.edu.
- *Anonymous ftp* for programs including the Perl interpreter source: Anonymous ftp sites include:

betwixt.cs.caltech.edu   131.215.128.4 (comp.lang.perl archives)
charon.mit.edu   18.70.0.224
chem.bu.edu   128.197.30.18 Formatted version of Perl (help) pages in texinfo and postscript.
convex.com   130.168.1.1
jpl-devvax.jpl.nasa.edu   128.149.1.143

lan_stuff.ucs.indiana.edu   129.79.16.96

uunet.uu.net   192.48.46.2

tut.cis.ohio-state.edu   128.146.8.60

Exception Handling in Perl

The following are tips and traps in dealing with error handling in Perl scripts:

1. Use the special (system) variables to capture return codes such as $? for SYS-TEM function calls, $@ for error codes from EVALs and REQUIREs. Also, $! usually has the current error number (errno). | ($!. under the Atari will not have the correct value when there is no error.)
2. Use the DIE function to print a message (and optionally $!) and then exit the script. Use the WARN function to print a message but not exit the script.
3. Use the EXIT and RETURN or last assignment statement (for subroutines) to pass exit(return) codes) between scripts and subroutines to the main script.
4. Use the KILL function to stop a series of processes (if supported such as OS/2 and UNIX).
5. Many operating systems send a "signal" when an error or an interruption has occurred. Perl recognizes these and can set a label that invokes an exception-handling sequence (error/attention routine). Here is an example of using signals in Perl.

```perl
$SIG{"INT"}= "bye1"; #Assigns bye to handle all common signals
$SIG{"QUIT"}= "bye1";
$SIG{"ABRT"}= "bye1";
print % SIG;
# The above prints system associative array that contains all cur-
#rently defined signals and their
#associated subroutines.
#later in the script...

sub bye 1 {
    local($stype) = @_; #Capture the type of signal.
    print "The signal is $stype\n";
    print "You asked to interrupt this script. Fine by me\n";
    print "Closing all files\n";
    close(FILE1);
    close(FILE2);
}
```

Other signals include:

SIG{'ALRM'}   Send alarm signal

SIG{'ABRT'}   Send abort signal

SIG{'FPE'}   Floating point signal

SIG{'ILL'}   Illegal instruction

SIG{'INT'}   Interrupt script. Breaks script when CTRL C is pressed (DOS, OS/2, and UNIX).

SIG {'QUIT'}   Quit script

Remember that signals apply only to the main package unless another package is explicitly specified (see a previous section on subroutines and Perl for how to do this). Also note that signal names and error numbers vary across operating systems. (Note that how signals work with Perl under AmigaDOS is untested.)

Portability of Perl Scripts

This section discusses concerns when porting Perl across the various operating systems. Here are some tips and guidelines when porting Perl across operating systems:

1. Create scalar variables to set the current operating system. Use this to define operating-system features such as file names, Perl functions used, and so on.
2. Use scalar variables to hold file names so you have to make a change in only one place.
3. Consider using file names that are portable across operating systems (such as text.txt, which can be used by DOS, OS/2, and UNIX).
4. In general, stay away from those functions that perform subprocess operations, socket operations, symbolic link operations, change file protection, run SETUID scripts, or perform database management operations.
5. Avoid using undump if porting a program. The result is unique to each operating system.
6. Minimize use of environment variables for portable programs—specific variables are not always available across operating systems.
7. Perl scripts may have different extensions across operating systems (.PL for UNIX, .BAT for DOS, and .CMD for OS/2).
8. System calls using the SYSCALL function are generally not portable across operating systems. (Such as the Atari's support for Gemdos |xbios|bios interfaces.)
9. Signals may be different across operating systems.
10. Library Perl scripts may be named slightly differently across operating systems (example: for UNIX, importenv.pl,, and DOS or OS/2, importen.pl).

11. If a nested Perl script is invoked by EVAL SYSTEM or SYSTEM and an EXIT code is passed, $? will not correctly capture it under DOS and OS/2.
12. AMIGA, MS-DOS, and OS/2 do not have either a creation or access time for a file.
13. Stay away from Macintosh-specific functions! Ask (ask user for value), answer (display dialog box), pick (choose a value), sgetfile/sgetfolder (get file or folder), and sputfile (write a file).

Migrating to Other Command Languages

Like REXX, Perl is a fairly complete language. So there will be only a few occasions that you will need to convert to other command languages. Many of the command languages in this book are available on the same platforms as Perl, so there is some variety from which to choose.

When Should I Consider Converting My Perl Script?

When any of the following becomes a need:

- When scripts require much interaction with the users
- When the emphasis is manipulating words rather than text files
- When programs need to be ported to VMS, CMS, or MVS.
- When you need to teach a command language to someone unfamiliar with C or UNIX.
- When a full-screen/windowing application needs to be developed (sometimes can be developed with Perl).
- When complex data structures need to be processed

What Command Language Should I Convert To?

1. A *compiled language program* remains a good possibility. The next best thing would be calling a compiled program from a Perl script (or using the SYSCALL function to do the same thing by accessing a desired system call).
2. The *batch language* would be a step back from Perl. It contains less sophisticated exception handling, flow control operators, variable types, and file operations. Batch files lack arrays, function libraries, system variables, the ability to capture user input, and real debugger. However, it is available on two of the same platforms that Perl is—DOS and OS/2—and is fairly portable between those two environments.
3. The *CLIST* language is available for MS-DOS (pCLIST). It offers some of the functionality of Perl but has less sophisticated data types—i.e. no true arrays or decimals—exception handling, report generation, and function library. However, clist code is also portable to the TSO environment found on IBM mainframes (which Perl currently is not).

4. A *DCL* interpreter is available for UNIX (various flavors) and DOS—two of the three environments where Perl is found. DCL offers some of the functionality of Perl but has less sophisticated data types and flow control structures and lacks a true debugger. However, DCL code is portable to VMS (which Perl currently is not).

5. *REXX* interpreters are available for all Perl platforms—DOS (Kilowatt, Quercus and Trodus); OS/2 (part of OS/2 since 1.2 for extended edition and 1.3 for standard edition.* AmigaDOS, and UNIX. It is also available on the entire line of operating systems for IBM mainframes and minicomputers. REXX offers nearly all the functions of Perl but is stronger in manipulating words instead of text files and does not have database and socket functions built into the standard language. Various additional packages do this.

Some of the preceding choices support a greater number of environments that Perl does (such as DCL and REXX). The rest of the chapter discusses the major issues in converting Perl scripts to other command languages.

Perl to Batch Language

1. The following Perl concepts have no equivalent in the batch language:
   a. Math functions
   b. Networking functions
   c. DBM functions (database)
   d. Awk to Perl, C header files to Perl, and sed to Perl converters
   e. Setuid and setgid scripts
   f. Associative arrays
   g. Report variables.
   h. Binary file mode.

2. Here are recommendations on Perl commands/functions that can be easily converted to batch language equivalents:
   a. @ARGV in main scripts and @_for subroutines to %1–%9
   b. Environment variables or scalar variables to environment variables
   c. Assignment statement to SET
   d. For (more powerful in PERL.) or foreach to FOR
   e. Exec or sys and DOS or OS/2 *command* to DOS or OS/2 commands
   f. Eval, perl *name* and syscall function to CALL, COMMAND, CMD (OS/2), DETACH (OS/2), and START
   g. A subprocedure (sub) or function to a heavily used module in a batch file. With return is a function, otherwise is a subprocedure.

Versions are also available from Quercus and Tritus.

h. $? to IF ERRORLEVEL (if supported by the DOS command or executable)

i. Print, printf, and sprintf to ECHO

j. IF $ARGV[1] to IF %1

k. Gmtime or localtime to ECHO. | DATE | FIND "1990"

l. Gmtime or localtime to ECHO. | TIME | FIND ":"

m. Statements that have the same names and perform similar functions (but not necessarily the same syntax): GOTO, Labels, IF, Multiple IFs, FOR

n. The signals sequences as indicated by the $SIG array are roughly equivalent to using BREAK=ON (in your CONFIG.SYS file) and capturing selected ERRORLEVELS (DOS 5 and later). Under DOS, an application is interrupted when a user presses CTRL-Break/Ctrl-C. Perl signal sequences include ABRT (abnormal script terminal), ILL (illegal command), INT (equivalent to CTRL/C and CTRL Break), QUIT (quit script), and TERM (termination request).

o. perl -d to ECHO ON

p. -e *filename* to IF EXIST *filename* and !-e *filename* to IF NOT EXIST *filename*

q. perl -v to VER

r. $ENV{'PATH'} = "path" to SET PATH="path"/ $ENV{'VAR'} = "value" to SET var=value

s. if-elsif to IF, do *block* while and do *block* until to FOR

Perl to Clist

The following are tips and traps in converting from Perl scripts to clist programs:

1. These useful Perl concepts and commands have no direct equivalent in the clist language:
   a. Environment variables—these are similar to global symbolic variables
   b. Converting DOS to TSO commands
   c. Math functions
   d. Networking functions
   e. Awk to Perl, C header files to Perl, and sed to Perl converters
   f. Setuid and setgid scripts
   g. Associative arrays
   h. Report variables
   i. Binary file mode

2. The following Perl commands/functions can be easily converted to clist equivalents:
   a. @ARGV for main scripts and @_ for subroutines to PROC positional operands

    b. Environment variables to local/global symbolic variables

    c. Multiple IFs to SELECT

    d. do *block* while and do *block* until to DO-WHILE, DO UNTIL, or Iterative DO

    e. exec/sys and the command to DOS command

    f. for or foreach to iterative or compound DO

    g. perl *script_name* to EXEC clist, or *clist_name*

    h. A subroutine or function (sub) to a subprocedure (SYSCALL)

    i. $?. to &LASTCC

    j. print to WRITE

    k. IF $ARGV[..] to PROC *var* ...if &*var*

    l. gmtime/localtime to &SYSDATE

    m. gmtime/localtime to &SYSTIME

    n. Statements that have the same names and perform similar functions (but not necessarily the same syntax): GOTO, Labels, IF, DO.

    o. The signals sequences as indicated by the $SIG array are the equivalent of the attention (ATTN) key being pressed. These include ABRT (abnormal script terminal), ILL (illegal command), INT (equivalent to CTRL/C and CTRL Break), QUIT (quit script), and TERM (termination request). So Perl signal sequences can be converted with some effort to ATTN and ERROR sequences.

    p. CONTROL CONLIST etc to Perl -d

    q. -e to &SYSDSN

    r. Perl -v to &SYSTSOE

    s. tr/a-z/A-Z/ to &SYSCAPS and tr/A-Z/a-z/ to &SYSLC

3. The following clist statements have no equivalent in Perl and have to be added after the clist is converted:

    a. DATA-ENDDATA and DATA-PROMPT-ENDDATA (The file handle DATA and the system variable _END_ are somewhat equivalent.)

    b. LISTDSI (somewhat the equivalent of the file test operators)

    c. NGLOBAL, SYSREF

    d. All functions and control variables not listed above

    e. Double ampersand symbolic variables

Perl to DCL

Here are recommendations on Perl commands that can be easily converted to DCL commands.

1. These useful Perl concepts and commands have no direct equivalent in the DCL language:

   a. Converting UNIX-based functions to VMS such as socket, dbms, password file, flock, ioctl, and others

2. The following Perl commands/functions can be easily converted to DCL equivalents:

   a. $ARGV[0]-$ARGV[$#ARGV] to P1–P8

   b. Environment variables to local and global symbols

   c. for to a loop sequence

   d. UNIX/DOS commands to VMS commands

   e. &subroutine to CALL

   f. A subroutine/function to a subprocedure (GOSUB or CALL)

   g. $? to $STATUS

   h. print to WRITE SYS$OUTPUT

   i. IF $ARGV[0] to IF P1

   j. gmtime/localtime to F$TIME

   k. gmtime/localtime to F$TIME

   l. Statements that have the same names and perform similar functions (but not necessarily the same syntax): GOTO, Labels, IF, Multiple IFs, assignment statements.

   m. The signals sequences as indicated by the $SIG array are the equivalent of the attention (CTRL-Y) key being pressed. You can use *ON CONTROL_Y sequences* to handle when the Control-Y is pressed within a DCL command procedure. The $SIG sequences include ABRT abnormal script terminal), ILL (illegal command), INT (equivalent to CTRL/C and CTRL Break), QUIT (quit script) and TERM (termination request).

   n. Perl -d to SET VERIFY and F$VERIFY

   o. -e to IF F$SEARCH

   p. Perl -v/$] to F$GETSYI("VERSION")

   q. tr/A-Z/a-z/ and tr/a-z/A-Z/ to F$EDIT

3. These DCL concepts and commands have no equivalent in the Perl language.

   a. **Logicals,** an alias for a file, tape, or disk device, or another logical (it may help you to substitute the word "location" when thinking about logicals) and **symbols** (an alias for a command, character string, another symbol or lexical function). For MS-DOS and UNIX users, these are similar to using environment variables where you can assign an alias to the directory or file name.

   b. All lexical functions not mentioned above

   c. File protections and system privileges (except for OS/2 and UNIX).

   d. Global symbols SEVERITY and RESTART

   e. STOP

Perl to REXX

1. Here are recommendations on Perl commands and functions that can be easily converted to REXX instructions and built-in functions:
   a. $ARGV[0]-$ARGV[$#ARGV] to PARSE ARG
   b. Environment variables to local and global symbols
   c. Assignment statement to assignment statement
   d. for/foreach to SELECT
   e. Multiple ifs to iterative or compound DO
   f. do *block* while and do *block* until to Iterative DO, DO WHILE, DO UNTIL.
   g. Host commands under Perl would be ADDRESS *environment* command or "command"
   h. Perl, eval, exec, or sys to cmd *execname* (OS/2), rexx *execname* (DOS, Quercus), ex *execname* (DOS, Kilowatt), exec execname (TSO), rxx programname (UNIX, Workstation Group). See Chapter 4's section on invoking a foreground REXX exec for further information.
   i. A subroutine to a subprocedure (CALL) and a function to a function
   j. $? to RC
   k. Print to SAY
   l. IF ($ARGV[0]...) to PARSE ARG val1;IF val1 (no predefined command-line variables)
   m. gmtime/localtime to DATE()
   n. gmtime/localtime to TIME()
   o. Statements that have the same names and perform similar functions (but not necessarily the same syntax): Labels, IF, Multiple IFs
   p. The signals sequences as indicated by the $SIG array are the equivalent of a SIGNAL sequence. You can use CALL ON HALT/SIGNAL ON HALT *sequences* to handle when a signal is detected. The $SIG sequences include ABRT (abnormal script terminal), ILL (illegal command), INT (equivalent to CTRL/C and CTRL Break), QUIT (quit script), and TERM (termination request).
   q. Perl -d to TRACE command and function
   r. Perl -v or print "$]\n"; to PARSE VERSION
   s. tr to TRANSLATE (to convert).

2. The following REXX instructions/concepts have no equivalent in Perl and have to be added after the command procedure is converted:
   a. Data buffer or stack operations (other than PULL or QUEUE)
   b. Compound symbols and related instructions
   c. ADDRESS
   d. Parsing templates

SUGGESTED READINGS

Bammi, Jwahari. "README. ST" textfile

Chen, Raymond, 1990. *Notes on the OS/2 Perl port,* Text file.

Christiansen, Tom, 1990. *Perl Course Notes.* (Handout).

Christiansen, Tom, 1991. Frequently Asked Questions Regarding Perl, with Answers. Text file.

Corrato, Tony, An Introduction to Regular Expressions. UNIX SIG Session Notes. *1991 Spring DECUS Symposium,* pp. 168–169.

Dilorio, Frank, 1989. Good Code, Bad Code: Strategies for Program Design. *NESUG 89 Conference Proceedings,* pp. 260–266.

Galligher, Gordon C. 1990. The Wisdom of Perl. *SUN Expert.* 2(4), pp. 62–67.

Grubbs, David C., 1990. *Porting PERL to the Amiga.* Text file.

Kellem, Jeff, and Larry Wall, 1991. *Perl Manual.* Text file.

Kerninghan, Brian W., and P.J. Plauger, 1978. *The Elements of Programming Style,* 2nd ed. New York: McGraw-Hill.

Kolstad, Ron, 1990 Perl: The Super-Language, *UNIX Review.* 8(5), pp. 30–40.

Kolstad, Ron, 1990 Perl: The Super-Language, Part II, *UNIX Review.* 8(6), pp. 79–85.

Kolstad, Ron, 1990 Perl: The Super-Language, Part III, *UNIX Review.* 8(7), pp. 44–48.

Manheimer, Ken, 1991 "A Comparison of UNIX Primary Shells" text file.

Morin, Richard, 1991. The Reference Library: Shell Scripting, *UNIX Review.* 9(1), pp. 83–7.

Reed, Len, 1990. *Additional MS DOS Perl Notes.* Text file.

Reisler, Kurt, 1991. A Swiss Army Knife for Building Utilities, *Digital Review,* 8(29), p. 30.

Ryan, Bob, 1990. Scripts Unbounded, *Byte.* August, pp. 235–240.

Salus, Peter H., 1990. SUGfest Preview. 1(13), pp. 70–76.

Spinellis, Diomidis, 1990. *Notes on the MS-DOS Perl Port.* Text file.

Wall, Larry, and Randall L. Schwartz, 1991. *Programming Perl.* Sebastopol, Calif.: O'Reilly & Associates.

Wall, Larry, 1991. The Mystery of the Perl Bug. *UNIX World.* 8(10), pp. 113–126.

Wall, Larry, 1991. The Perl of Least Resistance, *UNIX World.* 8(9), pp. 111–126.

Wall, Larry, 1991. Through the Perly Gates, *UNIX World.* 8(8), pp. 115–128.

8

Command Language Cookbook—The Grand Tour of the Major Command Languages

This chapter attempts to provide, for the first time, an overview of five of today's more popular command languages. It allows you to shop around before choosing the command language that's right for your application. Table 8-1 shows how you can use this chapter to do this. (Also look at Figure 1-1 which shows how you can use Chapters 2, 8, and the rest of the book in developing your command language application.)

CHOOSING A COMMAND LANGUAGE

Choosing a command language for any application is no easy task. When you decide which command language is best for an application, two major questions usually come to mind (see Figure 1-1 for an approach to develop command language applications and other places in the book to look for information):

Which command languages are available for my operating system/environment and can I port them to other operating systems?

Which command languages support the type of data and files that I plan to use in my application? (This assumes that you have a good understanding of your application **before** choosing a command language. Chapter 2 includes information that may help in reaching such an understanding by examining application types and command language components.)

The next two sections attempt to provide answers to these questions.

Table 8-1. Using This Chapter to Choose a Command Language

Step (section)	Tasks
Selecting command language candidates for your application (Choosing a Command Language)	Using the flow diagrams, decide which command languages are candidates for your application based on types of data, types of file, and operating system used. This is equivalent to the "information gathering stage" for new car buyers where they pick up brochures to read and also look at how various magazines rated their car
Comparing command languages (A Comparison of Command Languages)	Learn how your command language candidates compare on: • features (broken down by command language components, see Chapter 2) • ease of use/power • benchmarks This is the equivalent of the "pre-decision stage" for new car buyers where they are comparing features, looking at models, test driving, and "kicking the tires."
Comparison of command language commands (Comparing Commands Across Command Languages)	Learn the equivalent commands for each command language. These are broken down by: • components (see Chapter 2) • type (i.e. commands, system variables, built-in function) This is the equivalent of when new car buyers look for a model from a different company that is like their present car.

By Operating System

At least one command language is available for most operating systems/environments. Figure 8-1 shows the command languages by operating systems (including their portability).

Here are some notes explaining Figure 8-1's classification of portable/non-portable and some more information.

- Guidelines on porting between operating systems/environments for the command languages described in Chapters 3 through 7 can be found near the end of each chapter.
- Some command languages listed as non-portable do have versions available under other operating systems. But they do not offer the same high

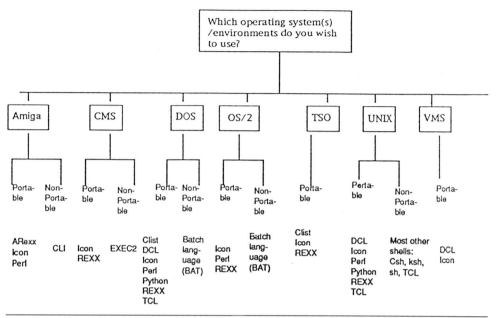

Figure 8-1. Command Language by Operating System

degree of portability (80 to 90 percent) as the other command languages shown here.

- DOS and OS/2 batch language files are somewhat portable (40 to 75 percent) across the other operating system. However, the OS/2 version has slightly greater functionality (and non-portable) features than DOS.
- Some UNIX shells (Csh, Ksh, and Sh) are available for AmigaDOS, DOS, and OS/2. It is unknown how portable these programs are across operating systems.
- There is a DOS product that is "EXEC2 like." (See Chapter 6's section on extending the DOS/OS/2 batch language for further information. How portable programs are between CMS and DOS remains unknown.
- The POSIX (Korn based) shell (1003.2), nearly finalized at this writing, will increase the portability of UNIX-like shells across operating systems. POSIX shells are or will be in Windows NT, VMS, and UNIX.
- Although Icon, Python, and TCL are not discussed at length in this book, they are included in Figure 8-1 for completeness. See Chapter 7's section on selecting Perl for more information on these languages.
- Icon, Perl, Python, and TCL are available on the Macintosh. Icon is also available on the Atari.
- REXX is not yet implemented as a commercial release under VMS. However, a REXX subset was developed for SLAC (Stanford Linear Accelerator Cen-

ter) that is running under VMS. It is rumored that the Workstation Group will soon come out with a VMS REXX interpreter.

- Unsupported copies of Perl do exist for VMS but have not been updated. This may be updated when VMS 5.5 comes out with POSIX support.

By Type of Data/Files

The other major consideration in choosing a command language is the type of data and files that an application uses. Figure 8-2 shows a classification of command languages by data/file type.

Here are additional notes on Figure 8-2:

- For Figure 8-2, a binary file means "a non-text file that can be accessed by a command language." DCL can store and retrieve data that is in indexed files. The advantages of doing this are more file operations can be performed and support for variable data records. Also Perl can use binary files, which result in smaller files because of compressing text.
- The REXX language does not explicitly support binary files. However, specific interpreters/compilers may include support. Watts (1990, p. 67) has a good discussion on REXX and binary files. Although more text-oriented than word-oriented, DCL or PERL may be used for binary file operations if available for your operating system.
- Python (not listed above) will support strings, numbers (with decimals), and arrays. It is more text-oriented than word-oriented. Text file operations are also supported.
- Icon (not listed above) supports strings, sets, and tables. Text file operations are supported.

The command languages listed in Figure 8-2 also support the following data types:

Arrays (simulated)   CLIST, DCL, DOS/OS/2 batch language
Arrays (true)   Perl, REXX
Associative arrays   Perl, REXX (compound symbols)
Boolean   DCL, Perl, REXX
Binary strings   DCL, REXX
Double byte characters   CLIST (TSO), REXX (CMS, TSO, OS/400, SAA)
Hexadecimal strings   CLIST, DCL, Perl, REXX
Octal strings   DCL, Perl
Scientific notation   REXX

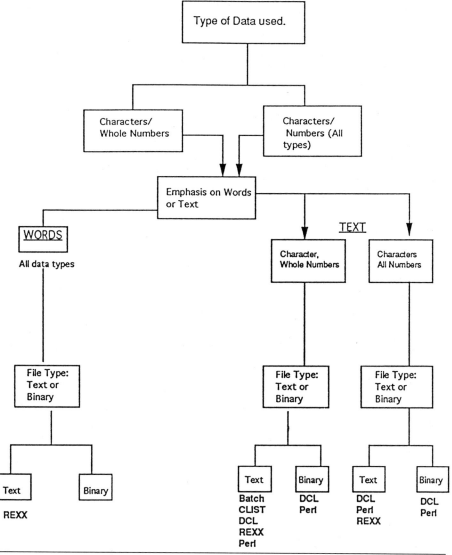

Figure 8-2. Command Language by Data/File Type

A COMPARISON OF COMMAND LANGUAGES

Until now, most studies comparing command languages have only compared two at a time. The section attempts to compare all **five** command languages discussed in this book by three different approaches.

- A comparison of command languages by power and ease of use
- A comparison of command languages by features
- A comparison of command languages by benchmarks

Power By Ease of Use

The following is an imperfect first attempt to measure the overall strength of a command language. Not finding any appropriate indices to do this, I created my own. The next section lists the components of two indices used to generate measures of a command language's *power* (which include rough measures of the command language's popularity) and *ease of use*. I assigned a 1 if a component was a standard part of that command language. Values less than 1 (such as 0.25, 0.5, and 0.75) were assigned based on the number of platforms on which a component was available. Values are subjectively based on my understanding on how each command language contains these components. No doubt, there will be advocates of the various command languages who will dispute the index components and the final results. I encourage them to come up with their own indices and do research in this area.

Table 8-2 lists the results of applying the two indices to the five command languages:

Table 8-2. Five Command Languages Compared

Command language	Power score and rank	Ease of use score and rank	*Unadjusted* total score and rank	*Adjusted* total score and rank
Batch	44.0	75.0	59.5	54
	(5)	(3)	(5)	(5)
CLIST	80.0	85.0	82.5	82
	(4)	(1)	(2)	(3)
DCL	86.25	77.5	81.9	83
	(3)	(2)	(3)	(2)
Perl	89.0	52.5	70.8	77
	(1)	(4)	(4)	(4)
REXX	88.75	85.0	86.9	88
	(2)	(1)	(1)	(1)

Here are three main conclusions you can draw from the table:

- The power index indicates that Perl and REXX are virtually tied for the highest rating of those examined. *Because there are only a few components to measure ease of use, one should rely more on the power index in choosing a command language for an application.*
- The ease of use index indicates that REXX and clist tied for the highest scores of those examined.
- REXX received the highest combined scores on ease of use and power. *Thus it appears that REXX is the best overall command language for general users and Perl is the best overall command language for power users. All other rankings* (except for the DOS batch language receiving low results from both indices command language of those examined) *may be the result of an inflation or deflation of the overall unadjusted score by the ease of use score—and should not be taken as the sole factor in choosing a command language.* An adjusted score was also calculated by giving ease of use a 0.5 weight to minimize this effect. This resulted in rankings similar to those produced by the power index.

Figure 8-3 displays the scores graphically.

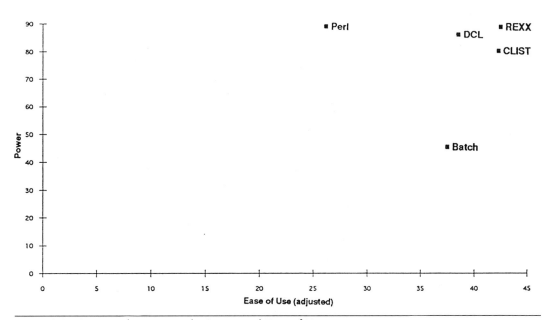

Figure 8-3. Command Languages by Power and Ease of Use

Table 8-3. Which Command Language Scored Highest in Various Categories

Command Language	Categories with Highest Scores
Batch	None
CLIST	System Variables (tie)
DCL	General I/O (tie)
	File I/O (tie)
	Exception handling (tie)
	Data types
	System variables (tie)
Perl	Invoking General I/O (tie)
	File I/O (tie)
	Flow control functions
REXX	General I/O (tie)
	Exception handling (tie)
	Interfaces to other environments
	Other

The above table breaks down scores by category and command language.

Features

Table 8-4 gives a comparison of the general features of command languages. This is also a listing of the components that made up the power and ease of use categories used in the previous section. See Figure 2-2 for information on the various commands to do this.

Table 8-4. Comparison of the General Features of Command Languages

Factor	Batch	CLIST	DCL	Perl	REXX
Invocation					
Invoke in foreground	Yes	Yes	Yes	Yes	Yes
Invoke in background	With Windows or OS/2	Yes Using JCL	Yes With Submit	UNIX OS/2 Windows	OS/2 TSO/E Windows
Capture output from script	Yes Redirection	Using Session Manager	Yes /OUTPUT	Yes Redirection	On some interpreters of REXX
Pass parameters on command line.	Yes	Yes	Yes	Yes	Yes
Ability to run command line "mini programs"	No	No	No (**VMS**) VCL -c (**DOS/UNIX**)	Yes -e	Yes Interpret and rxx -c (UNIX)
Interpreter has options	No	Yes	Yes	Yes	DOS TSO UNIX
General Input/Output					
Print text to screen	Yes	Yes	Yes	Yes	Yes
Print text and data to screen	Yes	Yes	Yes	Yes	Yes
Print to file	Yes	Yes	Yes	Yes	Yes
Print to other devices	Yes	Using Alloc	Yes	Yes	Yes
Input from keyboard	No If create program	Yes	Yes	Yes	Yes
Input from command line	Yes	Yes	Yes	Yes	Yes
Parse command line	Somewhat	Yes	Yes	Yes	Yes

Table 8-4. (continued)

File Input/Output

Factor	Batch	CLIST	DCL	Perl	REXX
Work with text files	Yes	Yes	Yes	Yes	Yes
Work with binary files	No	Yes	Yes	Yes	No
Open a file	Yes	Yes	Yes	Yes	Yes
Close a file	Yes	Yes	Yes	Yes	Yes
Sort a file	Yes but limited	Yes but add on or use ISPF/PDF Edit Macros	Yes	Yes	Yes
Tell the size of a file	No but can write program	Yes	Yes	Yes	On Some REXX interpreters
Tell if file exists	Yes	Yes	Yes	Yes	On some REXX interpreters
Tell file attributes	No but can write a program	Yes	Yes	Yes	On some REXX interpreters
Reading a record	Yes	Yes	Yes	Yes	Yes
Writing a record	Yes	Yes	Yes	Yes	Yes
Updating a record	No	Yes	Yes	Yes	Yes
Deleting a record	No	Yes	Yes	Yes	Yes

Flow Control

Factor	Batch	CLIST	DCL	Perl	REXX
IF	Yes	Yes	Yes	Yes	Yes
IF THEN-ELSE	No	Yes	Yes	Yes	Yes
SELECT (Case Logic)	No can be simulated	Yes	No can be simulated	No can be simulated	Yes

Table 8-4. (continued)

Factor	Batch	CLIST	DCL	Perl	REXX
Flow Control					
DO-END	Yes	Yes	No can be simulated	Yes	Yes
DO-WHILE-END	No	Yes	No can be simulated	Yes	Yes
DO-TO-BY (Same as For)	No	Yes	No can be simulated	No	Yes
FOR (Same as Do-To-By)	Yes	No	No can be simulated	Yes	No
BREAK	No Can simulate with GOTO	No Can simulate with GOTO	No Can simulate with GOTO	Yes	Yes
CONTINUE	No	No	No	Yes	Yes
GOTO	Yes	Yes	Yes	Yes	Simulated with SIGNAL (errors)
Multiple conditions	No	Yes	Yes	Yes	Yes
DATA-ENDDATA	No	Yes	Yes	Yes	No
Exception Handling					
Attention (interrupt) handling	No Rough detection	Yes	Yes	Yes	Yes
Error handling	No Rough detection	Yes	Yes	Yes	Yes
Error type detection	No Rough Detection and handling	Can capture error code and figure out	Yes	Yes	Yes
Capturing error codes	No Rough capturing	Yes	Yes	Yes	Yes
Generate EXIT codes	No Can create program	Yes	Yes	Yes, except for DOS or OS/2	Yes
Convert error code to text message	OS/2 only	No	Yes	Yes	Yes

Table 8-4. *(continued)*

Factor	Batch	CLIST	DCL	Perl	REXX
Debugging Features					
Trace Commands as being processed	Yes	Yes	Yes	Yes	Yes
Show symbolic substitution as being processed.	Yes	Yes	Yes	Yes	Yes
Establish breakpoints	No	No can be simulated	No can be simulated	Yes	Yes
Debug command/w subcommands	No	No	No	Yes	Yes
Data Types/General					
Labels	Yes	Yes	Yes	Yes	Yes
Comments	Yes	Yes	Yes	Yes	Yes
Symbolic Variables	Yes	Yes	Yes	Yes	Yes
Double Symbolic Variables (Names of symbolic variables)	No	Yes	Yes	No	Yes
Strings	Yes	Yes	Yes	Yes	Yes
Numbers	Yes	Yes	Yes	Yes	Yes
Decimals	No	No	Yes	Yes	Yes
Boolean	No	No	Yes	Yes	Yes
Hexadecimal	No	Yes	Yes	Yes	Yes
Octal	No	No	Yes	Yes	No
Binary	No	No	Yes	Yes	Yes
Bit operations	No	No	Yes	Yes	Yes
Scientific notation	No	No	No	No	Yes
Simulated arrays	Yes	Yes	Yes	No	No
True arrays	No	No	No	Yes	Yes

Table 8-4. *(continued)*

Factor	Batch	CLIST	DCL	Perl	REXX
Interfaces					
Functions	No but can create or obtain	Yes	Yes	Yes	Yes
Return from functions	Can create	Yes	Yes	Yes	Yes
External functions	No but can create or obtain	Yes	Yes	Yes	Yes
Subroutines	Can be simulated	Yes	Yes	Yes	Yes
Return from subroutines	Can be created	Yes	Yes	Yes	Yes
External subroutines	No but can create or obtain	No	Yes	Yes	Yes
External scripts	Yes with CALL in 3.3	Yes	Yes	Yes	Yes
Operating systems	Yes	Yes	Yes	Yes	Yes
Executables	Yes	Yes	Yes	Yes	Yes
Library	No	No	As Shareware	Yes	As Shareware
System Variables					
Version of interpreter	Yes	Yes	Yes	Yes	Yes
Version of operating system	Yes	Yes	Yes	No	If in PARSE VERSION string
Name of current operating system	Yes	Yes	Yes	No	If in PARSE VERSION string
Current user (multiuser systems)	No except for LANs	Yes	Yes	Yes	On CMS TSO UNIX
Name of currently executing script	Yes	Yes	Yes	Yes	Yes
Current date	No can be captured	Yes	Yes	Yes	Yes

319

Table 8-4. (continued)

Factor	Batch	CLIST	DCL	Perl	REXX
		System Variables			
Current time	No can be captured	Yes	Yes	Yes	Yes
Current directory	No	Yes	Yes	Using pwd library routine	On DOS OS/2 UNIX
Debug on/off	Yes	Yes	Yes	Yes	Yes
		Built-in Function			
Function library	No but can be created or obtained	Yes	Yes	Yes	Yes
Upper to lower function	No	Yes	Yes	Yes	Yes
Lower to upper function	No	Yes	Yes	Yes	Yes
Type conversion	No	Yes	Yes	Yes	Yes
Mathematical functions	No	No	No	Yes and additions as shareware	Yes and additions as shareware
Substring function	No	Yes	Yes	Yes	Yes
Index function	No	Yes	Yes	Yes	Yes
Date conversion	No	No but can easily create your own	Yes	Some formats included	Yes
String conversion	No	Yes	Yes	Yes	Yes
String length function	No	Yes	Yes	Yes	Yes
Data type format	No	Yes	Yes	Yes	Yes
Debug status	Yes	Yes	Yes	Yes	Yes

Table 8-4. *(continued)*

Factor	Batch	Other CLIST	DCL	Perl	REXX
Portable to other platforms	Limited portability to OS/2	Yes	Yes	Yes	Yes
Standard command language/ reference	IBM Microsoft Guide with OEM extensions	Yes IBM's manual and pclist manual	Yes DEC's	Yes Wall and Schwartz	Yes Cowlishaw and soon ANSI Standard in 93.
Magazine/column on command language	Yes	Yes	Yes	**No**	Yes
Usenet News Group on command language	Not dedicated group	Not dedicated group	Not dedicated group	Yes	Yes with various BITNET groups
Features or language to generate reports	**No**	**No**	Yes	Can be used as such	Yes

Table 8-4. *(continued)*

Factor	Batch	CLIST	DCL	Perl	REXX
		Ease of Use			
Comments	Yes	Yes	Yes	Yes	Yes
Blank Lines allowed	Yes	Yes	If prefixed by $	Yes	Yes
English commands	Yes	Yes	Yes	Yes	Yes
English system variables	Yes	Yes	Somewhat once know what variable means	No	Yes
English functions	No	Yes	Somewhat once know what function means	Yes	Yes
End of statement punctuation not required for a *single* statement	Yes	Yes	Yes	No Semicolon	Yes
Abbreviations of commands allowed.					
On-line help	In DOS 5.0 and as separate product	As separate product	Yes	For DEBUG and command-line options (OS/2) and man pages.	Yes CMS and TSO (separate product)
English Operators	No	Yes	Yes	Yes	No
Variables/keywords in any case	Yes	TSO commands and symbolic variables not key words	Enter in any case but converts symbols to upper	No for functions and key words. Variables, file handles, and subroutines YES	Yes

Benchmarks

This "bonus" section originally was not part of the book. For the first time ever, crude benchmarks will be performed for all five command languages on the only platform on which all exist—MS-DOS. Tests were performed on a PC XT with 640K—as close as possible to a "worst case" for speed. Benchmarks are presented "as is" without weighting for (1) the interpreter's implementation of the command language, (b) the interpreter's ability to run under 640K, (3) measurement error, (4) file buffering (which has a major effect on file operation speed), and so on. Note that the standard disclaimer applies here—"Your mileage may vary if performing these tests yourself."

Without any further hesitation—here are the results (the best time for each task by a command language is underlined):

Task	Batch	CLIST	DCL	Perl	REXX	BASIC
Read 10 80 byte records	2 seconds *	0 seconds	6 seconds	0 seconds	0 seconds	1 second
Read 100 80 byte records	2 seconds *	0 seconds	46 seconds	2 seconds	7 seconds	4 seconds (BASIC) 3 seconds (QUICK BASIC)
Read 1000 80 byte records	3 seconds *	0 seconds	7 minutes, 30 seconds	9 seconds	1 minute, 5 seconds	36 seconds (BASIC) 28 seconds (QUICK BASIC)
Write 10 80 byte records	4 seconds	2 seconds	7 seconds	1 second	1 second	1 second
Write 100 80 byte records	31 seconds	9 seconds	1 minute, 2 seconds	2 seconds	4 seconds	5 seconds (BASIC) 3 seconds (QUICK BASIC)
Write 1000 80 byte records	5 minutes, 41 seconds	24 seconds	10 minutes, 11 seconds	13 seconds	40 seconds	39 seconds (BASIC) 21 seconds (QUICK BASIC)
Print 10 80 byte lines	2 seconds	3 seconds	7 seconds	1 second	1 second	1 second
Print 100 80 byte lines	21 seconds	35 seconds	1 minute, 16 seconds	13 seconds	23 seconds	14 seconds (BASIC) 6 seconds

Task	Batch	CLIST	DCL	Perl	REXX	BASIC
Print 1000 80 byte lines	3 minutes, 22 seconds	5 minutes, 50 seconds	12 minutes, 31 seconds	<u>2 minutes, 15 seconds</u>	3 minutes, 53 seconds	2 minutes 30 seconds (BASIC) 1 minute 7 seconds (QUICK BASIC)
Concatenate String 1000 times	N/A	3 minutes, 26 seconds**	8 minutes, 58 seconds	<u>13 seconds</u>	28 seconds	10 seconds (BASIC) 6 seconds** (QUICK BASIC)
Create a 1000 element array	N/A	2 minutes, 24 seconds	12 minutes, 44 seconds***	24 seconds	31 seconds	4 seconds (BASIC) 5 seconds (QUICK BASIC)
Size of interpreter executable	46K	44K	86K	298K	114K	36K (BASIC) 254K (QUICK BASIC)

Notes:

* There is no READ command for DOS. This was done using a FIND command for the last record in the file.

** Estimated time. Failed test because exceeded clist value length limit.

*** Estimated time. Failed test because not enough memory.

1. The Interpreters used were:
   BASIC—Advanced BASIC 3.30 Interpreter (Comes with DOS 3.3)
   Batch—DOS 5.0
   CLIST—pCLIST 1.08c
   DCL—VCL 3.01
   Perl—Perl version 3.0.1 patch 41
   Quick BASIC—QUICK BASIC 5.0 (comes With DOS 5.0)
   REXX—Personal REXX 2.00D2

2. Notes on the tests themselves:
   - REXX I/O was done with LINEIN and LINEOUT and not EXECIO
   - VCL was run in -m (memory miser mode) to allow more memory
   - Regular arrays were used for Perl
   - The concatenation test consisted of concatenating the character b to a variable 1000 times.
   - The array test consisted of looping 1000 times and assigning the array element the value of the counter.

- Operating from within VCL or using the REXX resident version yielded about the same times.
- *Only two interpreters passed all tests—REXX and Perl.*

3. Perl appeared to be the fastest overall command language followed by REXX.

4. BASIC overall was not significantly faster than most command languages. However, QuickBASIC was significantly faster than all command languages except Perl.

5. The following reasons are likely for the slow performance of VCL:
   a. The limitations of the DCL language, including lacking a true DO-WHILE flow control structure.
   b. All files are OPENed to see if it is a directory or a special device file. Some time is also used converting from VMS to an internal filename syntax. Wildcards in filenames are allowed but this means that the files must be sorted first.
   c. Time is also lost because VCL uses the UNIX utilities YACC and LEX to internally parse VCL commands.
   d. Files operations are performed in non-buffered mode to save on memory. However, this is at the expense of speed of file operations.

      Later VCL releases should run significantly faster than the one tested.

6. Personal REXX 3.0, Tritus REXX, and Perl 4.10 for MS-DOS had just appeared at the time of the final draft of this book but arrived too late to run benchmarks on.

Another way to look at this is by ranking (such as 1 being assigned to first place, 2 to second, and so on). What follows is the average, *unadjusted* ranking for each command language **in descending order**:

Command Language	Rank without BASIC (out of 5)	RANK with BASIC 3.3 (out of 6)	Rank with QUICK BASIC (out of 6)	Overall average
Perl	**1.27**	**1.46**	**1.64**	**1.46**
BASIC/ QUICK/BASIC	- - - - - - - - - - -	2.09	1.72	1.91
REXX	2.36	2.9 (tie)	3 (tie)	2.75
CLIST	2.45	2.9 (tie)	3 (tie)	2.78
Batch	3	3.63	3.64	3.42
DCL	4.36	5.18	5.18	4.91

COMPARING COMMANDS ACROSS COMMAND LANGUAGES

This section provides the traditional command equivalence charts based on the command language components listed above. Table 2-4 is a less detailed version of the same chart.

General Features

Here is an overview of some basic topics for each command language:

Task	Batch	CLIST	DCL	Perl	REXX
What a program for this command language is called	Bat or Batch file	CLIST	Command procedure	Script	Exec
Extension of program for this command language	BAT (**DOS**) .CMD (**OS/2**)	CLIST (May be in PDS)	.COM	None required. Conventionally .PL	CMD (**OS/2**) EXEC (**CMS/TSO**) REX (**DOS/ UNIX**) REXX (**AMIGA**)
Comments Labels Continuation of line	REM *comment* :*labelname* None	/* *comment* */ *labelname*: Plus— eliminates leading blanks Hyphen— keeps leading blanks	$! *comment* *labelname*: Hyphen— with the last character on the previous line being a space or comma.	# *Comment* *labelname*: Comma for blank	/* *Comment* */ *labelname*: Comma

Invocation

All the command languages examined can be invoked a variety of ways (including in background) and usually have some options. Here is a summary of these:

Task	Batch	CLIST	DCL	Perl	REXX
Invoke in foreground	Name of batch file Start *name* (**OS/2**)	EXEC *execname*	@name VCL (**DOS/UNIX**)	perl *scriptname*	name (**CMS**) cmd *name* (**OS/2**) ex *name* (**DOS**) rexx *name*/ rx *name* (**DOS**) rx *name* (**AMIGA**) rxx *name* (**UNIX**)

Task	Batch	CLIST	DCL	Perl	REXX
Invoke in background	detach name **(OS/2)** Using Windows	JCL program including //STEP1 EXEC PGM =IKJEFT01 **(TSO)**	SUBMIT name	detach perl name **(OS/2)** Using Windows **(DOS)** perl name & **(UNIX)**	JCL program including //STEP1 EXEC PGM =IRXJCL **(TSO)**
Invocation options	None	CLIST (*name* is a CLIST) EXEC (*name* is a REXX exec) LIST/NOLIST (list commands at terminal) PROMPT NOPROMPT (prompts during clist)	/OUTPUT=file (capture output to file) VCL -c (execute mini programs) -m (Use less memory) -q no banner -v (turn on debug)	-c (syntax checker) -d (debugger) -e (execute miniprograms) -i (in-place editing) -s (simple)	rx /u (unload **DOS**) rxc -m (module generation **UNIX**) rxx -c (executes miniprogram **UNIX**)
Command line parameters	9 parameters stored in %1– %9	As many as needed. Both positional and keyword. Parsed by PROC.	8 parameters stored in P1– P8.	As many as needed stored in the array @ARGV	As many as needed. Parsed by PARSE ARG.

General Input/Output

Here is a look at the commands used by each command language to perform various input and output operations (*Text* is any valid combination of text, variables, and arrays. *File* is any valid file):

Task	Batch	CLIST	DCL	Perl	REXX
Print to screen	echo *text*	WRITE *text* WRITENR *text* (same line)	WRITE SYS$OUTPUT	print *text* printf *text* (formatted) sprintf *text*	say "*text*"

Task	Batch	CLIST	DCL	Perl	REXX
Print to file	echo *text>file*	PUTFILE	WRITE *file*	print *file text* printf *file text* (formatted) sprintf *file text*	EXECIO DISKW **(CMS, DOS, TSO)** LINEOUT **(DOS, OS2, UNIX)** CHAROUT **(DOS,OS2, UNIX)** WRITECH WRITELN **(AMIGA)**
Capture input from the keyboard	None must build your own	READ	INQUIRE READ (best choice)	getc substr(<STDIN >) while (<STDIN>)...	PULL/ PARSE PULL

File Input/Output

Except for batch language, the other command languages use very similar approaches to performing file operations. Here is a listing of file operations across command languages:

Task	Batch	CLIST	DCL	Perl	REXX
Opening a file for reading	N/A	OPENFILE INPUT	OPEN/READ	open(*handle, "file"*) or open (*handle," <file"*)	EXECIO DISKR **(CMS, DOS, TSO)** LINEIN **(DOS, OS2, UNIX)** CHARIN **(DOS,OS2, UNIX)** OPEN ('Read') READCH READLN **(AMIGA)**
Opening a file for writing	N/A	OPENFILE OUTPUT	OPEN/WRITE	open(*handle, ">file"*)	EXECIO DISKW

Task	Batch	CLIST	DCL	Perl	REXX
					(CMS, DOS, TSO) LINEOUT **(DOS, OS2, UNIX)** CHAROUT **(DOS,OS2, UNIX)** OPEN ('Write') WRITECH WRITELN **(AMIGA)**
Opening a file for updating/appending	N/A	OPENFILE UPDATE	OPEN/ APPEND OPEN/READ/ WRITE	open(handle, "+>file"); open(handle, ">>file");	EXECIO DISKRU (TSO) EXECIO DISKW OPEN ('Append') WRITECH WRITELN **(AMIGA)**
Closing a file	N/A	CLOSFILE	CLOSE	CLOSE	FINIS with EXECIO **(CMS, DOS, TSO)** Not needed for LINEIN/ LINEOUT CLOSE **(AMIGA)**
Binary file operations	N/A	N/A	OPEN READ DELETE WRITE CLOSE	binmode (DOS) Otherwise, automatically detected by Perl.	N/A
Sort a file	SORT up to 63K files	SORT must be purchased as a separate product unless ISREDIT SORT (PDF EDIT Macros) are used	SORT file	Use UNIX sort or SORT function	Use ADDRESS and operating system's SORT command.

Task	Batch	CLIST	DCL	Perl	REXX
Size of file	N/A	LISTDSI (&SYSBLK SIZE)	F$FILE_ATT RIBUTES (EOF)	-s file	LISTDSI function ($SYSBLK SIZE) **TSO**
File Attributes	N/A	LISTDSI	F$FILE_ATT RIBUTES	file test operators	*N/A*
Reading a record	FIND "*string*" *file*	GETFILE	READ	print $_; (in a while loop)	EXECIO DISKR **(CMS, DOS TSO)** LINEIN CHARIN READCH READLN **(AMIGA)**
Writing a record	ECHO *string>>file*	*PUTFILE*	*WRITE*	print *handle text* printf *handle text* sprintf *handle text*	LINEOUT CHAROUT WRITECH WRITELN **(AMIGA)**
Updating a record	N/A	PUTFILE	WRITE/ UPDATE (index)	print *handle text* printf *handle text* sprintf *handle text*	LINEOUT CHAROUT WRITECH WRITELN **(AMIGA)**
Deleting a record	N/A	PUTFILE	READ/ DELETE (index)	Use shift and unshift and then write out remaining records	LINEOUT CHAROUT

Flow Control

Each command offers some type of flow control statements (including GOTO except for REXX). Here is a comparison of these flow control structures across command languages.

Task	Batch	CLIST	DCL	Perl	REXX
IF	IF ERROR LEVEL IF EXIST *file*	IF THEN IF THEN DO END IF THEN ELSE	IF THEN IF THEN ELSE ENDIF	if *action* *action* if if elsif else	IF THEN ELSE
DO-END and miscellaneous forms	DO with implied end	DO-END	Can be simulated	do	DO number DO END DO FOREVER

Task	Batch	CLIST	DCL	Perl	REXX
DO-WHILE-END	N/A	DO-WHILE END	Can be simulated	while	DO WHILE END
DO-UNTIL-END	N/A	DO UNTIL END	Can be simulated	until	DO UNTIL END
FOR or DO TO BY	FOR IN DO	DO TO BY with UNTIL and WHILE	Can be simulated	for foreach	DO TO BY FOR with UNTIL and WHILE
BREAK	N/A	Can simulate with GOTO	Can simulate with GOTO	last	LEAVE
CONTINUE	N/A	N/A	N/A	next	iterate
GOTO	GOTO	GOTO	GOTO	GOTO	SIGNAL only for errors and interrupts
DATA-ENDDATA	N/A	DATA-ENDDATA DATA PROMPT ENDDATA	DECK-EOD	DATA as handle with _END_	N/A

Interfaces

An essential part of any command language is its interface to the operating system and various environments. This summarizes the commands used for each command language to provide such an interface:

Task	Batch	CLIST	DCL	Perl	REXX
Nest scripts	CALL COMMAND/C (**DOS**) CMD/C (**OS/2**)	*name* % *name* EXEC *name*	@*name*	eval exec/ /system exec	EXEC name EXEC (**TSO**) ADDRESS *command*
Function call	N/A	SYSCALL	GOSUB	&*function name* or do *function name*	*function name*
Function definition	N/A	label	label	sub *function name*	label
Subroutines	N/A	GOTO	CALL	&*function name*	CALL
Exit from subroutine	N/A	EXIT	EXIT	exit	EXIT
Return from function	N/A	RETURN	RETURN	return	RETURN

Task	Batch	CLIST	DCL	Perl	REXX
Execute operating system	*command*	*command* (**TSO**) DOS *command* (**DOS**)	*command* (**VMS**) SET VCL/PASSTH RU *command* (DOS) EXECUTE *command* (DOS)	exec(*command)* system(*command*	ADDRESS environment *"command"*
Capture output from system command	*command>file*	SMCOPY (Session Manager **TSO**) &SYSOUTLIN E/&SYSTRAP **TSO**) *command>file* (**DOS**)	/OUTPUT on most commands DEFINE /USER_MODE SYS$SOUT- PUT *file* *command* (**VMS**)	exec *(command>file)* system *(command>file)*	FIFO/LIFO (CMS) Some func- tions simulate DOS com mands and return output (**DOS**) *command>file* (**DOS**) SMCOPY (Session Manager **TSO**) OUTTRAP function (**TSO**) POPEN (**UNIX**)
Execute executable	*name*	CALL *name*	RUN *name*	exec *(name)* system *(name)*	ADDRESS *environment name*

Exception Handling

Command languages need to handle a variety of exceptions. The following sum-marizes the commands used to do this:

Task	Batch	CLIST	DCL	Perl	REXX
Attention detection	BREAK ON BREAK OFF	ATTN OFF ATTN DO END ATTN EXIT	ON CONTROL_Y	$SIG{'INT'}= *subname*	CALL ON HALT SIGNAL ON

Task	Batch	CLIST	DCL	Perl	REXX
Fatal error	N/A	ATTN RETURN ERROR OFF ERROR DO END ERROR EXIT ERROR RETURN	ON SEVERE_ ERROR	$#SIG ('ABRT') = *subname* die	HALT CALL ON FAILURE SIGNAL ON FAILURE
Serious error	N/A	ERROR OFF ERROR DO END ERROR EXIT ERROR RETURN IF $LASTCC=	ON ERROR IF .NOT. $STATUS	$SIG('error')= *subname* die	CALL ON ERROR SIGNAL ON ERROR Other CALL/ SIGNAL detections are ON NOVALUE ON NOTREADY ON SYNTAX
Warning error	N/A	IF &LASTCC=	ON WARNING IF .NOT. $STATUS	warn	N/A
Error type detection	N/A	By examining &LASTCC	IF $SEVERITY...	sub bye1{ {local($stype) = @_; print "$stype\ n";}	CONDITION
Capture error code	IF ERROR LEVEL (if supported)	IF &LASTCC =	IF .NOT. $STATUS	{$? (for system) $! $@ (do,eval,require)	CONDITION
Error sequences how invoked	IF ERROR LEVEL (if supported)	Error detected	ON SEVERE_ ERROR ON ERROR ON WARNING IF .NOT. $STATUS	$SIG{'error'} = *subname;*	CALL ON SIGNAL ON
Error Sequences how stored	Label	ERROR DO END	Label	sub *subname*	Label
Convert error code to text messages	HELP *messagenumber*	IF &LASTCC= *xxx* THEN WRITE Error is *yyy*	F$MESSAGE	$! $@ (do,eval, require)	ERROR TEXT CONDITION

Debugging

All the command languages examined have some degree of debugging with Perl and REXX the most complete. Here are the commands used by each command language for debugging:

Task	Batch	CLIST	DCL	Perl	REXX
Trace commands as being processed	ECHO ON	SET &SYSCONLIST =ON SET &SYSLIST =ON SET &SYSMSG =ON\SET &SYSSYMLIST CONTROL CONLIST etc	SET VERIFY F$VERIFY(1)	-w on invocation perl -d then s to process a line at a time	TRACE function TRACE command (with R)
Show symbolic substitution as being processed	ECHO *var*	CONTROL CONLIST	F$VERIFY(1) SET VERIFY	perl -d s perl -p	TRACE command (with R)
Enable/Disable	ECHO ON off	CONTROL CONLIST CONTROL NOCONLIST etc &SYSCONLIST =ON/OFF etc	F$VERIFY(0) (off) F$VERIFY(1) (on)	Just don't use -d option	TRACE(O) or TRACE O
Debug command with subcommands	None	None	None	Perl -d	TRACE ?

Data

Each command language can process a variety of data types. Here is a summary of the major data types across each command language:

Task	Batch	CLIST	DCL	Perl	REXX
Strings	*string* or "*string*"	*string* or &STR(*string*)	"*string*"	"*string*" or '*string*'	"*string*" or '*string*'
Whole numbers	number	number	number	number	number
Decimals	N/A	N/A	number	number	number
Scientific notation	N/A	N/A	N/A	N/A	number
Engineering notation	N/A	N/A	N/A	N/A	number

Task	Batch	CLIST	DCL	Perl	REXX
Boolean	N/A	&STRX=1	var=1	$var=1 $array[cnt] =1; $array {index}='1';	x=1
Hexadecimal	N/A	X'*number*'	%x*number*	0x*number*	'*string*'x
Octal	N/A	N/A	%O*number*	0*number*	N/A
Bit string/Binary	N/A	N/A	$x[0,8]=%x0E	pack(b or B,*number*)	"*string*"b or '*string*'b
Double byte	N/A	X's1' X's2' X's3' X's4'	N/A	N/A	Same as CLIST for CMS, OS/400, TSO
Simulated array	N/A	&&VAR&1	*var'cnt with cnt being a counter*	True Array	True Array
True array	N/A	N/A	N/A	@array—whole array $array[cnt]— element %array— whole associa- tive array $array{index}— element	a.—entire array (stem) a.george— element in array

System Variables

System variables provide command language users with a wealth of information about their operating system, current executing program, and much more. Here is a sample of system variables for each of the command languages:

Task	Batch	CLIST	DCL	Perl	REXX
Version of interpreter	No variable. Capture output of VER command.	&SYSTSOE (**TSO**) N/A (**DOS**)	No variable. Capture with F$GETSYI ("VERSION") or F$GETSYI ("NODE_ SWVERS")	$]	Can be simulated with PARSE VERSION (may not be available for all REXX interpreters/ compilers)
Version of the operating system	No variable. Capture output of VER command.	&SYSTSOE (**TSO**) N/A (**DOS**)	No variable. Can capture with F$GETSYI ("VERSION")	N/A	Can be simulated with PARSE VERSION

Task	Batch	CLIST	DCL	Perl	REXX
			or F$GETSYI ("NODE_ SWVERS")	N/A	(may not be available for all REXX interpreters/ compilers)
Name of the current operating script	%0	&SYSICMD (implicit invocation only)	No variable. Can be captured with F$ENVIRON-MENT ("PROCEDURE")	$0	N/A
Current date	None	&SYSDATE &SYSJDATE	No variable but can be captured by F$TIME()	$^T processed through gmtime or localtime Or gmtime/localtime	No variable but can be captured by DATE
Current time	None	&SYSTIME $SYSSTIME	No variable but can be captured by F$TIME()	$^T processed through gmtime or localtime Or gmtime/localtime	No variable but can be captured by TIME
Current user	N/A	&SYSUID	No variable can be captured with F$GETJPI	$< (real userid) $> (**effective** userid)	No variable but can be captured with SYSVAR (SYSUID— **TSO**) USERID (**CMS,TSO**) USERID/CUS USERID (**UNIX**)
Current mode	N/A	&SYSENV	No variable can be captured with F$MODE or F$GETJPI or F$ENVIRONMENT	N/A	SYSVAR (SYSENV— **TSO**)
Last error code	ERROR LEVEL	&LASTCC &MAXCC	$STATUS	$!, $@ (eval, require), $?(system)	RC
Last Return Code	ERROR LEVEL	&LASTCC &MAXCC	$STATUS	$!, $@ (eval, require), $?(system)	RC

Task	Batch	CLIST	DCL	Perl	REXX
Command line values	%1–%9	Stored in symbolic variables with the same name as the variables	Stored in symbols P1–P8	Stored in array @ARGV with no limit	Stored in symbols set by PARSE or ARG instruction

Built-in Functions

Each command language (except DOS) has built-in functions performing similar functions. Here is a summary of the major built-in functions for the various command languages:

Task	Batch	CLIST	DCL	Perl	REXX
Upper- to lower-case	None	&SYSLC	F$EDIT	tr/A-Z/a-z/	TRANS LATE
Lower- to upper-case	None. Use PATH variable	&SYSCAPS	F$EDIT	tr/a-z/A-Z/	TRANS LATE
Type conversion	None	&EVAL &STR	F$CVSI F$CVUI F$FAO F$IDENTI- FIER F$INTEGER F$STRING	hex int oct scalar	B2X C2D C2X D2C D2X X2B X2C X2D
Mathematical functions	None	&EVAL	F$FAO	atan2 cos exp log ord rand sin sqrt srand	ABS BITAND BITOR BITXOR MAX MIN RANDOM SIGN
Substring	None	&SUBSTR &SYSCSUB- STR	F$ELEMENT F$EXTRACT F$PARSE (FILES)	substr split	CENTER LEFT RIGHT SUBSTR SUBWORD WORD
Index	FIND	&SYSINDEX	F$LOCATE	index rindex	POS LASTPOS

Task	Batch	CLIST	DCL	Perl	REXX
					SUBSTR
					SUBWORD
					WORD
					WORD-INDEX
					WORDPOS
Length	None	&LENGTH &SYSCLENGTH	F$LENGTH	length	LENGTH WORD-LENGTH
Date/Time conversion	None	None but can be created	F$CVTIME	gmtime localtime	DATE TIME
Type of value	None	&DATATYPE	F$TYPE	if *regular expression*	DATATYPE

SUGGESTED READINGS

Cowlishaw, Michael F., 1990. *The REXX Language: A Practical Approach to Programming.* Prentice Hall: Englewood Cliffs, N. J..

Griswold, Ralph E., 1990. *An Overview of Version 8, the Icon Programming Language.*

Jones, Robert, 1990. pCLIST User's Guide.

Ousterhout, John K. TCL: An Embeddable Command Language

Van Rossum, Guido, 1991. *Python Library Reference.*

Van Rossum, Guido, 1991. *Python Tutorial.* (Draft).

Wall, Larry, and Randall L. Schwartz, 1991. *Programming Perl.* Sebastopol, Calif.: O'Reilly & Associates.

Watts, Keith, 1990. REXX language I/O and environment changes, *Proceedings of The REXX Symposium for Developers and Users,* pp. 66–74.

Appendix:
List of Command Language
Interpreters

The following is a sample of the command language interpreters and related products available. Others are presented throughout the rest of the book. The author makes no endorsement of any of these products:

CLIST

pCLIST—includes many of the features of TSO/E Version 1 Release 4 but runs on DOS.
Cost Trial Disk: $10, Registration: $39.
Vendor:
> Robert Jones
> 3534 Hawkwood Road
> Diamond Bar, Calif. 91765
> Compuserve: 72047,1154

DCL

DCP—a DCL to Fortran converter. Not a cure-all for all situations, but can help when faster execution times are needed.
Cost: $995
Vendor:
> Channel Islands Software Inc.
> P.O. Box 30942
> Santa Barbara, Calif. 93130
> (805) 682-3348
> Fax: (805) 682-1657

VCL—a DCL look-alike that runs on MS-DOS and a variety of UNIX flavors. The company also makes a variety of VMS look-alikes (such as mail and editors) that run on DOS and UNIX.
Cost: $195 (DOS) to $3995, depending on computer used.
Vendor:
> Boston Business Computing
> Three Dundee Park
> Andover, Mass. 01810
> (508) 470-0444

REXX

ARexx—a complete implementation of REXX for the Amiga (now also part of V2 of the AmigaDOS).
Cost: $50
Vendor:
> William S. Hawes
> P.O. Box 308
> Maynard, Mass. 01754
> (508) 568-8695
> Compuserve: 722030,367

Personal REXX—REXX (Language Version 4.0) for both DOS and OS/2. Also makes a communications product called REXXTERM. A MS-Windows version is also due out in early 1992.
Cost: $195
Vendor:
> Quercus Systems
> P.O. 2157
> Saratoga, Calif. 95070
> (408) 867-REXX
> Fax: (408) 867-7489

Portable REXX—REXX for the PC (Language Version 4.0). A MS Windows Version is due out in early 1992.
Cost: $95
Vendor:
> Kilowatt Software
> 1945 Washington Street #410
> San Francisco, Calif. 94109-2968
> (415) 346-7353

PROREXX—VM REXX Compiler
Cost: $500–$51,800
Vendor:
  Systems Center
  1800 Alexander Drive
  Reston, VA 22071
  (703) 264-8000
  Fax: (703) 264-1308

REXXTACY—in beta test, converts OS/2 REXX execs to Microsoft C code.
  The company plans to port to other environments as well.
Cost: Not available
Vendor:
  Anthony Green
  RoboCo
  108 Madison Avenue
  Toronto, Ontario
  M5R 2S4, Canada
  (416) 340-0887

REXXTools/MVS—A collection of subroutines, environments, and ISPF/PDF
  (ISREDIT) Edit Macros.
Cost: $3500 to $8500
Vendor:
  Chicago-Soft Ltd.
  6232 N. Pulaski Rd., Suite 402
  Chicago, Ill. 60646-9884
  (312) 525-6400

SPF/2—ISPF for OS/2 (also available for MS-DOS). Included here because it
  allows you to use ISREDIT edit macro commands with an OS/2 REXX
  interpreter.
Cost: $245
Vendor:
  Command Technology Corporation
  1040 Marina Village Parkway
  Alameda, California 94501
  Orders: (800) 336-3320
  Information: (415) 521-5900 or (800) 848-6700
  Fax: (415) 521-0369

Tritus REXX—SAA REXX for DOS and OS/2. Also makes Tritus-SPF
Cost: $75 until 3/3/92
Vendor:
>   Tritus Inc.
>   6034 W. Courtyard Dr., Suite 360
>   Austin, Texas 78730-5014
>   (512) 794-5800
>   Fax: (512) 794-3833

Uni-REXX—REXX for UNIX. Also makes UNI-XEDIT, UNI-SPF
Cost: $399–$40,000
Vendor:
>   The Workstation Group
>   6300 North River Road
>   Rosemont, Illinois 60018
>   (708) 696-4800 or (800) 228-0255
>   Fax: (708) 696-2277
>   UUNEX! wrkgrp! sales or sales%wrkgrp@uunet.uu.net.

UNIX SHELLS

MKS Toolkit—Access to UNIX tools and shells from DOS and OS/2.
Cost: $249 (DOS) $349 (OS/2) $399 (Both DOS and OS/2)
Vendor:
>   Mortice Kern Systems
>   35 King St North
>   Waterloo, Ontario
>   N2J 2W9, Canada
>   519-884-2251

EZ-BUILDER—Shell script builder
Cost: $699
Vendor:
>   Cora Computer Technologies
>   West Hempstead, NY

Appendix:
Your Turn

Please send to Dianne Littwin c/o Van Nostrand Reinhold, 115 Fifth Avenue, NY, NY 10003 or hhgl@bunny.gte.com via e-mail.

1. What sections did you find least interesting?   Why?

2. What sections would you like to see added or expanded?

3. What command languages would you like to see added to this book?

4. Use this space to add any corrections, suggestions, examples, or changes you would like to see in the next edition of this book.

5. We would appreciate if you identify yourself.

Name _____

Address _____

E-mail address _____

Index